AIDA Europe Research Series on Insurance Law and Regulation

Volume 12

The AIDA Europe Research Series on Insurance Law and Regulation is the first book series of its kind and area of specialization. It comprises volumes on topics researched and written with an international, comparative or European perspective.

The regulatory response to the financial crisis in 2008 has pushed towards the adoption of transnational principles and rules also in the field of insurance by encouraging the convergence of national regulations to common regulatory framework. The need for a common legal language emerges to fully understand the process of transnational convergence in place and its impact on national legislation. On the other hand, persisting national peculiarities must be examined in the light of the transnational convergence of rules and concepts. Moreover, new risks, business practices and customers' issues are emerging worldwide, so requiring increasingly global responses.

The scope of the series is to bring together academics, practitioners and policy makers in order to exchange views and approaches to the topics concerned, which are based on the new transnational dimension of insurance law, business and regulation. All contributions are peer reviewed.

Özge Tosun

The Law of Political Risk Insurance

Springer

Özge Tosun
Legal Department
Export Credit Bank of Turkiye (Turkiye
Eximbank)
Istanbul, Türkiye

ISSN 2662-1770 ISSN 2662-1789 (electronic)
AIDA Europe Research Series on Insurance Law and Regulation
ISBN 978-3-031-74674-1 ISBN 978-3-031-74675-8 (eBook)
https://doi.org/10.1007/978-3-031-74675-8

This Springer imprint is published by the registered company Springer Nature Switzerland AG
The registered company address is: Gewerbestrasse 11, 6330 Cham, Switzerland

Preface

I am thankful to King's College London for the research allowances; this book meets its readers in the end of opportunities King's provided to me. Many thanks are due to Claire Jervis, distinguished visiting researcher from King's College London who provided me with insight despite the paucity of her time and taught me the insignificance of the borders. And my gratitude goes to Ms. *Laura HOFMANN* from Springer whose endless support and understanding have allowed this book to reach readers. Warm thanks should go to my family, my mother *Peruze TOSUN*, my father *Metin TOSUN* and my sister Dr. *Özlem Deniz TOSUN* who have always stood by me in pursuit of my dream.

In preparing this book, I have benefited from the dissertations, articles or books of numerous academics; profound however, I must mention in particular two esteemed academics. I want to express my thanks to Associate Professor Kübra YETİŞ ŞAMLI from Istanbul University Faculty of Law who supervised me during my PhD studies. It was her persistence and dedication which encouraged me to publish my first book and which formed the very basis of this project.

In June 2021, in the shadow of COVID-19 outbreak and while strict travel restrictions were still in force, the feedback of Professor *Özlem GÜRSES* from King's College London on my research was the beginning of this journey, and without her supervision, never-ending support, sharp guidance and belief, this journey could have not been accomplished. I want to express my deepest and special gratitude to Professor *GÜRSES* for her outstanding contribution to my academic career and for everything in making this book possible. This book is dedicated to *Professor Özlem GÜRSES*.

Istanbul, Türkiye

Özge Tosun

Contents

Abbreviations

AAD	Arbitration award default
ACIA	ASEAN Comprehensive Investment Agreement
Arb.	Arbitration
art.	Article
BIT	Bilateral investment treaty
DFC	International Development Finance Corporation
DHAMAN	The Arab Investment & Export Credit Guarantee Corporation
DOJ	Denial of justice
ECA	Export Credit Agencies
ECHR	European Court of Human Rights
Ed	Editor
ed.	Edition
e.g.	Example
et al.	et alia 'and others'
etc.	Et cetera
et seq.	*et sequens*, *sequential* 'and the following'
FDI	Foreign direct investment
fn.	footnote
Ibid	ibidem 'in the same place,'
ICIEC	The Islamic Corporation for The Insurance of Investment and Export Credit
ICC	International Chamber of Commerce
ICISA	International Credit Insurance & Surety Association
ICSID	International Centre for Settlement of Investment Disputes
i.e.	id est
ILC	International Law Commission
ILO	International Labour Organization
IMF	International Monetary Fund
MIGA	Multilateral Investment Guarantee Agency

no.	Number
OECD	Organisation for Economic Co-operation and Development
OFAC	U.S. Treasury's Office of the Foreign Asset Control
OPIC	The Overseas Private Investment Corporation
para.	Paragraph
P	Page
PCA	Permanent Court of Arbitration
pp	Pages
SEC	The U.S. Securities and Exchange Commission
UNCITRAL	The United Nations Commission on International Trade Law
UNCTAD	United Nations Conference on Trade and Development
v.	versus
Vol.	Volume
WTO	World Trade Organization

Chapter 1
Introduction

An investment made with the purpose of obtaining a lasting interest in a country other than that of the investor, as is the case in developing countries, may face risks associated with doing business in a territory that does not enjoy a stable legal framework, political composition or governance. In the world of foreign investment, risky lands offer concessions or means alike to attract investments. However, reliance on the host country's statements can be an obedience to the unexpected. Once the investment is underway, it may be a point of no return, where the statements blur, and the host state takes advantage of the investor and behave recklessly. Therefore, in exchange for the potential of the risk exposure, investors should receive more than just words from the party with whom they enter into a transaction. In that regard, a third party's backing in the form of insurance coverage may address the investor's concerns.

Conventional insurance contracts are designed to mitigate losses, however, as this book will reveal, the presence of political risk insurance (PRI) may serve to avoid the occurrence of risks. In addition, PRI establishes a different relationship compared to conventional insurance; hence, it can be said that PRI is insurance for exceptional circumstances. Put differently, the gamut of perils that are covered by PRI policies does not fall within the scope of the conventional insurance, on the contrary, they are the 'excluded perils' of the customary insurance practices. In most cases, it is the sovereign who causes the peril whether through its direct or indirect actions. The primal need for the PRI coverage rests on the fact that sovereign powers may be predisposed towards interfering in the business activities of foreign investors. Thus, PRI acts as a form of protection to deter the wrongful sovereigns.

Political risks possess several defining attributes; They often develop gradually, and the consequences thereof may unfold over months or years. Tangible harm can arise without a physical injury befalling the investor's assets. Hence, one should anticipate that such risks may manifest in various forms and make it troublesome to trace the wrongdoer's footprints. The means by which the sovereign may achieve its objectives can take one of the following forms: unfair or arbitrary treatment by the sovereign power that deprives investors of their proprietary rights, transfer

Ö. Tosun, *The Law of Political Risk Insurance*, AIDA Europe Research Series on Insurance Law and Regulation 12, https://doi.org/10.1007/978-3-031-74675-8_1

restrictions; currency inconvertibility; the sovereign power's failure to honor its financial obligations; wrongful or unfair calling of guarantees, denial of justice; and arbitration award default.

In fact, certain political risks do not require deliberate actions from the sovereign, by contrast, these events are the ones over which sovereigns have no or limited control. Thus, risks such as war, terrorist attacks and other means of political force majeure or political violence deserve a distinct focus. International investments are shaped based on the mutual benefits and interests of the parties involved. While developing or less developed countries need capital export to support their economic growth and infrastructure projects, investors from the developed countries on the other hand engage in business with developing countries for various purposes, including political reasons, and for the purposes of expanding and diversifying their operations, accessing necessary natural resource and skilled labor force, lowering production costs and lastly even mitigating global warming. Despite the global economy having been following this economic trend within the last decades, wars and turmoil of every sort began to grip the world. Decision-makers of sovereigns kept pace with nationalist trends, and in so doing, led the foreign capitals to encounter severe reactions. Consequently, it may be accurate to say that PRI functions like an airbag, allowing investors to obviate the disaster when foreign capital and the sovereign clash.

The second chapter in this book recaps the history of PRI and the circumstances that led to the development of PRI. The following chapter employs a comparative analysis to make a distinction between regular insurance contracts and PRI contracts. Chapter 4 establishes the link between the three columns of international investment. The fifth chapter introduces the parties to PRI contract, provides an overview of the operations of global players, aims to fill the gap in the terminological differences and evaluates virtual form of investment along with the old-fashioned forms. In addition, it puts forward a brief discussion on recent political facts. In the sixth chapter, the discussion focuses on the techniques in mitigating the risks and losses.

The seventh chapter outlines forms of protection that investment treaties or agreements concluded between foreign investors and host states can offer. Chapter 8 presents the incidents that foreign investors fear the most. This chapter sets forth each political risk in great detail, and in doing so and by bearing the technological advancement in mind, visualizes what may be on the horizon. Moreover, it examines the legal concepts within the meaning of investment arbitration that serve to protect foreign investments. Chapter 9 addresses the incidents that are not covered by the PRI policies. The subsequent chapter explores the extent of the insurer's monetary obligation and distinguishes the mechanics of compensation. The book then proceeds to argue the concept of subrogation, assesses the place where the insurer stands and tackles the question by touching upon the immunity of the Sovereign. The same chapter provides a quasi-fruitful basis for insurers to induce treaty provisions to enable subrogation. And Chap. 12 concludes with the dispute resolution clauses and laws to govern both the PRI and the investment contract.

Chapter 2
The Origins of and the Need for the PRI

International trade gained momentum within the twentieth century, and less developed countries became more familiar with the concept of capital export. Investors were attracted by opportunities such as building and operating infrastructure projects in foreign countries or extracting and processing raw materials. While some of these less developed countries embraced liberalization as an end in itself, the idea of foreign nationals owning or controlling resources were seen as exploitation in the eyes of nationals of countries that either failed in or stood against liberalization. In addition, the way that the benefits were distributed intensified the social pressures leading to unpredictable interventions by the host states in foreign investments.[1]

The potential political risks compelled investors to seek assurance for their overseas transactions. In response to these needs, governments endeavored to provide guarantees to their investors. In the nineteenth century, state governments in the United States provided guarantees for the payment of interest and principal on railroad bonds sold in the capital markets of London and Paris.[2] As alluded, PRI did not arise miraculously; opinions diverge on its timeline. Some scholars assert that it originated from the marine insurance coverages provided to exporters.[3] Some authors suggest that PRI can be traced back to the inception of UK Export Finance in 1919 and the establishment of a guarantee facility for US investors in war-torn Europe under the Marshall Plan.[4] Some scholars on the other hand opine that true birth of private political risk insurance industry dates back to the 1930s when Lloyds of London began offering coverage for political risks.[5] The experience of the

[1] Rubins and Kinsella (2005), p. 5.

[2] For detail See Martin (1967), p. 282.

[3] Paul (1987), p. 710.

[4] Tan (2015), p. 175. Also see Jensen and Young (2008), p. 529. Also see Karagöz (2018), pp. 119, 131–134. Also see Papanastasiou (2021), p. 161, also see Khachaturian (2006), pp. 1044–1045, finally see Diaconis (1989), p. 272.

[5] DeLeonardo (2005), p. 742.

Ö. Tosun, *The Law of Political Risk Insurance*, AIDA Europe Research Series on Insurance Law and Regulation 12, https://doi.org/10.1007/978-3-031-74675-8_2

U.S. with PRI coverage began in 1948 through the 1948 Economic Corporation Act.[6] The US government launched a national investment program to contribute to rebuilding of Western Europe.[7] Initially, the US Investment Guarantee Program only covered non-convertibility risk. Eventually, the coverage expanded to include expropriation risk and after 1956 war risk.[8] From this date onwards the coverage broadened to encompass the risks of revolution and insurrection.[9]

In the late 1950s, a working group of Council of Europe's Consultative Assembly proposed a scheme to provide coverage against non-commercial risks.[10] This scheme was one of the first ones designed on a multinational level.[11] Following attempts to establish a multinational insurance program that designed to cover investments by the Europeans in the African countries failed. These attempts were not an end point but marked the beginning of a promising process. OECD drafted a report on 'Establishment of a Multilateral Investment Guarantee Corporation'.[12] On a global scale, the idea of establishing a political risk insurance provider was discussed at UNCTAD I. After pressure of OECD as well as the United Nations, the World Bank drafted the International Investment Insurance Agency's Articles of Agreement in 1966. However, U.S., the U.K., Japan, Canada and Germany had reservations. This insurance scheme was criticized due to the lack of the host state's financial participation and its bearing of a portion of the risk. Subrogation of the insurance agency to the claim of a compensated investor was another intractable problem.[13] Although amendments were made in 1972, differences in opinions stalled the negotiations.[14] In order for a political risk insurance, fruitless attempts did not come only from institutions; private bankers also made proposals for an insurance concept against political risks.[15]

In the twentieth century, a considerable number of foreign investments were exposed to political risks.[16] In the 1960s, widespread expropriation by the Castro regime after the Cuban revolution increased the need for insurance coverage at a multinational level. For the same reason, under the US insurance program, the

[6] See Peinhardt and Allee (2016), p. 211 and Martin (1967), p. 284, also see Dolzer and Schreuer (2012), pp. 228–229, McKellar (2010), p. 11.

[7] Rowat (1992), p. 119.

[8] Martin (1967), p. 284.

[9] Diaconis (1989), p. 272.

[10] Also see Radi (2020), p. 231.

[11] Berger (1988), pp. 23–24.

[12] Martin (1967), p. 286.

[13] Karagöz (2018), p. 106.

[14] Khachaturian (2006), pp. 1048–1049.

[15] Berger (1988), p. 22.

[16] Salacuse (2016), p. 382.

definitions of war and expropriation were implemented with broad language in the Foreign Assistance Act of 1961.[17]

The twenty-first century has also witnessed significant incidents giving rise to political risks. In the last twenty or so years, foreign investments in developing countries have boosted.[18] September 11, 2001[19] was a threshold in PRI that led to the inclusion of terrorism risk coverage alongside other risks, requiring an additional premium. Furthermore, the Turkey and Madrid bombings shifted the perception of the region as risky, and terrorist attacks added a remarkable level of uncertainty to the so-called risk-free legacy of the developed countries.[20] These attacks delivered a clear message that every place can be a potential target for political violence,[21] and due to the interdependent nature of national economies, political risks can have an effect similar to that of a butterfly. The occurrence of a political risk in one state may pose an economic threat to any other state or its exporters.

Terrorism coverage responded to the needs by offering investors a means for insuring against losses arising out of any form of violence that results in mass destruction. According to some scholars, after September 11, despite the obvious need, Exim banks ('ECAs'[22]) unexpectedly, inclined to stop offering coverage.[23] In this century, the US subprime mortgage crisis and global economic crisis drove sovereign powers to act with nationalist motives and threaten the profitability or continuity of investments. Moreover, investors encountered the quasi-war concepts of proxy wars and annexations. Viewed from this perspective, political risks are akin to taking a risky leap, and PRI acts as a parachute, providing a safe landing. The insurance coverage is vital for the investor insomuch as in its absence, the investor may not ever need it again. However, PRI was not then and is not now the main mechanism investors prefer, as we shall explore in the subsequent chapters, investors are prone to opt for protections provided by international law.

---

[17] Peinhardt and Allee (2016) p. 213, also see Martin (1967), p. 286. With the passage of this Act, investment(political) insurance against political risks began to be supported by the US government. See Hansen (2004), p. 80.

[18] Torrado (2005), p. 304.

[19] McKellar (2010), pp. 18, 49.

[20] Also see Jarvis Darryl and Griffiths (2007), p. 9.

[21] DeLeonardo (2005), p. 772.

[22] ECAs may be in the form of Export-Import banks and abbreviated to 'Exim bank'. Export Credit Agency is an agency in a creditor country that provides insurance, guarantees, or loans for the export of goods and services. Please visit IMF library, available at https://www.elibrary.imf.org/display/book/9781589060609/back-1 xml accessed 02.09.2024. *Heard* and *Laryea* define them as "*governmental or intergovernmental agencies or institutions in creditor-countries that provide insurance, guarantees or loans for the export of goods, services or capital by businesses and entities from the creditor-countries to other countries, usually debtor-countries considered to present high sovereign risks.*" See Heard and Laryea (2021), p. 616. For Exim banks also see Williams (1993), p. 89 et seq. For more about ECAs, please visit: https://www.eca-watch.org/ accessed 02.09.2024.

[23] Brown (2004), p. 20.

Online Database

https://www.eca-watch.org
https://www.elibrary.imf.org

References

Berger KP (1988) The new Multilateral Investment Guarantee Agency globalizing the investment insurance approach towards development. Syracuse J Int Law Commer 15(1):13

Brown V (2004) Political risk insurance after September 11 and the Argentine crisis: a public provider's perspective. In: Moran H, Theodore (ed) International political risk management, Vol. 2: The Brave New World, World Bank Publications, Washington: 15-26

DeLeonardo JM (2005) Are public and private political risk insurance two of a kind? Suggestions for a new direction for government coverage. Virginia J Int Law 45(3):737

Diaconis JS (1989) Political risk insurance: OPIC's use of a 'Fiduciary Agent' to facilitate resolution of subrogation claims. Int Lawyer 23(1):271–279

Dolzer R, Schreuer C (2012) Principles of international investment law, 2nd edn. Oxford University Press, Oxford

Hansen KW (2004) PRI and the rise (and Fall?) of private investment in public infrastructure. In: Moran HT (ed) International political risk management, vol. 2: The Brave New World. World Bank Publications, Washington, pp 75–100

Heard J, Laryea ET (2021) Export credit agencies, international investment law and the spectre of unsustainable developing countries' debts. Afr J Int Comp Law 29(4):612–643

Jarvis Darryl SL, Griffiths M (2007) Learning to fly: the evolution of political risk analysis. Glob Soc 21(1):5–21. https://doi.org/10.1080/13600820601116435

Jensen NM, Young DJ (2008) A violent future? Political risk insurance markets and violence forecasts. J Confl Resolut 52(4):527–547

Karagöz T (2018) The influence of investor-centered values in the operation of political risk insurance. J World Investment trade 19(1):118–153

Khachaturian A (2006) Are we in good hands? The adequacy of American and multilateral political risk insurance programs in fostering international development. Conn Law Rev 38(5):1041

Martin EM (1967) Multilateral investment insurance: the OECD proposal. Harv Int Law J 8(2): 280–338

McKellar R (2010) A short guide to political risk. Gower, Farnham

Papanastasiou TN (2021) The implications of political risk insurance in the governance of energy projects: the case of Japan's public insurance agencies. In: Titi C (ed) Public actors in international investment law, 1st edn. Springer International Publishing, Cham, pp 155–179

Paul DA (1987) New developments in private political risk insurance and trade finance. Int Lawyer 21(3):709–718

Peinhardt C, Allee T (2016) Political risk insurance as dispute resolution. J Int Disp Settlement 7(1): 205–224

Radi Y (2020) Insurance against political risks. In: Rules and practices of international investment law and arbitration. Cambridge University Press, pp 231–242

Rowat M (1992) Multilateral approaches to improving the investment climate of developing-countries - the cases of ICSID and MIGA. Harv Int Law J 33(1):103–144

Rubins N, Kinsella NS (2005) International investment, political risk and dispute resolution "A practitioner's Guide". Oxford University Press

Salacuse JW (2016) The law of investment treaties, 3rd edn. Oxford University Press, Oxford

Tan C (2015) Risky business: political risk insurance and the law and governance of natural resources. Int J Law Context 11(2):174–194

Torrado PM (2005) Political risk insurance and breach of contract coverage: how the intervention of domestic courts may prevent investors from claiming insurance. Pace Int Law Rev 17(2):301

Williams S (1993) Political and other risk insurance: OPIC, MIGA, EXIMBANK and other providers. Pace Int Law Rev 5:59–113

Chapter 3
Insuring the Loss Through a Contract

3.1 Identifying Insurance Contracts

Insurance contracts can be defined in numerous ways, according to *Merkin*, an insurance contract is "*a contract under which one person (the insurer) is legally bound to pay a sum of money or its equivalent to another person (the insured), upon the happening of a specified event involving some element of uncertainty as to whether it will occur (or, if it is certain to occur, as to when it will occur), and which event adversely affects the insured's interest in the subject matter of the insurance.*"[1] Another esteemed scholar contributed to terminology with the following definition, in his view; "*insurance is a contract whereby one person (the insurer), agrees to pay money or to provide a corresponding benefit on the occurrence of an event, which is both certain and adverse in return for money, usually called a premium*".[2]

The definition of a contract should be both broad and narrow in scope.[3] Put differently, it should be broad enough to encompass the basic elements of the contract, such as what parties owe to one another and the relation upon which the contract is built. In addition, the definition should also be narrow and disregard the issues that are not vital to readers. The definitions provided above encompass essential components of an insurance contract and offer different perspectives. However, in our opinion, insurance can be characterized as involving the following:

---

[1] Merkin (2013), pp. 1–3, for other definitions please see Merkin and Steele (2013), pp. 27, 28, 42, 43.

[2] Clarke (2013), p. 5, for another definition see Eggers and Picken (2018), p. 9. Another scholar defines in the following way "*a contract by which one party (the insurer) for a stipulated consideration or "premium" agrees to compensate another party (the insured) for loss on a specified subject by the happening of specified perils.*" Salacuse (2013), p. 246.

[3] According to one scholar, "*Definitions are like belts. The shorter they are, the more elastic they need to be. A short belt reveals nothing about its wearer: by stretching, it can be made to fit almost anybody.*" For the quotation of Stephen Toulmin, see Rubins (2004), p. 284.

Ö. Tosun, *The Law of Political Risk Insurance*, AIDA Europe Research Series on Insurance Law and Regulation 12, https://doi.org/10.1007/978-3-031-74675-8_3

the meaning, uncertainty and the impact of the risk, parties' monetary obligations and form of those obligations (if any). Moreover, as the following chapters will reveal, the party entitled to compensation can be referred to by different terms in different jurisdictions. Finally, one must note that the insured must have an insurable interest.[4] In the exercise of PRI, the insured must hold a title to tangible or intangible asset (own the asset or hold a right of enjoyment over the asset) and moreover, its interest must be 'at risk'.[5]

Even if one were to argue that the subject matter to be insured is of no consequence and that interest of any kind can be insurable, the loss caused by the materialization of the risk must have a calculable monetary value.[6] It's important to note that mental distress, being subjective in nature, are types of harm whose value cannot be objectively determined. Grief, anger, agony or disappointment -feelings specific to human beings- cannot be assessed and be fixed by monetary means.[7] It is a hazy area where a fine line cannot easily be drawn. Damages of a moral character are subjective; consequences of the incident may vary from one person to another. Valuation of an incorporeal damage is difficult to estimate or incapable of quantification and thus, its reparation function does not place the legal person in the situation where it could have been prior to occurrence of the risk, and neither monetary means can eradicate the signs of moral harm. In light of these facts and within the context of investment law, we define the insurance contract as *a contract by which the insurer undertakes; in exchange for the agreed contribution (premium), to provide coverage to insured or policyholder against an event occurrence of which is uncertain, adverse and upon the occurrence of this insured event, whether in cash or in kind, to compensate the concerned person's interest that is measurable by money.*

Insurance contracts are synallagmatic, executed on a reciprocal basis. The obligation of one party is correlative to the obligation of the other. The insurer assumes the duty to cover and is responsible for the compensation if the insured event occurs. The commencement of the insurer's liability may differ among jurisdictions, unless the law governing the contract states otherwise, the insurer's liability should begin when the premium is paid or in case of installments, when the first installment is paid. However, in an unconventional insurance concept like PRI, to the extent

[4] Also see Roach et al. (2022), chapter 27.

[5] Budd (1993), p. 30.

[6] In the view of the OECD Insurance Committee, the technical conditions that make a risk insurable are: "assessability (probability and severity of losses should be quantifiable); randomness (the time at which the insured event occurs should be unpredictable when the policy is underwritten, and the occurrence itself must be independent of the will of the insured); mutuality (numerous persons exposed to a given hazard should be able to join together to form a risk community within which the risk is shared and diversified)." See Gordon (2008), p. 93.

[7] *Dumberry* argues that even if the amount allocated will admittedly often be largely symbolic, monetary compensation remains the appropriate remedy for moral damages affecting a corporation. See Dumberry (2012), p. 228.

possible,[8] it should be left to the parties' discretion. For instance, the period of coverage is of significant importance in construction projects, hence, parties must state the dates when the liability of the insurer commences and expires.

Insurance contracts may be classified as guarantee contracts. However, the warranty function they serve is not identical to the ones provided by banks. As some may know, under German and Turkish law, insurance contracts differ from letter of guarantees on the basis of; the conditional nature of the insurance contract, the law applied thereto and the obligation of the parties. Finally, although an ECA incorporated in the form of an Exim bank may provide a PRI coverage, insurance contracts are not blanket guarantees,[9] the insured party is a juridical person and a merchant rather than a real person consumer, and the insured item is not money deposited in a bank.

Insurance contracts are also aleatory in nature. In this regard, it is worth noting the difference between wagering contracts and insurance contracts. In a wagering contract each party, by entering into the contract, takes the risk of a certain loss and depending on the occurrence or non-occurrence of an event, one party wins from the other. Simply put, a wagering contract is not built upon a win-win basis. In a PRI contract however, one party pays a premium for the protection of his/her interest and even if the risk is not materialized and notwithstanding the fact that the premium is paid, the insured still benefits from being relieved from a possible financial loss. Besides, if the insured is a bank, it may take advantage of risk mitigation by using the insured credit amounts in calculating its capital requirements. In accordance with the Basel Accord, banks are allowed to utilize insurance policies for capital relief so that they may allocate less capital against the risk of debtors' default.[10]

---

[8]Turkish Commercial Code (TCC) deals with the obligations of the parties to insurance contracts. In accordance with art. 1421 of the TCC, insurance coverage begins upon the payment of the premium or its installment. TCC is available at http://www.aida.org.uk/pdf/turkish%20insurance%20contract%20law.pdf accessed 02.09.2024. A similar provision exists in German Insurance Contract Act 2008, according to section 51 "*The commencement of the insurance cover may be made dependent on the payment of the premium insofar as the insurer has drawn the policyholder's attention to this condition in writing in a separate communication or by means of a conspicuous note in the insurance policy.*" However, if PRI is assumed to cover jumbo risks, (it may be so in accordance with the subparagraph 2(2) of section 210), parties will be free to decide the terms of their PRI contract since section 210 of the same Act states "*The restrictions on the freedom of contract under this Act shall not apply to jumbo risks*". English version of the Act is available at https://www.gesetze-im-internet.de/englisch_vvg/englisch_vvg.html#p0015 accessed 02.09.2024.

[9]A blanket guarantee is a declaration by authorities that, in addition to the protection provided by limited coverage deposit insurance or other arrangements, certain deposits and perhaps other financial instruments will be protected. Please visit: https://www.dicgc.org.in/pdf/CorePrinciplesOfIADI_Nov2014.pdf accessed 02.09.2024. Also see HAY (1997), p. 158.

[10]Section 30.19 of Basel framework reads as follows "*Under the AMA (Advanced Measurement Approaches), a bank will be allowed to recognize the risk mitigating impact of insurance in the measures of operational risk used for regulatory minimum capital requirements. The recognition of insurance mitigation will be limited to 20% of the total operational risk capital requirements calculated under the AMA*". For the criteria set for insurance policy as well as insurance companies,

Finally, in conventional practice, agents and brokers may execute the contracts. Using intermediaries, however, may raise some concerns regarding the scope of the authority conferred upon the intermediary. Therefore, actions of the intermediary may require a ratification. Put differently, in order to justify whether the insurer is directly bound by the transactions concluded by the intermediary, the insured may wish to ascertain whether the intermediary has actual or apparent authority. Besides, in conventional insurance practice, intermediaries may assume pre-contractual onuses namely the duty to inform, to advise or to warn. The relation between intermediary and the insurer sets whom to bear the consequences of violating these duties. Prudent merchant foreign investors, however, cannot benefit from the principles meant to protect real person insureds. PRI might seem old-fashioned; due to specificity of the investments and the amount of the coverage, due diligence is a must. Thus, the last thing parties may want is an envoy (intermediary) who may, even unintentionally, bar or hinder a direct correspondence and cause delays in the circulation of documents.[11]

3.2 PRI Defined by Artificial Intelligence

Artificial intelligence (AI) has literally taken the world by storm; its use has proliferated in insurance practice, as well as in all aspects of life. In insurance, AI can provide accurate data and lower the number of human-induced errors, in addition AI can facilitate the performance of contractual obligations. In the following sections, we will discuss the impact of artificial intelligence on the PRI, in doing so we wanted to shed light on the prospective role of technology in PRI. As we applied to AI (namely 'ChatGPT') it provided a basic and expected definition for PRI,[12] surprisingly, it claimed that PRI might offer coverage for evacuation costs or expenses related to relocating the insured's operations. The coverage for these expenses is not irrational; by contrast, it will serve to mitigate the insurer's loss. By way of illustration, in trade credit insurance, in case the buyer refuses to receive the goods, the insurance policy may cover the additional costs (such as freight, demurrage, customs clearance, and storage at customs or insurance) accrued at the time of repatriation of the goods to the country of the supplier (exporter).

---

also see section 30.20 Available at https://www.bis.org/basel_framework/index.htm?export=pdf accessed 02.09.2024.

[11] Also see Gilbert (1986), pp. 407–415.

[12] According to ChatGPT, PRI is "*a type of insurance that protects businesses, investors, lenders, and other parties from losses resulting from political risks such as political violence, expropriation, currency inconvertibility, and other forms of government action or inaction that can adversely affect investments or operations in foreign countries.*"

3.3 A Humble Attempt to Define PRI

PRI can serve as a management strategy in unfamiliar environments that require attention.[13] It covers a composite of different threats[14] and serves as a major tool; to shift political risks from the foreign investor to the insurance provider[15] and to assist investors and lenders in reducing the probability or severity arising from the adverse actions or inactions by host governments.[16] This specialized line of insurance protects traders, investors and lenders against non-commercial risks that can disrupt the successful completion of trade contracts, and the effective ownership or operation of investments.[17]

As the name suggests PRI, in short, is the insurer's payment guarantee to natural or juridical persons (investors) against losses arising from political risks. This simplified definition fails to highlight the most notable part of PRI, which is the various forms of political risk and is therefore far from being accurate. As will be elucidated below, expecting a consensus on a single definition is impractical; however, some may wish to delve into its meaning.

Risk stands as the probability of an event; in insurance practice, it signifies the deteriorative nature of the event. For instance, in life insurance, it takes the form of an event, the occurrence of which is only a matter of time. In PRI, however, it indicates the possibility of investors not reaping benefits from their investment due to events beyond their control. The term 'country-risk' on the other hand captures various risks, including those political.[18] Country risk denotes a variety of instances such as macroeconomic risks (instability, inflation) and environmental risks (natural disasters and labor disruptions).[19] Hence, the meaning of the term is broad in scope and echoes the risks of all forms with regard to the country in question. Amidst

[13] Brink (2016), p. 4.

[14] DeLeonardo (2005), p. 739.

[15] Hyder and Attanasio (2021), pp. 450–451.

[16] Baroudi (2017), p. 406.

[17] Wagner (2012), p. 97.

[18] OECD classifies countries into eight categories (according to the likelihood of whether they will service their external debts). The indictors are basically as follows; general moratorium on repayments, political events and/or economic difficulties which prevent or delay the transfer of funds paid in respect of the credit, legal provisions adopted in the obligor's/guarantor's country declaring repayments made in local currency to be a valid discharge of the debt, any other measure or decision which prevents repayment under a credit, cases of force majeure (war [including civil war]), expropriation, revolution, riot, civil disturbances, cyclones, floods, earthquakes, eruptions, tidal waves and nuclear accidents) See OECD's Arrangement on Officially Supported Export Credits available at https://one.oecd.org/document/TAD/PG(2022)1/en/pdf accessed 02.09.2024. Also see Burnett and Bret (2017), pp. 30–31.

[19] In the wording of the *Tidewater* tribunal "*country risk premium quantifies the general risks, including political risks, of doing business in the particular country, as they applied on that date and as they might then reasonably have been expected to affect the prospects, and thus the value to be ascribed to the likely cash flow of the business going forward.*" see para. 186 of the award dated 13.03.2015. Available at https://www.italaw.com/sites/default/files/case-documents/italaw4206_0.

almost unlimited definitions of 'political risk' we simply chose to quote a few to create a distinction. In the narrowest sense it is "the amalgam of unwanted consequences of political activity[20]", or "*the possibility that investments will be impaired by certain types of government measures*".[21] One scholar proposes the following definition which is "*governmental or societal actions and policies, originating either within or outside the host country, and negatively affecting either a select group of, or the majority of, foreign business operations and investments.*[22]" While other scholars extend this definition to "*governmental or societal actions, policies or omissions that negatively affect the business operations and investments of a specific firm or a group of firms in the form of physical damages or economic losses in its home or a host country*[23]". Finally, *Rubins and Kinsella* introduced a definition and referred to facet of political risk insurance that is most salient. According to authors, political risk is "*the probability that a host government will, by act or omission, reduce the investor's ability to realize an expected return on his investment*[24]".

Political risks manifest in foreign lands, and the sources of this risk are multifaceted, but they mainly involve politically motivated actions/omissions by the ruler of those lands that sweep away foreign investments. It is therefore, prior to defining PRI, it is essential to explain some key terms peculiar to this concept of insurance. Every sovereign craves to control, whether of its nationals or of others, the actions taken on its territory. Hence, *sovereignty* can be defined as the public authority that commands in civil society, and orders and directs what each citizen is to perform to obtain the end of its institution.[25] *Sovereign* on the other hand, is the person invested

pdf accessed 02.09.2024. Also see Burgstaller and Ketcheson (2017), p. 195 and Dorobantu et al. (2016), p. 219, also see the chapter dealing with the valuation of investment.

[20] Jarvis Darryl and Griffiths (2007), p. 11.

[21] Kantor et al. (2011), p. xx. (Introduction part).

[22] Simon (1982), p. 68.

[23] See Braun and Fischer (2018), p. 4. Due to its broad scope, political risk has been defined in several ways, for instance, in some authors' view, political risk is "*the risk associated with the effect that actions of agents pursuing political objectives may have on the value of the assets of agents pursuing economic objectives.*" See Restrepo et al. (2012). Another scholar defines political risk in the following words: "*the probability that the profitability of an investment be negatively affected by circumstances ascribable either to unforeseen changes (e.g. revolutions, even when linked to democratization processes) in the domestic or international political arena, or to governmental policy choices affecting the international investor's property rights.*" See Emma Sottilota (2013), p. 6. One author opines that political risks are "*threats to the profitability of a project that derive from some sort of governmental action or non-action rather than from changes in economic conditions in the marketplace.*" See Moran Theodore (1999), at 3 [citing Harvard Professor Louis Wells, Jr.] as cited in Ibid, p. 3. Some scholars also define as "*the risk that a sovereign host government will unexpectedly change the 'rules of the game' under which businesses operate.*" See Butler and Joaquin (1998), p. 599. For other definitions please see Jiang et al. (2021), p. 127. Also see Han et al. (2018), p. 124. Similarly, see McDowell (2021), p. 639 and finally, see Tan (2015), p. 180.

[24] Rubins and Kinsella (2005), p. 3.

[25] Sovereignty is also defined as "*the supreme and independent authority of the nation state within its own territory*". For the quoted definition and detail, please see Salacuse (2013), p. 76.

in with the authority.[26] Lastly, the term '*political*' denotes matters pertaining to politics; of or relating to the conduct of government.[27]

Despite its scope, the literal interpretation of '*political risk insurance*' may mislead those unfamiliar with this concept. At first glance, for some, PRI may connote an insurance coverage against the harms resulting from political disputes. A more accurate phrase could have been 'sovereign risk insurance[28] (SRI)' which better captures what this insurance protects against. Although practitioners employ the term 'investment insurance', some may suppose that it provides coverage against physical damage that investments incur, whereas most political risks are intangible in nature. In order to avoid confusion and to highlight its substantial component, in this study we opt for 'political risk insurance' ('PRI').

As all contracts do, PRI contracts encompass a purposive activity where the foreign investor and the insurer aim to gain a benefit. Since risks are diversified and complex, in our view, PRI in the broadest sense can be defined as an *insurance that provides coverage against losses foreign investors incur as a result of: a) events, namely; arbitrary, discriminatory or unfair measures or decisions attributable to the host state that deprive the investor of the enjoyment of proprietary rights and adversely affect fair, reasonable, justifiable and legitimate expectations*[29] *from*

[26] de Vattel (1852), pp. 71, 84. After discussions at the deliberations of 'Draft articles on Jurisdictional Immunities of States and Their Property', the International Law Commission(ILC) employed "sovereign authority" as the corresponding term for "prerogatives de la puissance publique de l'Etat". According to some members of the ILC, this French text appeared to be intended to refer to public institutions and to distinguish them from private institutions. Although some members took the view that "sovereign authority" was associated with the international personality of the state they expressed that "governmental authority" was the nearest translation of this French term within the context of the draft articles. Please see footnote 36 at page 16 and 17 of the commentary to 'Draft articles on Jurisdictional Immunities of States and Their Property'available at https://legal.un.org/ilc/texts/instruments/english/commentaries/4_1_1991.pdf accessed 02.09.2024. Also see Fox and Webb (2013), pp. 302–303.

[27] Definition can be found in the Black's Law Dictionary. (In this book references in regard to the Black's law Dictionary were made to its ninth ed.).

[28] Also, see Heard and Laryea (2021), p. 617.

[29] The ECHR uses this concept in its jurisprudence, See Ratner (2008), p. 498. According to *Newcombe*, legitimate expectations of the investor must also be assessed in the context that investments are made for commercial returns and inevitably involve risk. See Newcombe and Paradell (2009), p. 350. In *Potočnik's view*, legitimate expectations are based on the concept of specific assurances made by the host state to the investor at the time the investment was made. See Potočnik (2019), p. 158. According to *Tudor*, following criteria are of significance. Investor's expectations must stem from an authority's (State) conduct, the expectations must be reasonable and justifiable in the light of circumstances and finally the investor's loss must be directly linked to or caused by the host state's failure to respect these expectations. Tudor (2008), pp. 166, 168. And finally, in the view of the ECHR, to be legitimate, the expectation must be of a nature more concrete than a mere hope and be based on a legal provision or a legal act such as a judicial decision, bearing on the property interest in question. The court also opines that a license provided to a company becomes component part of its property and if a contract is signed then the legitimate expectation is based on a legal act which has a sound legal basis. See "page 9 of the Guide on Article 1 of Protocol

his/her investment or b) acts and/or omissions in the form of political violence/force majeure that takes place in the territory of and attributable to the host state.

Cases

Tidewater: (1) Tidewater Investment srl (2) Tidewater Caribe, c.a., v. The Bolivarian Republic of Venezuela, (ICSID Case No. ARB/10/5), Award.

Online Database

http://www.aida.org.uk
https://www.bis.org
https://www.dicgc.org
https://rm.coe.int/guide-art-1-protocol-1-eng/1680a20cdc
https://www.gesetze-im-internet.de
https://www.italaw.com
https://www.iadi.org
https://www.legal.un.org
https://www.oecd.org
https://www.researchgate.net

References

Baroudi MM (2017) Innovation in political risk insurance: experience from the multilateral investment guarantee agency. Global Pol 8:406–413. https://doi.org/10.1111/1758-5899.12480

Braun A, Fischer M (eds) (2018) Handbook of political risk insurance. University of St. Gallen. ISBN: 978-3-7297-2011-4 https://www.researchgate.net/publication/335395711_Handbook_of_Political_Risk_Insurance

Brink CH (2016) Measuring political risk: risks to foreign investment. Routledge Taylor & Francis Group

Budd N (1993) Making sense of political risk insurance policies. Int Financ Law Rev 12(6):29–32

Burgstaller M, Ketcheson J (2017) Should expropriation risk be taken into account in the assessment of damages? ICSID Rev 32(1):193–215

Burnett HG, Bret L (2017) Arbitration of international mining disputes: law and practice. Oxford University Press

Butler KC, Joaquin DC (1998) A note on political risk and the required return on foreign direct investment. J Int Bus Stud 29(3):599–607

Clarke MA (2013) The law of liability insurance. Informa Law from Routledge, New York

No. 1 to the European Convention on Human Rights" available at https://rm.coe.int/guide-art-1-protocol-1-eng/1680a20cdc accessed 02.09.2024.

de Vattel E (1852) The law of nations, or principles of the law of nature applied to the conduct and affairs of nations and sovereigns. T. & J.W. Johnson, Pennsylvania

DeLeonardo JM (2005) Are public and private political risk insurance two of a kind? Suggestions for a new direction for government coverage. Virginia J Int Law 45(3):737

Dorobantu FA, Dupont N, Maniatis MA (2016) Country risk and damages in investment arbitration. ICSID Rev 31(1):219–231

Dumberry P (2012) Satisfaction as a form of reparation for moral damages suffered by investors and respondent states in investor-state arbitration disputes. J Int Disp Settlement 3(1)

Eggers PM, Picken S (2018) Good faith and insurance contracts, 4th edn. Routledge Taylor & Francis Group

Emma Sottilota C (2013) Political Risk: Concepts, Definitions, Challenges. LUISS School of Government Working Paper Series, 1. https://sog.luiss.it/sites/sog.luiss.it/files/SOG%20Working%20Papers%20Sottilotta%20ISSN_0.pdf

Fox H, Webb P (2013) The law of state immunity, 3rd edn. Oxford University Press, Oxford

Gilbert PR (1986) Acquiring and utilizing political risk insurance; a practitioner's perspective. Hast Int Comp Law Rev 9(3):407–415

Gordon K (2008) Investment guarantees and political risk insurance: institutions, incentives and development. OECD, Investment Policy Perspectives, Paris

Han X et al (2018) Chinese multinational enterprises in Europe and Africa: how do they perceive political risk? Manag Int Rev 58(1):121–146

Hay R (1997) Protecting assets from political risk. Priv Client Bus 3:152–164

Heard J, Laryea ET (2021) Export credit agencies, international investment law and the spectre of unsustainable developing countries' debts. Afr J Int Comp Law 29(4):612–643

Hyder AA, Attanasio DL (2021) International investment protection of global banking and finance: legal principles and arbitral practice. Kluwer Law International

Jarvis Darryl SL, Griffiths M (2007) Learning to fly: the evolution of political risk analysis. Glob Soc 21(1):5–21. https://doi.org/10.1080/13600820601116435

Jiang W et al (2021) Political risk management of foreign direct investment in infrastructure projects: bibliometric-qualitative analyses of research in developing countries. Eng Constr Archit Manag 28(1):125–153

Kantor M, Nolan MD, Sauvant KP (2011) Reports of overseas private investment corporation determinations, vol 1. Oxford University Press

McDowell D (2021) Financial sanctions and political risk in the international currency system. Rev Int Polit Econ RIPE 28(3):635–661

Merkin RM (2013) Insurance law: an introduction. Routledge, London

Merkin RM, Steele J (2013) Insurance and the law of obligations, 1st edn. Oxford University Press, Oxford

Moran Theodore H (1999) Political and regulatory risk in infrastructure investment in developing countries: introduction and overview. CEPMLP J 5(6)

Newcombe A, Paradell L (2009) Law and practice of investment treaties. Standards of Treatment Kluwer Law International

Potočnik M (2019) Arbitrating brands: international investment treaties and trademarks. Edward Elgar Publishing Limited, Cheltenham, Gloucestershire

Ratner SR (2008) Regulatory takings in institutional context: beyond the fear of fragmented international law. Am J Int Law 102(3):475–528

Restrepo D et al (2012) Political risk and corporate investment decisions, Working Paper 04. Business Economic Series 03. https://e-archivo.uc3m.es/bitstream/handle/10016/13114/wb120403.pdf?sequence=1

Roach L et al (2022) Additional chapter principles of insurance law. In: Commercial law. Oxford University Press

Rubins N (2004) The notion of 'investment' in international investment arbitration. In: Horn N, Kröll SM (eds) Arbitrating foreign investment disputes: procedural and substantive legal aspects, studies in transnational economic law, vol 19. Kluwer Law International, pp 283–324

Rubins N, Kinsella NS (2005) International investment, political risk and dispute resolution "A practitioner's Guide". Oxford University Press

Salacuse JW (2013) The three laws of international investment: national, contractual, and international frameworks for foreign capital. Oxford University Press

Simon J (1982) Political risk assessment: past trends and future prospects. Columbia J World Business 1762–71

Tan C (2015) Risky business: political risk insurance and the law and governance of natural resources. Int J Law Context 11(2):174–194

The Black's Law Dictionary. 9th edn

Tudor I (2008) The fair and equitable treatment standard in the international law of foreign investment. Oxford University Press, Oxford

Wagner D (2012) Managing country risk a practitioner's guide to effective cross-border risk analysis. CRC Press, Boca Raton

Chapter 4
Treaties, Arbitration and PRI

4.1 Investment Treaties and, Arbitration in General

An investment treaty is defined as "*an agreement by which two or more states agree to accord specified legal treatment to investments undertaken in their territory by nationals of another treaty party and to resolve related disputes in the event that a state is alleged to have denied such legal treatment to a protected investment*".[1] A BIT on the other hand aims at protecting foreign direct investment[2] and is an agreement between two countries that establishes the term and conditions for private investment by nationals and companies of one state in the other state.[3]

Treaties are binding instruments of international law imposing enforceable legal obligations on the host state, rather than being 'expressions of good will'. The assumption upon which treaties rest is that enforceable rules would protect foreign investment, reduce the risks that the investors may otherwise face and encourage investment.[4] Accordingly, it might be said that investment treaties sustain hegemonic balance and therefore prevent an anarchic system of trade between sovereign states.

Most of the PRI practitioners neglect the relation between investment arbitration and PRI. In PRI, insureds are foreign investors, wrongdoers are the sovereigns (host state), and the wrongs are acts or omissions attributable to the sovereign. In the absence of PRI, the investor will resort to arbitration; in the presence of PRI, the insurer will. Therefore, as far as we are concerned, investment arbitration is the source of PRI and in this chapter, we will discuss the irregular bond between international procedural law and insurance law.

[1] Salacuse (2013), p. 364, similarly, Salacuse (2016), p. 168.

[2] Comeaux and Kinsella (1994), p. 5.

[3] Please visit: https://www.law.cornell.edu/wex/bilateral_investment_treaty accessed 02.09.2024.

[4] Salacuse and Sullivan (2005), p. 77 and Salacuse (2016), pp. 7,9,10. For an empirical analysis of the impact of the BITs, see Swenson (2009), pp 438–457.

Ö. Tosun, *The Law of Political Risk Insurance*, AIDA Europe Research Series on Insurance Law and Regulation 12, https://doi.org/10.1007/978-3-031-74675-8_4

4.2 Interaction of Treaties, Arbitration and PRI

BITs and investment arbitration, along with PRI, are synergistic and not strangers to each other; they are not merely alternatives.[5] Political risks are one of the main reasons for reduced capital flows to developing countries.[6] A great risk requires a greater potential profit, hence, in the absence of BITs[7] or PRI, investors would be more vulnerable to risks and, as a matter of course, would be reluctant to engage in overseas business.

The exclusive sway of domestic law is mitigated to an extent due to commitments made by a country under the BITS entered into by the host and source countries.[8] Albeit BITs play a prominent role in the creation of and claim determination in PRI, they are not the only instruments at play. Along with BITs, PRI serves to manage political risks and stands as the second pillar for protecting foreign direct investment.[9] Examples of political risks, therefore, deviation of states from their commitments, are abounded in the context of the investment arbitration cases.[10]

International law serves as a lighthouse for PRI in defining perils such as expropriation, as evidenced by some PRI policies referencing 'international law' for such definitions.[11] Finally, as chapter eleven will put forward, if the insurer claims rights against the sovereign, in deciding whether the insurer's claims are valid, arbitrator(s) must examine the merits of the dispute between the foreign investor and the sovereign. Hence, one may need to note that, since arbitrator (s) will determine on the legality of the disputed event or the sovereign's measure, arbitral awards are an ineluctable end in the implementation of PRI.

Although PRI claims are, by definition, investor-state disputes, but not the kind that is subject to investment arbitration.[12] Arguments can be made in support of the

[5] See 'Chapter 8: Third-Party Funding in Investment Arbitration', ICCA Reports No. 4: Report of the ICCA-Queen Mary Task Force on Third-Party Funding in International Arbitration, ICCA Reports Series, Vol. 4 International Council for Commercial Arbitration; ICCA & Kluwer Law International 2018 p 212.

[6] Alfaro et al. (2005), p. 7.

[7] Although we will discuss in detail in the following chapters BITs reduce risks stemming from obsolescence bargaining, by incorporating six core elements, which are as follows: 1- Host states' obligation to ensure that the investment receive fair and equitable treatment (FET), 2-The investor is compensated for expropriation, 3- Host state incorporates NT (National treatment) and MFN(Most favored nation) which binds the host state to treat BIT investors no less favorably than 'like' foreign and local investors, 4- Investors transfer their investments and returns therefrom into a freely convertible currency, 5- Host states incorporate umbrella clauses that result in extending their liability to any dispute relating covered investments 6- BITs provide binding third-party arbitration of disputes between investor and home state, and home state and host state. For detail, please see Soopramanien (2017), p. 589, also see Ginsburg (2013), p. 948. Garver (2009), p. 83.

[8] Haque and Burdescu (2004), p. 250.

[9] Tita (2010), p. 656.

[10] Rubins and Kinsella (2005), p. 6.

[11] Kantor (2015), p. 176. Similarly, Ginsburg (2013), p. 949.

[12] See Peinhardt and Allee (2016), p. 206.

presumption that PRI contracts cannot delineate the boundaries of, therefore be the basis for the state-state disputes. Subrogation,[13] however transforms the initial investor-state dispute into a state-state dispute once the insurer indemnifies the insured.[14] For instance, in 2004, the United States instituted arbitration against India due to DFC's claim payment to one of its insurers.[15] Some Latin American constitutions, however, have placed reservations against subrogation and have avoided allowing disputes between the host state and the investor to escalate into a political confrontation between governments.[16]

BITs undoubtedly provide guidance for risk-taking; however, they are not crucial components or determinants of PRI underwriting. Correspondingly, tribunals in investment arbitration are not bound by the decisions of PRI providers, however, drew consequences. In *Enron v. Argentina*, despite OPIC's finding was that there was an expropriation in the dispute, in the tribunal's view, OPIC's conclusion responded to a different kind of procedure and context that cannot influence or be taken into account in the case.[17] In *Generation Ukraine*, however, the tribunal's finding was that the investor failed, under the insurance contract with OPIC, to generate certain documents established a negative impact.[18] In the view of scholars, the case reflects an important insight as to the tribunals' rising awareness of the prerequisites set by PRI providers.[19]

The similarities between BITs and PRI are so extensive that their differences are subtle. We can inspect the dissimilarities of BITs and PRI in three groups. *Formation-wise*; BITs are not an insurance against business risk,[20] they are elements of

[13] Most of the BITs remove ambiguities as to the post-indemnification era and do contain articles where each state recognizes the rights of the insurers of the other.

[14] Heard and Laryea (2021), p. 623.

[15] Salacuse (2013), p. 261. See, *Offshore Power v. India*, also see, Artemis and Kabir (2024). Defending the rights of their nationals or the corporations incorporated within their borders before courts is not a new concept for states. In *Barcelona Traction* case where a Canadian company supplying electricity to a Spanish city was expropriated, Belgium sought to assert the expropriated rights of its nationals who held shares in the company. However, the International Court of Justice rejected this claim, stating that the company had the right to pursue its own claims. See Salacuse (2013), p. 313. The case is available at https://www.icj-cij.org/case/50 accessed 02.09.2024.

[16] Shihata (1986), p. 20.

[17] See paras. 235, 247, available at https://www.italaw.com/sites/default/files/case-documents/ita0293.pdf accessed 02.09.2024, also see Kantor et al. (2011), p. xxiv.

[18] The tribunal viewed that "*in accordance with the OPIC insurance policy maintained by the Claimant in relation to its investment in Heneratsiya, the Claimant was obliged to "maintain in the United States true and complete copies of the records, books of account and current financial statements for the foreign enterprise necessary to compute and substantiate compensation, including (1) records documenting the investment..." Either Generation Ukraine failed to keep such records in breach of its obligations under the OPIC policy, or they were withheld from the Tribunal despite their importance.*" See para. 19.22, the case is available at https://www.italaw.com/sites/default/files/case-documents/ita0358.pdf accessed 02.09.2024.

[19] Kantor et al. (2011), p. xxiv.

[20] See *MTD Equity v. Chile*, para.178. Available at https://www.italaw.com/sites/default/files/case-documents/ita0544.pdf similarly, *Maffezini v. Spain*, para. 64, available at https://www.italaw.com/

international law that outline favorable conditions for investment by nationals and companies of one state in the territory of another state, providing the basis for the reciprocal protection. The states promise each other to not to take certain actions defined in the BIT[21] and nationals of each party enjoy the rights stated therein. Unlike a regular contract, modifying a document of international law to which states are parties can be a lengthy process, making BITs orthodox in nature. On the other hand, a PRI policy is a contract of private law concluded between the insurer and the investor who is in the hopes of deterring the host state's wrongful acts. It is a contract which does not necessarily root for reciprocity and where, the insurer promises to indemnify the investor for the losses arising from the host state's interference with its investment or project.[22] PRI policies are liberal, flexible and may provide more favorable substantive protection[23] and amendments thereto are slightly easy. According to *Schill*, PRI schemes cannot serve as an alternative to the rights investors hold in investor-state arbitrations. In the scholar's view, this limitation arises from the non-obligatory nature of PRI on the host state. Instead of promoting investment flows, the PRI provider may become subject to externalizing the negative consequences of the host state's treatment of foreign investors.[24] This perspective undermines the subrogation mechanism, where the insurer is subrogated to all rights its insured held prior to subrogation, including those that may be alleged at the time of investment arbitration. Therefore, if the insured incurs losses due to the host state's unfair and inequitable treatment and if such losses were covered by the policy, the insurer must be entitled to seek reimbursement from the host state based on the lack of fair treatment.

Scope and availability-wise; BITs extend their benefits to citizens and companies incorporated within the signatory states. Public PRI providers or private insurers mandated by the governments may require the prospective insured to be a citizen of their own country or a company to be incorporated under the laws of that country. In connection with this, insurers may impose further requirements, and coverage may be provided to eligible exporters or investors.[25] Additionally, the condition of

sites/default/files/case-documents/ita0479.pdf both accessed 02.09.2024. Also see Tudor (2008), p. 167.

[21] Ginsburg (2013), p. 948.

[22] PRI is also described as an example of a creative and ingenious insurance solution. Rayman-Bacchus and Webb (2012), p. 396.

[23] Waters (2015), p. 366.

[24] Schill (2010), pp. 47–49.

[25] Prior to providing coverage, due to ECAs' commitments to conventions or multilateral agreements, ECAs may require their potential clients: to a) present certain declarations (for instance in accordance with Recommendation of the Council on Bribery and Officially Supported Export Credits, a declaration that exporter have not been engaged or will not engage in bribery in the transaction) b) be a member of export/foreign investment related unions and finally c) verify their capacity and therefore submit documents that they had already exercised export or foreign investment in the amount required by the government. For the Recommendation of the Council on Bribery and Officially Supported Export Credits, please visit: https://legalinstruments.oecd.org/en/instruments/OECD-LEGAL-0447 accessed 02.09.2024.

national content[26] must be met on all exports, Public PRI providers offer insurance coverage for exports where a certain percentage of the transaction value originates in the exporter's country. As we shall see, multinational insurers may introduce their own musts. A distinguishing feature of PRI is that it may require compliance with environmental guidelines,[27] while dated BITs may not keep up with the evolving nature of matters imperative in combating climate change. While both mechanisms require investors to take all reasonable efforts to mitigate the damage,[28] PRIs go further and impose obligations on the insured to immediately notify of losses or anticipated losses. Finally, while most investment arbitration awards are publicly available, PRI providers are secretive about the terms of their insurance contracts,[29] and determinations of claims are less likely publicized.[30]

Another remarkable difference lies within their *monetary terms.* BITs do not specify an amount, whereas PRIs set a cap, thereby limiting the amount of indemnification by the insurer. The calculation method for indemnification may also vary; while PRI policies mostly take net book value, damages under BITs are calculated using the discounted cash flow method.[31] Compared to investment arbitration, triggering payment provisions of PRI policies will be less time-consuming, and filing a claim may be sufficient. However, the process of obtaining an award will be lengthy,[32] whereas the average claim determination by PRI providers is more

---

[26] In response to foreign investors' enthusiasm to expand their operations, developing countries offer cheaper labor force, concessions and other means. Domestic manufacture can be crucial for the employment of nationals; however, a government subsidy should be availed to production in foreign territory. Hence, it is almost today's requisite to replace 'made in' concept with 'made by' concept and shift "national content" with the 'national interest'. For a discussion, see Søndergaard-Jensen (2019), pp. 427–431.

[27] Waters (2015), p. 377.

[28] As we will see later, investment tribunals seek claimant investors to first exhaust local remedies. When it comes to PRI, art. 17th of the MIGA Convention employs the following wording" *Contracts of guarantee shall require holders of guarantees to seek, before a payment is made by the Agency, such administrative remedies as may be appropriate under the circumstances, provided that they are readily available to them under the laws of the host country.*" See Muchlinski et al. (2008), p. 545 and also see Soopramanien (2017), pp. 604, 605.

[29] Tan (2015), p. 186.

[30] DFC, in this regard, is an exception since it makes decisions publicly available on its website. Please visit: https://www.dfc.gov/who-we-are/transparency-and-accountability accessed 02.09.2024.

[31] Although we will discuss valuation methods in the following chapters, in *Waters'* expression, since MIGA calculates compensation based on the 'book value' the method of which excludes the goodwill of the company, a MIGA payout after expropriation can be unsatisfactory for the investors building a company which requires developing substantial goodwill. See Waters (2015), p. 372 also see Salacuse (2013), p. 257.

[32] ICSID secretariat reviewed 63 cases concluded with an award in the period January 1, 2015 to June 30, 2017, the average length of a case was 3 years 7 months. See schedule 9: Addressing time and cost in arbitration in Proposals for Amendment of the ICSID Rules—Working Paper please visit: https://icsid.worldbank.org/sites/default/files/publications/WP1_Amendments_Vol_3_WP-updated-9.17.18.pdf p. 898, para. 3, accessed 02.09.2024.

expedited.[33]Even if some policies as a condition precedent, entail the elapse of a 'cooling off' or 'waiting' period,[34] such period is shorter than the time required to obtain an arbitral award.

Cases

Barcelona Traction: Barcelona Traction, Light and Power Company, Limited (Belgium v. Spain) (1970) ICJ Rep 3; (1970)

ENRON v. Argentina: Enron Corporation Ponderosa Assets, L.P v. The Argentine Republic, (ICSID Case No. ARB/01/3), Award

Generation Ukraine: Generation Ukraine Inc. v. Ukraine, (ICSID Case No. ARB/00/9), Award

Maffezini v. Spain: Emilio Agustín Maffezini v. The Kingdom of Spain, (ICSID Case No. ARB/97/7), Decision of the tribunal on objections to jurisdiction

MTD Equity v. Chile: MTD Equity Sdn. Bhd. and MTD Chile S.A. v. Republic of Chile, (ICSID Case No. ARB/01/7), Award

Offshore Power v. India: *Offshore Power Production C.V., Travamark Two B.V., EFS India-Energy B.V., Enron B.V., and Indian Power Investments B.V. vs. Republic of India (Ad hoc Arbitration)*

Online Database

https://www.dfc.gov
https://www.jusmundi.com
https://www.icj-cij.org
https:// www.icsid.worldbank.org
https://www.italaw.com
https://www.law.cornell.edu

[33] *Bekker and Ogawa* state that the mean length of time between filing a claim of loss and a claim determination by OPIC was 4.75 months. Scholars reached this number by taking the average duration of several cases. See Bekker and Ogawa (2013), p. 327, fn 90.

[34] Waiting period is assumed to enable the insurer and insured to test intention of the host government as well as to resolve the dispute without having to trigger the loss provision under the policy. Gilbert (1986), p. 411.

References

Alfaro L et al (2005) Why Doesn't capital flow from rich to poor countries? An empirical investigation. National Bureau of Economic Research, Cambridge

Artemis M, Kabir AND (2024) Political risk insurance. https://jusmundi.com/en/document/publication/en-political-risk-insurance

Bekker P, Ogawa A (2013) The impact of bilateral investment treaty (BIT) proliferation on demand for investment insurance: reassessing political risk insurance after the 'BIT bang'. ICSID Rev 28(2):314–350

Comeaux PE, Kinsella N (1994) Reducing political risk in developing countries: bilateral investment treaties, stabilization clauses, and MIGA & (and) OPIC investment insurance. New York Law School J Int Comp Law 15(1):1–48

Garver P (2009) The changing face of political risk. In: Lu KW et al (eds) Investing with confidence understanding political risk management in the 21st century. World Bank, Washington DC, pp 81–90

Gilbert PR (1986) Acquiring and utilizing political risk insurance; a practitioner's perspective. Hast Int Comp Law Rev 9(3):407–415

Ginsburg R (2013) Political risk insurance and bilateral investment treaties: making the connection. J World Investment Trade 14(6):943–977

Haque I, Burdescu R (2004) Monterrey consensus on financing for development: response sought from international economic law. Boston Coll Int Comp Law Rev 27(2):219

Heard J, Laryea ET (2021) Export credit agencies, international investment law and the spectre of unsustainable developing countries' debts. Afr J Int Comp Law 29(4):612–643

ICCA Reports No. 4: Report of the ICCA-Queen Mary Task Force on Third-Party Funding in International Arbitration, ICCA Reports Series, Vol. 4 International Council for Commercial Arbitration; ICCA & Kluwer Law International 2018

Kantor M (2015) Indirect expropriation and political risk insurance for energy projects. J World Energy Law Bus 8(2):173–198

Kantor M, Nolan MD, Sauvant KP (2011) Reports of overseas private investment corporation determinations, vol 1. Oxford University Press

Muchlinski P et al (2008) The Oxford handbook of international investment law. Oxford University Press

Peinhardt C, Allee T (2016) Political risk insurance as dispute resolution. J Int Disp Settlement 7(1):205–224

Rayman-Bacchus L, Webb K (2012) Political risk insurance, CSR and the mining sector: an illustration of the regulatory effects of contracts. Int J Law Management 54(5):394–415

Rubins N, Kinsella NS (2005) International investment, political risk and dispute resolution "a practitioner's guide". Oxford University Press

Salacuse JW (2013) The three laws of international investment: national, contractual, and international frameworks for foreign capital. Oxford University Press

Salacuse JW (2016) The law of investment treaties, 3rd edn. Oxford University Press, Oxford

Salacuse JW, Sullivan NP (2005) Do BITs really work?: an evaluation of bilateral investment treaties and their grand bargain. Harv Int Law J 46(1):67–130

Schill SW (2010) Part I chapter 2: private enforcement of international investment law: why we need investor standing in BIT dispute settlement. In: Waibel M, Kaushal A et al (eds) The backlash against investment arbitration. Kluwer Law International

Shihata IFI (1986) Toward a greater depoliticization of investment disputes: the roles of ICSID and MIGA. ICSID Rev Foreign Investment Law J 1(1):1–25. https://doi.org/10.1093/icsidtakingreview/1.1.1

Søndergaard-Jensen M (2019) Will OECD governments avoid the path towards a new credit war? Global Pol 10(3):427–431

Soopramanien RD (2017) Mind the GAP: tailoring the form and substance of political risk Insurance in order to bridge the 'enforcement gap' in investment arbitration. Int Lawyer 50(3):585–611

Swenson DL (2009) Why do developing countries sign bits? In the effect of treaties on foreign direct investment. Oxford University Press, New York

Tan C (2015) Risky business: political risk insurance and the law and governance of natural resources. Int J Law Context 11(2):174–194

Tita A (2010) Investment Insurance in International law: a restatement on the regime of foreign investment. J World Investment Trade 11(4)

Tudor I (2008) The fair and equitable treatment standard in the international law of foreign investment. Oxford University Press, Oxford

Waters JJ (2015) A comparative analysis of public and private political risk insurance policies with strategic applications for risk mitigation. Duke J Comp Int Law 25(3):361

Chapter 5
Parties to PRI Contract and the Wrongdoer

The terminology in insurance contracts is diverse; therefore, it is appropriate to add an observation regarding the terminology. Some may suppose that insurance contracts consist of two parties, namely 'the insurer', and 'the insured'. However, in jurisdictions such as Germany and Turkey, an insurance contract can be made for another party, and in that case, 'the insured' denotes 'the party for the account of whom the insurance contract is made or in other words the party entitled to compensation'. On the other hand, 'the policyholder' may denote 'the party making the contract in his/her own name and assuming the premium'. In this book, we give weight to the investment-related risks; hence, we mostly used 'the investor' however it is denominated in conventional insurance contracts or BITs.

5.1 Insurer and Global Outlook

5.1.1 Insurer

The insurer, in short, may be defined as 'the party to the insurance contract, providing coverage and undertaking to indemnify the loss caused by the materialization of the risk in exchange for the premium'. From the investors' standpoint, whether the insurer is public or private is of immense importance. Public insurers are not on a par with private insurers as far as flexibility is concerned. As inspected in the previous chapter, governments may impose social or environmental conditions on public insurers or mandate that insurers seek national content in the exported commodities. In addition, public insurers may operate on a last resort basis.[1]

[1] *Gordon* believes that public providers position themselves as platforms for promoting responsible business conduct at the same time investment is being promoted. See Gordon (2008), p. 104.

Ö. Tosun, *The Law of Political Risk Insurance*, AIDA Europe Research Series on Insurance Law and Regulation 12, https://doi.org/10.1007/978-3-031-74675-8_5

Private insurers can charge exorbitant premiums if they find the scope of the transaction is too risky to cover, at that moment public insurers can come into play and provide coverage. Public insurers typically have long tenors,[2] often operate on a break-even basis, and are less profit-driven enabling them to offer lower premiums.[3] Another distinctive advantage of public insurers is their ability to work in close consultation with the home state's relevant departments such as the embassy or commercial attaché. This provides them with valuable intelligence and information[4] prior to taking on the risk. Host states may fear negative repercussions from the home country (investor's/public insurer's country). The political engagement of the home country can facilitate amicable dispute resolution.[5] In the worst-case scenario, the insurer can seek assistance in subrogation through diplomatic pressure. Nevertheless, even if a host state's decision-makers resist diplomatic pressure, the public insurer, when compared to the private insurer, will be in a better position to pursue an investor's subrogated claim. There may be cases where the private insurers are mandated to serve as a country's official PRI provider ('public insurer in disguise'), despite their private status and supposed independence, the insurer is likely to face interference of the government in its policies when export and, therefore national interests are at stake.

Private carriers of political risks on the other hand are profit-oriented. Therefore, private insurers must be more flexible and speedier than their public counterparts, and must be able to offer coverage for wider range of risks[6] without regard to national origin, ownership[7]or domestic presence of foreign corporations.[8] Although they may set higher caps on the amount of the insurable item/investment,[9] private insurers have two drawbacks. During a crisis, they tend to reduce risk exposure by lowering the number of the insureds along with the amount of coverage as this results in a foregone profit boost.[10] Some scholars are of the view that PRI sends a

[2]Dolzer and Schreuer (2012), p. 229. However, some authors state that private companies, as of today, can provide coverage up to 15 years. Wagner (2012), p. 104.

[3]Private insurers are believed to charge as much as 7% for coverage of investments in high-risk countries. See Rowat (1992), p. 126.

[4]Waters (2015), pp. 375, 376, DeLeonardo (2005), pp. 739, 753–755.

[5]Also see Johnson et al. (2019), p, 7.

[6]See Peinhardt and Allee (2016), p. 208. However, some authors believe otherwise, please see Soopramanien (2017), p. 597 and Tan (2015), p. 177.

[7]Peinhardt and Allee (2016), p. 208.

[8]Tan (2015), p. 176.

[9]ECAs like Turk Eximbank set coverage limits on the basis of country and risk factor. In doing so, ECAs rely on OECD's risk classification and aim to diversify the risk and manage the overall risk amount to be assumed. For the practice of Turkish ECA, please visit: https://www.eximbank.gov.tr/content/files/c1913d02-bddb-4df0-96f1-074680820448/ulke-limitleri-listesi accessed 02.09.2024.

[10]According to *Waters*, during the crisis in 2008 and 2009, the growth in total coverage provided by public providers increased much faster than that of private providers. Waters (2015), p. 380.

signal to the host government, retaining sovereignty, that government actions that are interventionist in nature will have consequences for current and future investments.[11]

MIGA's mandate is to enhance the flow of private foreign investment in developing countries.[12] *Tan* argues that this mandate, coupled with its international status, grants MIGA a deterrence power and access to host states' officials at the highest level and occasions to resolve potential disputes.[13] Thus, the second drawback is that private insurers lack quasi-governmental status and do not operate on a full faith and credit basis, hence do not have the deterrent power[14] public insurers carry.[15]

Along with insurers being private or public, the nationality or multinational status of the insurer can deter the host state from taking action.[16] A host state's non-compliance with BITs can affect the decision-making of the insurer's home state in further commercial or diplomatic activities, and the political capacity or economic strength of the country where the insurer is seated has the primary deterrent effect. Moreover, if the insurer were a multinational agency of which the host state is a member, any decision by the host state disrupting the investment by any means would come with a significant cost. Such a decision would give rise to the suspension of membership as well as a decrease in the host state's credit ratings and credibility. Therefore, political or economic advantages in interfering with a foreign investor's assets will not outweigh the strain on bilateral or multilateral relations.

5.1.2 Global Outlook

5.1.2.1 Multinational Insurers and DFC

5.1.2.1.1 In General

The coexistence of PRI providers at both national (ECAs) and international levels fosters the global economic growth, economic integration, alleviates abysmal poverty, and generates job opportunities and wealth. The burden of bringing an end to or reducing the actions of wronged states falls on both domestic and international insurers. Numerous multinational institutions provide insurance or guarantees

[11] Khachaturian (2006), p. 1053.

[12] Please visit: https://ieg.worldbankgroup.org/sites/default/files/Data/reports/chapters/rap2013_vol2updated.pdf accessed 02.09.2024.

[13] Tan (2015), p. 186.

[14] DFC's insurance coverage is considered 'deterrent'. See DeLeonardo (2005), p. 744. According to some scholars OPIC's links to the U.S. government allow OPIC to compensate investors for a wider range of governmental regulations than other institutions. See Ratner (2008), p. 493.

[15] Waters (2015), p. 381.

[16] See Papanastasiou (2021), p. 167. *Karagöz* states that the involvement of public investment insurer is an effective deterrent against the host government. See Karagöz (2018), p. 129.

against political risks. For instance, while the African Trade Insurance Agency[17] provides insurance, the Asian Development Bank[18] and the Inter-American Development Bank[19]offer partial guarantees. Multinational insurers possess several advantages over public providers. The multinational character of these insurers has a greater impact on investment climate. These providers focus on enhancing the economies of the members countries through promoting cash flow and supporting the growth of foreign trade.[20] A member state hosting an investment insured by one of these providers can face isolation from the global community as it engages in activities involving political risks. Moreover, these providers possess the necessary expertise and financial capacity to pioneer the PRI industry. They are autonomous, free from political considerations (at least on the surface), facilitating a focus on the welfare of less developed countries.

5.1.2.1.2 DHAMAN

DHAMAN, established in 1974, provides coverage against a number of distinct types of events, including expropriation/nationalization, inconvertibility, arbitration award defaults and wars/civil disturbances.[21] According to article 15 of its convention, eligible investments shall comprise all investments between the contracting countries and towards them. These include direct investments such as enterprises and their branches or agencies; ownership of equity shares, real estate, warranties, licensing, franchising and intellectual property rights; portfolio investments, including ownership of shares and bonds, and loans with a term exceeding 3 years as well as shorter-term loans as the Board may decide to treat as eligible for insurance in exceptional cases.

Speaking of requirements pertaining to investors, 'nationality' seems to be the decisive element for obtaining insurance coverage. A typical eligibility criterion

---

[17] Please visit: https://www.ati-aca.org/about-us/who-we-are/ accessed 02.09.2024.

[18] Please visit: https://www.adb.org/what-we-do/private-sector-financing/guarantees#partial-risk-guarantees accessed 02.09.2024.

[19] Please visit: https://www.iadb.org/en/who-we-are/about-idbaccessed 02.09.2024.

[20] The 3rd art. titled "Objective and Purposes" of the MIGA's Convention reads as follows "*The objective of the Agency shall be to encourage the flow of investments for productive purposes among member countries, and in particular to developing member countries…*" https://www.miga.org/history MIGA Convention available at https://www.miga.org/sites/default/files/archive/Documents/MIGA%20Convention%20(April%202018).pdf both accessed 02.09.2024. Also see Muchlinski et al. (2008), pp. 538–539. Similarly, art. 2 of the Convention Establishing the Arap Investment and Export Credit Guarantee Corporation (the Convention), available at https://www.dhaman.org/establishing-convention.html accessed 02.09.2024 and art. 5 ICIEC AoA, available at https://iciec.isdb.org/wp-content/uploads/2021/10/ICIEC-ARTICLE-OF-AGREEMENTALL-compressed_1.pdf accessed 02.09.2024.

[21] See art. 18 of the Convention Establishing the Arap Investment and Export Credit Guarantee Corporation (the Convention), available at https://www.dhaman.org/establishing-convention.htmlaccessed 26.08.2024.

required by an ECA is that the investor or exporter is domiciled in the same country as the ECA. For a multinational insurer, that the investor's seat is located in one of the contracting counties[22] The nationality of a juridical person is identified by its country of domicile and accordingly the laws that govern it. Insurers can extend the content of the nationality and can base eligibility on the ownership of the investment. DHAMAN does not confine the content of nationality solely to the investor's home country.[23] In a simplified language, a juridical person domiciled in a non-contracting country may qualify if a national or juridical person from a contracting country possesses a certain portion of its shares, as required by the multinational insurer.[24] With regard to the eligibility of the investment, DHAMAN favors nationals of its member countries. Investments (subject to obtaining a prior approval of the competent official authority in the host state[25]), with a wide range of varieties are eligible.[26]

5.1.2.1.3 MIGA

MIGA is considered to stand to fill a certain market niche.[27] The idea of multilateral political risk insurance dates back to 1948, and it is almost another 40 years before

[22] According to art. 17(1) of the Convention, a juridical person having a seat located in a non-contracting country, by a resolution of the Board of Directors, may obtain insurance coverage provided that at least fifty percent of such juridical person is owned by one or more of the contracting countries or by their nationals or by the juridical persons who are, under the provisions of this paragraph, acceptable as party to the insurance contract.

[23] Also see Williams (1993), p. 95.

[24] Art 17(2) of the Convention is as follows: "*Nevertheless, a juridical person may, by a resolution of the Board of Directors, be accepted as a party to an insurance contract, even if his main seat is located in a non-contracting country, provided that such juridical person is owned by not less than fifty percent by one or more of the contracting countries or by their nationals or by the juridical persons who are, under the provisions of this paragraph, acceptable as party to the insurance contract.*"

[25] According to Article 15(6) of the Convention, approval may be either formal or silent, provided that the official authority does not communicate a rejection of the offer to the corporation within 60 days.

[26] Eligibility criteria for receiving insurance coverage are stated under art. 15 of the Convention which reads as follows: "*1-Investments eligible for insurance shall comprise all investments between the contracting countries and towards them, whether they are direct investments including enterprises and their branches or agencies, ownership of equity shares, real estate, warranty, licensing, franchising and intellectual property rights, portfolio investments including ownership of shares and bonds, and loans for a term exceeding three years as well as such shorter term loans as the Board may in exceptional cases decide to treat as eligible for insurance. 2. Pursuant to the procedures adopted by the Board and following the proposal of the Director General, the Corporation may: a. provide insurance for foreign investments which are owned by nationals of non-member states if those investments are in the member countries. b. provide insurance for Arab nationals' investments in their Arab countries of nationality when the investments pertain to their funds which are repatriated from abroad.*"

[27] Rowat (1992), p. 128.

the World Bank created MIGA.[28] MIGA's establishment did not get off the ground until 1985,[29] and it entered the political risk insurance market in 1988.[30] Article 11 of the MIGA Convention, in principle[31] stipulates the risks to be covered as currency transfer, expropriation, breach of contract, war, and civil disturbance. The convention requires host states to approve the issuance of the insurance.[32] However, article 38(b) of the Convention indicates a 'silent approval' mechanism. According to the article, unless the host state presents an objection within a reasonable period, MIGA can deem that it obtained approval.[33]

Although the Convention introduces certain prerequisites,[34] it is generous in terms of the scope of eligible investments and brings broad eligibility criterion for the investments. The drafters seemingly left the door open on purpose. According to the article 12 of MIGA Convention "*Eligible investments shall include equity interests, including medium- or long-term loans made or guaranteed by holders of equity in the enterprise concerned, and such forms of direct investment as may be determined by the Board. (b) Loans other than those mentioned in Section (a) above are eligible for coverage (i) if they are made to finance or are otherwise related to a specific investment or project in which some other form of direct investment is present, whether or not guaranteed by the Agency and regardless of when such other investment was made, or (ii) as may be otherwise approved by the Board by special majority. (c) The Board, by special majority, may extend eligibility to any other medium- or long-term form of investment.*" As explained in the commentaries on the MIGA Convention, this provision aims at striking a balance between the need to preserve the Agency's scarce capital to promote flows of direct investment and the

[28]See Rowat (1992), p. 119 and Martin (1967), pp. 286–290. Also see St. John (2018), pp. 104–107.

[29]Baker (1995), p. 25 and Salacuse (2013), pp. 266–272.

[30]Comeaux and Kinsella (1994), p. 40.

[31]Article 11 (b) of the Convention Establishing the Multilateral Investment Guarantee Agency (the MIGA Convention) grants the Board the necessary authority to broaden the scope of the non-commercial risks to be covered, however imposes a limitation on inclusion of the risk of devaluation or depreciation of currency. The Convention is available at https://www.miga.org/sites/default/files/archive/Documents/MIGA%20Convention%20(April%202018).pdf accessed 02.09.2024.

[32]Art. 15 of the MIGA Convention is as follows: "*The Agency shall not conclude any contract of guarantee before the host government has approved the issuance of the guarantee by the Agency against the risks designated for cover.*"

[33]Also see Williams (1993), p. 84.

[34]Prospective insured is required to satisfy MIGA that their investment: (a) economically sounds, contributes to the host country, (b) complies with the laws and regulations of the host country, (c) is consistent with the declared development objectives and priorities of the host country; and (d) fair and equitable treatment and legal protection for the investment is available in the host country. See art. 12(e) of the MIGA Convention.

need to assure future flexibility by allowing the Board to extend coverage to other types of investment.[35]

In terms of requirements pertaining to investors, the MIGA Convention imposes a twofold nationality condition. As a preliminary condition, natural persons must be 'nationals of a member other than the host country'. Juridical persons are deemed to be eligible if they are incorporated and have their principal place of business in a member, or the majority of their capital is owned by a member or members, or nationals thereof, provided that such a member is not the host country in any of the above cases. Article 13 (c), on the other hand, lifts the orthodox barriers to eligibility and paves the way for the natural and juridical persons of the host country to receive coverage.[36] *Williams* states that the provision will assist developing countries reverse capital flight.[37] Commentary on the MIGA Convention suggests these exceptions align with the 'Agency's central objective of channeling the flow of investments to developing countries, some of which now have nationals living abroad with considerable offshore funds'.[38] Municipal laws govern the relationship between the host state and its nationals. For this reason, due to ongoing nationalist trends, the state may employ more political risk-like measures towards its citizens who also hold an investor title than it would towards foreign investors. Hence, providing insurance coverage to nationals of the host state can be complicated.

One scholar seems to premise his/her view on the commentary to the article 12 of the MIGA Convention, in the view of the scholar, the presence of such article dealing with eligibility criteria reflects the 'drafters' efforts to balance the need to preserve MIGA's scarce capital resources with maintaining sufficient flexibility in its eligibility determination'.[39] As stated elsewhere, PRI is a device to boost foreign capital flow and prosperity in developing countries. Therefore, expanding the amount or the scope of coverage, even if the prospective insured is the national of the wrongdoer, would serve MIGA's purpose. Given the fact that the eligibility of

[35] See para. 19 of the Commentary on the MIGA Convention, available at https://www.miga.org/sites/default/files/archive/Documents/commentary_convention_november_2010.pdf accessed 02.09.2024.

[36] According to said article "*Upon the joint application of the investor and the host country, the Board, by special majority, may extend eligibility to a natural person who is a national of the host country or a juridical person which is incorporated in the host country, or the majority of whose capital is owned by its nationals, provided that the assets invested are transferred from outside the host country.*" In *Toprak Mahsulleri Ofisi,* Turkish buyers undertook to open a letter of credit confirmed by a first-class United States or West European bank. However, Turkish buyers faced challenges to obtain exchange control permission from the Turkish Ministry of Finance to open such a letter of credit and argued the impossibility of opening a letter of credit without exporting money from Turkey. While there was not an asset transfer, extension of the scope of the coverage to the nationals or juridical persons incorporated or domiciled in the host country could have been useful in such a circumstance. The case is cited from McKendrick (1995), p. 83.

[37] Williams (1993), p. 84.

[38] See para. 23 of the Commentary on the Convention Establishing the Multilateral Investment Guarantee Agency 'Commentary on the MIGA Convention'.

[39] Berger (1988), p. 32.

the form of investments may be expanded by a special majority of the Board, forms of investment have less importance compared to other conditions in place that lack similar exceptions. Investments are territorially circumscribed under article 14 and are deemed eligible only if they are to be made in the territory of a developing member country. BITs are of relevance to the underwriting process of MIGA,[40] however if the fair and equal treatment of the host state is not satisfactory to the MIGA, it can enter into separate agreement with the host state by which MIGA will be assured that '*it has treatment at least as favorable as that agreed by the member concerned for the most favored investment guarantee agency or state in an agreement relating to investment'*.[41]

5.1.2.1.4 ICIEC

ICIEC, a member of the Islamic Development Bank (IsDB) Group, was established in 1994.[42] The covered risks provided in article 19 of its Articles of Agreement (AoA) are much the same as those the MIGA covers.[43] The AoA provides coverage against currency transfer, expropriation, breach of contract, war and civil disturbance. In terms of eligible investments. Article 17(1) is broad in scope and leaves the discretion of forms of direct investment to Board of Directors.[44] The same AoA indicates that banks, and any natural person who is a national of a member state other than the host country, as well as any juridical person incorporated or carrying on business in a member state, are entitled to apply for insurance coverage. Similar to DHAMAN's implementation, a juridical person located in a non-member state may also apply for coverage.[45] And finally, article 18(4) implies the existence of an unspoken consensus among multinational insurers to extend coverage to nationals or juridical persons of the host country. As per the article, insurance coverage might be extended to a natural person who is a national of or a juridical person which is incorporated in the host country, or the majority of whose capital is owned by its

[40] Poulsen (2010), p. 17. In order to settle the disputes between MIGA, (acting as subrogee of an investor) and member state, parties may enter into agreement in accordance with art. 57 of the MIGA Convention.

[41] See MIGA Convention art.23(b)(ii), also see Williams (1993), p. 85.

[42] Please visit: https://iciec.isdb.org/who-we-are/ accessed 02.09.2024.

[43] The AoA can be found at https://iciec.isdb.org/wp-content/uploads/2022/04/ICIEC-ARTICLE-OF-AGREEMENT-ALL-2022.pdf accessed 02.09.2024.

[44] The article defines eligible investment as "*all investments in Member States by Eligible Investors including direct investments in enterprises, their branches and agencies; investments in the share capital of enterprises including principal amounts of loans made or guaranteed by holders of equity in the enterprise concerned; and all other forms of direct investments which shall be considered eligible for insurance by the Board of Directors.*"

[45] According to art. 18 of the Agreement, a juridical person may, by a resolution of the Board of Directors, be accepted as a party to an insurance or Reinsurance Contract even if its principal office is located in a non-Member State, provided that such juridical person is owned, by not less than 50%, by one or more Members or by a national or nationals of one or more Member States.

nationals. However, in such a case, the same article requires a joint request from the host country and the applicant for insurance and the ICIEC expects transfer of the assets (that are to be insured) from outside the host country.

5.1.2.1.5 DFC

DFC, established in 2019 through the passage of BUILD[46] (the Better Utilization of Investments Leading to Development) operates as the U.S. Government's development finance institution and is the successor of OPIC. OPIC, now known as DFC, was created in 1971 by the Foreign Assistance Act of 1969.[47] In fact, OPIC was formed in 1969 after a presidential advisory committee recommendation stating that the United States Agency for International Development (AID) (former insurance provider of the government) was not well-equipped and focused on supporting governments rather than private individuals or entities. Besides, the agency could not cope with the volume of requests for political risk insurance.[48] The same committee recommended that an insurer with a corporate structure having a hybrid of a public and private board would offer more effective support by acting in a more businesslike manner with flexibility,[49] and OPIC began to operate in 1971.[50] Some scholars express that OPIC's goal was to spur development of the private insurance sector, thereby and in time, replacing private players with OPIC.[51] However, due to the disinclination of the private market or their inability to offer coverage on conditions similar to those available through DFC, such replacement did not take place.[52] In fact, the OPIC suffered a variety of predicaments. OPIC inherited insurance contracts issued by the Agency for International Development (AID), and claims existed therein amounting to almost a half billion dollars. However, the

[46]The BUILD Act combined the capabilities of the Overseas Private Investment Corporation (OPIC) and the Development Credit Authority which had previously been housed in the U.-S. Agency for International Development (USAID). Please visit: https://www.dfc.gov/sites/default/files/2019-08/BILLS-115hr302_BUILDAct2018.pdf accessed 02.09.2024. Also see Kantor et al. (2011), p. xxi.

[47]See https://www.govinfo.gov/content/pkg/STATUTE-83/pdf/STATUTE-83-Pg805.pdf#page=22 accessed 02.09.2024 and also for detail See Muchlinski et al. (2008), pp. 533–535, similarly Comeaux and Kinsella (1994), p. 33. And as stated in the section 1434 of BUILD act, DFC serves in accordance with full faith and credit of the United States. Please visit: https://www.dfc.gov/who-we-are/overview accessed 02.09.2024. Also see Berger (1988), p. 38, finally for the detail, see Diaconis (1989), pp. 271–275.

[48]Rubins and Kinsella (2005), p. 71.

[49]DeLeonardo (2005), p. 741.

[50]Khachaturian (2006), p. 1045, also see Williams (1993), p. 71.

[51]The privatization of the OPIC was on the Congress's agenda. However, the private sector was disinclined to assume political risks under the same terms as the OPIC and they lacked the resources to proceed with the U.S. government's objectives. As a result, the Congress withdrew the mandate to require the complete privatization of OPIC. See Diaconis (1989), p. 273.

[52]DeLeonardo (2005), p. 741. Rubins and Kinsella (2005), p. 71.

amount exceeded OPIC's initial reserves, and this heritage was about to end with its insolvency. The claims were based on expropriation of US investments by the Chilean government, which afterwards were settled by the successor government.[53] And in 1996, the US Congress failed to re-authorize OPIC which could lead to its eradication.[54]

In the insurance market, the disclosure of claims and decisions is an element of forecasting the horizon, albeit in exceptional cases. This is where DFC comes into play, as it enables such decisions to be publicly accessible.[55] DFC offers coverage against currency inconvertibility, expropriation, arbitral award default, denial of justice, wrongful calling of bonds, political violence and breach of contract for capital markets[56] The scope of investment, as well as eligible investors are defined in section 238 of the Foreign Assistance Act of 1961. The scope of the investments seems to be broad, and since DFC is a U.S.-based insurer, drafters seek a link (citizenship or otherwise) between the investor and the United States.[57] Finally, DFC enters into its own inter-governmental agreements with the host states[58] and by

---

[53] See Hansen (2004), p. 81.

[54] Rubins and Kinsella (2005), p. 71.

[55] Available at https://www.dfc.gov/who-we-are/transparency-and-accountability accessed 02.09.2024. Also see Reisman et al. (2014), pp. 381–436.

[56] Please visit: https://www.dfc.gov/what-we-offer-our-products/political-risk-insurance accessed 02.09.2024.

[57] Investments refer to contribution or commitment of funds, commodities, services, patents, processes, or techniques, in the form of (1) a loan or loans to an approved project, (2) the purchase of a share of ownership in any such project, (3) participation in royalties, earnings, or profits of any such project, and (4) the furnishing of commodities or services pursuant to a lease or other contract. Eligible investors are: (1) United States citizens; (2) corporations, partnerships, or other associations including non-profit associations, created under the laws of the United States any State or territory thereof, or the District of Columbia, and substantially beneficially owned by United States citizens; and (3) foreign corporations, partnerships, or other associations wholly owned by one or more such United States citizens, corporations, partnerships, or other associations: Provided however, that the eligibility of such foreign corporation shall be determined without regard to any shares, in aggregate less than 5 per centum of the total issued and subscribed share capital, held by other than the United States owners: Provided further, That in the case of any loan investment a final determination of eligibility may be made at the time the insurance or guaranty is issued; in all other cases, the investor must be eligible at the time a claim arises as well as the time the insurance or guaranty is issued. Please visit: https://www.foreign.senate.gov/imo/media/doc/Foreign%20Assistance%20Act%20Of%201961.pdf and https://www.congress.gov/congressional-report/115th-congress/house-report/814 both accessed 02.09.2024.

[58] For instance, art. 2(c) of the Investment Incentive Agreement between the Government of the United States and the Government of the Lao People's Democratic Republic, 8 March 1996 reads as: "*If the Issuer [OPIC} makes a payment to any person or entity, or exercises its rights as a creditor, in connection with any Investment Support, the Government of the Lao People's Democratic Republic shall recognize the transfer to, or acquisition by, the Issuer of any cash, accounts, credits, instruments or other assets in connection with such payment, as well as the succession of the Issuer to any right, title, claim, privileged or cause of action existing, or which may arise, in connection therewith*" Available at https://www.dfc.gov/sites/default/files/2019-08/bl_lao_peoples_democratic_republic_03-08-1996.pdf accessed 02.09.2024. See Poulsen (2010),

virtue of these agreements, it may receive the most favored treatment.[59] The claim determinations of this US-based insurer were made during its 'OPIC' era, therefore, throughout this book, we find it appropriate to mention this name in referring to its determinations.

5.1.2.2 International Associations

The presence of multinational insurers does not put an end to the need for another international-level insurance associations. Associations focusing on credit and political risk insurance are non-profit organizations that lend support to international trade by creating networks and facilitating the exchange of expertise among their members, include ECAs, private insurers and financial institutions. These associations offer various forms of support, such as briefings and educational resources for underwriters. In addition, members meet on a regular basis to discuss recent developments and trends in the industry. Finally, these associations conduct and publish research[60] to assess risk attitudes and the global impact of certain events. Given that only a small number of Lloyd's syndicates offer insurance against political risk, in this chapter, we have chosen to focus on the unions pioneering the market.

5.1.2.2.1 Berne Union

The International Union of Credit and Investment Insurers was founded by four members in 1934 in Berne, the city that gave its name to the Union. The same city hosted meetings of the Union for the following 5 years. The Union has been domiciled in London since 1975 and was previously in Paris.[61] Its day-to-day operations are managed by the secretariat, and the Union is led by the president, vice president and management committee.[62] Some find the Union 'the peak organization' of the export credit and PRI sector.[63] As its name suggests, it is the union of investment insurers, thus apart from its century-long experience, what makes the Union 'unique' in terms of PRI is that the association brings together the world's leading PRI providers as members under the same roof.

---

p. 16, Salacuse (2013), p. 260, Salacuse (2016), p. 453. Dolzer and Schreuer (2012), pp. 230–231 and similarly, see "Chapter 8: Third-Party Funding in Investment Arbitration', ICCA Reports No. 4: Report of the ICCA-Queen Mary Task Force on Third-Party Funding in International Arbitration, ICCA Reports Series, Vol. 4 International Council for Commercial Arbitration; ICCA & Kluwer Law International 2018 p 214, similarly see Tan (2015), p. 184, finally, see Diaconis (1989), p. 276.

[59] Williams (1993), p. 85.

[60] Unions, on a regular basis, publish non-enforceable guiding principles. Also, see Heard and Laryea (2021), p. 621.

[61] Ward (1986), p. 246.

[62] Please visit: https://www.berneunion.org/Stub/Display/169 accessed 07.09.2024.

[63] Spagnoletti and O'Callaghan (2011), p. 3.

5.1.2.2.2 Aman Union

The Aman Union, established in 2009, is a relatively young association. Although article 2 of its charter provides that the seat of the Union should be in Muscat, the Sultanate of Oman, Muscat was one of several cities where the Union's operations were conducted. The Secretariat General of the Union has been managed by its members over time in various cities. The Aman Union appears to take on the mission of the Berne Union in the gulf region. The Union is composed of a general assembly, an executive council and a general secretariat. Similar to the Berne Union, the Aman Union dedicates itself to providing a forum of network on a global scale and nurtures the establishment of new export credit agencies in the member countries.[64]

5.1.2.2.3 ICISA

The origins of ICISA can be traced back to the first international conference on trade credit insurance held in 1926 in London. Two years later, ICISA was established in Paris. The operations of ICISA were conducted across several countries. From its inception until 1999, ICISA was based in Switzerland, and the same year the association's head office was moved to London. Interestingly, it shared its premises with the Berne Union until 2003. From that date onwards, the secretariat of the association has been domiciled in Amsterdam.[65]

The Association advocates on behalf of its members on issues related to surety[66] and credit insurance. It is important to note that trade credit insurance (TCI) shoulders buyers' or importers' default risk. In comparison with PRI, TCI, has a

[64] Article 4 of the Charter outlines a long list of objectives, including the encouragement of efforts towards enhancing the investment climate in member countries, encouragement of exchange of information, technical assistance, expertise and consultation in relation to commercial and non-commercial risk insurance. Also visit: https://amanunion.net/uploads/userprofiles/Aman%20Union%20Charter%202023%20(Vf).pdf accessed 02.09.2024.

[65] https://icisa.org/who-are-we/ accessed 02.09.2024.

[66] The legal structure of the surety and subrogation therein deviates from the conventional insurance. First, a surety bond is a tripartite relationship, the principal assumes responsibility under the primary contract concluded with the obligee and pays the premium to the insurer (surety) in return for the issuance of a bond in favor of the obligee, whereby the surety guarantees the performance of the principal's contractual undertaking. Should the principal fail to honor its obligation, the surety indemnifies the obligee. Subrogation in surety is also complex; the surety recoups its damages from the principal. To put it another way, in conventional insurance, the party paying the premium is indemnified and the loss typically stems from the actions of a third party to which the insurer eventually recourses. In surety bond, however, the wrongdoer is the principal which is responsible for payment of the premium. After indemnification, the insurer is subrogated to the rights of the obligee and seeks recourse from the principal.

shorter lifespan and holds the lion's share of ECAs.[67] The political risks that TCI addresses are not entirely distinct from those of PRI. As a well-recognized union for TCI, ICISA deals with commercial matters, and makes a meaningful contribution to the development of political risk insurance, playing a vital role among PRI providers throughout the world.

5.2 Investor as 'Insured', The Notions of Property Rights and Investment

5.2.1 Investor as 'Insured'

The term "investor" can be articulated in various ways, essentially, it refers to the real or legal (juridical) person having proprietary rights over an investment in the foreign territory.[68] PRI contracts typically do not emphasize ownership or address control mechanisms, unless the PRI provider is a multinational institution, a juridical person incorporated within the jurisdiction[69] where the insurer is based, or a real person investor sharing the same nationality as the insurer, is eligible to enter into an insurance contract. However, during the process of subrogation, the host (respondent) state may challenge the insurer's standing, by claiming the lack of ICSID

[67] To illustrate, in 2021, claims paid under short term and medium long term credit insurance programs worth a total of USD 6.780 while PRI claims remained USD 1.443. See Berne Union, Istanbul Spring Meeting and H2 2021 Data available at https://www.berneunion.org/Stub/Display/62 accessed 02.09.2024. Also see Wagner (2012), p. 101.

[68] An investor can also be defined as "*a physical or legal person in one country who invests funds or capital in another country by means of an investment transaction*" See Salacuse (2013), p. 8. Sources defining the investment also define the investor. For instance, according to Model International Agreement on Investment for Sustainable Development 'investor' is a "*national or company of a home State Party that makes, or is making, an investment into the territory of another Party*". Asean Comprehensive Investment Agreement (ACIA) defines investor as "*a natural person of a Member State or a juridical person of a Member State that is making or has made an investment in the territory of any other Member State*". Please visit: https://www.italaw.com/sites/default/files/archive/ita1027.pdf and http://investasean.asean.org/files/upload/Doc%2005%20-%20ACIA.pdf both accessed 02.09.2024.

[69] In fact, according to the scholars, 'place of constitution', 'place of incorporation' or 'company seat' are the tests applied by international tribunals to determine the nationality of company. See Susler and Wilson (2018), pp. 38–51 also see Baltag (2012), pp. 105–106.

jurisdiction,[70] if a natural person insured holds dual nationality[71] (belonging to both the home state and the host state) or if the investor is a legal entity (non-natural person) owned or controlled by a natural person holding such dual nationality simultaneously. Even if the BIT between the host state and home state or a multinational treaty to which they are party may design a non-ICSID mechanism and remains silent on the dual nationality,[72] identifying ownership or control (including

---

[70] In *CSOB v. Slovak Republic*, the respondent objected to the tribunal's jurisdiction based on its dissatisfaction with article 25 of the ICSID Convention. The respondent argued that CSOB was an agent of the Czech Republic and that the assignments made to the Czech Republic of CSOB's interest in the receivables transformed the Czech Republic into the real party in interest to this case. Therefore, the Czech Republic should have been disqualified under the same provision from stepping into CSOB's shoes. The tribunal rejected this argument, noting that '*at the time when these proceedings were instituted, neither of these assignments had been concluded.'* See *para. 10,28 and 31* and also see, Chap. 12 of this book. If one were to wonder whether a person possessing nationality of both the home state and the host state could enjoy protection of the BIT concluded by these states. The article 25 of the ICSID Convention contains an absolute prohibition, the article reads as: *(1) The jurisdiction of the Centre shall extend to any legal dispute arising directly out of an investment, between a Contracting State (or any constituent subdivision or agency of a Contracting State designated to the Centre by that State) and a national of another Contracting State, which the parties to the dispute consent in writing to submit to the Centre. When the parties have given their consent, no party may withdraw its consent unilaterally. (2) "National of another Contracting State" means: (a) any natural person who had the nationality of a Contracting State other than the State party to the dispute on the date on which the parties consented to submit such dispute to conciliation or arbitration as well as on the date on which the request was registered pursuant to paragraph (3) of Article 28 or paragraph (3) of Article 36, but does not include any person who on either date also had the nationality of the Contracting State party to the dispute; and (b) any juridical person which had the nationality of a Contracting State other than the State party to the dispute on the date on which the parties consented to submit such dispute to conciliation or arbitration and any juridical person which had the nationality of the Contracting State party to the dispute on that date and which, because of foreign control, the parties have agreed should be treated as a national of another Contracting State for the purposes of this Convention.*

[71] In *Champion Trading v. Egypt*, the tribunal took the position that it has no jurisdiction over the claims by individual claimants as they had both the American as well as the Egyptian nationality and therefore cannot invoke the Convention, see p 17. The case is available at https://www.italaw.com/sites/default/files/case-documents/ita0147.pdf accessed 02.09.2024. Also see Baltag (2012), pp. 95–96 and similarly, Olmedo (2017).

[72] *In Uzan v. Turkey,* the claimant initiated arbitration with the SCC in accordance with the ECT. Despite being a Turkish national, the claimant based his allegations his permanent residence in the United Kingdom and his current residency in France. Article 1(7)(a)(i) of the ECT defines a real person investor "*a natural person having the citizenship or nationality of or who is permanently residing in that Contracting Party in accordance with its applicable law*". However, the tribunal was persuaded to believe that the claimant was permanently residing in the host state. With regard to his residence in France, the tribunal stated that "*permanently residing in a Contracting Party is not sufficient to determine that the Claimant is an Investor in accordance with Articles 1(7)(a)(i) and 26(1) of the ECT, as the Claimant is not an Investor "of another Contracting Party." According to the tribunal "the object and purpose of the ECT is to protect "the international flow of investments," and hence to protect international investors. The Claimant, no matter how he frames his arguments, is missing this essential transnational link, in relation both to the time his "investment" was made and when he alleges it was interfered with. The ECT was intended to protect Investors investing into Turkey, not nationals within Turkey who make investments in their own country"* and

any indirect control, and potentially piercing the corporate veil) may still be of interest to the insurer.

The rationale behind adopting broad or narrow definitions of investor or investment in PRI contracts depends on a variety of factors. The first factor that comes to mind is the PRI providers' risk appetite and profit enthusiasm. However, if the PRI provider is an entity owned or mandated by a government, rather than the insurer's interest, market demand and inclinations of policymakers will likely determine the scope of these definitions. Moreover, the adjective 'investor' carries a connotation linked to investment, thus, necessitates exploring the scope of the investment. Assets with the same characteristics of an investment defined in the insurance policy enjoy PRI coverage. In contrast to natural persons, legal entities to a greater or lesser extent make more investments and justification lies in the PRI practice. In other words, juridical persons, such as corporations, companies or business associations, by their nature, engage in more investment activities abroad, rendering them vulnerable to sovereign conduct and therefore requiring insurance.

One may cogently argue that the size of the investment may be determinative in obtaining PRI coverage. While large investors have greater capacity to diversify their risks and protect their investment by other means,[73] small and medium investors are more vulnerable and not too big to not to fail. Whereas the larger the investment, the greater the potential loss. Therefore, big companies' weathering political risks may not be easier than that of small ones. Hence, the need for PRI is essential, irrespective of the size of the investment. In a PRI contract, the investor assumes the role of the insured party. While navigating through each page, readers might notice that the terms 'insured', and 'investor' can sometimes become intertwined. However, we have endeavored to employ the term "investor" in the context of investment law, and 'insured' when highlighting the insurance element.

5.2.2 *The Concept of Property, Property Rights and Investment*

5.2.2.1 Property and Property Rights

The right to own a thing is endowed in each and every person. Whether tangible or not, individuals are constitutionally entitled to the right of property. The entitlement to a property does not only play a role in meeting the needs of human beings, but it also satisfies the intrinsic attribute of the human beings, that is to feel secure. In the domain of international investment, an investment represents a means to produce

therefore it concluded that it had no jurisdiction to hear the individual claimant's claims. See paras. 152,187 and 191, also see Judgment of the Svea Court of Appeal upholding this decision, available at https://www.italaw.com/sites/default/files/case-documents/italaw10344.pdf accessed 02.09.2024.

[73] Shihata (1987), p. 687.

wealth.[74] An investor gains certain property as a result of making an investment.[75] However, the host state's interference adversely affects the investor's right to possess and manage the property. Therefore, understanding the foundations of the rights that are being violated is crucial. The roots of property rely on the Latin word '*proprietas*' meaning 'ownership'.[76] In the eyes of law, property means an entitlement of a person that is related to a thing[77] which is capable of being appropriated.[78] Property, in common-law terminology involves realty—personality, and tangible—intangible assets. In civil-law terminology, property rights refer to 'things' that are divided into the corresponding categories of immovables—movables and corporal—incorporeal[79] and it is a social institution that serves social functions.[80]

Property rights represent the formal and informal claims and obligations of individuals against the resources of a society.[81] It comprises three main Roman law-based powers namely, *usus*, *abusus* and *fructus*.[82] *Usus* is the right to use, in other words the owner's personal enjoyment and use of the thing. *Abusus* refers to the right to dispose of or sell the property.[83] Finally, *fructus* is the right to fruits of the property such as interest and rental. *Usufructs* on the other hand, is a real right, granting holders, exclusive possession and use of a thing, along with the right to fruits it produces, however, differs from ownership in key respects. *Usufructs* are time-limited (the entitlement is for a certain duration) and holder of the right is prohibited from causing damage to the thing.[84] Although PRI policies and investment treaties mostly employ the term 'investment', the subject of the political risk may be other than tangible or immovable property. This may reveal why multinational insurers have designed a broad scope and extended the meaning of

[74] According the oft-quoted interpretation of *Salacuse*" *the restrictive notion of property as a material 'thing' is obsolete and has ceded its place to a contemporary conception which includes managerial control over components of a process that is wealth producing*" See Salacuse (2016), p. 389.

[75] Salacuse (2013), p. 4.

[76] Civil law and common law approach the concept of ownership differently, English law was premised on the assumption that only the king could own land. See Sprankling (2014), pp. 23, 24.

[77] Sprankling (2014), pp. 23, 24.

[78] Lawson and Rudden (2002), p. 20.

[79] Rubins and Kinsella (2005), pp. 3–4.

[80] Newcombe (2005), p. 22.

[81] Anon (2004), p. 5.

[82] For instance, in *Glamis Gold Ltd.* (para.357) the tribunal referred to "*economic rights, i.e. ownership, use, enjoyment or management of the business*". Available at https://www.italaw.com/sites/default/files/case-documents/ita0378.pdf accessed 02.09.2024.

[83] Usus, fructus and abusus are regarded as patrimonial attributes of the investment. Kunoy (2005), p. 468.

[84] Sprankling (2014), p. 30.

investments even to concession agreements, which are considered to be a form of usufructs.[85]

5.2.2.2 Investment

5.2.2.2.1 Scope and Legality

While investment has a wide range of definitions, investment cannot be degraded into one single definition. However, basically, it denotes "one type of human action in which the profit sought is economic or monetary in nature".[86] In Salacuse's view, investment entails "*the commitment of resources by a physical or legal person to a specific purpose in order to earn a profit or to gain a return*".[87] *Lawson and Rudden*, on the other hand, use phrasing reminiscent of socialist jargon to describe it as "*a thing in which people or corporations possessing wealth beyond what they need to survive find something permanent, safe, limited in supply, income producing and appreciating in capital value*".[88]

The scope of an investment is shaped by multiple sources; BITs[89] have been influential, and so have multinational investment treaties[90] and international model

[85] In *Railroad Development Corp.* (29 June 2012, award, para. 30) 50-year right to rebuild and operate the Guatemalan rail system considered to be Usufruct Contract. Available at https://www.italaw.com/sites/default/files/case-documents/ita1051.pdf accessed 02.09.2024.

[86] Rubins and Kinsella (2005), p. 1.

[87] Salacuse (2013), p. 3, Salacuse (2016), p. 30.

[88] Lawson and Rudden (2002), p. 25.

[89] In the wording of the BIT between UK and Turkey investment means "*every kind of asset and in particular, though not exclusively, includes: (i) movable and immovable property and any other property rights such as mortgages, liens or pledges; (ii) shares in and stock and debentures of a company and any other form of participation in a company; (iii) claims to money or to any performance under contract associated with any investment having a financial value; (iv) industrial and intellectual property rights, technical processes, knowhow and goodwill; (v) business concessions conferred by law or under contract, including concessions to search for, cultivate, extract or exploit natural resources.*" Please visit: https://investmentpolicy.unctad.org/international-investment-agreements/treaty-files/2355/download accessed 02.09.2024.

[90] Under article 1(6) of Energy Charter Treaty, 'Investment' means "*every kind of asset, owned or controlled directly or indirectly by an Investor and includes: (a) tangible and intangible, and movable and immovable, property, and any property rights such as leases, mortgages, liens, and pledges; (b) a company or business enterprise, or shares, stock, or other forms of equity participation in a company or business enterprise, and bonds and other debt of a company or business enterprise; (c) claims to money and claims to performance pursuant to contract having an economic value and associated with an Investment; (d) Intellectual Property; (e) Returns; (f) any right conferred by law or contract or by virtue of any licences and permits granted pursuant to law to undertake any Economic Activity in the Energy Sector.*" https://www.energycharter.org/fileadmin/DocumentsMedia/Legal/ECTC-en.pdf accessed 02.09.2024.

agreements.[91] Typical features of an investment can be listed as certain duration, an expectation of profit and return, assumption of risk by both sides, commitment, and finally, contribution to the development of the host state.[92] Some BITs may require an investment to be tangible assets and located in a specific territory[93] while others may limit investment to certain sectors and may adopt a non-exhaustive list.[94]

---

[91] According to ACIA, investment means: every kind of asset, owned or controlled, by an investor, including but not limited to the following: (i) movable and immovable property and other property rights such as mortgages, liens or pledges; (ii) shares, stocks, bonds and debentures and any other forms of participation in a juridical person and rights or interest derived therefrom; (iii) intellectual property rights which are conferred pursuant to the laws and regulations of each Member State; (iv) claims to money or to any contractual performance related to a business and having financial value; (v) rights under contracts, including turnkey, construction, management, production or revenue-sharing contracts; and business concessions required to conduct economic activities and having financial value conferred by law or under a contract, including any concessions to search, cultivate, extract or exploit natural resources. The term "investment" also includes amounts yielded by investments, in particular, profits, interest, capital gains, dividend, royalties and fees. Any alteration of the form in which assets are invested or reinvested shall not affect their classification as investment; http://investasean.asean.org/files/upload/Doc%2005%20-%20ACIA.pdf accessed 02.09.2024. Model International Agreement on Investment for Sustainable Development defines "investment" as: (i) a company; (ii) shares, stock and other forms of equity participation in a company, and bonds, debentures and other forms of debt interests in a company; (iii) contractual rights, such as under turnkey, construction or management contracts, production or revenue-sharing contracts, concessions or other similar contracts; (iv) tangible property, including real property; and intangible property, including rights, such as leases, mortgages, hypothecs, liens and pledges on real property; (v) rights conferred pursuant to law, such as licenses and permits provided that (a) such investments are not in the nature of portfolio investments which shall not be covered by this Agreement; (b) that there is a significant physical presence of the investment in the host state; (c) that the investment in the host state is made in accordance with the laws of that host state; (d) the investment is part or all of a business or commercial operation; and (e) the investment is made by an investor as defined herein. For greater certainty, an investment does not include: market share, whether or not it is based on foreign origin trade; claims to money deriving solely from commercial contracts for the sale of goods and services to or from the territory of a Party to the territory of another country, or a loan to a Party or to a state enterprise; a bank letter of credit; or the extension of credit in connection with a commercial transaction, such as trade financing. https://www.italaw.com/sites/default/files/archive/ita1027.pdf accessed 02.09.2024.

[92] See Baltag (2012), pp. 177–178, 215, 217.

[93] The impetus behind narrowing the definition of investment within a territory may rest in the old-fashioned purpose of establishing a tangible asset in the host country. The blind side of such an approach is the exclusion of loans and pre-shipments. For instance, in *Fedax v. Venezue*la, the tribunal discussed whether promissory notes the investor acquired constitute an investment made in the territory of the contracting state. In the tribunal's view, promissory notes were invested in the territory of Venezuela within the meaning of the treaty. Available at https://www.italaw.com/sites/default/files/case-documents/ita0316_0.pdf accessed 02.09.2024. Also see Salacuse (2013), pp. 372, 373 and Dolzer and Schreuer (2012), p. 76 and finally Baltag (2012), pp. 195–196.

[94] BITs can illustrate the scope of covered investment in several ways. The commonly adopted method, familiar to practitioners is to adopt a list (exhaustive or non-exhaustive). Some BITs, however, provide for certain kinds of property that are not considered investments and while others combine attributes of both methods. In this hybrid concept, a BIT encompasses a non-exhaustive list and the activities or assets that are not to be qualified as investments. For detail see Rubins (2004), pp. 293–295.

Arbitral decisions can expand the traditional definition of 'asset' in the context of investments, as much as, or in the same way that BITs do. Of relevance to the discussion on investment can be the case of the 'letter of intent' held, or expenditures made by investors. While one tribunal did not accept 'letter of intent' as a valid denomination of investment due to its association with pre-contractual expenses,[95] in a contrasting situation, another tribunal held that expenditures dedicated to a specific purpose and made by the claimant in the territory of the host sate pursuant to the agreement concluded with the host state, constituted a valid investment within the meaning of the relevant treaty.[96]

The scope of the definition is crucial for both the investor -as the prospective insured- and the underwriter of the PRI, for two reasons. Firstly, PRI contracts specify covered investments; consequently, the investor must ensure that their investment falls within one of the categories stated therein. Secondly, investors, and consequently the PRI provider as the subrogee, can secure ICSID jurisdiction if the investment fits in with the BIT signed between the investor's country and the host country. According to *Ginsburg*, the scope of the BIT's provision should be equal to or similar to the equivalent under the PRI policy. If the BIT is narrow in scope, the insurer will compensate the insured for events that would not be covered under the BIT, and therefore, the value of the insurer's subrogation rights will be diminished.[97] Hence, given the vast difference among investment treaties, underwriters should pay attention to wording during the drafting phase, and PRI providers need to review the BITs. It is imperative that investors or their legal advisers have a general understanding of how BITs and PRI work. If the BIT and PRI mismatch and the BIT is narrower in scope. after compensating the insured, the insurer may have limited rights in accordance with the BIT.

Finally, one should note that the legality of the investment is as important as its scope. While a PRI underwriter delves into the definition of investment and strives to ensure that the investment falls within the definition provided in the BIT, the same BIT contains a so-called 'legality clause' which disqualifies investments from the

---

[95] See *Mihaly* case, paras.55–61, available at https://www.italaw.com/sites/default/files/case-documents/ita0532.pdf accessed 02.09.2024. While agreeing with the award's conclusion, David Suratgar, in his concurring opinion, expressed that the letter of intent could have been admissible as an investment, had the claimant demonstrated that the expenditures were made by a Sri Lankan company in which it held a share. See Rubins (2004), pp. 303–304 and similarly see Baltag (2012), pp. 204–206.

[96] See SGS v. Pakistan para. 140. The case is available at https://www.italaw.com/sites/default/files/case-documents/ita0779.pdf In *SGS v. Philippines*, the tribunal arrived at same conclusion. The case is available at https://www.italaw.com/sites/default/files/case-documents/ita0782.pdf both accessed 02.09.2024. Also see Salacuse (2013), p. 373. See *Mihaly* case, paras.55–61. In *PSEG v. Turkey*, however, despite the fact that no work had commenced, the contract was considered a protected investment. Available at https://www.italaw.com/sites/default/files/case-documents/ita0695.pdf accessed 02.09.2024.

[97] Ginsburg (2013), p. 969.

BIT's protection if the investment concerned was procured by fraud.[98] The reason is that states consent to grant protection to investments only if they are obtained through lawful means.

5.2.2.2.2 Forms of Investment

A company, a manufacturing facility or a smoking chimney are no longer considered as typical images of an investment under PRI policies. PRI policies can easily catch up with the dynamics that the international investments may take on their own. In other words, insurance policies do not lag behind the international investment practice. Due to technological innovations and the adaptation of financial markets thereto, new forms of investments have come into being. Hence, as will be discussed in this chapter, assets or rights of an intangible nature—such as shares, loans, copyrights, and even digital assets on the internet or in the metaverse realm—are recognized by law and can thus be subject to insurance protection.

Salacuse focuses on the attributes of investment. According to the scholar, the crucial attributes of investments include (a) property and contractual rights resulting from the investment (b) control attributes of the investment and (c) the enterprise form in which the investment is made.[99] The host state's law may provide a variety of investment forms with different legal attributes as well as it may condition the investment to take a particular form. The scope of the rights that parties to PRI are entitled to or the obligations they assume thereunder are designed according to the form of the investment. In this chapter, we will present not only the conventional forms but also novel forms and discuss their availability within the PRI context.

5.2.2.2.2.1 Contractual Rights

5.2.2.2.2.1.1 In General

The contracts in which foreign investors possess, whether fully or partially an entitlement over an asset, are undoubtedly considered investments. Investors may own a fixed asset or shares of a company (whether in the form of minority shares[100]

---

[98] The tribubal in *Plama v. Bulgaria* rejected to apply the protections of the ECT. In its view "*the investment was obtained by deceitful conduct that is in violation of Bulgarian law .... It would also be contrary to the basic notion of international public policy - that a contract obtained by wrongful means (fraudulent misrepresentation) should not be enforced by a tribunal.*" See paras. 139–143. The case is available at https://www.italaw.com/sites/default/files/case-documents/ita0671.pdf accessed 02.09.2024. For discussion on the 'legality clause', see Bottini (2010), pp. 297–314 and also see Baltag (2012), pp. 197–199.

[99] Salacuse (2013), p. 4.

[100] An investor may own shares less than %10 of a company. In terms of international law, there should be a cut-off point to prevent every shareholder of the same company from bringing endless claims. Salacuse (2016), pp. 217–222, 243.

or indirect shareholding[101]) that provide ownership interest, and this so-called *equity investment* entitles investors to both profits and the right to manage the enterprise. In terms of the shareholders' protection, although the ILC's rules provide limitations,[102] and courts have been prone to interpret the scope of the protection narrowly,[103] arbitral tribunals see no impediment to extending protection to shareholders and have acknowledged their legal standing in arbitration.[104]

In the case of *debt investment,* as is in loans or bonds,[105] the investor is promised repayment of the principal and interest on the maturity date specified in the related agreement. From a management aspect, investment may take the form of either direct or portfolio management. By way of portfolio investment, investors aim for short-term financial gains without the right to manage and a need to engage in the daily operations of the enterprise. However, there is endless room for debate among

[101] An investor may participate in a company through intermediaries. In *ENRON v. Argentina*, the indirect ownership did not stand as a bar to adjudicate the dispute. The case is available at https://www.italaw.com/sites/default/files/case-documents/ita0293.pdf accessed 02.09.2024.

[102] Article 11 of the ILC's Draft articles on Diplomatic Protection provides two exceptions for the shareholders to enjoy protection, the article reads as: "*A State of nationality of shareholders in a corporation shall not be entitled to exercise diplomatic protection in respect of such shareholders in the case of an injury to the corporation unless: (a) the corporation has ceased to exist according to the law of the State of incorporation for a reason unrelated to the injury; or (b) the corporation had, at the date of injury, the nationality of the State alleged to be responsible for causing the injury, and incorporation in that State was required by it as a precondition for doing business there.*" The text is available at https://legal.un.org/ilc/texts/instruments/english/draft_articles/9_8_2006.pdf accessed 02.09.2024.

[103] In *Barcelona Traction*, the International Court of Justice made a distinction between shareholders' rights and those of the company itself, and held that "n*otwithstanding the separate corporate personality, a wrong done to the company frequently causes prejudice to its shareholders. But the mere fact that damage is sustained by both company and shareholder does not imply that both are entitled to claim compensation. Thus, no legal conclusion can be drawn from the fact that the same event caused damage simultaneously affecting several natural or juristic persons. Creditors do not have any right to claim compensation from a person who, by wronging their debtor, causes them loss.*" See Judgment of 5 February 1970 para. 44. Also see Baltag (2012), pp. 118,119 and Salacuse (2013), p. 313.

[104] For instance, in *Gami v. Mexico*, (para.35), Mexico expropriated a number of mills belonging to GAMI in which a U.S. company held 14,18% equity interest. In the tribunal's view, although shares were not expropriated, Mexico's conduct impaired the value of the shares to such an extent that it was deemed tantamount to expropriation. Available at https://www.italaw.com/sites/default/files/case-documents/ita0353_0.pdf accessed 02.09.2024, also see Dolzer and Schreuer (2012), p. 56. For other decisions see Baltag (2012), pp. 123–128.

[105] Financial institutions extend loans to sovereigns through syndication by several banks, in so doing each institution spreads its risk. Sovereigns can also meet their capital needs through issuing bonds to investors in other countries. While in the first kind of debt mechanism the bank itself lends its funds directly to the debtor it found, in the latter, the bank acts as an intermediary, responsible for selling the bonds to investors in the primary market. Although will be discussed in the subsequent chapters, due to its immunity from judicial enforcement mechanisms, transactions in which the sovereign is the debtor are of particular importance. For detail see Salacuse (2013), pp. 16, 17, 123, 124.

tribunals and scholars as to whether contracts concluded between the investor and the host state[106] or arbitral awards can qualify as an investment.

5.2.2.2.2.1.2 Arbitral Awards

The attributes of the arbitral award as defined in BITs hold significant importance. If the investment gives rise to arbitration, the question that must be tackled is that whether the arbitral award can be considered a 'continuation of an original investment[107]'? Similarly, can the non-enforcement of the award be regarded as a 'deprivation of investment'? *Saipem v. Bangladesh* is the first known case where a tribunal evaluated the responsibility of the state.[108] Saipem, the prevailing party of a commercial arbitration case (ICC case) sought enforcement of the award rendered in its favour. However, the respondent set aside the award, and the High Court Division of the Supreme Court of Bangladesh denied acknowledging the existence of the award.[109] Saipem then filed a claim before investment arbitration (ICSID), alleging that the state partook in sabotaging the ICC arbitration.[110] According to article 1(1)(c) of the related BIT,[111] the investment could be comprised of 'credit for sums of money' and the ICSID tribunal stated that "*the rights accruing from the ICC Award fall squarely within the notion of 'credit for sums of money*".[112] However, this view did not support the claimant's argument. By contrast, in the furtherance of the evaluation, the same tribunal ruled in Bangladesh's favor and did not qualify the award as an investment. In the tribunal's belief, the rights arising out of the ICC award would only indirectly relate to the investment.[113] Despite rejecting the allegation, the tribunal remained skeptical, leaving the door open by admitting that it was not prepared to accept that the award would constitute an investment under Article 25(1) of the ICSID Convention.[114]

---

[106] Contracts may be regarded as an investment on the grounds that the investor's right to transfer the benefits or to claim the performance of monetary obligations from the host state, derives from the contract. Also see Lawson and Rudden (2002), p. 25.

[107] Clasmeier (2016), p. 69.

[108] Mistelis (2013), p. 73.

[109] In the wording of the court "*A non-existent award can neither be set aside nor can it be enforced.*" See para. 36 in *Saipem v. Bangladesh*. Available at https://www.italaw.com/sites/default/files/case-documents/ita0733.pdf accessed 02.09.2024.

[110] See para. 61.

[111] Bilateral investment treaty; specifically, "Agreement Between the Government of the Republic of Italy and the Government of the People's Republic of Bangladesh on the Promotion and Protection of Investments" of 20 March 1990.

[112] See para.125.

[113] See para. 113.

[114] See para. 113. The ICSID Convention is a treaty ratified by 156 Contracting States. It entered into force on October 14, 1966, ICSID is an institution devoted to international investment dispute settlement. States have agreed on using ICSID as a forum for investor-state dispute settlement in most international investment treaties and in numerous investment laws and contracts. See https://icsid.worldbank.org/About/ICSID accessed 02.09.2024.

By the same token, in *ATA v. Jordan,* the tribunal assessed the validity of the annulment by the Jordanian court of a commercial arbitration award rendered in favor of ATA, a Turkish construction company. The tribunal was of the opinion that a 'claim to money' or a 'right to financial performance' which were provided for in article I(2)(a) of the Turkey-Jordan BIT constitutes discrete investments.[115] The tribunal adhered to its progenitor *Saipem* case and refrained from deciding whether an award comprised an investment.[116] In *Mistelis*' belief, this case reinforces the decision of the Saipem tribunal as to the liability of states which interfere with arbitral rights and lawfully obtained arbitral awards.[117] The findings in both cases are in line; however, the tribunal in *ATA v. Jordan* was courageous in finding that the right to arbitration was a distinct 'investment' within the meaning of the BIT.

Previous cases shed light on the potential of arbitral awards to constitute an investment, thus the tribunal in *GEA v. Ukraine* could have adopted a different position. Instead, in the tribunal's mind, an award is merely a legal instrument, which provides for the disposition of rights and obligations arising out of the investment and therefore cannot constitute an 'investment.'[118] It observed the required attributes of the investment and by discussing the test applied in *Salini v. Morocco,*[119] the tribunal came to the conclusion that an award itself involves no contribution to, or relevant economic activity within the scope of the term 'investment' as defined in ICSID.[120]

---

[115]See *ATA v. Jordan* (para. 112) Available at https://www.italaw.com/sites/default/files/case-documents/ita0043.pdf accessed 02.09.2024.

[116]However, the tribunal did acknowledge that "*Now, measured by the standards in Saipem, the Final Award at issue in the present arbitration would be part of an 'entire operation' that qualifies as an investment. Since the first legal confrontation between the parties over the Final Award occurred prior to the entry into force of the Turkey-Jordan BIT, as previously concluded, the Tribunal cannot claim jurisdiction ratione temporis over any issue concerning the annulment of the Final Award.*" See *ATA v. Jordan* para. 115.

[117]Mistelis (2013), p. 78.

[118]See *GEA v. Ukraine,* para. 161. Available at https://www.italaw.com/sites/default/files/case-documents/ita0356.pdf accessed 02.09.2024. For a detailed analysis, see Clasmeier (2016), pp. 77–91.

[119]In *Salini v. Morocco* (para. 52) the tribunal held that" *The doctrine generally considers that investment infers: contributions, a certain duration of performance of the contract and a participation in the risks of the transaction… In reading the Convention's preamble, one may add the contribution to the economic development of the host State of the investment as an additional condition.* Available at https://www.italaw.com/sites/default/files/case-documents/ita0738.pdf accessed 02.09.2024. See Salacuse (2016), pp. 217–222, 233–234, However, in *Fakes v. TURKEY,* (para. 121), the tribunal ruled to apply only three criteria (contribution, duration and risk) to the investment. Available at https //www.italaw.com/sites/default/files/case-documents/ita0314.pdf accessed 02.09.2024. See Dolzer and Schreuer (2012), pp. 66–67.

[120]See *GEA v. Ukraine,* para. 162. Also, in *White Industries v. India* the tribunal stated the following *"Tribunal considers that the conclusion expressed by the GEA Tribunal represents an incorrect departure from the developing jurisprudence on the treatment of arbitral awards to the effect that awards made by tribunals arising out of disputes concerning "investments" made by "investors" under BITs represent a continuation or transformation of the original investment"* See

In *Frontier v. Czech Republic*, the claimant initiated an investment arbitration against the Czech Republic before the PCA on the basis of an alleged mistreatment which was a result of inaction by the Czech judiciary in recognition of an arbitral award.[121] Article 1 of the Canada—Czech Republic BIT provided a broad definition of investment in which "claims to money, and claims to performance under contract having a financial value" were included in the definition of investment and the tribunal held that "*by refusing to recognize and enforce the Final Award in its entirety, the Tribunal accepts that the Respondent could be said to have affected the management, use, enjoyment, or disposal by the Claimant of what remained of its original investment.*"[122]

In the cases above, the investment arbitration tribunals discussed the investment character of the awards that were rendered by commercial arbitration tribunals and were far from accepting that awards were investments. By way of contrast, in *Stran Greek Refineries* case, the ECHR interpreted the arbitral award as a 'debt' in claimant's favor that was sufficiently established to be enforceable. The claimant was conferred upon a right in the sums awarded and that right constituted a 'possession' within the meaning of Article 1 of Protocol No. 1.[123] The court determined that claimant was deprived of its possessions because the outcome was literally to cancel the debt arising out of an award against which no ordinary or special appeal laid.[124] As is likewise clear from the position of the court in *BTS Holding, A.S. v. Slovakia*, a claim could constitute a possession that non-enforcement of such a claim amount to interference with it.[125] As far as 'deprivation' is concerned, some may be prone to limit it to rights on tangible assets. In fact, precluding the investor from enjoying its rights, regardless of whether it is pertained to an asset or enforcement of an award, leads to a deprivation within the same meaning. Scholars also reach similar conclusion, with *Douglas* noting that if an arbitral award is not subject to further judicial review, "*it is a chose-in-action*

White Industries v. India para. 7.6.8. Available at https://www.italaw.com/sites/default/files/case-documents/ita0906.pdf accessed 02.09.2024.

[121] See Frontier *v. Czech Republic*, para. 28. Available at https://www.italaw.com/sites/default/files/case-documents/ita0342.pdf accessed 02.09.2024.

[122] See para. 231.

[123] Art. 1 of Protocol 1 of the European Convention on Human Rights which is worded as follows: "*Every natural or legal person is entitled to the peaceful enjoyment of his possessions. No one shall be deprived of his possessions except in the public interest and subject to the conditions provided for by law and by the general principles of international law. The preceding provisions shall not, however, in any way impair the right of a State to enforce such laws as it deems necessary to control the use of property in accordance with the general interest or to secure the payment of taxes or other contributions or penalties.*" Also see Guide on Article 1 of Protocol No. 1 to the European Convention on Human Rights, p. 24.

[124] Available at https://hudoc.echr.coe.int/eng#{%22fulltext%22:[%2213427/87%22],%22documentcollectionid2%22:[%22CHAMBER%22],%22itemid%22:[%22001-57913%22]} accessed 02.09.2024.

[125] See paras. 47–49, 62–64. Available at https://hudoc.echr.coe.int/eng#{%22itemid%22:[%22001-218080%22]} accessed 02.09.2024.

(intangible property) that is capable of being expropriated by the exercise of the State's enforcement powers".[126]

The wording of the BITs may be vague and may call for interpretation. In any case, the term 'investment' should be interpreted broadly. It should not be disregarded that the award, enforcement of which is sought, is the outcome of an investment-related dispute. Thus, the award is a continuation of the original investment, and if the form of the investment is considered to have changed, such a change should not affect its character as an investment.

5.2.2.2.2.2 Foreign Direct Investment

The element of 'control' qualifies an investment as direct and distinguishes it from portfolio investment.[127] Investors choose a hands-on approach either to build an enterprise from scratch so that gain full control, or actively participate in its management by owning at least %10 of its shares [128] The diversification of investment in the global market calls for a broader definition of this direct investment concept. In one scholar's definition, foreign direct investment (FDI) is "*the creation, acquisition or endowment in the host country, of enterprises either incorporated as branches, subsidiaries or associate companies, or in the form of unincorporated enterprises or joint ventures*".[129] The World Bank[130] and IMF[131] brought definitions focusing on the 'control' element over the investment.

Control is deemed to exist if the direct investor owns more than 50 percent of the voting power in the direct investment enterprise or a significant degree of influence is determined to exist if the direct investor owns from 10 to 50 percent of the voting

[126] Douglas (2014), p. 897, fn 124.

[127] An investor of the portfolio investment has no right to participate in the control and management of the enterprise. According to *Salacuse*, direct investment gives the investor a voice in control over the enterprise, whereas the portfolio investment is too small to permit such control. See Salacuse (2013), pp. 6, 15, 121. Portfolio investments are foreign-owned passive assets, and extension of jurisdiction to these assets where the investor has limited or no control may not align with the intention of states. Therefore, such investments might not qualify as 'investments' for the purposes of jurisdiction under the relevant bilateral investment agreements. See Rubins (2004), pp. 319, 320.

[128] https://www.imf.org/external/pubs/ft/fandd/basics/20_direct-invest.htm accessed 02.09.2024.

[129] Berger (1988), p. 17, also see Shihata (1987), p. 671, fn 1. For another definition see Salacuse, (2013), p. 14.

[130] According to the World Bank, FDI is "*net inflows of investment to acquire a lasting interest in or management control over an enterprise operating in an economy other than that of the investor. It is the sum of equity capital, reinvested earnings, other long-term capital, and short-term capital, as shown in the balance of payments.*" For the broad definition see https://databank.worldbank.org/metadataglossary/international-debt-statistics/series/BX.KLT.DINV.CD.DT accessed 02.09.2024.

[131] In the IMF's wording, FDI is "*a category of cross-border investment associated with a resident in one economy having control or a significant degree of influence on the management of an enterprise that is resident in another economy.*" See IMF's Balance of Payments and International Investment Position Manual Sixth ed., p 100. Available at https://www.imf.org/external/pubs/ft/bop/2007/pdf/bpm6.pdf accessed 02.09.2024.

power in the direct investment enterprise. Lastly, there is a form of an 'indirect' direct investment where control is exercised indirectly through the ownership of voting power in one direct investment enterprise that, in turn, owns voting power in another enterprise.[132] According to OECD, FDI provides a means for creating direct, stable and long-lasting links between economies. Under the right policy environment, it can serve as an important vehicle for local enterprise development, and it may also enhance the competitive position of both the recipient ('host') and the investing ('home') economy. In particular, FDI encourages the transfer of technology and know-how between economies.[133]

It is accurate to say that both BITs and PRIs are crafted to safeguard FDIs.[134] While FDIs can grant less developed countries managerial and technical expertise and competitive market, host states may perceive risks in that foreign investment, instead of fostering local enterprise, in fact, stultifies the competition. Unlike a debt-creating financial instrument, FDI fosters lending for future projects.[135]

5.2.2.2.2.3 Enterprise Forms

The final categorization can be made based on the ownership structure. To illustrate, an investment can take the form of a *subsidiary* when it is owned by a separate legal entity where the investor holds and equity interest.[136] Conversely, in the case of a *branch*, the investor directly owns the investment. The distinction reveals itself in the legal ramifications when the investment incurs liabilities. In such a case, a subsidiary may provide a degree of protection for its owner, an investor may not enjoy limited liability if the investment is structured as a branch.[137]

5.2.2.2.2.4 Investments in Virtual World

Technology is the thrust of alteration in the law of property. As the internet has permeated our lives, computer coding systems have enabled the possibility of ownership akin to entitlement to land or chattel in the real world, extended to objects in the virtual world. The artificial or fictitious nature of this virtual world does not

---

[132] IMF's Balance of Payments and International Investment Position Manual Sixth ed., p. 101.

[133] See OECD Benchmark Definition of Foreign Direct Investment (4th ed., 2008), available at https://www.oecd-ilibrary.org/finance-and-investment/oecd-benchmark-definition-of-foreign-direct-investment-2008_9789264045743-en accessed 02.09.2024.

[134] Several studies have examined the effects of BITs on foreign direct investment. Different scholars have made different assessment about these studies. One scholar believes that the data are insufficient that studies are not capable of implicating that BITs catalyze investments into developing countries. Conversely, other scholars are of the opinion that econometric studies have found a positive correlation between the conclusion of BITs and the increase in foreign investment flows. Please see respectively, Kerner (2018), p. 13 and Schill and Djanic (2018), pp. 31, 34 et seq.

[135] Khachaturian (2006), p. 1042, similarly see Shihata (1987), p. 675.

[136] Salacuse (2013), p. 6.

[137] Salacuse (2016), pp. 36, 37, Salacuse, (2013), p. 7.

mean that it falls entirely outside the ambit of the reality.[138] Although this world is unreal, investors are intrigued by this virtuality because profits generated therefrom are real.

A virtual property, also known as a virtual asset, is an object in the virtual world and can be described in several ways. According to one definition, a virtual property is two or three-dimensional graphic representations of intangible objects that are perceived by humans as existing in a computer-generated virtual world. This includes avatars, buildings, clothing, furniture, and terrain in an online game,[139] a player's account in a virtual world, intellectual property interests held by both players and developers in the objects that they create, import and use within virtual worlds.[140]

In order for interacting with the virtual world, individuals are provided with certain licensed rights which are delineated by End User License Agreements (EULA).[141] The intellectual property rights (IP rights) fall far short of full ownership, they do not govern the ownership of physical property, by contrast, govern the ownership regime of the non-tangible elements of a physical property.[142] Ownership remains vested in the service provider[143] and the extent of software lays down the limits of protection of these property rights.[144] The recognition of virtual property rights does not negate intellectual property; in fact, the ownership of the virtual property is distinct from the ownership of the intellectual property embedded therein. Property owners are not entitled to generate copies of it. However, if the intellectual property law is applied to virtual property, holders of IP rights may invalidate emerging virtual property rights by the use of EULAs.[145]

The internet provides the basis for absolute freedom in acquiring virtual assets. While the virtual estates in the digital world mimic real-world properties, they are not confined to mere imitations of tangible assets.[146] This leads to challenges in classifying intangible assets and parsing various forms of virtual assets. On the flip side of entitlement to virtual property there lies the metaverse objects.[147] If credence is given to ordinary meanings of the words in metaverse, 'meta' is a Greek term denotes after or beyond and 'universe' is used to describe the concept of a future

---

[138] Lastowka and Hunter (2003), p. 6.

[139] Sprankling (2014), p. 94.

[140] See Erlank (2013), p. 771, fn 10.

[141] Chein (2006), p. 1084, also see Lastowka and Hunter (2003), pp. 67–68.

[142] Ramos (2022).

[143] Erlank (2013), p. 772, fn 16.

[144] Erlank (2013), p. 776.

[145] Fairfield (2005), p. 1050.

[146] Also see Lastowka and Hunter (2003), p. 37 et seq.

[147] Neal Stephenson first coined the 'metaverse' concept in his book "Snow Crash" in which he described it as a virtual world through which people escape a dystopian reality by creating a customized virtual avatar to represent themselves in this world. Ernest Cline's "Ready Player One" depicts a similar virtual world. See Goldberg and Schär (2023), p. 2. Also visit: https://www.blockchain-council.org/metaverse/metaverse-guide/ both accessed 02.09.2024.

iteration of the internet, made up of persistent, shared, 3D virtual spaces linked into a perceived virtual universe.[148]

The advent of the metaverse smooths the way for recognition of rights on the new objects that are reminiscent of the real world. The assets in metaverse are of peculiar nature.[149] Metaverse is a 3D(3-dimensional) world accessed through a browser where human interaction occurs through avatars. Although, the real world is not the same as the servers on which the metaverse object resides, the metaverse reaps the profits off the real world. As far as metaverse is concerned, the line between the virtual world and the physical world becomes blurred, and transactions within it are likely to be the norm in the future.

If a BIT requires a territorial nexus between the investment and the host state, the location of where the virtual property is deployed will pose a challenge in determining whether the digital asset is admissible within the meaning of ICSID Convention. The internet or metaverse do not have specific geographical locations for tagging.[150] Consequently, the criteria applied to virtual property in satisfying the territorial nexus requisite should not be the same as those applied to investments involving physical property.[151] Speaking of territorial link, the tribunal in *Abaclat v. Argentina,* discussed the benefit of the investment to the host state. In the tribunal's view, the territorial link in investments is of a purely financial nature and could be shifted to "where and/or for the benefit of whom the funds are ultimately used".[152] Applying this idea to the metaverse, the 'ultimate beneficiary' might not be an individual owning an asset, but rather the juridical person operating the server. This blurred concept will sit on a more concrete footing in the chapters where we will discuss the possibility of expropriation of these assets.

---

[148] See Hackl (2021). Also visit: https://www.independent.co.uk/tech/facebook-meta-metaverse-rename-meaning-b1947654.html both accessed 02.09.2024.

[149] It is interoperable, different platforms, technologies, and services work together and communicate with each other.

[150] See Lau (2022), p. 80.

[151] Some scholars differentiate digital assets into three categories based on their location. The first category of digital assets includes those contained on a device that is in the owner's control. The assets in the second category are those held on a device that is owned by a third party. And finally, assets in the third category, as in domain names, do not need to be stored on a device; put it another way, their existence is not dependent upon storage. For the classification of Jonathan Bick, see Chaisse and Bauer (2019), p. 564.

[152] See paras. 372–380. Available https://www.italaw.com/sites/default/files/case-documents/ita0236.pdf accessed 02.09.2024.

5.3 Host State 'The Wrongdoer'

5.3.1 *Definition*

States are political bodies, societies of individuals united together for the purpose of promoting their mutual safety and advantage by the joint efforts of their combined strength.[153] In PRI practice, the term 'host' serves more than a catchy adjective; in its ordinary parlance, it implies the state 'hosting the investment' and therefore, a host state denotes the sovereign power considering itself as having full authority over foreign investment.[154] In practice, along with 'host sate', underwriters employ terms such as 'host country' and 'host government'. Scholars on the other hand, may use 'transgressor country'.[155] Regardless of the modification of the adjective 'host', in this study, we mostly employed the term 'host state'. However, the term 'host country' can be more accurate in referring to the territorial zone of the state (as in 'transfer restrictions and inconvertibility' risk). The term 'host government' may be appropriate in cases where the political move of status quo requires specific attention.

The host state may engage in a variety of actions or may avoid engaging in actions that ultimately lead to political risks. The host state is not a party to insurance contract; in hindsight, it is the wrongdoer and faces the insurer's claim at the stage of subrogation.[156] Investigations may assume the innocence of the host state (except for political force majeure) until she has been proven responsible for the harm. Hence, in order to deem that a political risk has occurred, actions (whether direct or not) or omissions must be attributable to the host state.

5.3.2 *Attributability*

5.3.2.1 In General

In legal terminology, the meaning given to the term cause[157] slightly deviates from its conventional use. Cause is defined as "*something that produces an effect or*

[153] de Vattel (1852), pp. 49, 71.

[154] *Kantor* provides the following definition" *(a) the present or any succeeding governing authority (without regard to the method of its succession or as to whether it is internationally recognized) in effective control of all or any part of territory of the Host Country or any political or territorial subdivision thereof (including any dependent territory); and (b) any other public authority in or of the Host Country on which regulatory powers are conferred by the laws of the Host Country (emphasis added)*". See Kantor (2015), p. 182.

[155] DeLeonardo (2005), p. 739.

[156] Karagöz (2018), p. 120.

[157] PRI providers give weight to causation. The case of *Joseph Companies* is instructive in understanding how OPIC considered the issue of causation. The case concerned the lifting of

result". Causation, on the other hand, denotes "*the causing or producing of an effect*".[158] It deals with whether occurrence of the risk triggers the coverage within the language of the insurance policy[159] and acts as the connector between the loss and the occurrence of the peril.[160] The occurrence of the insured peril must be sufficient to bring about the loss by itself.[161] In insurance practice, indemnification to some degree is a process of justification; the insurer's liability does not commence[162] until it finds that a peril that the insurance contract covers caused the loss. That is to say, for indemnification, PRI providers do not adopt a probability approach; instead, they seek the presence of the actions or omissions by the host state as contained in the insurance contract.

The host state is an abstract person, thus, the conduct of its agencies, officials, employees,[163] and institutions may cause political risks. Investment law employs the term '*attribution*' to connect the actor or the act to the state.[164] The concept of attribution is devised to bridge the gap between the unity of the state and the multitude of its organs and instrumentalities,[165] and it finds its foundation under international law.[166] The Articles on Responsibility of States for Internationally Wrongful Acts (ILC articles) adopted by the International Law Commission

---

prohibitive import duties on the products of JSPI (60% of the equity was owned by the government and 40% by the insured), which had enabled the company to operate without being swamped by offshore competition. The recent regulation permitting imports without subjecting them to any duty resulted in the deterioration of the insured's (Josco) finance, despite having received oral assurances from the Government of Jamaica that various tariff protections would be continued. OPIC determined that "Josco would not have made its additional equity investment but for express oral assurances that were, in hindsight, misleading and unfair". In determining that direct causation was established, OPIC held that "to establish a direct causation, Josco must demonstrate that the loss was not the result of exogenous factors, such as the failure to derive benefits from the marketplace. Relevant questions in establishing causation are (i) whether JSPI was financially sound prior to the government action, and (ii) whether the loss would have occurred even in the absence of the government action. For the summary of the case, see Kantor et al. (2011), pp. 692–707, Kantor (2015), p. 183. Also see Memorandum of Determinations, Expropriation Claim of Joseph Companies Incorporated of Minneapolis Jamaica-Contract of Insurance No. E197. And please visit: https://www.dfc.gov/sites/default/files/2019-08/josephcompanies.pdf accessed 02.09.2024.

[158] See the Black's Law Dictionary.

[159] Stempel et al. (2012), p. 687.

[160] Randall and Fred (2006), p. 313.

[161] Due to subrogation, the proximate cause principle is of no use in PRI practice. Also see Roach et al. (2022), chapter 27.

[162] Peril is defined as" *fortuity; in other words, not something which is bound to happen.*" See Gürses (2016), p. 166.

[163] In the case of an individual's conduct, the rules of obedience and respondeat superior may be applied and it is worthy to note that such conduct should occur during his/her tenor. Stefano (2020), p. 44.

[164] Kovács (2018), pp. 25–28.

[165] Stefano (2020), p. 6.

[166] Muchlinski et al. (2008), pp. 553–554.

(a subsidiary organ of the United Nations General Assembly) address the attribution concept (articles 4 through 11). The ILC articles are more of an authoritative codification without a binding effect.[167] However, there is a consensus that these articles accurately reflect customary international law[168] on state responsibility.

The most generic form of attribution is stipulated under article 4 of the ILC.[169] The principle is that the state[170] which, by conduct of its organs'[171] has committed a breach of an international obligation[172] will be regarded as having committed an

---

[167] In *Clayton,* (para. 307) the tribunal held that "*The ILC Articles quoted here are considered as statements of customary international law on the question of attribution for purposes of asserting the responsibility of a State towards another State, which are applicable by analogy to the responsibility of States towards private parties.*" Available at https://www.italaw.com/sites/default/files/case-documents/italaw4212.pdf accessed 02.09.2024. Also see Muchlinski et al. (2008), p. 555.

[168] According to the art. 38 of the Statue of International Court of Justice, sources of international law fall under 4 categories which are as follows; (a) international conventions, whether general or particular, establishing rules expressly recognized by the contesting states; (b) international custom, as evidence of a general practice accepted as law; (c) the general principles of law recognized by civilized nations; and (d) subject to the provisions of Article 59, judicial decisions and the teachings of the most highly qualified publicists of the various nations, as subsidiary means for the determination of rules of law. Available at https://www.icj-cij.org/en/statute accessed 02.09.2024.

[169] According to the 4th art. of ILC Articles that was adopted in 2001 "*1- The conduct of any State organ shall be considered an act of that State under international law, whether the organ exercises legislative, executive, judicial or any other functions, whatever position it holds in the organization of the State, and whatever its character as an organ of the central Government or of a territorial unit of the State. 2- An organ includes any person or entity which has that status in accordance with the internal law of the State*" Please see https://legal.un.org/ilc/texts/instruments/english/draft_articles/9_6_2001.pdf accessed 02.09.2024.

[170] The tribunal in *Tulip v. Turkey* (award para. 289] held that "*ownership of a corporate entity by the State triggers the presumption of statehood. … whilst state ownership may, in certain circumstances, be a factor relevant to the question of attribution, it does not convert a separate corporate entity into an "organ" of the State.*" Available at https://www.italaw.com/sites/default/files/case-documents/italaw3126.pdf accessed 02.09.2024. However, in *Ampal v. Egypt* (para. 137), the institutions subject to dispute (EGPC) was considered to be corporate entity within the overall structure of the Ministry of Petroleum, despite its separate legal personality. Available at https://www.italaw.com/sites/default/files/case-documents/italaw8487.pdf accessed 02.09.2024.

[171] According to the commentary on the ILC Articles" *In determining what constitutes an organ of a State for the purposes of responsibility, the internal law and practice of each State are of prime importance. The structure of the State and the functions of its organs are not, in general, governed by international law. It is a matter for each State to decide how its administration is to be structured and which functions are to be assumed by government." See Commentary on the ILC Articles, Chapter II, para. 6, p 39. Available at* https://legal.un.org/ilc/texts/instruments/english/commentaries/9_6_2001.pdf accessed 02.09.2024. In *Almås* (para.207), the tribunal stated that "*internal status does not necessarily imply that an entity is not a state organ if other factors, such as the performance of core governmental functions, direct day-to-day subordination to central government, or lack of all operational autonomy, point the other way.*" Available at https://www.italaw.com/sites/default/files/case-documents/italaw7531.pdf accessed 02.09.2024.

[172] International obligations of the state may arise from treaties, decisions of a competent international organ or customary law. We have employed this broad term without taking into consideration

internationally wrongful act. In this sense, the conduct of de jure state's organs[173] such as legislative/judiciary body[174] (including acts of the persons exercising a public function on behalf of the Parliament, such as the speaker[175] of the parliament[176]), government, privatization agency,[177] administration of state property,[178] central banks,[179] armed forces or police, judiciary (courts,

---

the nature of and without referring to, the document or organization that may have bearing on the formation of the sources of international obligations.

[173] Kovács (2018), p. 65 et seq.

[174] In *Paushok* (para. 289), the tribunal stated that "*Actions by legislative assemblies are not beyond the reach of bilateral investment treaties. A State is not immune from claims by foreign investors in connection with legislation passed by its legislative body, unless a specific exemption is included in the relevant treaty.*"Available at https://www.italaw.com/sites/default/files/case-documents/ita0622.pdf also see *EDF Limited v. Romania case (*Award, 8 October 2009, para. 186). Available at https://www.italaw.com/sites/default/files/case-documents/ita0267.pdf both accessed 02.09.2024.

[175] Actions of individual members, not representing any constituencies, or acting in a similar capacity would not be attributable to the host state. In *Burlington Resources (*para. 305) tribunal stated that" *By calling attention to this congressional debate, the Tribunal does not intend to attribute responsibility to Ecuador for the statements of individual congressmen.*" Available at https://jusmundi.com/en/document/decision/en-burlington-resources-inc-v-republic-of-ecuador-decision-on-liability-friday-14th-december-2012 accessed 02.09.2024.

[176] See Kovács (2018), p. 65. For case law, see Stefano (2020), pp. 137–138, fn 155.

[177] In *Noble Ventures* (Award, 12 October 2005, para. 80), the tribunal concluded that "*State Ownership Fund (SOF), later reorganized into the Authority for Privatization and Management of the State (APAPS) were entitled by law to represent the Respondent and did so in all their actions as well as omissions. The acts allegedly in violation of the BIT are therefore attributable to the Respondent for the purposes of assessment under the BIT*". Available at https://www.italaw.com/sites/default/files/case-documents/ita0565.pdf accessed 02.09.2024.

[178] However, the tribunal in *Almås (para. 37]* opined that" *ANR (Polish Agricultural Property Agency (Agencja Nieruchomości Rolnych) which is a Polish institution under the supervision of the Ministry of Agriculture and Rural Development, is responsible for administering, leasing and selling Polish State-owned land is not a state organ under the domestic law of Poland, and the Claimants do not argue otherwise. It has separate legal personality and exercises operational autonomy. Under Article 3 of the 1991 Act, ANR is 'a state legal entity' that is 'supervised by the minister for rural development'. 345 It is authorized under Article 5 of the 1991 Act to 'perform on its own behalf the rights and obligations' related to State agricultural property. In light of this, ANR cannot be considered a state organ de jure under Polish law.*" Also see Stefano (2020), pp. 137–138, fn 161.

[179] Central banks, although they appear to be independent, are placed in the organizational structure of the states representing the authority conferred power to regulate monetary policies of the government. In *Paushok* case (para. 582) the tribunal held that" *...the fact that the Mongolian Parliament has created it as an institution independent of the Government does not per se make it lose its status as an organ of the State. In fact, it fulfills a major State function, and the list of its responsibilities clearly demonstrates that it fulfills a role that only a State can fulfill: exclusive right to issue currency, formulation and implementation of monetary policy, acting as the Government's financial intermediary; supervising activities of other banks; holding and managing the State's reserves of foreign currencies. As stated in the Commentary to the ILC Articles: "The reference to a "State organ" covers all the individual or collective activities which make up the organization of the State and act on its behalf." Like other central banks in the world, MongolBank assumes part of the executive responsibility of the State; and, if one were to argue for a more limited definition of the*

prosecutions,[180] enforcement authorities,[181] arbitral institutions[182]) or de facto organs,[183] political or administrative subdivisions,[184] violating international obligations incumbent upon the state entail its responsibility.[185] It is also undisputed that

---

executive power of the State, Mongolbank would still qualify as an organ of the State under the words "any other functions" mentioned in article 4 of the ILC Articles." Also see *Genin case*. Available at https://www.italaw.com/sites/default/files/case-documents/ita0359.pdf accessed 02.09.2024. Also See Stefano (2020), p. 40.

[180]Mostly in the form of 'denial of justice' risk.

[181]See *Rumeli Telekom,* available at https://www.italaw.com/sites/default/files/case-documents/ita0728.pdf , similarly, *OAO Tatneft*, available at https://www.italaw.com/sites/default/files/case-documents/italaw8622.pdf and finally, *Dan Cake* case, https://www.italaw.com/sites/default/files/case-documents/italaw4457.pdf all accessed 02.09.2024.

[182]In *Clayton (*para. 308), Joint Review Panel (JRP) was an ad hoc body constituted in relation to a particular project, and its members were appointed by the Minister of the Environment for Canada, the tribunal concluded that *"A body that exercises impartial judgment, however, can well be an organ of the state; Article 4 of the ILC Articles, just quoted, specifically includes those exercising "judicial" functions*." Also see Kovács (2018), pp. 110–111. For case law, see Stefano (2020), p. 138, fn 153.

[183]As the principle of the de facto organ is in place, a close attachment with the state or a lack of autonomy in its entirety would allow the grasp this fact. The Iranian Revolutionary Committees (Komitehs) (which, during the Iranian Revolution, served as local security forces empowered to arrest, confiscate property, and imprison, but were not officially recognized until May 1979), are considered to be one of the chief examples of de facto organs. Also see Stefano (2020), p. 51. Commentary on ILC Articles, Chapter II, para. 6. states that" *the conduct of certain institutions performing public functions and exercising public powers (e.g., the police) is attributed to the State even if those institutions are regarded in internal law as autonomous and independent of the executive government*." In *Salini v. Morocco,* (para. 35), the tribunal held that "*the State uses a varied spectrum of modes of organisation, among which are in particular semi-public companies, a State may act through the medium of a company having its own legal personality is no longer unusual if one considers the extraordinary expansion of public authority activity.*" And in *Almås (*para. 207) the tribunal held that "*internal status does not necessarily imply that an entity is not a State organ if other factors, such as the performance of core governmental functions, direct day-to-day subordination to central government, or lack of all operational autonomy, point the other way.*" Finally, in *Flemingo DutyFree (*para. 432) the tribunal noted that *"compared to the many restrictions and forms of government control and interference, the above expressions of quasi-independence and quasi-autonomy do not tip the scales*." Available at https://www.italaw.com/sites/default/files/case-documents/italaw7709_3.pdf accessed 02.09.2024.

[184]It does not matter for this purpose whether the territorial unit in question is a component unit of a federal state or a specific autonomous area, and it is equally irrelevant whether the internal law of the state in question gives the federal parliament power to compel the component unit to abide by the state's international obligations. See Commentary on ILC Art. 4, para. 9. In *Generation Ukraine, (*Award, 16 September 2003, para. 10.3) the tribunal noted that "*there is no doubt that the conduct of a municipal authority such as the Kyiv City State Administration, which is listed as an organ of State power by the Ukrainian Constitution, is capable of being recognised as an act of the State of Ukraine under international law*." In *Vivendi v. Argentina* II (para. 49) the tribunal opined that "*it is well established that actions of a political subdivision of federal state, such as the Province of Tucumán in the federal state of the Argentine Republic, are attributable to the central government*". Available at https://www.italaw.com/sites/default/files/case-documents/ita0206.pdf accessed 02.09.2024.

[185]Stefano (2020), p. 8.

states are responsible for the acts of territorial units (such as states of the federal states, autonomous regions, overseas provinces, territories under military occupation, counties, municipalities[186]), and mayors of the municipality or municipal police.[187]

Article 5 of the ILC Articles deals with the conduct of persons or entities that are not state organs but are delegated and exercise elements of governmental[188] authority.[189] A state is deemed liable if the failure on the part of persons or entities over whom it exercises significant control to carry out its international obligations causes damage to the assets of the foreigners located on the territory of the concerned state. The article stipulates that the act of the entity (mostly parastatal[190]) or of the person in question (state instrumentality[191]) must involve an exercise of governmental

[186] Art. 23/1 of ECT states" *Each Contracting Party is fully responsible under this Treaty for the observance of all provisions of the Treaty and shall take such reasonable measures as may be available to it to ensure such observance by regional and local governments and authorities within its Area.*" For ECT case law related to attribution *see Nykomb Synergetics* where Latvenergo, a monopolist electricity supplier failed to pay the contractually-agreed tariff to the claimant. The tribunal, also relying on the fact that government failed to act in order to correct the situation, came to the conclusion that "*Latvenergo had no authority of its own to decide or negotiate purchase prices for electric power produced in Latvia. The average price tariff at any time was determined by regulatory authorities... Latvia was responsible for Latvenergo's actions under the rules of attribution in international law.*" See pp. 30–32. Available at https://www.italaw.com/sites/default/files/case-documents/ita0570.pdf accessed 02.09.2024. Similarly, see Muchlinski et al. (2008), p. 563. Also see Dolzer and Schreuer (2012), pp. 217–218.

[187] Stefano (2020), p. 42.

[188] The Commentary on ILC art. 5 states that" Beyond a certain limit, what is regarded as "governmental" depends on the particular society, its history and traditions." The Commentary further states that" *The generic term "entity" reflects the wide variety of bodies which, though not organs, may be empowered by the law of a State to exercise elements of governmental authority. They may include public corporations, semi-public entities, public agencies of various kinds and even, in special cases, private companies, provided that in each case the entity is empowered by the law of the State to exercise functions of a public character normally exercised by State organs, and the conduct of the entity relates to the exercise of the governmental authority concerned.*" See Commentary on ILC art. 5 para.2, p 43.

[189] Art. 5 of ILC articles reads as: *"The conduct of a person or entity which is not an organ of the State under* art. *4 but which is empowered by the law of that State to exercise elements of the governmental authority shall be considered an act of the State under international law, provided the person or entity is acting in that capacity in the particular instance.*" In *Jan de Nul case* (para. 170), the tribunal noted that "*What matters is not the "service public" element, but the use of "prérogatives de puissance publique" or governmental authority*". Available at https://www.italaw.com/sites/default/files/case-documents/ita0440.pdf accessed 02.09.2024.

[190] " Company or organization which is owned by a country's government and often has some political power" https://dictionary.cambridge.org/dictionary/english/parastatal accessed 02.09.2024. For case law see Stefano (2020), pp. 150–151, fn 214–220.

[191] For instance, state agencies are not organs of the state, however, are considered a category of state instrumentalities. For detail, see Kovács (2018), p. 141.

authority.[192] State instrumentalities do not exist in the organic structure of the state; however, their impugned conduct is attributable to the state if their power has been delegated by the government and they acted in a governmental capacity.[193]

Drawing up an exhaustive list or defining the state organs that may interfere with foreign investments may not be feasible.[194] The key connector to attribute the conduct of the entity to the state is whether the organ or individual acting in an official capacity.[195] Doctrine offers a non-exhaustive list for the symptoms of the status of the parastatal entities implied under 5th article of the ILC.[196] In ascertaining

---

[192] In some cases, states may aim for total management therefore, whether direct or indirect or whether through influence or total management, discovering the palpable degree of affiliation between the entity and the government is essential. Also see Stefano (2020), pp. 63–64.

[193] See Stefano (2020), pp. 54–57. For sample case, see *Gustav* available at https://www.italaw.com/sites/default/files/case-documents/ita0396.pdf and *Toto Costruzioni* available at https://www.italaw.com/sites/default/files/case-documents/ita0869.pdf both accessed 02.09.2024.

[194] Institutions of an administrative nature, corporate or non-corporate forms exercising state functions or holding a statutory authorization to issue regulations, or entities under the state's ownership or control (for instance, where the state is in charge of appointing and removing the board of directors or where the state de facto controls) are the formations or correlations that are pinpoint targets of attribution.

[195] In *Deutsche Bank*, (para. 405 and 356 respectively) the tribunal noted that *"While it may be unusual for a state enterprise to be considered an organ of the State, this is only the case where the state enterprise is genuinely independent – the fact that it takes the form of a separate legal entity is not decisive."* Also in the same decision, the tribunal referred to Sri Sri Lankan Supreme Court decision and held that" *a legal hybrid bred by the Government to enable it to engage in commercial business tailor made to suit its style of business. It is a government creation clothed with juristic personality so as to give it an aura of independence, but in reality, it is just a business house doing only the State's business for and on behalf of the State.*" Available at https://www.italaw.com/sites/default/files/case-documents/italaw1272.pdf accessed 02.09.2024.

[196] (a) establishment by statutory act or decree(including privatization laws); (b) mission to provide a public service or to pursue a public purpose; (c) entitlement to acquire, hold, and dispose of property; (d) management of State-owned property; (e) capacity to sue and to be sued; (f) autonomous budget; (g) funds deposited in a special account or accounts at the central bank of the establishing State; (h) subsidization by the government; (i) exercise of a delegated monopoly (including the power to set prices); (j) board of directors appointed (and revoked) by the government or political power; (k) ministers sitting as president or members of the board of directors; (l) applicability to employees of the labour regime governing public servants; (m) registration on the Treasury's accounts of the charges collected and revenues received by the parastatal; (n) auditing of accounts and balance sheets by the General Auditor of the State; (o) palpable governmental oversight (also through a Conseil d'État), mandatory approval of resolutions and operations, and mandates; (p) jurisdiction of administrative courts over the activities of the parastatal entity; (q) applicability of the administrative regulation for public contracts (including concessions and procurements) (r) general and broad power to issue regulations to implement a parastatal's mandate; (s) empowerment to impose coercive measures, such as charges, fines, and penalties (t) protection of immunity from suit. See Stefano (2020), pp. 155–156.

whether actions or omissions are imputable, a twofold test is exercised: First, the organ of the state[197] undergoes a structural examination[198] and in the second phase, functions of the state entity or instrumentality is observed.[199]

The remaining ILC articles set out a variety of conducts that may be attributable to the states; According to article 6, the conduct of organs placed at the disposal of a state by another state may result in the state's liability.[200] Article 7 introduces another form of attribution. As per the article, the state can be held to have incurred international responsibility if the conduct of its organs, persons or entities acting in a governmental capacity.[201] This article differs from the 5th article and covers

---

[197] If a body is not characterized as a 'state organ' under internal law, this fact does not mean that it is not a state organ for the purposes of attribution. See Muchlinski et al. (2008), p. 556, similarly, Stefano (2020), pp. 29, 30.

[198] In order to identify the structural designation (legal establishment and the status) of the organ in question, such a test is made. *Maffezini v. Spain* is a good illustration of structural and functional tests.

[199] To determine whether a person or entity acts as a state organ, the legal function, role of the person or entity is observed. In *Maffezini v. Spain* (para. 79) the tribunal noted that "*Because of the many forms that State enterprises may take and thus shape the manners of State action, the structural test by itself may not always be a conclusive determination whether an entity is an organ of the State or whether its acts may be attributed to the State. An additional test has been developed, a functional test, which looks to the functions of or role to be performed by the entity.*" For the detailed explanation of the structural and functional tests, see Stefano (2020), pp. 59–60, 158–166. and Kovács (2018), pp. 61–62.

[200] Art. 6 of ILC Articles reads as: "The *conduct of an organ placed at the disposal of a State by another State shall be considered an act of the former State under international law if the organ is acting in the exercise of elements of the governmental authority of the State at whose disposal it is placed*".

[201] Art. 7 of the ILC Articles reads as: "The *conduct of an organ of a State or of a person or entity empowered to exercise elements of the governmental authority shall be considered an act of the State under international law if the organ, person or entity acts in that capacity, even if it exceeds its authority or contravenes instructions.*" The authority or functions of organs, entities or persons are entrusted as well as circumscribed by specific regulations or instructed by their superior. It is fair and proper to protect a foreign legal or real person from conduct that took place in the territory of the state, regardless of whether the state has the capacity to guide, control or prevent every single conduct of its persons. Since the provision is in relation to situations in which state officials abuse their power or act contrary to directives, the principle of ultra vires is at stake. It is worthy to note that private actions or omissions by individuals who happen to be representatives do not fall within the scope of this book. See Muchlinski et al. (2008), p. 555. Also, a state organ using the means put at its disposal by virtue of its office and duties is interpreted as sufficient ground for the operation of the ultra vires rule. See Stefano (2020), p. 48. In *Kardassopoulos v. Georgia*, (para. 273), the tribunal noted that"*It is also immaterial whether or not SakNavtobi and Transneft were authorized to grant the rights contemplated by the JVA and the Concession or whether or not they otherwise acted beyond their authority under Georgian law. Art. 7 of the Articles on State Responsibility provides that even in cases where an entity empowered to exercise governmental authority acts ultra vires of it, the conduct in question is nevertheless attributable to the State*". Available at https://www.italaw.com/sites/default/files/case-documents/ita0445.pdf accessed 02.09.2024. And in *Southern v. Egypt* (para. 83], the tribunal decided that "*Whether legal under Egyptian law or not, the acts in question were the acts of Egyptian authorities, including the highest executive authority of the Government. These acts, which are now alleged to have been in violation of the*

situations where the official exceeds their competence or contravenes provisions they should have obeyed. In other words, the state is responsible even if the person in question surpasses the state's authority or violates instructions. In general perception of attributability, whether manifest or veiled, the will of the state in orchestrating the conduct is sought, and a link is established between the conduct of the persons or entities and the machinery of the state. Article 7, however, deals with the exceptional situations in which the official acts against the rules or instructions laid down by the state. It therefore reminds the state's strict liability and whether the state may be called upon to answer 'personal' conduct of perpetrators in question. Moreover, the article emerges the question of attributability in case of misconduct of the official acting out of the range of its apparent authority. In a similar vein, attributability will be disputed if the official has acted in its capacity but outside its competence under internal law[202] or has acted on its own account and actions were unconnected with its official duties.

Attribution can be implicated, if the conduct is directed or controlled by the state under article 8 of the ILC Articles.[203] Additionally, states can be charged with the

---

Egyptian municipal legal system, created expectations protected by established principles of international law." https://www.italaw.com/sites/default/files/case-documents/italaw6314_0.pdf accessed 02.09.2024. Also see Stefano (2020), pp. 147–149.

[202] See Draft articles on state responsibility with commentaries thereto adopted by the ILC on first reading", January 1997. p. 40. Text is available at https://legal.un.org/ilc/texts/instruments/english/commentaries/9_6_1996.pdf accessed 02.09.2024.

[203] This principle is enunciated in ILC art. 8 as follows: "*The conduct of a person or group of persons shall be considered an act of a State under international law if the person or group of persons is in fact acting on the* instructions of, or under the direction or control of, that State in carrying out the conduct." This probability includes a de facto situation where the state's intervention may take place through its binding instructions or effective or specific control 'as a vehicle" over non-state actors (persons or groups of persons not falling under the attribution mechanisms pertaining to the category of organs) and thereby states may exploit non-state actors to achieve its objective. (See *Tulip v. Turkey*) In Commentary on ILC Art. 8, para. 3, the following statement is made" conduct *will be attributable to the State only if it directed or controlled the specific operation and the conduct complained of was an integral part of that operation. The principle does not extend to conduct which was only incidentally or peripherally associated with an operation and which escaped from the State's direction or control*." Also, in para. 3 it was stated that "*As a general principle, the conduct of private persons or entities is not attributable to the State under international law. Circumstances may arise, however, where such conduct is nevertheless attributable to the State because there exists a specific factual relationship between the person or entity engaging in the conduct and the State.* Art.*8 deals with two such circumstances. The first involves private persons acting on the instructions of the State in carrying out the wrongful conduct. The second deals with a more general situation where private persons act under the State's direction or control. Bearing in mind the important role played by the principle of effectiveness in international law, it is necessary to take into account in both cases the existence of a real link between the person or group performing the act and the State machinery.*" For cases where states were held liable for its binding instructions, see *EDF Limited v. Romania*. For a sample case of the state's control, see *UAB E Energija v. Latvia*, also see *EnCana v. Ecuador,* please visit respectively https://www.italaw.com/sites/default/files/case-documents/italaw9481.pdf and https://www.italaw.com/sites/default/files/case-documents/ita0285_0.pdf both accessed 02.09.2024 *and Ampal v. Egypt.* And for detail see Stefano (2020), pp. 78, 173–177 and Kovács (2018), p. 226.

conduct carried out in the absence or default of the official authorities as per article 9.[204] Organs of the state not carrying out certain tasks make use of persons who are not formally part of the state machinery. The conduct in which the persons or groups in question engage on behalf of the state should therefore be regarded under international law, as acts of the state. Determining with precision the status of private persons, who, acting on their own initiative, assume military functions is challenging; their conduct must effectively relate to exercising elements of governmental authority. In the second place, their conduct must occur due to the absence of official authorities.[205] Finally, an internationally wrongful act occurs so long as there is a violation of an international obligation by conduct acknowledged and adopted by a State as its own.[206]

5.3.2.2 State-Owned Enterprise, the Victim or the Wrongdoer?

Some may presume that only private individuals or entities engage in international investment. In fact, as governments become concerned about the lack of private investors or reserving important areas of economic activity for themselves, they actively take part in the international trade as investors and provide services or goods to the inhabitants of their countries.[207] Studies put forward that there is a trend to include state-owned enterprises (SOE) in the definition of investors in investment treaties.[208] Thus, although its practice is scant, within the definitions of the investor,

---

[204] Art. 9 of the ILC Articles provides: "*The conduct of a person or group of persons shall be considered an act of a State under international law if the person or group of persons is in fact exercising elements of the governmental authority in the absence or default of the official authorities and in circumstances such as to call for the exercise of those elements of authority*".

[205] See Draft articles on state responsibility with commentaries thereto adopted by the international law commission on first reading", p. 34. The document is available at https://legal.un.org/ilc/texts/instruments/english/commentaries/9_6_1996.pdf accessed 02.09.2024.

[206] Art. 11 of the ILC Article reads as: "*Conduct which is not attributable to a State under the preceding articles shall nevertheless be considered an act of that State under international law if and to the extent that the State acknowledges and adopts the conduct in question as its own*". In this probability, the State should unequivocally adopt the impugned conduct and make it its own. Hence, a word of caution may be opportune at this stage that that adoption should not be in the form of a silent approval. Commentary to the article 11 of the ILC articles states that "*Conduct will not be attributable to a State under article 11 where a State merely acknowledges the factual existence of conduct or expresses its verbal approval of it*". For case law See *Saint-Gobain v. Venezuela* available at https://www.italaw.com/sites/default/files/case-documents/italaw8286_0.pdf accessed 02.09.2024, also see *Ampal v. Egypt,* and for detail, see Stefano (2020), pp. 73–74. And Kovács (2018), p. 228.

[207] Salacuse (2013), p. 10.

[208] See McLaughlin (2019), pp. 609, 610, for the treaties explicitly defining SOEs as investors, see Ibid, p 616 and similarly, see Wang (2016), p. 47.

SOEs[209] or sovereign wealth funds[210] can be qualified as 'investor'.[211] Some model multilateral treaties do not require investment to be profit-oriented, thereby enabling SOEs to enjoy protection of the treaty.[212] However, as discussed in following chapters, states enjoy jurisdictional immunity; accordingly, one may well raise the question of whether an SOE's linkage with the sovereign hinders its access to PRI or whether PRI coverage is essential for an SOE that sits under the umbrella of immunity. In our opinion, as long as the SOE uses the means that are more commercial than diplomatic, it would be absurd not to treat the SOE as an investor.[213] The intention of treaty drafters must be to permit states to enjoy benefits of being investor only if they act in a commercial capacity.[214] Some scholars support this idea by arguing that claimants' acts can be attributable to the state but given that the drafters anticipated the possibility of claims by governments as investors, the attribution should not interfere with the claimant's ability to qualify as an 'investor'.[215]

The government agency or the instrumentality must have the legal capacity to enter into a transaction with the foreign investor. Otherwise, the sovereign may advance the argument that the agreement on issues over which its agency has no power of commitment is void and does not generate rights to the foreign investor. The transaction can only be covered by its apparent acquiescence. Hence, according to scholars this places a heavy due diligence burden on companies to ascertain the legal powers of their government partner.[216]

In addition, the sovereign, should not evade or avoid its responsibilities for wrongful acts or omissions by hiding behind a veil[217] through contractual or

---

[209] OECD defines SOEs as "*any corporate entity recognized by national law as an enterprise, and in which the state exercises ownership*" See OECD Guidelines on Corporate Governance of State-Owned Enterprises, 2015 ed. available at https://www.oecd-ilibrary.org/docserver/9789264244160-en.pdf?expires=1676984028&id=id&accname=guest&checksum=D065852D74E970D12A7CB6AD031C4FD2 accessed 02.09.2024.

[210] Sovereign Wealth Funds (SWFs) are state agencies holding a portion of a country's foreign currency reserves. Salacuse (2013), p. 11.

[211] Some scholars opine that SOEs are 'constrained investors' that refrain from taking an active corporate governance role in target companies to avoid attracting host state regulatory backlash. Blyschak Paul (2016), p. 7.

[212] See Henin et al. (2019), p. 47.

[213] Also see Baltag (2012), pp. 131–134.

[214] Feldman (2016), p. 30, McLaughlin (2019), pp. 607, 608.

[215] Feldman (2016), p. 28.

[216] For detail see Waelde and Ndi (1996), pp. 235, 236.

[217] The commercial activities of export credit and insurance institutions, whether conditional or not, are backed or subsidized by governments. In a case where Czech Export Bank, a.s. (CEB) and Export Guarantee and Insurance Corporation (EGAP) did not respond exporter's financial requests on anti-money laundering grounds, as a result, the exporter declared bankrupt, and its assets were sold. Although the tribunal did not consider the attribution issue since it found that there is a conduct capable of breaching the expropriation standard in the BIT. The tribunal discussed whether CEB and EGAP were performing ordinary commercial actions or performing governmental functions

commercial means.[218] The responsibility of the state will be disregarded if the breach is not of an international obligation, but of a pure commercial nature. The performance of a mere act,[219] such as termination of a contract that a regular commercial entity[220] conducts in the ordinary course of trade life, by a state instrumentality vested with power within the framework of those governmental powers, may not necessarily imply the exercise of a governmental authority.[221]

In *Al Tamimi* case, OMCO (a state-owned enterprise) terminated the agreement concluded with Al Tamimi. In the tribunal's view, the relevant provision of the US-Oman FTA[222] limits the number of the grounds on which attribution could be based. Thus, circumstances related to imputability set out in the ILC Articles on State Responsibility are not applicable to the case. Although a number of OMCO's board members also served as government ministers, the tribunal did not find any conduct imputable to the Omani State under the US–Oman FTA.[223]

On the other hand, a state's responsibility may not apply even if an investment contract is signed by a state-owned association. In the *Bridas* case, Bridas entered into a joint venture agreement ('JVA') with a production association, Turkmenneft, formed and owned by the Turkmenistan government at the time when the JVA was signed. The government did not sign the JVA, nor was it defined as a party to the agreement. Although some clauses in the contract suggested that there would be particular government actions or inactions[224] there was no clear indication that Turkmenneft acted in the government's capacity or represented the government which could have been accomplished in a myriad of ways. In the court's wording

---

and found that the case involved serious issues as to attributability. See *WNC Factoring Limited,* available at https://www.italaw.com/sites/default/files/case-documents/italaw8533.pdf accessed 02.09.2024. Also see Kovács (2018), pp. 158–160, also see *Barcelona Traction* (Judgment, 5 February 1970) and see Stefano (2020), pp. 81–82, 152.

[218] See *Maffezini v. Spain.*

[219] The Commentary on ILC art. 5 states that "*The justification for attributing to the State under international law the conduct of "parastatal" entities lies in the fact that the internal law of the State has conferred on the entity in question the exercise of certain elements of the governmental authority. If it is to be regarded as an act of the State for purposes of international responsibility, the conduct of an entity must accordingly concern governmental activity and not other private or commercial activity in which the entity may engage. Thus, for example, the conduct of a railway company to which certain police powers have been granted will be regarded as an act of the State under international law if it concerns the exercise of those powers, but not if it concerns other activities (e.g., the sale of tickets or the purchase of rolling stock).*"

[220] See *Gustav* case, also see Muchlinski et al. (2008), p. 567.

[221] For the detail case law see Stefano (2020), pp. 160–161.

[222] The related article of the US-Oman FTA provides "*A Party's obligations under this Section shall apply to a state enterprise or other person when it exercises any regulatory, administrative, or other governmental authority delegated to it by that Party.*"

[223] For the discussion of the case, see Stefano (2017), pp. 267–274. See paras. 317–335 of the case, available at https://www.italaw.com/sites/default/files/case-documents/italaw4450.pdf accessed 02.09.2024.

[224] Rubins and Kinsella (2005), p. 66.

"*Bridas could have requested that the Government sign the agreement or inserted a prominent and direct statement as to Turkmenneft's status....*" and the court concluded that "*a signatory may not estop a nonsignatory from avoiding arbitration regardless of how closely affiliated that nonsignatory is with another signing part.*"[225]

As will be discussed under the topic of 'creeping expropriation', a state will jeopardize its reputation as well as its economic future if it enjoys sovereign authority in a wrongful or illegal manner aimed at foreign investors' assets. Thus, in order to escape such consequence, it will abstain from direct conduct. In essence, attributability is a game of 'hide and seek' in international investment, where the host state cloaks its intention and exercises various indirect expropriatory actions and in response arbitrators and PRI providers make efforts to ascertain the illegal conduct of the entity that bears the 'attributes of statehood'.[226]

5.3.2.3 Case Studies

5.3.2.3.1 Ukraine

In 2022, an armed conflict broke out in Ukraine. To grasp the causation at play, a variety of views should be ventured. According to some views, it is a pure invasion of Ukrainian soil[227] to restore the dissolved Soviet Union[228] by claiming NATO's (North Atlantic Treaty Organization) possible enlargement toward the east and ratification of Ukraine's accession.[229] Others who oppose this view suppose that these are the West's (led by the U.S.) efforts to prevent multipolarity in the world by

[225] Please visit: https://www.courtlistener.com/opinion/32595/bridas-sapic-v-govt-of-turkmenistan/ accessed 02.09.2024.

[226] Frischknecht and Poplinger et al. (2018), p. 311.

[227] Please visit: https://www.nato.int/cps/en/natohq/115204.htm and https://www.defense.gov/News/News-Stories/Article/article/3737058/ and, see Shifrinson (2022) available at https://nationalinterest.org/feature/what-americas-interest-ukraine-war-205555 all accessed 18.09.2024.

[228] Experts are of the opinion that Russia's attempt to invade Ukraine might aim to restore as much of the Soviet Union's territory as possible. Please visit: https://www.ox.ac.uk/news/2022-04-21-expert-comment-putin-s-russia-people-increasingly-identify-soviet-union-here-s-what also visit: https://foreignpolicy.com/2023/11/05/russia-ukraine-empire-imperialism-war/ and https://www.aljazeera.com/news/2014/9/14/ukraine-pm-putin-wants-to-restore-the-ussr all accessed 18.09.2024.

[229] In the authors' view, if NATO's presence in the countries sharing borders with Russia were to pose a threat to its security concerns, Russia would likely react—though probably not in the same way it did in Ukraine—to forestall the accession of Finland and Sweden to NATO. See Dickinson (2023) available at https://www.atlanticcouncil.org/blogs/ukrainealert/russias-invasion-of-ukraine-was-never-about-nato/ similarly, please visit: https://blogs.lse.ac.uk/europpblog/2022/04/27/nato-enlargement-is-not-to-blame-for-russias-war-in-ukraine/ both accessed 18.09.2024.

distracting Russia and weakening its military and financial capacity,[230] thereby averting growing solid ties between Russia and China[231] and encircling China in the Pacific.[232] Supporters of this view go further and opine that this action will have served the U.S. to gain full trust and support from Europe and to steer them away from engaging in business with Russia. In 2014, Russia's and Crimea's leadership agreed on Crimea and Sevastopol becoming a part of Russia.[233] After the territorial change, a decision which allowed nationalizing businesses and property was adopted. In the same vein, Russia recognized the independence of Donetsk and Luhansk in 2022 amid the ongoing war.[234] The establishment of the *de facto entities/ breakaway republics* was premised on violations of peremptory norms of international law.[235] The presence of one country's military personnel on the soil of another holds the purpose of subverting the sovereignty.[236] Ukrainian sovereignty in these regions appears to be displaced and the dubious sovereignty of the breakaway republics is likely to wear off over time. These two republics, along with the Zaporozhye and Kherson regions, have undergone the same fate with that of Crimea. Although condemned by the international community, in late September of 2022, referendums on these regions' joining Russia were staged. While there is no official recognition by the authorities of the incorporation of these regions into Russia, Russia signed treaties on accession of the mentioned regions to the Russian Federation,[237] in line with the outcome of these referendums.

The *Montevideo Convention on the Rights and Duties of States (*The Montevideo Convention*)* provides the qualifications indispensable for a state to be a person of international law. According to article 1 of the Convention, a state should have a

---

[230] Please visit: https://www.romney.senate.gov/the-u-s-should-continue-to-support-ukraines-war-effort/ accessed 18.09.2024.

[231] Harris et al. (2023) and similarly, Sagild and Hsiung (2024). Also please visit: https://edition.cnn.com/2024/09/17/china/china-russia-military-drills-analysis-intl-hnk/index.html accessed 18.09.2024.

[232] Bachulska and Leonard (2023).

[233] Azarova (2018), p. 58, for the background of this decision and timeline see Tsybulenko and Kelichavyi (2018), pp. 279, 282. And finally, see Kemp and Lyubashenko (2018), p. 344.

[234] Please visit: https://www.bbc.com/news/av/world-europe-60470900, similarly visit: https://www.independent.co.uk/news/world/europe/russia-ukraine-donetsk-luhansk-putin-b2019840.html both accessed 02.09.2024.

[235] Azarova (2018), p. 44.

[236] As is known to everyone, paramilitary means have been deployed on Ukrainian soil. According to article 5 of the ILC, the engagement of mercenaries who are empowered by the law of the state and who exercise elements of the governmental authority (military operations in this case) can be attributable to the state in question. Since art. 5 specifically requires "empowerment *by the law*", some may argue that the wording refers to the constitution, a decree or statutory law, however the language should be construed in a broader sense and private contracts of a delegation nature would also be involved. Also see Stefano (2020), pp. 64–66.

[237] Please visit: https://www.reuters.com/world/europe/russias-federation-council-ratifies-annexation-four-ukrainian-regions-2022-10-04/ accessed 02.09.2024.

permanent population, a defined territory, a government and the capacity to enter into relations with other states.[238] In terms of these attributes, in the view of some scholars, the population of breakaway republics consists of Ukrainian citizens and groups with separatist aspirations cannot be qualified as recognized state at international level.[239] Capacitating the prospective state can be an intention of a tacit recognition[240] however, Russia's actions have received a commensurate reaction, and international community has avoided recognition of those states.[241]

A territory can be transferred from one state to another, or a state can be replaced by another. The Vienna Convention on Succession of States in respect of treaties deals with state succession[242] however, applies only to the effects of a succession of states occurring in conformity with international law.[243] One may raise the question of whether Russian investment treaties will govern foreign investments in the annexed territories or whether political risks can be attributed to Russia.[244] Military occupation of a territory does not constitute a succession of states.[245] Illegal annexation will not produce a legitimate effect and will not have a different bearing on attributability.[246] A state cannot claim sovereignty over the territory it annexed and while holding a position that treaties binding upon it do not apply with respect to that territory.[247]

---

[238] The Convention is available at https://www.oas.org/juridico/english/treaties/a-40.html accessed 02.09.2024. According to some scholars, the lawfulness of a state requires obtaining following principles: territorial integrity, inviolability of borders, non-interference, and the legitimate use of the principle of peoples' right to self-determination. See Korotkyi and Hendel (2018), p. 148, similarly, see Fox and Webb (2013), p. 341.

[239] Korotkyi and Hendel (2018), p. 149.

[240] According to art. 7 of the Montevideo Convention recognition may be express or tacit and in the latter one the Convention requires "the intention to recognize the new State".

[241] Please visit; https://press.un.org/en/2022/sgsm21153.doc.htm accessed 02.09.2024. Also see Korotkyi and Hendel (2018), pp. 158–160.

[242] Russia has not signed, and therefore, is not bound by the Convention. Please visit: https://treaties.un.org/pages/ViewDetails.aspx?src=IND&mtdsg_no=XXIII-2&chapter=23&clang=_en accessed 02.09.2024.

[243] See article 6, the Convention is available at https://legal.un.org/ilc/texts/instruments/english/conventions/3_2_1978.pdf accessed 02.09.2024.

[244] For the discussion see Papaefstratiou Athina (2023).

[245] Article 40 of the Convention reads as "*The provisions of the present Convention shall not prejudge any question that may arise in regard to a treaty from the military occupation of a territory.*" Also see commentary to art. 39 of the Convention, para. 2, 4, p. 268, available at https://legal.un.org/ilc/texts/instruments/english/commentaries/3_2_1974.pdf accessed 02.09.2024.

[246] According to article 15 of the Convention, "*when part of the territory of a State becomes part of the territory of another State: (a) treaties of the predecessor State cease to be in force in respect of the territory to which the succession of States relates from the date of the succession of States; and (b) treaties of the successor State are in force in respect of the territory to which the succession of States relates from the date of the succession of States…*"

[247] For detail, see Costelloe (2016), pp. 343–378.

What concerns PRI is that the Russia's abovementioned conduct lacked a provision for obtaining any compensation for damages[248] and several companies, in reliance on article 5 of the Russia-Ukraine BIT,[249] claimed compensation for the loss caused by the belligerent annexation[250] of Crimea.[251] Moreover, as debated elsewhere in this study, the key figure in the political risk is the sovereign, and the causal link is the attributability of the actions or omissions to her. Some may want to ascertain an answer to who will assume the loss deriving from the political risk (most likely in the form of political force majeure) taking place in these regions. The answer is more complicated than the situation itself, as the US appears to have shifted its foreign policy in a way that may upend the balance in Russia's favor by considering the recognition of occupied territories as part of Russia. In one scholar's view, in accordance with article 8 of the ILC Articles crimes, committed by the breakaway republics should be attributed to Russia.[252] A similar conclusion may be reached within the context of insurance.[253] Insurers should bear in mind that states are entitled to restore or maintain their territorial integrity and the fact is that Russian military interference is being exercised on Ukrainian soil. In this regard, insurers may wring their hands over how to reduce their costs, however, definitely, Ukraine cannot be a target for recourse.

5.3.2.3.2 Taiwan

As the writing of this book comes to an end in late 2024, relations between China and the US have become strained over the issue of Taiwan, and the ongoing war between Russia and Ukraine has driven interest in insuring operations located in

---

[248] Tsybulenko and Kelichavyi (2018), p. 283.

[249] See Agreement Between the Cabinet of Ministers of Ukraine and the Government of the Russian Federation on the Encouragement and Mutual Protection of Investments. Available at https://investmentpolicy.unctad.org/international-investment-agreements/treaty-files/2233/download accessed 02.09.2024.

[250] According to art. 42 of Convention (IV) respecting the Laws and Customs of War on Land and its annex: Regulations concerning the Laws and Customs of War on Land. The Hague, 18 October 1907. "*Territory is considered occupied when it is actually placed under the authority of the hostile army.*" Available at https://ihl-databases.icrc.org/applic/ihl/ihl.nsf/Article.xsp?action=openDocument&documentId=01D426B0086089BEC12563CD00516887 accessed 02.09.2024.

[251] Butkevych (2018), p. 206.

[252] See Merezhko (2018), p. 117.

[253] Ukrainian government also enacted a law concerning the actions has taken place in its territory, according to the article 2 of the law with the number of 2268-VIII dated on 18.01.2018 "*The temporary occupation of Ukrainian territories by the Russian Federation determined by section one of article one of this Law, regardless of its duration, is illegal and does not create for the Russian Federation territorial rights of any kind.* The same provision indicated the following: "*Liability for material and non-material damage caused to Ukraine as a consequence of the armed aggression of the Russian Federation is borne by the Russian Federation, in accordance with the principles and standards of international law*". Available at https://ips.ligazakon.net/document/T182268?an=1 accessed 02.09.2024.

Taiwan against political violence risks.[254] As opposed to the Russian-Ukrainian conflict, attributability is far less complicated due to the lack of any actual skirmish on Taiwan's soil, however, Taiwan poses a risk in terms of subrogation.

Any entity claiming the status of a state must possess the attributes of statehood, including the exercise of sovereignty over territory, authority over its nationals and the capacity to make international law with other states. Needless to say, the latter criterion calls for 'recognition by other states'.[255] Taiwan has not received recognition from the majority of the international community. On the other hand, article 3 of the Montevideo Convention provides that "*The political existence of the State is independent of recognition by the other states*". But PRI-wise such an article is of no use on the grounds that prior to concluding the insurance contract, a public insurer or mandated private insurer may seek a respondent or interlocutor within the meaning of diplomacy. Furthermore, as we shall discuss in the subsequent chapters, BITs may contain clauses that recognize the subrogation rights of the insurer, hence, insurers are prone to provide coverage against the risks of the country that has concluded a BIT with the home state. In the absence of the BIT, the PRI provider must obtain a commitment to a similar effect from the host state. In a different way of saying, the recognition of a host state, for the sake of subrogation (to claim and liquidate the subrogated rights), by the international community, is of vital importance.

5.3.2.3.3 Afghanistan

Distinctive care should be given to insurrectional or other movements and an up-to-date example is the political shift in Afghanistan where myriad de facto governments existed in some rural districts.[256] The Taliban acted semi-autonomously, quasi-sub national in furtherance of its insurgent[257] mode,[258] and has taken over the capital city.[259] ILC article 10 would offer fertile ground for the application of the principles of attribution[260] for the conducts of the Taliban. Recognizing an insurrectional

[254] Please visit: https://www.wsj.com/articles/ukraine-war-drives-interest-in-china-taiwan-risk-insurance-11652108581 and https://www.ft.com/content/bfa317e0-743b-4994-a4f5-7c0b25ed9cec both accessed 02.09.2024.

[255] Fox and Webb (2013), pp. 339–341.

[256] See Wani (2021), pp. 220–237.

[257] One may argue that insurgency, a semblance of a para-state is not a state. However, it is of great importance to demarcate the line for responsibilitisation of the sovereign. See Maloney (2010), p. 405.

[258] Terpstra (2020), p. 1157.

[259] Please visit: https://www.washingtonpost.com/world/2021/08/15/afghanistan-taliban-islamic-emirate/ accessed 02.09.2024.

[260] Art. 10 of the ILC articles reads as follows: "*1. The conduct of an insurrectional movement which becomes the new Government of a State shall be considered an act of that State under international law. 2. The conduct of a movement, insurrectional or other, which succeeds in establishing a new State in part of the territory of a pre-existing State or in a territory under its*

movement as the new sovereign or attributing liability to its actions can find its foundations in several theories, namely, the continuity of states, the legitimacy of the struggle, the resurrection of the state, and organic structural continuity. The continuity of the state basically suggests that the new state must be held responsible for the acts of rebellion prior to its acquisition of power. The second theory, as implied by its name, relies on rhetoric, asserting that the struggle of the rebels represents the true national will, eventually legitimizing their rule over the country. The third theory implies that the new state, in fact, was an ancient one that had ceased to exist but came into being through a liberation movement. The fourth theory does not distinguish the identity of the group succeeding in forming a new state and is based on the presumption that rebels and the new state share the same identity, preventing a break in continuity.[261] Although the grounds on which these theories rest may not be as solid as expected, it is necessary to acknowledge that the continuity of the state, regardless of the identity of the rebels or the methods employed to acquire power, holds significance.

On 11.02.2022, the U.S. Treasury announced an executive order allowing Federal Reserve Bank of New York to transfer USD of 3.5 billion to a special account "*for the benefit of the people of Afghanistan, including to an international financing mechanism (in which the United States is a member) holding and disbursing funds for the benefit of the people of Afghanistan, or to a United Nations fund, programme, specialized agency, or other entity or body for the benefit of the people of Afghanistan*"[262] This order raised the question of whether Taliban is recognized by the U.S.[263] As the targeted incentive of this order is humanitarian aid, even while the Taliban regime appears to be in effective control of the country, the international community is most likely to engage in diplomatic relations in the absence of formal recognition for the coming months or years.[264] Despite reluctance of or inconsistency among international community in recognizing Taliban as the official government.[265] Considering the definitions/role ascribed to an army in international agreements[266] and the Taliban's control over Afghan territory (the fact that the

administration shall be considered an act of the new State under international law. 3. This article is without prejudice to the attribution to a State of any conduct, however related to that of the movement concerned, which is to be considered an act of that State by virtue of articles 4 to 9."

261 For a detailed analysis of and the critiques on these theories, see Dumberry (2006), pp. 605–621.

262 Please visit: https://home.treasury.gov/system/files/126/afghanistan_bank_eo.pdf accessed 02.09.2024.

263 Wuerth (2022).

264 Also, see Anderson (2021).

265 Please visit: https://crsreports.congress.gov/product/pdf/R/R46879 accessed 02.09.2024.

266 Art. 43(1) of Protocol Additional to the Geneva Conventions of 12 August 1949, and relating to the Protection of Victims of International Armed Conflicts (Protocol I) 8 June 1977 reads as: The armed forces of a Party to a conflict consist of all organized armed forces, groups and units which are under a command responsible to that Party for the conduct of its subordinates, even if that Party is represented by a government or an authority not recognized by an adverse Party. Such armed forces shall be subject to an internal disciplinary system which, 'inter alia', shall enforce compliance

capital city was handed over), the Taliban's legal status appears to be that of any sovereign power.

Cases

Abaclat v. Argentina: Abaclat and others v. The Argentine republic (ICSID Case No. ARB/07/5), Decision on jurisdiction and admissibility

Almås: Mr Kristian Almås and Mr Geir Almås v. The Republic of Poland, (PCA Cas, 27 June 2016), Award

Al Tamimi: Adel a hamad i Al Tamimi v. Sultanate of Oman, (ICSID Case No. ARB/11/33), Award

Ampal v. Egypt: Ampal-American Israel Corporation and others v. Arab Republic of Egypt, (ICSID Case No. ARB/12/11), Decision on Liability and Heads of Loss, 21 February 2017)

ATA v. Jordan: ATA Construction, Industrial and Trading Company v. The Hashemite Kingdom of Jordan, (ICSID Case No. ARB/08/2), Award

Barcelona Traction: Barcelona Traction, Light and Power Company, Limited (Belgium v. Spain) (1970) ICJ Rep 3; (1970)

Bridas: Bridas S.A.P.I.C. v. Government of Turkmenistan, 345 F.3d 347 (5th Cir. 2003),Court of Appeals for the Fifth Circuit

BTS Holding, A.S. v. Slovakia: ECHR, (Application no. 55617/17), JUDGMENT (Merits)

Burlington Resources:Burlington Resources Inc. v. Republic of Ecuador, (ICSID Case No. ARB/08/5), Decision on Liability

Champion Trading v. Egypt: Champion Trading Company, Ameritrade International, Inc. v. Arab Republic of Egypt, (formerly Champion Trading Company, Ameritrade International, Inc., James T. Wahba, John B. Wahba, Timothy T. Wahba v. Arab Republic of Egypt), ICSID Case No. ARB/02/9, Decision on Jurisdiction

Clayton: William Ralph Clayton, William Richard Clayton, Douglas Clayton, Daniel Clayton and Bilcon Delaware Inc. v. Government of Canada, (PCA Case No. 2009-04), Award on Jurisdiction and Liability

CSOB v. Slovak Republic: Ceskoslovenska Obchodni Banka, A.S. v. The Slovak Republic, (ICSID Case No. ARB/97/4), Decision of the Tribunal on Objections to Jurisdiction

Dan Cake: Dan Cake (Portugal) S.A. v. Hungary, (ICSID Case No. ARB/12/9), Decision on Jurisdiction and Liability

with the rules of international law applicable in armed conflict. Please visit: https://ihl-databases.icrc.org/applic/ihl/ihl.nsf/Article.xsp?action=openDocument&documentId=AF64638EB5530E58C12563CD0051DB93 accessed 02.09.2024.

Deutsche Bank: Deutsche Bank AG v. Democratic Socialist Republic of Sri Lanka, (ICSID Case No. ARB/09/2) Award

EDF Limited v. Romania: EDF (Services) Limited v. Romania, (ICSID Case No. ARB/05/13), Award

EnCana v. Ecuador: EnCana Corporation v. Republic of Ecuador, (UNCITRAL Rules), Award

ENRON v. Argentina: Enron Corporation Ponderosa Assets, L.P v. The Argentine Republic, (ICSID Case No. ARB/01/3), Award

Fakes v. TURKEY: Mr. Saba Fakes v. The Republic of Turkey, (ICSID Case No. ARB/07/20), Award

Fedax v. Venezuela: Fedax n. v. The Republic of Venezuela, (ICSID Case No. ARB/96/3), Award

Flemingo DutyFree: Flemingo DutyFree Shop Private Limited v. The Republic of Poland, (UNCITRAL Arbitration, PCA), Award

Frontier v. Czech Republic: Frontier Petroleum Services v. The Czech Republic, (UNCITRAL Rules, PCA), Final Award

Gami v. Mexico: Gami Investments Inc. v. The government of the United Mexican States, (UNCITRAL Arbitration), Final Award

GEA v. Ukraine: Group Aktiengesellschaft v. Ukraine, (ICSID Case No. ARB/08/16), Award

Generation Ukraine: Generation Ukraine Inc. v. Ukraine, (ICSID Case No. ARB/00/9), Award

Genin: Alex Genin, Eastern Credit Limited, INC. and A.S. Baltoil v. Republic of Estonia, (ICSID Case No. ARB/99/2), Award

Glamis Gold Ltd.:Glamis Gold, Ltd. v. United States of America, (ICSID case), Award

Gustav: Gustav F W Hamester GmbH & Co KG v. Republic of Ghana, (ICSID Case No. ARB/07/24, Award

Jan de Nul: Jan de Nul N.V. Dredging International N.V. v. Arab Republic of Egypt, (ICSID Case No. ARB/04/13), Award

Joseph Companies: Joseph Companies Incorporated of Minneapolis (Jamaica: 1999) 1999 OPIC Contract Type 234 KGT 12-85 (Second Revision) NS equity OPIC Contract of Insurance No E197, OPIC Claim Determination

Kardassopoulos v. Georgia: Ioannis Kardassopoulos v. The Republic of Georgia, (ICSID Case Nos. ARB/05/18 and ARB/07/15), Award

Maffezini v. Spain: Emilio Agustín Maffezini v. The Kingdom of Spain, (ICSID Case No. ARB/97/7), Decision of the tribunal on objections to jurisdiction

Mihaly: Mihaly International Corporation v. Democratic Socialist Republic of Sri Lanka, ICSID Case No. ARB/00/2

Noble Ventures: Noble Ventures Inc. v. Romania, (ICSID Case No. ARB/01/11), Award

Nykomb Synergetics: Nykomb Synergetics Technology Holding AB (Nykomb) v. The Republic of Latvia, SCC, Award.

OAO Tatneft: OAO Tatneft v. Ukraine, (UNCITRAL Arbitration), Award on the Merits

Paushok: Sergei Paushok, CJSC Golden East Company and CJSC Vostokneftegaz Company v. The Government of Mongolia, (UNCITRAL Arbitration), Award on Jurisdiction and Liability

Plama v. Bulgaria: Plama Consortium Limited v. Republic of Bulgaria, (ICSID Case No. ARB/03/24), Award

PSEG v. Turkey: PSEG Global Inc., the North American Coal Corporation, and Konya Ilgin Electrik Uretim ve Ticaret Limited Sirketi v. The Republic of Turkey, (ICSID Case No. ARB/02/5), Award

Railroad Development Corp.: Railroad Development Corporation v. Republic of Guatemala, (ICSID Case No. Arb/07/023), Award

Rumeli Telekom: Rumeli Telekom A.S. and Telsim Mobil Telekomunikasyon Hizmetleri A.S. v. Republic of Kazakhstan, (ICSID Case No. ARB/05/16), Award and Decision of the Ad Hoc Committee on Annulment Proceedings

Saint-Gobain v. Venezuela: Saint-Gobain Performance Plastics Europe v. Bolivarian Republic of Venezuela, ICSID Case No. ARB/12/13, Decision on Liability and the Principles of Quantum

Saipem v. Bangladesh: Saipem S p.A. v. The People's Republic of Bangladesh, (ICSID Case No.ARB/05/07), Decision on jurisdiction and recommendation on provisional measures

Salini *v. Morocco:* Salini costruttori s.p.a. and Italstrade s.p.a. v. Kingdom of Morocco, (ICSID Case No. ARB/OO/4), Decision on jurisdiction

SGS v. Pakistan: Société Générale de Surveillance (SGS) vs. Pakistan, (ICSID Case No. ARB/01/13), Decision of the tribunal on objections to jurisdiction

SGS v. Philippines: Société Générale de Surveillance (SGS) v. Philippines, (ICSID Case No. ARB/02/6) Decision of the Tribunal on Objections to Jurisdiction

Southern v. Egypt: Southern Pacific Properties (middle east) Limited v. Arab Republic of Egypt, (ICSID Case No. ARB/84/3), Award on the Merits

Stran Greek Refineries: Stran Greek Refineries and Stratis Andreadis v. Greece, ECHR Case No 13427/87, Judgment of 9 December 1994

Toprak Mahsulleri Ofisi: Toprak Mahsulleri Ofisi v. Finagrain Compagnie Commerciale Agricole et Financière S.A.

Toto Costruzioni: Toto Costruzioni Generali S.p.A. v. The Republic of Lebanon, (ICSID Case No. ARB/07/12), Decision on Jurisdiction

Tulip v. Turkey: Tulip Real Estate Investment and Development Netherlands B.V. v. Republic of Turkey, (ICSID Case No. ARB/11/28), Award

UAB E Energija v. Latvia: UAB E Energija v. Latvia, (ICSID Case No. ARB/12/33), Award

Uzan v. Turkey: Cem Cengiz Uzan v. The Republic of Turkey, SCC, Award On Respondent's Bifurcated Preliminary Objection, 2014/023

Vivendi v. Argentina II: Compañía de Aguas del Aconquija, S.A. & Compagnie Générale des Eaux, Claimants v. Argentine Republic, (ICSID Case No. ARB/97/3), Award

White Industries v. India: White Industries Australia Limited v. The Republic of India, UNCITRAL Arbitration, Final award

WNC Factoring: WNC Factoring Limited v. The Czech Republic, (PCA Case No. 2014-34), Award

Online Database

https://www.adb.org
https://www.amanunion.net/
https://www.ati-aca.org
https://www.bbc.com
https://www.berneunion.org
https://www.blockchain-council.org
https://www.congress.gov
https://www.courtlistener.com
https://www.crsreports.congress.gov
https://www.databank.worldbank.org
https://www.dfc.gov
https://www.dhaman.org
https://www.dictionary.cambridge.org
https://www.eximbank.gov.tr
https://www.forbes.com/sites
https://www.foreign.senate.gov
https://www.ft.com
https://www.govinfo.gov
https://www.home.treasury.gov
https://www.hudoc.echr.coe.int
https://www.iadb.org
https://www.iciec.isdb.org
https://www.icj-cij.org
https://www.ieg.worldbankgroup.org
https://ihl-databases.icrc.org/en/
https://www.imf.org
https://www.independent.co.uk
http://www.investasean.asean.org
https://www.investmentpolicy.unctad.org
https://www.ips.ligazakon.net
https://www.italaw.com
https://www.jusmundi.com
https://www.lawfaremedia.org
https://www.legal.un.org
https://www.miga.org
https://www.oas.org
https://www.oecd.org
https://www.press.un.org
https://www.reuters.com
https://www.scholarship.law.columbia.edu
https://www.treaties.un.org
https://www.washingtonpost.com

https://www.wipo.int
https://www.wsj.com

References

Anderson SR (2021) History and the recognition of the Taliban. https://www.lawfaremedia.org

Anon (2004) Property rights institutions and investment. World Bank

Azarova V (2018) An illegal territorial regime? On the occupation and annexation of Crimea as a matter of international law. In: The use of force against Ukraine and international law. T.M.C. Asser Press, The Hague

Bachulska A, Leonard M (2023) China and Ukraine: the Chinese debate about Russia's war and its meaning for the world. Available at https://ecfr.eu/publication/china-and-ukraine-the-chinese-debate-about-russias-war-and-its-meaning-for-the-world/

Baker JC (1995) Global foreign investment insurance the case of MIGA with comparisons to OPIC and private insurance. Manag Financ 21(4):23–39

Baltag C (2012) Chapter 3: natural persons and legal entities as investors under the energy charter treaty. In: The energy charter treaty: the notion of investor, international arbitration law library, vol 25. Kluwer Law International

Berger KP (1988) The new multilateral investment guarantee agency globalizing the investment insurance approach towards development. Syracuse J Int Law Commerce 15(1):13

Blyschak Paul M (2016) State-owned enterprises in international investment. ICSID Rev 31(1): 5–11

Bottini G (2010) Part III Chapter 12: legality of investments under ICSID jurisprudence. In: Waibel M, Kaushal A et al (eds) The Backlash against investment arbitration. Kluwer Law International, pp 297–314

Butkevych O (2018) The operation of international treaties and contracts in the event of armed conflict: problems reopened by russian aggression against Ukraine. In: The use of force against Ukraine and international law. T.M.C. Asser Press, The Hague

Chaisse J, Bauer C (2019) Cybersecurity and the protection of digital assets -- assessing the role of international investment law and arbitration. Vanderbilt J Entertain Technol Law 21(3)

Chein A (2006) Practical look at virtual property. St John's Law Rev 80(3):1059–1090

Clasmeier M (2016) Arbitral awards as investments: treaty interpretation and the dynamics of international investment law, international arbitration law library, vol 39. Kluwer Law International

Comeaux PE, Kinsella N (1994) Reducing political risk in developing countries: bilateral investment treaties, stabilization clauses, and MIGA & (and) OPIC investment insurance. New York Law School J Int Comp Law 15(1):1–48

Costelloe D (2016) Treaty succession in annexed territory. Int Comp Law Quart 65(2):343–378

de Vattel E (1852) The law of nations, or principles of the law of nature applied to the conduct and affairs of nations and sovereigns. T. & J.W. Johnson, Pennsylvania

DeLeonardo JM (2005) Are public and private political risk insurance two of a kind? Suggestions for a new direction for government coverage. Virginia J Int Law 45(3):737

Diaconis JS (1989) Political risk insurance: OPIC's use of a 'fiduciary agent' to facilitate resolution of subrogation claims. Int Lawyer 23(1):271–279

Dickinson P (2023) Russia's invasion of Ukraine was never about NATO

Dolzer R, Schreuer C (2012) Principles of international investment law, 2nd edn. Oxford University Press, Oxford

Douglas Z (2014) International responsibility for domestic adjudication: denial of justice deconstructed. Int Comp Law Quart 63(4)

Dumberry P (2006) New state responsibility for internationally wrongful acts by an insurrectional movement. Eur J Int Law 17(3):605–621
Erlank W (2013) Acquisition of ownership inside virtual worlds. De Jure 46(3):770–782
Fairfield J (2005) 'Virtual Property' Boston University Law Review. Vol. 85, Indiana Legal Studies Research Paper No. 35: 1047–1102
Feldman M (2016) State-owned enterprises as claimants in international investment arbitration. ICSID Rev 31(1):24–35
Fox H, Webb P (2013) The law of state immunity, 3rd edn. Oxford University Press, Oxford
Frischknecht A, Poplinger A et al (2018) Chapter 18: special considerations with respect to recognition and enforcement of foreign arbitral awards and judgments against sovereigns. In: Frischknecht A et al (eds) Enforcement of foreign arbitral awards and judgments in New York. Kluwer Law International
Ginsburg R (2013) Political risk insurance and bilateral investment treaties: making the connection. J World Investment Trade 14(6)
Goldberg M, Schär F (2023) Metaverse governance: an empirical analysis of voting within decentralized autonomous organizations. J Bus Res. https://reader.elsevier.com
Gordon K (2008) Investment guarantees and political risk insurance: institutions, incentives and development. OECD, Investment Policy Perspectives, Paris
Gürses Ö (2016) Marine insurance law. Taylor and Francis
Hackl C (2021) Defining the Metaverse Today. Available at https://www.forbes.com/sites
Hansen KW (2004) PRI and the rise (and fall?) of private investment in public infrastructure. In: Moran HT (ed) International political risk management, vol 2. The Brave New World, World Bank Publications, Washington, pp 75–100
Harris P, Marinova I, Gricius G (2023) War in Ukraine in a polarised America. LSE Public Policy Rev 3(1):1–8. https://doi.org/10.31389/lseppr.89
Heard J, Laryea ET (2021) Export credit agencies, international investment law and the spectre of unsustainable developing countries' debts. Afr J Int Comp Law 29(4):612–643
Henin P et al (2019) Innovating international investment agreements: a proposed green investment protocol for climate change mitigation and adaptation. J Int Arbitr 36(1). Kluwer Law International BV, The Netherlands, pp 37–70
ICCA Reports No. 4: Report of the ICCA-Queen Mary Task Force on Third-Party Funding in International Arbitration, ICCA Reports Series, Vol. 4 (International Council for Commercial Arbitration; ICCA & Kluwer Law International 2018
Johnson L et al (2019) Alternatives to investor-state dispute settlement. Columbia Law School, Columbia Center on Sustainable Investment Staff Publications. Available at: https://scholarship.law.columbia.edu/sustainable_investment_staffpubs/153
Kantor M (2015) Indirect expropriation and political risk insurance for energy projects. J World Energy Law Bus 8(2)
Kantor M, Nolan MD, Sauvant KP (2011) Reports of overseas private investment corporation determinations, vol 1. Oxford University Press
Karagöz T (2018) The influence of investor-centered values in the operation of political risk insurance. J World Investment Trade 19(1):118–153
Kemp G, Lyubashenko I (2018) The conflict in Ukrainian Donbas: international, regional and comparative perspectives on the jus post bellum options. In: The use of force against Ukraine and international law. T.M.C. Asser Press, The Hague
Kerner A (2018) What can we really know about BITs and FDI. ICSID Rev 33(1):1–13
Khachaturian A (2006) Are we in good hands? The adequacy of American and multilateral political risk insurance programs in fostering international development. Conn Law Rev 38(5):1041
Korotkyi T, Hendel N (2018) The legal status of the Donetsk and Luhansk "peoples' republics". In: The use of force against Ukraine and international law. T.M.C. Asser Press, The Hague
Kovács C (2018) Attribution in international investment law. Kluwer Law International
Kunoy B (2005) Developments in indirect expropriation case law in ICSID transnational arbitration. J World Investment Trade 6(3):467–492

Lastowka G, Hunter D (2003) The Laws of the virtual worlds. Calif Law Rev 92(1). Available at https://papers.ssrn.com/sol3/papers.cfm?abstract_id=402860

Lau PL (2022) The murky waters of the metaverse: addressing some key legal concerns. Commun Law 27(2):77–83

Lawson FH, Rudden B (2002) The law of property. Oxford University Press, Oxford

Maloney SM (2010) Can we negotiate with the Taliban? Small Wars Insurg 21(2):404–408

Martin EM (1967) Multilateral investment insurance: the OECD proposal. Harv Int Law J 8(2): 280–338

McKendrick E (1995) Force majeure and frustration of contract, 2nd edn. Lloyd's of London, London

McLaughlin M (2019) Defining a state-owned enterprise in international investment agreements. ICSID Review 34(3):595–625

Merezhko O (2018) International legal aspects of Russia's war against Ukraine in eastern Ukraine. In: The use of force against Ukraine and international law. T.M.C. Asser Press, The Hague

Mistelis LA (2013) Award as an investment: the value of an arbitral award or the cost of non-enforcement. ICSID Rev 28(1):64–87

Muchlinski P et al (2008) The Oxford handbook of international investment law. Oxford University Press

Newcombe A (2005) The boundaries of regulatory expropriation in international law. ICSID Rev 20(1):1–57

Olmedo JG (2017) Claims by dual nationals under investment treaties: are investors entitled to sue their own states? Forthcoming. J Int Disp Settlement, pp 1–33. Available at SSRN: https://ssrn.com/abstract=3043229

Papaefstratiou Athina F (2023) Crimea as Russian territory for the purposes of the Russia-Ukraine-BIT: Consent v. international law? Kluwer Arbitration Blog. Available at https://arbitrationblog.kluwerarbitration.com

Papanastasiou TN (2021) The implications of political risk insurance in the governance of energy projects: the case of Japan's public insurance agencies. In: Titi C (ed) Public actors in international investment law, 1st edn. Springer International Publishing, Cham, pp 155–179

Peinhardt C, Allee T (2016) Political risk insurance as dispute resolution. J Int Disp Settlement 7(1): 205–224

Poulsen L (2010) The importance of BITs for foreign direct investment and political risk insurance: revisiting the evidence. In: Sauvant KP (ed) Yearbook on international investment law & policy. Oxford University Press, New York

Ramos A (2022) The Metaverse, NFTs and IP rights: to regulate or not to regulate? WIPO Magazine, Issue 2. Available at https://www.wipo.int/wipo_magazine/en/2022/02/

Randall LS, Fred AS (2006) Causation in insurance law. South Texas Law Rev 48(2):305–426

Ratner SR (2008) Regulatory takings in institutional context: beyond the fear of fragmented international law. Am J Int Law 102(3):475–528

Reisman WM, Crawford JR et al (eds) (2014) Foreign investment disputes: cases, materials and commentary, 2nd edn. Kluwer Law International

Roach L et al (2022) Additional chapter principles of insurance law. In: Commercial law. Oxford University Press

Rowat M (1992) Multilateral approaches to improving the investment climate of developing-countries - the cases of ICSID and MIGA. Harv Int Law J 33(1):103–144

Rubins N (2004) The notion of 'investment' in international investment arbitration. In: Horn N, Kröll SM (eds) Arbitrating foreign investment disputes: procedural and substantive legal aspects, studies in transnational economic law, vol 19. Kluwer Law International, pp 283–324

Rubins N, Kinsella NS (2005) International investment, political risk and dispute resolution "A practitioner's Guide". Oxford University Press

Sagild RÅ, Hsiung CW (2024) Chinese re-examinations of Russia? The strategic partnership in the wake of Russia's War Against Ukraine. J Contemp China, pp 1–16. https://doi.org/10.1080/10670564.2024.2358876

Salacuse JW (2013) The three laws of international investment: national, contractual, and international frameworks for foreign capital. Oxford University Press
Salacuse JW (2016) The law of investment treaties, 3rd edn. Oxford University Press, Oxford
Schill SW, Djanic V (2018) Wherefore art thou? Towards a public interest-based justification of international investment law. ICSID Rev 33(1):29–55
Shifrinson (2022) What Is the America's Interest in the Ukraine War, MIT Center for International Studies, please visit: https://cis.mit.edu/publications/analysis-opinion/2022/what-americas-interest-ukraine-war accessed 18.03.2025.
Shihata IFI (1987) Factors influencing the flow of foreign investment and the relevance of a multilateral investment guarantee scheme. Int Lawyer 21(3):671–694
Soopramanien RD (2017) Mind the GAP: tailoring the form and substance of political risk insurance in order to bridge the 'enforcement gap' in investment arbitration. Int Lawyer 50(3)
Spagnoletti B, O'Callaghan T (2011) Going undercover: the paradox of political risk insurance. Asia-Pac J Risk Insur 5(2):1064
Sprankling JG (2014) The international law of property, 1st edn. Oxford University Press, Oxford
St. John T (2018) The rise of investor-state arbitration: politics, law, and unintended consequences, 1st edn. Oxford University Press, Oxford
Stefano CD (2017) CASE COMMENT Adel a Hamadi Al Tamimi v Sultanate of Oman attributing to sovereigns the conduct of state-owned enterprises: towards circumvention of the accountability of states under international investment law. ICSID Rev 32(2):267–274
Stefano CD (2020) Attribution in international law and arbitration, 1st edn. Oxford University Press, Oxford
Stempel JW, Swisher PN, Knutsen ES (2012) Principles of insurance law ISBN: 978-1-5791-1650-7
Susler O, Wilson T (2018) Restoring balance in investor state dispute settlement: addressing treaty shopping and indirect expropriation claims and consistent approaches to decision-making. Chart Inst Arbitr J Arbitr Int J Arbitr Mediat Disp Manage 84(1):38–51
Tan C (2015) Risky business: political risk insurance and the law and governance of natural resources. Int J Law Context [Online] 11(2):174–194
Terpstra N (2020) Rebel governance, rebel legitimacy, and external intervention: assessing three phases of Taliban rule in Afghanistan. Small Wars Insurgen 31(6):1143–1173
The Black's Law Dictionary. 9th edn
Tsybulenko E, Kelichavyi B (2018) International legal dimensions of the Russian occupation of Crimea. In: The use of force against Ukraine and international law. T.M.C. Asser Press, The Hague
Waelde TW, Ndi G (1996) Stabilizing international investment commitments: international law versus contract interpretation. Tex Int Law J 31(2):215–268
Wagner D (2012) Managing country risk a practitioner's guide to effective cross-border risk analysis. CRC Press, Boca Raton
Wang L (2016) Special focus issue note non-discrimination treatment of state-owned enterprise investors in international investment agreements? ICSID Rev 31(1):45–57
Wani ZA (2021) Afghanistan's Neo-Taliban Puzzle. South Asia Res 41(2):220–237
Ward DA (1986) The management of international trade risks: the role of the Berne union. Geneva papers on risk and insurance. Iss Pract 11(4):246–248
Waters JJ (2015) A comparative analysis of public and private political risk insurance policies with strategic applications for risk mitigation. Duke J Comp Int Law 25(3):361
Williams S (1993) Political and other risk insurance: OPIC, MIGA, EXIMBANK and other providers. Pace Int Law Rev 5:59–113
Wuerth I (2022) Does foreign sovereign immunity apply to sanctions on central banks? Lawfareblog Online https://www.lawfaremedia.org

Chapter 6
Mitigating the Risk and the Loss

6.1 Risk Mitigation

The concept of risk aversion is the tendency of individuals to avoid taking risks. An individual with a low-risk tolerance tends to seek a modest investment return. To put it differently, the more risk-averse an individual is, the less likely that individual will invest in risky assets.[1] Inflation can be one of the core factors that can outpace and erode investment returns over time. Hence, individuals mostly favor investments that preserve the value of their original investment. By way of illustration, an individual will likely choose a return on capital that matches or slightly exceeds the level of inflation rate over the potential for growth that can double or triple the returns over time. As a consequence of asymmetric information, inexperience, or imperfect rationality, individuals or consumers may lack awareness in the matter of terms of the contract which they are party to and fail to appreciate certain risks. The likely outcome of this situation is a disparity between the performances of the parties[2] involved; the individual/consumer may not receive the equivalent of what was bargained for, and the opposing party reaps the benefit over the disparity between the performances. Therefore, the legal consequences attached to consumers' acts are undeniably different from those of investors. Lawmakers lay down specific rules, and consumers receive a higher degree of protection for economic interest in their contractual relation.[3]

Being a foreign investor, however, comes at a price. A foreign investor can be as risk averse as an individual; it can be predictable in decision-making and choose the option that will yield the probable expectation of utility. However, as a merchant, the

[1] See O'Donoghue and Somerville (2018), p. 106.

[2] *Lesion* is a concept known as such to civil law and is defined as "*a detriment to one of the parties to a contract which results from an imbalance or disparity between the performance promised on the two sides.*" See the Black's Law Dictionary.

[3] To illustrate, the ambiguities in insurance contracts are interpreted in consumer-insured's favor.

Ö. Tosun, *The Law of Political Risk Insurance*, AIDA Europe Research Series on Insurance Law and Regulation 12, https://doi.org/10.1007/978-3-031-74675-8_6

foreign investor is assumed to have anticipated, identified and assessed the perils associated with doing business in foreign countries. Hence, unless the foreign investor has opted for a risk-mitigation instrument that is most functional to itself, the foreign investor must be on guard, carry on business in a prudent manner and bear the outcomes of its 'conscious choice'.[4]

6.2 Investor's 'To Do' List

6.2.1 Risk-Mitigating Strategies

The robust appetite for investment into developing countries combined with salience of host states' nationalist and unstable behavior towards foreign investments urged the sustained need for tools to mitigate risks. Nevertheless, the willingness to obtain a risk mitigation mechanism must be greater than its price.[5] The foreign investor must pick an instrument that has the probability of achieving its goal at a level of cost that it can live with. Suppose the foreign investor has the PRI coverage, the price of the protection (PRI premium) may diminish the expected value of the investment made in a high-risk country. Besides, reasonably avoidable losses are not recoverable.[6] An investor can never fully know what risks the host state may pose to its investment. Therefore, it should give consideration to preparing a 'to do list' prior to investment.

As for the conclusion in risk-mitigating strategies domain, in order to implement a fruitful risk management, the foreign investor must first rank the risks properly[7] and then put the most sound strategy in place. Foreign investments have the potential for a large positive return; this profit-intensive nature of the investments makes them susceptible to risks. Hence, it is almost imperative for the investor to benefit from an array of options in the choice set of risk-mitigating strategies. Strategies can be classified upon a variety of parameters.

---

[4]The tribunal in *Starrett Housing v. Iran* held that "..... *investors in all other countries, have to assume a risk that the country might experience strikes, lock-outs, disturbances, changes of the economic and political system and even revolution. That any of these risks materialized does not necessarily mean that property rights affected by such events can be deemed to have been taken. A revolution as such does not entitle investors to compensation under international law.*" Interlocutory Award, para.73. Available at https://jusmundi.com/en/document/decision/en-starrett-housing-corporation-starrett-systems-inc-and-others-v-the-government-of-the-islamic-republic-of-iran-bank-markazi-iran-and-others-final-award-award-no-314-24-1-friday-14th-august-1987 accessed 03.09.2024.

[5]Also, see O'Donoghue and Somerville (2018), pp. 94,104.

[6]Clarke (2013), p. 80.

[7]Kerur and Marshall (2012), p. 10.

6.2.1.1 Strategies Associated with the Operation of Investment

Elaborate risk management strategies are now being implemented in international business, with a focus on methods for the operation of the investment featured prominently. In the context of PRI, risk management primarily rests with the party that expects to generate profit from its investment. Faced with political risks to a prospective investment, the investor may opt out of entering the host state's market. The major risk management strategy lies in the hands of the host state and local people.[8] In any given country, these local solutions serve to mitigate risks while also solidifying and advancing economic cooperation with the host state and its populace.

Emerging countries aim for vacuuming foreign capital, and in doing so, they make representations and commitments to foreign investors. Some of these commitments can be embodied in agreements such as concessions upon which investors will rely in making decision.[9] Because of its privileges accorded to foreign investors, they can operate in the local market in ways that the local entrepreneurs cannot. Moreover, the form of the investment or the techniques used in operations may have adverse effect on the local people. For instance, conducts harmful to the environment or displacing the local labor can lead to local resentment. Thus, these methods necessitate the establishment of partnerships either with the host state or with parties whose reactions the host state will be wary of.

6.2.1.1.1 The Correlation Between the Risk and the Investment

Political risks may manifest themselves at industry or firm-behavior level. Industry-sourced political risk may transpire itself in the form of sophisticated procedures or quota systems. In addition, the tenor of the investment or investment's crucial features that are of similar nature can increase the probability of events considered as political risks. International investments can be sophisticated, have a longer duration, and are not subject to the same kinds of political risks as trade contracts dealing with a single exchange of a commodity. For instance, the characteristics of mining projects require a long period of exploration, appraisal, and development. The risk the investor may face at the time of exploration will not be as great as it may incur when the facility is in place and the production is underway. The reason is that the investor contributes capital and technology that the host state needs[10] however, it takes long time to recoup such expenditures. The agreements concluded between the investor and the host state can be ill-suited to accommodate changes leading to an

[8] Scholars suggest that negotiating contracts with the state means "*pulling the state down from its sovereign pedestal, replete with powers of command, to a level of equality among business partners*". See Waelde and Ndi (1996), p. 234.

[9] Incentives carry risks and may not render all the outcomes that the host state sought. If the host state lacks information as to the investor's capabilities, intentions, and goals, the incentive may cost more than the benefit it may produce. Also see Salacuse (2013), p. 102.

[10] Van de Putte et al. (2012), pp. 285,286.

increase in political pressure in the long run.[11] To put the matter in another way, the continuing relation between the investor and the host state subjects the investment to the sovereignty of the host state, thus, the longer the duration of the agreement requires years to generate profit, the riskier it places the investment, as it will be more vulnerable to the government's unjustified interference.[12]

Some sectors are vital for preserving a country's sovereignty, economic independence and national security. The dominance of foreign investors in specific or critical sectors may place host states in a position of permanent dependence on the foreign investor and therefore compel the government to replace the investor in question with local entrepreneurs. Scarce or non-renewable sources, along with geopolitical tensions, may trigger resource nationalism. While the laws of some developing countries vest exclusive exploration, extraction, and selling rights in the state, others may adopt a more liberal approach. In the case of the latter, the resources of the host state must be employed in such a way as to prevent their depletion. Perceptions within a host country, held by the population, that the investor exploits the resources of the host country or that the economy is dependent on outsiders are often at the core of local opposition to a foreign investment. Besides, if the quality and quantity of the raw material are higher than projected, or if the prices or income shoot beyond the levels contemplated, the host state may change its open-minded policy and wish to benefit from the income that has been generated from the investment to a much greater extent than the actual operation of the contract's fiscal regime allows.[13]

In *Tan's view,* in the fragile legal and political systems, investments extracting natural resources are susceptible to violence over territorial rights and states may wish to rebalance the revenue rights and access to domestic recourses.[14] In the mining sector, investments are typically permanent and cannot be deployed to other jurisdictions. Investors and host states often sign long-term concession agreements that are ill-suited to accommodate significant operational or economic changes, resulting in a higher risk of politically motivated renegotiation pressures.[15] For instance, despite the rich material deposits in Africa, the tendency has been to concentrate on deposits in 'safe' industrialized countries.[16]

6.2.1.1.2 Cooperation with the Host State and Its Nationals

Cooperative risk management is premised on the idea that both parties stand to gain benefits. While cooperation offers the host state an occasion to reduce the perception of political risk, the foreign investor will distance itself from the risk occurrence. As

[11] Also see Burnett and Bret (2017), pp. 30–31.

[12] Also see Salacuse (2013), p. 23.

[13] Waelde and Ndi (1996), p. 225.

[14] Tan (2015), p. 176.

[15] See Burnett and Bret (2017), pp. 30–31 also, see Papanastasiou (2021), pp. 157–160.

[16] Shihata (1987), p. 687.

a result, both sides of these collaborations may wish to show their potential in coming to terms with political risks.[17] The foreign investor may conduct operations with the host state or with third parties that the host state is familiar with. The reactions of these parties can serve as an effective deterrent to the host state. In the first scenario, the investor may establish a joint venture or public-private partnership in which the host state either holds the majority of the shares or owns the privileged/golden shares. Participation of the host state in the venture may prevent the foreign investors from gaining control of the enterprise, at the same time ensure that the enterprise will operate in conformity with the national interest and thus, act as a deterrent against political risks.[18] The foreign investor also has the opportunity to establish its investment on a multinational basis. While acting towards such an investment, host states will likely avoid having diplomatic problems with numerous countries whose nationals are participants in the investment in question.

The 'keep your enemy closer' is an indirect/informal risk-mitigation technique that can yield a low-or-no-cost solution for the investor. The current political risk approach minimizes the much greater potential for collaboration between both sides in coming to terms with a present risk that is mostly beyond the control of either party. In the latter strategy, the foreign investor may collaborate with a local subsidiary or a key political figure.[19] If it is in the interest of the nationals, this form of cooperation can be initiated at the insistence of either them or the investor. In so doing, the investor will be able to both reduce its jurisdictional risk and tap into its partners' local expertise and market knowledge.[20] An investor who has engaged in unethical conduct or exploited the local labor force will experience zero tolerance. The investor may foster domestic benefits associated with the investment;[21] it will have anchored in the safe harbor if it structures its business in a manner that the local population has a stake in the project's success. In this circumstance, the host state must be as meticulous as possible if it wishes to avoid a united front composed of the investor and nationals opposing intervention in the investment.

The last strategy is of a political nature; a host state prone to political risk must keep its eyes wide open and avoid interfering with the projects that are financed by ECAs of other countries or by syndication of lenders in which multinational banks such as the World Bank participate. The occurrence of a political risk will impede the host state's own borrowings, and the rebound in host state's credit ratings will be cumbersome. Some authors suggest that structuring the investment, where possible, in the form of project finance, might minimize the risk. The authors highlight that the

---

[17] Waelde and Ndi (1996), p. 237.

[18] Also see Salacuse (2013), p. 97.

[19] Also see MIGA (2009) World Investment and Political Risk, p. 34. Available at https://openknowledge.worldbank.org/bitstream/handle/10986/2688/520190PUB0flag10Box345548B01PUBLIC1.pdf?sequence=1&isAllowed=y accessed 03.09.2024. Commercial-wise, If the local subsidiary acts as a subcontractor, the investor may transfer the risk only if it assumes high or full portion of it. Finally, see Kerur and Marshall (2012), p. 11.

[20] Kerur and Marshall (2012), p. 12.

[21] Waelde and Ndi (1996), p. 234.

non-recourse nature of SPV (special purpose vehicle incorporated by the sponsors/ shareholders of the project) financing avails debt structuring of the SPV without recourse to the project sponsors.[22] In such a case, the investor's interest in SPV must not be on par with its interest in the parent company, thereby, the investor will have fended of the risk as SPV incurs the risk instead of the parent company.

6.2.1.1.3 The Effects of Home State's Activities

The activities of the home state can be one of the factors increasing the probability of the risks-occurrence. According to scholars, a growing number of countries leverage their political influence for export promotion.[23] States grant export credits at rates below the market rate or cover the costs incurred by the exporters in obtaining credits.[24] The financial contribution extended by the home state might make its investor 'better off'. By way of illustration, the credit terms offered by the home state can be materially more favorable than the terms that would otherwise have been available in the marketplace. If the investor is equipped or backed with subsidies or low-cost loans, the host state's exporters/investors might not be on a level playing field. In response to such trade-distorting financial means, and in an effort to protect its traders, the host state may introduce measures that could give rise to political risks.

In *Brazil—Aircraft,* the panel and Appellate Body discussed whether Brazil's 'export financing program for aircraft (PROEX)[25]'conferred a material advantage in the field of export credit terms. The Appellate Body appeared to have identified the minimum interest rates (CIRR)[26] as a 'market benchmark'. In the view of the Panel, material advantage could not be determined on the basis of the applicable interest rate alone, irrespective of other export credit terms. The Panel further concluded that operating the program did not constitute a prohibited export subsidy.[27] The appellate body, in its article 21.5 report on Brazil—Aircraft stated that to establish that

[22] See Van de Putte et al. (2012), p. 290.

[23] See Jennekens and Klasen (2022).

[24] Illustrative list of export subsidies can be found in ANNEX I of WTO's AGREEMENT ON SUBSIDIES AND COUNTERVAILING MEASURES. According to the WTO, these subsidies are prohibited "*in so far as they are used to secure a material advantage in the field of export credit terms*" Please visit: https://www.wto.org/english/docs_e/legal_e/24-scm.pdf accessed 03.09.2024.

[25] Central Bank of Brazil (BCB) Resolution No. 2799 of 6 December 2000. Resolution 2799 is entitled: "Redefining the rules applicable to transactions under the interest rate equalization system of the Export Financing Program—PROEX" See https://docs.wto.org/dol2fe/Pages/SS/directdoc.aspx?filename=Q:/WT/DS/46RW2-01.pdf&Open=True accessed 03.09.2024.

[26] Commercial Interest Reference Rates (CIRRs) that are published monthly by the OECD corresponding to the currency and maturity of the operation. Please visit: https://www.oecd.org/en/topics/sub-issues/arrangement-and-sector-understandings.htmland https://www.wto.org/english/res_e/publications_e/ai17_e/subsidies_anni_jur.pdf both accessed 03.09.2024.

[27] See paras. Between 5.229–5.268 and paras. 6.1–6.3 in the Second Recourse by Canada to Article 21.5 of the DSU - Report of the Panel, available at https://docs.wto.org/dol2fe/Pages/FE_Search/

PROEX III payments are not used to secure a material advantage, Brazil needs only to prove that the net interest rates under the revised terms are at or above that benchmark. However, Brazil had not identified an appropriate 'market benchmark' for a comparison with the export credit terms available under the measure at issue and the appellate body found that "the Panel's findings on these issues were moot, and, thus, of no legal effect".[28]

Lastly, certain foreign investors might carry out political missions of their home country and, therefore, their commercial activities can be a threat to the host country's national security. The link is somewhat discernible when foreign investors appoint officials from the home country within the company. If the investor operates in industries or develops technologies strategic to the host state, concerns will arise among nationals as to whether their government waives critical resources or expertise into the hands of foreign investors.[29]

6.2.1.2 Financial Instruments, Due Diligence and Bilateral Treaties

6.2.1.2.1 Credit Default Swap, Hedging and Bill Discounting

According to MIGA, PRI is by no means the most widespread form of political risk mitigation.[30] Financial instruments may not be the most prevalent approach, but they are intrinsically effective tools and 'heavy hitters' that can offer rapid solutions for risk-mitigation. Three of the foremost instruments are credit default swaps, operational hedging[31] and factoring/forfeiting.

A credit default swap (CDS)[32] is a credit derivative in which the protection buyer and the protection seller exchange the risk that the sovereign will default. The concept functions in a way similar to insurance. The buyer pays regular premiums in return for a payoff when the sovereign defaults, and then hands over the possession of the underlined defaulted loan. Economic difficulties of every sort may give rise to an increase in insurance coverage cost; however, the low transaction costs and quicker payments can place the CDS in a position to expand its reach.

FE_S_S006.aspx?Query=(@Symbol=%20wt/ds46/rw2*)&Language=ENGLISH&Context=FomerScriptedSearch&languageUIChanged=true# accessed 03.09.2024.

[28] Please visit: https://www.wto.org/english/tratop_e/dispu_e/cases_e/1pagesum_e/ds46sum_e.pdf accessed 03.09.2024.

[29] Authors reach this conclusion by making several interviews with the foreign investors. For details see Han et al. (2018), pp. 130–138.

[30] Similarly, MIGA (2011), World Investment and Political Risk. p. 47. Available at https://www.miga.org/sites/default/files/archive/Documents/WIPR11.pdf accessed 03.09.2024.

[31] See MIGA (2009), pp. 31, 34. similarly, MIGA (2011), p. 47.

[32] Credit Default Swap (CDS) is a contract where a "protection buyer" agrees to make periodic payments (the CDS "spread" or premium) over a predetermined number of years (the maturity or term of the CDS) to a "protection seller" in exchange for a payment from the protection seller in the event of default by a "reference entity." See Bomfim (2022), p. 1.

The foreign investor may implement currency hedging[33] to minimize exposure to fluctuations; nevertheless, this may erode the margin on the project.[34] Political risk can also be associated with de-using of the US dollar as a medium of exchange. It is taken for granted that the US dollar is the dominant international reserve asset[35]; thus, concerns are afoot that a third country's misbehavior in using dollar will provide a legitimate basis for the U.S. sanctions.[36] Put succinctly, states must adhere to the U.S. authorities' regarding the use of the US dollar.[37]

The shift towards a multi-polar world system could bring the question of whether sanctions can generate political risks to the fore. In our opinion, de-dollarization is correlated with the negative perception of governments' attempt to change the foreign currency composition. Moreover, sanctions have more to do with the U.S.'s attitude towards countries' policies regarding the reduction of the dependence on the dollar per se. Geopolitical tensions, economic sanctions, and the host state's intentional conduct towards the foreign investment all have an impact on political risk occurrence. High levels of foreign currency debt strongly imply economic vulnerability to sanctions.

Sanctions could be weaponized to disrupt the macroeconomic equilibrium of the host state and amplify the effect of political risks if the state has insufficient reserves of foreign currency to bail out banks with dollar shortfalls. Given that sanctions could trigger a liquidity crisis and thus a local currency meltdown[38] the host state can pursue de-dollarization in its economy in an attempt to shield the banking system. Toward this end, the host state could impose stifling transfer restrictions to prevent the foreign currency outflow, peg the denomination of the domestic currency, and diversify the composition of foreign exchange reserves in order for lessening its exposure to risks associated with holding official reserves in dollar.[39] On the other hand, some scholars allege that even if the political environment remains stable,

---

[33] Hedging is a strategy that attempts to reduce the impact of adverse fluctuations in the price of one asset by taking an offsetting position in another (often notional) asset. See The Book of Jargon–European Capital Markets and Bank Finance, available at https://www.lw.com/ accessed 03.09.2024.

[34] Kerur and Marshall (2012), p. 11.

[35] The dollar's share of international reserves in 2023 was around %60. Please see the report of Congressional Research Service, available at https://crsreports.congress.gov/product/pdf/IF/IF11707#:~:text=The%20dollar%20has%20functioned%20as,in%20dollars%20(Figure%201). A recent IMF study shows the ongoing gradual decline in the dollar's share of allocated foreign reserves of central banks and governments. As of Q1 of 2024 this rate has been reduced to almost %55. For the chart by years, please visit: https://data.imf.org/?sk=e6a5f467-c14b-4aa8-9f6d-5a09ec4e62a4 both accessed 03.09.2024.

[36] According to the same scholars "*The US earns the 'exorbitant privilege' of having the global reserve currency by daring to impose penalties when justified by the behavior of the owners of reserves.*" See Dooley et al. (2022).

[37] For detail, please see McDowell (2021), pp. 637, 642, 646.

[38] See Honohan (2006), p. 21.

[39] For instance, after OFAC enacted sanctions, Turkey has increased its gold holding reserves. For the reasons of the dispute between Turkey and United States, see McDowell (2021), pp. 651–654.

capital can leave the country in reaction to an economic downturn.[40] In 2011 and 2002, Argentina converted domestic loans denominated in foreign currency into local currency at the post-devaluation exchange rate and froze bank deposits after converting them to pesos at the pre-devaluation parity. The economic breakdown resulted in political risk claims including breach of contract, transfer restriction and civil disturbance.[41] Finally, as will be discussed in detail in the chapter dealing with sovereign immunity, sanctions may take the form of expropriation.

The foreign investor may gain advantages from operational hedging which entails a degree of geographic diversification.[42] The idea of parking overall investment portfolio in a single country or single industry can be risky. Take, for example, nationalization, when it occurs, the sovereign takes ownership or control of a particular industry. Hence, spreading out the risk can reduce the investor's share in the risk. The investor may set up multiple plants across several countries and diversify its portfolio across several types of asset categories, in so doing; only the nationalized segment or portion of the portfolio would suffer a loss.[43]

In factoring, the supplier (exporter) sells its receivables to a financial institution and receives early funding based on the future payments approved by the financial institution, at a discount rate and on a without-recourse basis. Forfaiting, on the other hand, is the non-recourse purchase by a bank or a specialized financial institution (forfeiter) of receivables arising from the export of deferred goods and services, with payment collected according to a certain payment plan. Forms of bill discounting may not be the major tools in the overall toolbox of risk-management techniques. The reason is that the investments may not always be established and operated in a manner in which they generate a firm and transferrable amount of receivable/bill undertaken by the host state.

Although the last two financial instruments are commonly used in international sales, they are among 'excluded events' in the trade credit insurance policies. The reason is that the supplier/exporter relinquishes its right to receive payment from the buyer in advance, preventing the subrogation principle where the receivables are assigned to the insurer. We are of the opinion that these mechanisms can be adapted into PRI. The amounts that the host state undertakes to pay in return for the performance of the foreign investor which complies with the terms of the concession agreement can be transferred to third parties.

And Russia, to minimize the risk related to use of the US dollar, decided to shift its economy away from dollar and pitched China's currency "the yuan" as an alternative. See Ibid., p. 645.

[40] See Ramon-Ballester and Wezel (2007), p. 25.

[41] For detail, please see MIGA (2009), p. 50, also see Salacuse (2013), p. 142.

[42] Kim et al. (2005), p. 835.

[43] Also see Salacuse (2013), p. 147.

6.2.1.2.2 Due Diligence

Circumstances in the host state may not always lend themselves to foreign investments. Scholars believe that there are several factors influencing the investment climate. The first factor is the political stability of the host government (the host state's propensity to political risks) and its economic policies, along with its behavior towards foreign investors in terms of predictability and perseverance in the implementation of these policies.[44] The second parameter is the availability and efficiency of physical facilities and human resources. The final component is legal in nature, simply put, specific regulations concerning foreign direct investments can be introduced or investor-friendly municipal laws and international agreements (BITs or multilateral investment agreements) can be adopted.[45]

In addition, the track records of nationalist reactions, the existence of the rule of law can be identified as key paradigms that can trigger the factors capable of wreaking havoc upon the investment. If the history of the host state is replete with examples of political risk-related disputes, unlawfulness towards foreign investment might be imminent. Therefore, foreign investors might need to monitor certain parameters. Toward this end, the foreign investor must observe the financial reports

---

[44] *Newcombe* highlights the importance of the equilibrium between stability, security, predictability and fairness for the foreign investor with state regulation in the public interest. According to the author, stability and regulatory standstill are not synonyms and investors must not expect unchanging laws. See Newcombe (2005), p. 35.

[45] For detail, see Shihata (1987), pp. 679–685, similarly, see Rowat (1992), p. 104.

of professionals such as The Economist Intelligence Unit (The EIU),[46] the PRS Group,[47] Control Risks[48] or Business Environment Risk Intelligence (Beri).[49]

PFC Energy's Petroleum Risk Manager (PRM) rating weighs five factors, namely, Political Violence, Political Legitimacy, Government Volatility, Rule of Law, Political Competition and Rogue Factor. The rogue factor, among these, might be unfamiliar concept to readers; it denotes the assessment of a country's political behavior in the international system.[50] However, in *Yackee's* view, the rating of these companies suffers from a number of important limitations. The most crucial one is that they provide ratings at country level, not estimates of firm- or project-level risk. The author provides the following example; While the United States is a low-risk country, if the investment is a nuclear power generation facility in the United States, the risk of a permit being denied is high.[51]

---

[46] This unit was created in 1946 and provides a Country Risk Service that assesses risks to businesses posed by the political and economic situation in each country. The report encompasses 5 rating categories: sovereign, currency, banking, politics and economic structure. Along with the analysis, the report includes a two-year forecast of the political, economic, and external payment situations. Please visit: https://www.eiu.com/n/ accessed 03.09.2024.

[47] This institution drafts a Country Report (with 18-month and five-year risk ratings and forecasts, key macroeconomic forecasts, 10 years of historical data and extensive textual analysis of risk to business) Country Forecasts, a Political Risk Letter (includes 18-month and five-year forecasts for turmoil, investment, transfer, and export risk in countries and forecasts of real GDP growth, inflation and, current account), Political Risk Yearbook and Country Data. Please visit: https://epub.prsgroup.com/products/political-risk-yearbook accessed 03.09.2024. For instance, the PRS system has variables for scoring the political risk of a country. In this system 100 points are distributed according to the importance of the variables. A country is scored out of 12 points for each of the following components which are Government Stability, Socioeconomic Conditions, Investment Profile, Internal Conflict and External Conflict. The same country is scored out of 6 points for Corruption, Military in Politics, Religious Tensions, Law and Order, Ethnic Tensions and Democratic Accountability. Finally scored out of 4 points for Bureaucracy Quality. For Turkey's political risk evaluation between 2002–2019 see Arslan and Furtuna (2020).

[48] Please visit: https://www.controlrisks com/our-services/political-and-country-risk accessed 03.09.2024.

[49] Beri was founded in 1966, it publishes the Business Risk Service(analysis and forecasts for fifty countries three times per year and includes each country's Political Risk Index, Operations Risk Index, and Remittance & Repatriation Factor ratings together with the Composite Score and Political Information including the governmental system, changes in government, and the most probable political scenario) Forelend (provides perspective on the capacity and willingness of 50 countries to meet obligations in convertible currency during a five-year period) The Historical Ratings Research Package (HRRP) (data of 53 countries from 1980 to 2019) Financial Ethics Index (FEI) The Quality of Workforce Index (QWI) and finally The Mineral Extraction Risk Assessment (MERA). See https://beri.com/publications/ accessed 03.09.2024.

[50] See Van de Putte et al. (2012), p. 288.

[51] Yackee (2014), p. 484.

6.3 Loss Mitigation

Under conventional insurance, whether deriving from the contract or the law, the insured assumes a range of obligations. In order to prevent or mitigate loss,[52] and to protect the insurer's right to seek reimbursement, the investor must take all reasonable efforts and comply with the reasonable instructions of the insurer. The insurer must not be held liable for harm suffered by the insured to the extent that the harm could have been reduced by the insured taking reasonable steps. The insured must be recouped for the expenses it incurred on behalf of the insurer in accordance with those instructions. Where possible and if necessary, the insured must allow the insurer to examine the site where the risk took place and furnish the documentation as requested by the insurer.

In fact, the insured is obliged to disclose events material to the risk throughout the insurance contract. It should make full disclosure of the material facts that it knows or ought to know in the ordinary course of business. '*Material*' is a term with a subjective characteristic that may barely lend itself to a precise definition but can be defined as "*the facts to which a prudent underwriter would have acted otherwise in terms of acceptance of the risk, the premium charged, or the terms imposed if the insurer had been aware of it*".[53] Take a project or concession agreement that is not faring well, the insurer may be well aware of the host state's risk attitudes however, the scope of the agreement or the developments pertaining to the project are of significant importance. In the event of, or ideally prior to, material changes in the project agreement or implementation of the project, the insured must inform the insurer regarding those changes.[54] If the disclosed facts are later found to be untrue, incomplete or misleading[55] underwriters are within their rights to void the Policy and refuse a claim for compensation.[56] To the extent the insured is, whether partial or full, at fault in fulfilling its obligations, the insurer's loss increases. In simpler terms, the insured's failure can be likened to "a step on the insurer's shoulders causing him to drown". According to *Williams*, the insurance contract should require a provision by which the insured assumes the above-mentioned obligation.[57] One may need to note that, certain jurisdictions like Turkey, impose statutory obligations on insureds;

---

[52] In insurance practice, net book value of the investment in question on the date prior to expropriatory event is paid and claim payments are based on the lesser of fair market value or replacement cost. See Wagner (2012), p. 104.

[53] The concept of utmost good faith is related to duty of disclosure which according to *Merkin and Steele*, diminished in significance. On utmost good faith, please see Merkin and Steele (2013), pp. 52–54.

[54] See Kantor (2015), p. 196.

[55] Budd (1993), p. 30.

[56] For instance, under New York Law, misrepresentation or concealment of material facts are grounds to cancel the contract. See Williams (1993), p. 104.

[57] See Williams (1993), p. 102.

put it another way, irrespective from whether the insurance contract contains or not, the insured assumes obligations to mitigate the loss and disclose material facts.

PRI does not offer a free haven to foreign investors, nor does it serve to protect investments under all circumstances. The conditional nature of the insurance contract posits the investor as the vulnerable party. To put it another way, since indemnification is at the insurer's sole discretion, it must be satisfied that the insured has presented the necessary documents and fulfilled its obligations. Interpretation in favor of the insured is a basic principle and some jurisdictions identify foreign investments as 'jumbo (or large)' risk. In Turkish law however, the insurer of jumbo risks is not granted complete freedom to determine the terms of the insurance contract. Following the principle of interpretation in favor of the insured, which captures both commercial parties and consumers, merchant insureds receive the same level of protection as consumer insureds do.

In a typical contractual relationship, the obligor might be excused for lacking information concerning an impediment that accrues in the course of the contract. In PRI, the insured should be held responsible to the extent that it contributes to an increase in the loss. The insurer should not face alone the burden of loss that could have been diminished by the insured's efforts. For instance, the loss resulting from the investor's(insured) employees' actions will fall beyond the scope of the PRI if it could have been resolved by the investor. That is to say, the investor should bear the consequences of its intentional actions in its entirety. In the case of negligence, to the extent measurable, indemnity should be diminished in the same proportion of negligence.[58] However, a mere contribution to causation is, not sufficient; the action or omission must represent negligent and reproachable behavior.[59] Although it concerns the responsibility of the states, article 39 of the ILC Articles adopts a similar approach and attributes state liability based on its contributory negligence.[60]

Finally, according to some policies the insurer is not responsible for the loss if it is not notified by the insured within a certain period following the materialization of the risk. Such policies oblige the insured to immediately serve a notification upon the occurrence of the risk or when he/she becomes aware. At first glance, this principle seems to be '*cutting off one's nose to spite one's face*' and some might argue that

---

[58] In *Occidental v. Ecuador*, in the tribunal's belief, the claimants acted negligently. Hence, the tribunal concluded that "*the Claimants have contributed to the extent of 25% to the prejudice which they suffered when the Respondent issued the Caducidad Decree. The resulting apportionment of responsibility as between the Claimants and the Respondent, to wit 25% and 75%, is fair and reasonable in the circumstances of the present case.*" See para. 687, available at https://www.italaw.com/sites/default/files/case-documents/italaw1094.pdf accessed 03.09.2024.

[59] In *Copper v. Ecuador*, (para.676), the tribunal, by referring to *Delagoa Bay Railway Arbitration* held that "*All these circumstances that can be put forward against the concessionaire and to the credit of the Portuguese government lessen the responsibility of the latter and justify [...] a reduction in the damages to be granted]*". Available at https://www.italaw.com/sites/default/files/case-documents/italaw7443.pdf accessed 03.09.2024.

[60] The article is as follows "*In the determination of reparation, account shall be taken of the contribution to the injury by willful or negligent action or omission of the injured State or any person or entity in relation to whom reparation is sought.*"

rather than foreclosing avenues for the insurer, the insurer must first examine whether belated notification increased the amount of indemnity and if so, reduce the indemnity by taking into consideration of the degree of the insured's negligence. International agreements contain 'time bar' provisions, requiring investors to submit their claims within a specified time.[61] While the results linked to the omission or violation of basic duties might seem catastrophic, the conclusion of a PRI contract which deals with an exceptional situation must be interpreted as an implication of the insured's awareness. Therefore, the insured must come to terms with his/her wrongdoings.

Cases

Brazil – Aircraft: Brazil – Export Financing Programme for Aircraft (Canada v. Brazil WTO dispute)

Copper v. Ecuador: Copper Mesa Mining Corporation v. The Republic of Ecuador, (UNCITRAL Arbitration, PCA Case No. 2012-2), Award

Occidental v. Ecuador: Occidental Petroleum Corporation Occidental Exploration and Production Company v. The Republic of Ecuador, (ICSID Case No. ARB/06/11), AWARD

Starrett Housing v. Iran: Starrett Housing International, Inc v. The Government of the Islamic Republic of Iran, Bank Markazi, Others, (IUSCT Case no. 24), Final Award, Award No. 314-24-1 and See; Interlocutory Award No ITL 32-24-1

Online Database

https://www.beri.com
https://www.controlrisks.com
https://www.crsreports.congress.gov
https://www.eiu.com
https://www.jusmundi.com
https://www.imf.org/
https://www.italaw.com
https://www.lw.com/
https://www.oecd.org

[61] For instance, Article 1116(2) of the North American Free Trade Agreement provides the following "*An investor may not make a claim if more than three years have elapsed from the date on which the investor first acquired, or should have first acquired, knowledge of the alleged breach and knowledge that the investor has incurred loss or damage*." Text is available at https://jusmundi.com/en/document/treaty/en-north-american-free-trade-agreement-nafta-thursday-17th-december-1992 accessed 03.09.2024.

https://www.prsgroup.com
https://www3.tcmb.gov.tr
https://www.wto.org

References

Arslan K, Furtuna TK (2020) Political risk and Turkey 2002-2019. Int J Commerce Finance 6(2)

Bomfim AN (2022) Credit default swaps. Finance and economics discussion series 2022–023. Board of Governors of the Federal Reserve System, Washington

Budd N (1993) Making sense of political risk insurance policies. Int Financ Law Rev 12(6):29–32

Burnett HG, Bret L (2017) Arbitration of international mining disputes: law and practice. Oxford University Press

Clarke MA (2013) The law of liability insurance. Informa Law from Routledge, New York

Dooley MP et al (2022) US Sanctions Reinforce the Dollar's Dominance. Open economies review

Han X et al (2018) Chinese multinational enterprises in Europe and Africa: how do they perceive political risk? Manag Int Rev 58(1):121–146

Honohan P (2006) Dollarization and exchange rate fluctuations. Prepared for the Central Bank of Turkey 75th Anniversary Conference: Dollarization: Consequences and Policy Options. https://www3.tcmb.gov.tr/dollarization/sunumlar/Honohan1.pdf

Jennekens B, Klasen A (2022) How "safe" is the WTO "safe haven"? A need to modernise disciplines for officially supported export credits. J Int Trade Law Policy. https://doi.org/10.1108/JITLP-05-2022-0012

Kantor M (2015) Indirect expropriation and political risk insurance for energy projects. J World Energy Law Bus 8(2)

Kerur S, Marshall W (2012) Identifying and managing risk in international construction projects. International Review of Law

Kim YS, Mathur I, Nam J (2005) Is operational hedging a substitute for or a complement to financial hedging? J Corp Finance, Vol. 12. Pace University Finance Research Paper No. 2005/04 https://papers.ssrn.com/sol3/papers.cfm?abstract_id=799524

McDowell D (2021) Financial sanctions and political risk in the international currency system. Rev Int Polit Econ 28(3):635–661

Merkin RM, Steele J (2013) Insurance and the law of obligations, 1st edn. Oxford University Press, Oxford

MIGA (2009) World Investment and Political Risk. https://openknowledge.worldbank.org/bitstream/handle/10986/2688/520190PUB0flag10Box345548B01PUBLIC1.pdf?sequence=1&isAllowed=y

MIGA (2011) World Investment and Political Risk. https://www.miga.org/sites/default/files/archive/Documents/WIPR11.pdf

Newcombe A (2005) The boundaries of regulatory expropriation in international law. ICSID Rev 20(1):1–57

O'Donoghue T, Somerville J (2018) Modeling risk aversion in economics. J Econ Perspect 32(2):91–114

Papanastasiou TN (2021) The implications of political risk insurance in the governance of energy projects: the case of Japan's public insurance agencies. In: Titi C (ed) Public actors in international investment law, 1st edn. Springer International Publishing, Cham, pp 155–179

Ramon-Ballester F, Wezel T (2007) International financial linkages of Latin American Banks: the effects of political risk and deposit dollarization. ECB Working Paper No. 744 https://papers.ssrn.com/sol3/papers.cfm?abstract_id=975684

Rowat M (1992) Multilateral approaches to improving the investment climate of developing-countries - the cases of ICSID and MIGA. Harv Int Law J 33(1):103–144

Salacuse JW (2013) The three laws of international investment: national, contractual, and international frameworks for foreign capital. Oxford University Press

Shihata IFI (1987) Factors influencing the flow of foreign investment and the relevance of a multilateral investment guarantee scheme. Int Lawyer 21(3):671–694

Tan C (2015) Risky business: political risk insurance and the law and governance of natural resources. Int J Law Context 11(2):174–194

The Black's Law Dictionary

The Book of Jargon– European Capital Markets and Bank Finance. https://www.lw.com/

Van de Putte A, Gates DF, Holder AK (2012) Political risk insurance as an instrument to reduce oil and gas investment risk and manage investment returns. J World Energy Law Bus 5(4)

Waelde TW, Ndi G (1996) Stabilizing international investment commitments: international law versus contract interpretation. Tex Int Law J 31(2):215–268

Wagner D (2012) Managing country risk a practitioner's guide to effective cross-border risk analysis. CRC Press, Boca Raton

Williams S (1993) Political and other risk insurance: OPIC, MIGA, EXIMBANK and other providers. Pace Int Law Rev 5:59–113

Yackee JW (2014) Political risk and international investment law. Duke J Comp Int Law 24(3)

Chapter 7
International Standards to Protect Investors

7.1 In General

Host states aim to attract investors to devote their money or expertise to the country in question through laws, roadshows,[1] policies, specific and unambiguous representations[2] and statements directed at foreign investors, such as concession undertakings or any similar means of action.[3] In doing so, the host state induces an influence and legitimate expectations[4] in the minds of potential investors that investments can be profitable and enjoy the privileges and rights granted by the host state.

Expectations are a matter of degree; investors expect legal certainty and governments to act in a transparent manner.[5] Inconsistent legislation and amendments entailing interpretation are detrimental to foreign investors. According to some authors, "*investors should know beforehand the rules of the game and so that be protected against unfair surprise*".[6] As discussed earlier, due diligence is as much an exercise of care by the investor as it is a series of sessions where the host state makes representations. It may unearth such an 'unfair surprise', however, facts such as pandemic or global warming, whether to the benefit of investors or not, may force

---

[1] PAKISTAN signed most of its BITs as a part of road shows. See Poulsen (2010), p. 9.

[2] Newcombe and Paradell (2009), pp. 285–286.

[3] Statements, advertisements made at promotional 'road shows', or at negotiations may also create legitimate expectations in investors. Salacuse (2013), p. 100; Salacuse (2016), p. 413. Also see Newcombe and Paradell (2009), p. 279.

[4] According to *Tudor*, in indirect expropriation 'deprivation of property' is replaced by violation of the 'legitimate expectations' of the investor. Tudor (2008), p. 164.

[5] In, *Maffezini v. Spain, (para. 83),* transferring of a loan from the claimant's account to a public institution, without its consent was found by the tribunal "*the lack of transparency with which this loan transaction was conducted is incompatible with Spain's commitment to ensure the investor a fair and equitable treatment.*" Available at https://www.italaw.com/sites/default/files/case-documents/ita0481.pdf accessed 03.09 2024.

[6] Abba and Wälde (2008), p. 236.

Ö. Tosun, *The Law of Political Risk Insurance*, AIDA Europe Research Series on Insurance Law and Regulation 12, https://doi.org/10.1007/978-3-031-74675-8_7

governments to drastically change the 'rules of the game'. Hence, except for such facts, transparency expected from host states should be interpreted as *'a reasonable time given to investor to adapt its conduct of business prior to legislation enters into force[7]'*.

The legal framework existed prior to or at the time of the investment forms a strong basis for legitimate expectations. Alteration[8] or repudiation[9] of legislation may weigh in finding a political risk.[10] The degree of fairness and reasonableness of the investor's expectations rest upon the clarity of the state's representations, which also can assist in gauging any potential deviation.[11] However, in cases where the host state solely implies its intentions, the assessment of the political, socioeconomic, cultural, and historical conditions prevailing in the host state may be of immense importance. That being said, historical instabilities or financial breakdowns must not be grounds for host states to avoid incurring responsibility.

In the realm of investment, the host state may dishonor the promises given to investors and may shift from its previous stance. Such treatment lacking a legal basis would undermine the investor's business, and a frustrated investor may be compelled to abandon its expectations once the state itself has been instrumental in creating.[12] Internationally recognized standards, below which the investor should not fall, are intended to impose discipline on host states' actions[13] and assist in protecting investors, however, they may dilute their regulatory power and exhibit some degree of uncertainty in their nature.

Whether through introduction of specific municipal laws concerning foreign direct investments or through BITs, host states may adopt principles serving to protect foreign investments. However, one may need to note that such laws may regulate only the basics of these principles[14] and provide a few of the protections to be discussed in this chapter. *Salacuse* identifies six standards that provide protection

[7]For instance, certain legislation or administrative decisions come into effect after a period following their official announcement. Therefore, persons, whose businesses are governed and affected by the said legislation are provided time to adapt their businesses. Also, see Newcombe and Paradell (2009), pp. 291–292.

[8]See *Metalclad v. Mexico.*

[9]See *CMS v. Argentina, available at* https://www.italaw.com/sites/default/files/case-documents/ita0184.pdf accessed 03.09.2024.

[10]In *Biloune v. Ghana*, the investor began work before it applied for a building permit, which was in the eyes of investor "*a formality and would eventually be discharged and was not necessary prior to starting work.*" And according to the tribunal the investor was entitled to rely on the indications. See para. 78. Available at https://jusmundi.com/en/document/decision/en-biloune-and-marine-drive-complex-ltd-v-ghana-investments-centre-and-the-government-of-ghana-award-on-jurisdiction-and-liability-friday-27th-october-1989 accessed 03.09.2024.

[11]Dolzer and Schreuer (2012), p. 145.

[12]Salacuse (2016), p. 308.

[13]Salacuse (2013), p. 383.

[14]By way of illustration, the Foreign Direct Investment Law of Turkey, (Law no. 4875) deals only with equal treatment and national treatment. To see the unofficial translation of the Law, please visit: http://www.lawsturkey.com/law/foreign-direct-investment-law-4875 accessed 03.09.2024.

to investors.[15] In our opinion, the international minimum treatment and protection from unreasonable or discriminatory measures introduced by the scholar are subsumed within the meaning of the standards discussed below. Therefore, we find no need to further discuss these treatments.

International standards serve to shelter foreign investors at the time of dispute settlement. What lies behind discussing these standards is not to establish a comparison with PRI. By contrast, as one scholar well notes, "*in the country of the blind, the one-eyed man is king*";[16] hence, in the absence of PRI, international standards are investors' only-choice. Besides, in our opinion, insurers may benefit from these standards as the subrogee or require, to the extent possible, insureds to invoke all protections that should have been accorded to them under the relevant BIT.[17] The protection insurance contract provides may not operate on a last-resort basis; however, it must not also imply a 'set-and-forget' principle where insureds neglect to manage their duties with a reasonable degree of prudence and care. Finally, due to subrogation, if the PRI provider steps into the shoes of the insured and is entitled to all rights derived from the international law or from the contract concluded with the host state, the PRI provider will claim the host state's failure to accord the necessary treatment that the investor could have received.

7.2 Fair and Equal Treatment

Fair and equal treatment (in short 'FET') stands one of the most- frequently quoted[18] and sought-after standards[19] in international investment law. It serves as a form of protection accorded to aliens. Arbitrators, entitled to interpret the meaning given to

[15] Salacuse (2013), p. 384.

[16] Hartwell et al. (2005), p. 8.

[17] As discussed earlier, loss mitigation is of paramount importance to the insurer and is the foremost obligation of the insured. Virtually all insurance contracts explicitly impose this obligation on the insured.

[18] Sprankling (2014), p. 286.

[19] The tribunal in *Tecmed v. Mexico* came with the following definition "*The foreign investor expects the host State to act in a consistent manner, free from ambiguity and totally transparently in its relations with the foreign investor, so that it may know beforehand any and all rules and regulations that will govern its investments, as well as the goals of the relevant policies and administrative practices or directives, to be able to plan its investment and comply with such regulations. The foreign investor also expects the host State to act consistently, i.e., without arbitrarily revoking any preexisting decisions or permits issued by the State that were relied upon by the investor to assume its commitments as well as to plan and launch its commercial and business activities. The investor also expects the State to use the legal instruments that govern the actions of the investor or the investment in conformity with the function usually assigned to such instruments, and not to deprive the investor of its investment without the required compensation.* See *Tecmed v. Mexico* para. 154, available at https://www.italaw.com/sites/default/files/case-documents/ita0854.pdf accessed 03.09.2024. Also, in *Genin* case, minimum standard, in the

this standard in case of a dispute, must ensure that the alien concerned received what he/she rightfully deserved based on a reasonable assessment of the situation.[20] For a better understanding, assessment of whether the standard corresponds with the meaning attached to each adjective involved in the standard can be crucial.[21] The notion of '*fairness*' refers to reasonable treatment[22] and respecting the rights of the alien. On the other hand, under the principle of '*equitableness*', parties receive what they should legitimately possess.[23] The vagueness of these terms endows us with the necessary flexibility, while also allowing us to forge it further in the practice of investment disputes.

Host states must act towards the investor, fairly,[24] non-discriminatorily, reasonably, in good faith[25] and with transparency[26] while amending their regulations.[27] If the legal framework had induced foreign investors, the question of to what extent the

---

tribunal's view would include "*acts showing a willful neglect of duty, an insufficiency of action falling far below international standards, or even subjective bad faith.*" See para. 367.

[20] See Tudor (2008), pp. 123–126.

[21] Some scholars argue that the meaning of FET is of a generic kind that is capable of being changed over time; thus, interpreters may need to follow the evolution of contemporary standards in investment protection. Others oppose this view for several reasons. First, the conclusion of BITs may be for a short period and may lack the purpose to provide a contemporary level of protection; second, evolution of the FET through a bilateral treaty may not reflect a consensus. The third reason is the conceptual problem; the classification of FET as a generic term may distort the clear dichotomy between the starting point of the argument requiring contemporary meaning and conclusion of the argument providing it. For the debate among scholars, please see Paparinskis (2013), pp. 122–124.

[22] The ordinary meaning of 'treatment' within the context of investment includes the rights and privileges granted and the obligations and burdens imposed by a Contracting State on investments made by investors covered by the treaty. See *Suez v. Argentina (para. 55)* available at https://www.italaw.com/sites/default/files/case-documents/ita0807.pdf accessed 03.09.2024.

[23] Tudor (2008), pp. 126–128.

[24] Arbitral proceedings lift the vagueness given to the terms 'fair' and 'equitable'. The golden rule treaty interpretation is provided under art. 31 of the Vienna Convention on the Law of Treaties (1969) which states that "*A treaty shall be interpreted in good faith in accordance with the ordinary meaning to be given to the terms of the treaty in their context and in the light of its object and purpose.*" and tribunals while interpreting and applying these terms take the objective and purpose of the treaties. Convention is available at https://legal.un.org/ilc/texts/instruments/english/conventions/1_1_1969.pdf accessed 03.09.2024.

Also see Salacuse (2016), pp. 73. 303–304 and Weiler (2003), p. 234.

[25] Good faith means absence of deceit and artifice during the negotiation and execution of instruments that gave rise to the investment, as well as loyalty, truth and intent to maintain the equilibrium between the reciprocal performance of the parties, see *Inceysa v. El Salvador* (para. 231), available at https://www.italaw.com/sites/default/files/case-documents/ita0424_0.pdf accessed 03.09.2024.

[26] In defining the term, weight should be given to whether amendments are publicly available and, in some cases, whether amendments adopted in a short period without a debate with practitioners. Also see Salacuse (2016), pp. 448–452, similarly see Kriebaum et al. (2022), pp. 213–215.

[27] In doing so, host states are prevented from; biased decision-making, denial of justice, disregarding fundamental principles of due process of law, coercion and harassment of the investor. Also see Potočnik (2019), p. 157.

host state must avoid altering the regulations may remain unanswered. Although, the tribunal in *Electrabel v. Hungary* held that *the host State is entitled to maintain a reasonable degree of regulatory flexibility to respond to changing circumstances in the public interest,*[28] investors' legitimate expectations mature over time, so may the regulatory flexibility of the host state. However, a regulatory shift must not be seen as a complete swing towards granting unlimited regulatory flexibility to the host state.[29] The breadth definition of these concepts may beg the question of whether the FET standard must be regarded as a part of customary international minimum standard.[30] We can suffice it to say that a duality exists in doctrinal views. While some scholars support this statement, another approach considers that FET is a standard of an independent character.[31] The reason is that scholars in the latter group suggest that parties to a BIT must have explicitly linked FET and the international minimum standard if that was their intention.[32]

Fair treatment can also be the case if the treatment in question has adverse consequences on the part of another alien. For instance, the host state must avoid compensating the foreign investor if the investor, in its operations, has not been acting in good faith. The wide scope and the lighter standard of proving its violation make fair and equitable treatment[33] the most relied upon provision by claimants in

[28] See para. 7.77, available at https://www.italaw.com/sites/default/files/case-documents/italaw1071clean.pdf accessed 03.09.2024.

[29] Also, see Reed and Consedine (2015) pp. 292–293.

[30] The tribunal in *Glamis Gold Ltd.* opined that minimum standard of treatment is "*a floor below which the international community will not condone conduct*". See para. 619. In *Sharpe*'s view, the minimum standard treatment is not a singular obligation towards the foreign investor. The treatment may capture a range of several international standards including affording fair and equitable treatment, full protection and security, and providing prompt, adequate, and effective compensation for the expropriation of investments. See Sharpe (2015), p. 281.

[31] According to *Tudor*, an investor must be aware of the laws of the host state, and by entering to a foreign territory, the investor acknowledges the local levels of treatment. This implicit choice constitutes an invisible agreement between the investor and the host state. However, inadequacy of national treatment and local standards has urged the need to rely on international standards to protect aliens. In this regard, the author defines international minimum standard (IMS) as "*a norm of customary international law which governs the treatment of aliens by providing for a minimum set of principles which States, regardless of their domestic legislation and practices, must respect when dealing with foreign nationals and their property*". Tudor (2008), pp. 56, 60, 61.

[32] Also see Salacuse (2013), p. 386.

[33] In *MTD Equity v. Chile*, (para. 113) the tribunal defined FET as "*treatment in an even-handed and just manner, conducive to fostering the promotion of foreign investment. Its terms are framed as a pro-active statement – "to promote", "to create", "to stimulate"- rather than prescriptions for a passive behavior of the State or avoidance of prejudicial conduct to the investors.*" In *Metalclad v. Mexico*, (para. 89), in the tribunal's opinion, "*Metalclad was entitled to rely on the representations of federal officials and to believe that it was entitled to continue its construction of the landfill. Metalclad was merely acting prudently and in full expectation that the permit would be granted.*" Available at https://www.italaw.com/sites/default/files/case-documents/ita0510.pdf accessed 03.09.2024. Also see Dolzer and Schreuer (2012), p. 108.

investment disputes.[34] *Dumberry*'s relatively recent findings show that more than 95 percent of BITs contain an FET obligation for host states of investments.[35] Events giving rise to indirect expropriations may, in some cases, result in a lack of such treatment.

In the thoughts of some scholars, the norm of FET has a great deal of teeth in penalizing states for actions against foreign investors.[36] Other scholars hold the view that, PRI that could provide coverage against the host state's failure to afford 'fair and equal treatment' is not availed to investors.[37] The host state's objective conduct induces legitimate expectations on the part of the foreign investor. If the host state is to pursue its interests aligned with new circumstances, it must consider the interests of the foreign investor who has earlier adjusted his conduct to the previous course required by the host state. Reversing the investor's position in a frustrating manner with serious negative effects upon him must base on exceptional yet convincing reasons that must also necessitate the investor to re-adapt its business.[38] In support of the latter scholars' argument, it might be said that a PRI policy addressing the host state's dishonoring of its subjective, evolving, and therefore vague obligation, may not offer a satisfactory solution for the investor,[39] even if the causation and burden of proof mechanics have been well established in the policy.

7.3 Full Protection and Security

States are regarded as responsible for all harms that befall the investment.[40] In other words, along with acts purposefully directed at the foreign investment, states may prejudice investments through inactions or providing inadequate security means.[41] A

[34] Abba and Wälde (2008), p. 235.

[35] Dumberry (2017), p. 117.

[36] Ratner (2008), p. 480.

[37] Hyder and Attanasio (2021), p. 458.

[38] See Dolzer (2014), p. 21.

[39] The standard should be applied only if the same expectations should have been formed by another investor under similar circumstances.

[40] Salacuse and Sullivan (2005), p. 83.

[41] The conduct of armed forces is of great importance in political violence, since they are in charge and under obligation to protect investments against physical harms. In *Ampal v. Egypt*, the tribunal found the state responsible for failing to prevent the unrest that gave rise to the damage. And, in *AMCO* case (Award, 20 November 1984) partially annulled by Ad hoc Committee Decision on the Application for Annulment (16 May 1986), but the first tribunal's findings on the role of the army and the police were found to be res judicata in the Award of the second tribunal in the resubmitted proceedings (31 May 1990). The illegal acts of the army and police resulted in loss of the right to operate the investment(hotel) Available at https://www.italaw.com/sites/default/files/case-documents/italaw8885.pdf accessed 03.09.2024. Also, see Stefano (2020), pp. 34–36, for case law, see Ibid, 138, fn 156–157.

representative formulation of *full protection and security* standard (FPS)[42] can be found in the China - Turkey BIT(2015) which provides that; "*Full protection and security requires that Contracting Parties shall take reasonable and necessary police measures when performing the duty of guaranteeing investment protection and security.*[43]"

In practice, FET and FPS may be used one for another[44] and in some cases, FET is believed to absorb FPS[45] and treatment that is not fair and equitable automatically believed to imply a lack of full protection and security.[46] FPS places on the host state an obligation in regard to the physical protection of the investment;[47] however, this obligation cannot be construed as a warranty that property will never, in any circumstances, be occupied or disturbed.[48] The expected level of care of the host state should be the same as that which could be accorded for another investor under similar circumstances.[49] The investment may face physical harm when a political violence risk arises; therefore, FPS may beget an inquiry into the presence of political force majeure risk, and we will explore further this in the subsequent chapters.

[42] The OECD Convention states a "most constant protection and security".

[43] Available at https://investmentpolicy.unctad.org/international-investment-agreements/treaty-files/6085/download accessed 03.09.2024.

[44] Art. 2 of the BIT between UK and Turkey reads as: "Neither *contracting party shall, in any way, impair by unreasonable or discriminatory measures the management, maintenance, use, enjoyment or disposal of investments in its territory of nationals or companies of the other Contracting Party.*"

[45] Giuditta (2008), p. 133.

[46] See *Azurix v. Argentina,* available at https://www.italaw.com/cases/118 accessed 03.09.2024.

[47] Newcombe and Paradell (2009), pp. 309–310. Article 2(4) of the Hungary - Oman BIT provides the following: "For *greater certainty, "full protection and security" refers to the Contracting Party's obligations to provide the physical security of Investors and Investments.*"

[48] See *ELSI* case (para. 108), available at https://www.icj-cij.org/public/files/case-related/76/076-19890720-JUD-01-00-EN.pdf accessed 03.09.2024.

[49] The tribunal in *AMT v. Zaire* noted that "*The obligation incumbent upon the host State is an obligation of vigilance, in the sense that the host State as the receiving State of investments made by claimant, shall take all measures necessary to ensure the full enjoyment of protection and security of its investment and should not be permitted to invoke its own legislation to detract from any such obligation*" and tribunal further expressed that the treatment to be accorded to the foreign investor must not be any less than one recognized by the international law. See *AMT v. Zaire*, paras. 6.05–6.06. Available at https://www.italaw.com/sites/default/files/case-documents/ita0028.pdf accessed 03.09.2024.

7.4 National Treatment

The *national treatment* (NT) protects investors against discrimination based on nationality, allowing foreign investors benefiting from equal competitive opportunities.[50] Under *NT,* the host state is required not to treat foreign investors less favorably than its domestic investors in like circumstances.[51] Exceptional circumstances may arise where differences in treatment can be justified with legitimate rationales and policies that are neither motivated by a preference of domestic investments over foreign-owned ones nor they compose a disproportionate disadvantage.[52]

To measure the treatment accorded to foreign investor; a three-step test must be taken. First, an appropriate domestic comparator 'in like circumstances' must be identified.[53] If the allegedly favored entity is not in 'like circumstances[54]', the national treatment claim will fail.[55] The second limb of the test requires an investigation as to whether the treatment accorded to the foreign investor was less favorable than that given the domestic comparator.[56] At the last stage, it should be determined whether the different treatment might be justified by legitimate reasons.[57] The drawback of NT is that, irrespective of the treatment a state accords to its own nationals, the international minimum standard,[58] as the backbone of international

[50]Newcombe and Paradell (2009), pp. 150–151.

[51]Salacuse (2016), pp. 177, 334; Salacuse and Sullivan (2005), p. 85. Some BITs employ different wording such as 'like situation', 'similar situation' and 'same circumstance', see Newcombe and Paradell (2009), p. 160.

[52]Newcombe and Paradell (2009), p. 177.

[53]In case of no comparator, proving the discriminatory treatment will be difficult. *In Occidental* case, para. 176, although Petroecuador (the State-owned oil company) and Occidental were treated in a similar fashion, in the tribunal's perspective, interpretation had to be made in a broader sense and treatment accorded to the investor could be compared with exporters from other sectors. Thee tribunal explained this opinion in the following wordings "*no exporter ought to be put in a disadvantageous position as compared to other exporters.*" Available at https://www.italaw.com/sites/default/files/case-documents/ita0571.pdf accessed 07.09.2024. Also see Newcombe and Paradell (2009), pp. 160–167, 181.

[54]Host states may afford discriminatory treatment provided that they have valid reasons. In *Enron v. Argentina* the tribunal did not find a capricious, irrational or absurd differentiation in the treatment accorded to the Claimants compared to other entities or sectors. In the tribunal's conclusion, (para. 287) "*different solutions might have been sought, but it could not be said that any such sector has been singled out, in particular either to apply to it measures harsher than in respect of others, or conversely to provide a more beneficial remedy to one sector to the detriment of another.*"

[55]Bjorklund (2008), p. 31.

[56]Bjorklund (2008), p. 38.

[57]Reinisch (2015), pp. 395, 396.

[58]According to the correspondence between US Secretary of State Cordell Hull and Mexican Minister of Foreign Affairs Eduardo Hay, while Hay viewed that when an investor moves to another country, along with enjoying benefits, he/she should be assumed to have accepted exposing itself to certain risks. Hull, however, opposed Hay's position and made the famous statement

law, provides a higher level of protection to aliens. To avoid such end, nationals of the host state may be accorded with the same degree of treatment that the foreign investors receive.[59]

7.5 Most-Favored Nation

Most-favored nation (MFN) treatment is one of the common features of BITs, along with the other standards to protect investors. However, foreign investors cannot benefit from its advantages under custom.[60] While NT sets the minimum standards for foreign investors by taking the rights of national investors as a precedent, under *MFN*,[61] the minimum standards taken as precedents are those of the investor from a third country.[62] In a simpler language, for the purpose of applying MFN treatment, the comparator is a third-country investor entitled to more favorably protection. Both treatments may appear as stand-alone obligations; in most BITs, NT is combined with MFN obligations.[63]

It is uncontested that MFN clauses in BITs prohibit discrimination of foreign investors and the imposition of different transaction costs based on their nationality. These clauses enable equal competition and establish a level playing field for all foreign investors.[64] By its very nature and similar to NT, 'like circumstances' or 'like situations' are also considered as an inherent principle in ascertaining MFN treatment.[65] As the host state commits to treating an investor no less favorably than it treats an investor from any other country,[66] investors from less powerful country

---

concerning international minimum standard "*when aliens are admitted into a country the country is obligated to accord them that degree of protection of life and property consistent with the standards of justice recognized by the law of nations.*" Quoted from Salacuse (2013), pp. 309, 310.

[59] Tudor (2008), pp. 61, 127.

[60] It is a treaty-based obligation that is not considered as part of custom. See Dumberry (2017), p. 118.

[61] The Turkey–Pakistan BIT contained no provision specifically guaranteeing fair and equitable treatment for Turkish investors; nonetheless, Pakistan had concluded investment treaties with various European countries explicitly promising such treatment. In a dispute, a Turkish claimant argued, and the tribunal eventually agreed, that by virtue of the MFN clause in the Turkey–Pakistan BIT, Pakistan was obliged to treat the claimant in a fair and equitable manner. Salacuse and Sullivan (2005), p. 85, also see Salacuse (2016), pp. 177, 333, 342.

[62] For the illustration of the treatment, please see Dumberry (2017), pp. 118–119.

[63] Reinisch (2015), p. 390.

[64] Schill (2009), p. 123 and similarly see Caron and Shirlow (2015), p. 400.

[65] Ziegler (2008), p. 77.

[66] In *Maffezini v. Spain*, investor, relying on Argentina – Spain BIT, requested to benefit from the Chile – Argentina BIT, however, in the tribunal's view, application of MFN clause was not covering jurisdictional matters, therefore it rejected the investor's arguments. Similarly, in *Salini v. Jordan*, in *Plama v. Bulgaria* and *Telenor v. Hungary*, requests to borrow the dispute settlement clauses were rejected by the tribunals. See respectively, https://www.italaw.com/sites/default/files/

gain benefits and advantages that investors from more powerful country secured during treaty negotiations. In this way, the MFN clause operates similar to an insurance coverage against oversights and errors in treaty drafting and changing conditions.[67] On the other hand, the inclusion of MFN clauses in BITs may discomfort host states on several grounds. First and foremost, incorporation[68] of more favorable treatment granted by a third-party investment treaty may constrain the host state in bilateral bargaining. Furthermore, it may prevent the state from making preferential concession in return for a desired counter-concession.[69]

Some may question whether the investor could claim the benefit of FET treatment by invoking the MFN clause if the BIT concerned lacks an FET clause. The tribunal in *Bayindir v. Pakistan,* dealt with whether the claimant was entitled to rely on Pakistan's obligation to treat Turkish investors fairly and equitably, as stipulated in other BITs concluded by Pakistan. The tribunal adopted the position that Pakistan is bound to treat investments of Turkish nationals 'fairly and equitably.[70]' If states deliberately omitted an FET clause from their BIT, and did not draft the MFN clause accordingly, in *Dumberry*'s view, these states should have to live with the consequences of such a choice.[71] Tribunals may also be prone to permit recourse to the umbrella clauses of third-country treaties.[72] Tribunals' positions on importation of a

---

case-documents/ita0737.pdf and https://www.italaw.com/sites/default/files/case-documents/ita0858.pdf both accessed 03.09.2024 In *MTD Equity v. Chile*, tribunal agreed to incorporate the provisions of the Croatian and Danish treaties into the Treaty between Malaysia and Chile which contained more detailed treaty language on fair and equitable treatment. In the tribunal's view "including as part of the protections of the BIT those included in Art. 3(1) of the Denmark BIT and Art. 3(3) and (4) of the Croatia BIT is in consonance with this purpose." Also see Ziegler (2008), pp. 69–71.

[67] Newcombe and Paradell (2009), p. 195 and for cases see Ibid, pp. 208–222.

[68] MFN clauses are characterized as "drafting by reference." See Schill (2009), p. 127.

[69] Schill (2009), pp. 124, 128.

[70] See paras. 230–232, available at https://www.italaw.com/sites/default/files/case-documents/ita0074.pdf accessed 03.09.2024. In *İçkale v. Turkmenistan,* the relevant BIT contained the following article "Each Party shall accord to these investments [i.e., investments permitted into its territory pursuant to Article II(1)], once established, treatment no less favourable than that accorded in similar situations to investments of its investors or to investments of investors of any third country, whichever is the most favorable." According to the tribunal, the scope of application of the MFN clause was limited to "similar situations" and it was not satisfied whether a "similar situation" existed. By contrast, in its view, MFN treatment obligation exists *"only insofar as the investments of the investors of the home State and those of the investors of the third State can be said to be in "a similar situation."* See paras. *326–329.* Available at https://www.italaw.com/sites/default/files/case-documents/italaw7163_1.pdf accessed 03.09.2024.

[71] Dumberry (2017), p. 129.

[72] The tribunal in *EDF v. Argentina*, concluded that "*the MFN clause does in fact permit recourse to the —umbrella clauses|| of third-country treaties, which leads to arbitration rather than the administrative courts of the City of Mendoza*" See para. 929, https://www.italaw.com/sites/default/files/case-documents/ita1069.pdf accessed 03.09.2024. Conversely, some tribunals opted not to accept invocation of umbrella clause. In *Impregilo v. Pakistan*, the tribunal, rejected claimant's arguments on the basis that it concluded contract with the Pakistan Water and Power

BIT clause through the MFN clause of the base treaty can be crucial with respect to insurance law. MFN provisions are invoked to expand the standards of treatments;[73] if the relevant BIT lacks express exceptions, some may debate whether PRI providers can avail themselves of subrogation if such a right exists in a comparator treaty. In the forthcoming chapter dealing with subrogation, we will analyze in depth whether the extension of an MFN clause to subrogation is possible.

7.6 Umbrella Clauses

Umbrella clauses are known as the 'observance of undertaking' clauses and as the name clearly suggests, this clause guarantees the observance of obligations assumed by the host state vis-à-vis the investor[74] and requires the host state to honor its commitments made in an investment protection treaty.[75] The presence of this clause in a treaty renders an international character to the commitments. Therefore, by virtue of an umbrella clause, a mere contractual breach by the host state can amount to breach of the BIT, providing a basis for tribunals in investor-state disputes to exercise jurisdiction over the dispute. Hence, the foreign investor may no longer need to exhaust local legal remedies, by contrast, the clause will permit arbitration of claims for breach by the host state of any obligation owed to the investor, thereby allowing investors to arbitrate a wide range of disputes with the host state.[76]

According to scholars, the purpose of including such a provision in a treaty is to impose an international obligation on host states to uphold their commitments related to foreign investments and provide additional protection to foreign investors when the actions of the host states cannot be addressed by the FET or FPS clauses.[77] However, the query revolves around whether a tribunal, based upon a provision of a BIT, can extend its jurisdiction and adjudicate a claim in respect of a pure commercial contract that explicitly lacks an arbitration provision. *SGS v. Pakistan* marked the first instance where a tribunal dealt with the umbrella clause. Tribunal assigned no significance to the umbrella clause, in tribunal's appreciation, the article 11 of the

Development Authority, not with the host state. See para. 223 available at https://www.italaw.com/sites/default/files/case-documents/ita0422.pdf accessed 03.09.2024.

[73] Also see Caron and Shirlow (2015), pp. 405–406.

[74] Kriebaum et al. (2022), p. 273.

[75] For instance, article 2(II-c) of the Argentina–U.S. BIT (1991) provides "*Each Party shall observe any obligation it may have entered into with regard to investments*". Available at https://investmentpolicy.unctad.org/international-investment-agreements/treaty-files/127/download accessed 03.09.2024. Also see Konrad (2013), pp. 34–35.

[76] Born (2021), pp. 510, 516.

[77] Salacuse (2013), pp. 390, 391.

Switzerland-Pakistan BIT[78] falls short of elevating the breach of the contract by the state to the level of breaches of international treaty law.[79] The tribunal, citing another arbitration case, opined that a violation of contract between the foreign investor and the host state is not, by itself, a violation of international law. In the tribunal's analysis, giving effect to umbrella clause would "*render mutually agreed procedure of dispute settlement a dead-letter, at the investor's choice*[80]". However, the tribunal in *SGS v. Philippines* strongly debated this restrictive interpretation. The reason was that the relevant BIT in the *SGS v. Pakistan* case, to which the tribunal referred, did not contain an equivalent provision to the one found in the Switzerland-Pakistan BIT. Therefore, in the tribunal's conclusion, 'the ad hoc Committee did not need to consider whether a clause in a treaty requiring a state to observe specific domestic commitments has an effect in international law.' Additionally, despite sharing the concern that the umbrella clause may potentially override dispute settlement clauses negotiated in specific contracts, the clause does not convert; non-binding domestic blandishments into binding international obligations and questions of contract law into questions of treaty law.[81]

An umbrella clause necessarily mirrors the principle of treaty-shopping and can override the exclusive jurisdiction clause in contracts. The language of umbrella clauses is broad, encompassing every conceivable obligation of the host state. Tribunals may be prone to read the clause broadly and attribute far-reaching legal consequences to it. Foreign investors might wish to elevate all their contractual disputes to BIT claims. The second drawback is related to the international nature of the clause. One may suggest that whether in the form of commitments or not, the host state will have enabled an international scrutiny over its actions.[82] If foreign investors can avoid what they agreed upon in an investment contract through the umbrella cluse, specifically with regard to the forum selection, PRI providers might seek to cover foreign investments in countries which have concluded BITs containing such a clause.

---

[78] The article is as follows: "*Either Contracting Party shall constantly guarantee the observance of the commitments it has entered into with respect to the investments of the investors of the other Contracting Party.*"

[79] See Kunoy (2005), p. 484.

[80] See paras. 163–173.

[81] See paras 115–127.

[82] For discussions on the umbrella clause, see Golcuklu (2018) and similarly, Sureda (2015).

7.7 Setting the Boundaries of Sovereigns Through Stabilization Clauses and BITs

7.7.1 Stabilization Clauses in General

Investment transactions embody risks; in *Salacuse*'s succinct definition, they are a wager on the unknown.[83] Therefore, they may suffer from vagueness and a lack of predictability. The reason is not difficult to surmise; investors carry out high-risk investments in reliance on the host state's 'promise of regulatory stability'. Thus, a wary foreign investor might wish to associate with an 'investor-friendly' state in the jurisdiction of which the legal framework is steady, consistent and thus utterly predictable.[84] However, as the nature and the practice of commercial transactions evolve over time, so must the legislation that govern them.

Rubins and Kinsella mention the theory of '*obsolescing bargain*'. Host states can be inclined to disrespect the privileges they grant to foreign investor to the extent that the benefits that they have gained from the investment begin to fall short of expectations or the economic costs of altering the laws or contractual terms outweigh the mentioned benefits.[85] Along with increasing economic concerns, states' eagerness to alter their commitments might be politically driven. Commissioning foreign investments that do not contribute to local employment, welfare, or, *Salacuse's* words drain national resources through profit repatriation, will draw local people's repercussions.[86] For these reasons, the original bargain between the foreign investor and the host state can become obsolete, and the contractual terms can be subject to change at the host state's initiative.

The sector and phase of the project determine the scope of investor's vulnerability. If a significant investment has been sunk into the project (for instance, if equipment and machinery used for the project cannot be sold or repurposed) the host government may have a great deal of leverage over the foreign investor[87] and may tend to exploit the shift in bargaining power by requesting renegotiations.[88] In fact, foreign investment is the transfer of certain means such as technology, know-how and capital from one country to another in return for the repatriation of profits or

---

[83] Salacuse (2013), p. 167.

[84] According to *Waelde and Ndi*, life cannot be squeezed into a human plan for eternity, same scholars underline the simple dichotomy of lawyers who wish to "play the God" under a delusion of drafting away all the vagaries of the future. See Waelde and Ndi (1996), p. 220.

[85] Salacuse (2013), p. 141.

[86] Salacuse (2013), pp. 19, 27, 28, 141.

[87] According to *Rubins and Kinsella*, If the occurrence of the risk is unavoidable, prior to it and to the extent possible, the investor may transfer equipment, machinery or the currency out of the host state.

See Rubins and Kinsella (2005), pp. 5, 38–40. Also see Yackee (2014), pp. 484–485.

[88] Waelde and Ndi (1996), p. 225.

sources from the latter country. If the nature of the investment requires particular know-how, the bargaining power may not shift in favor of the host government.

The host state and the foreign investor may become embroiled in a dispute over changes in the laws. The investor will want to ensure that the host state either does not introduce new laws or exempts the investor from new taxes or fiscal levies imposed by subsequent regulations. Irrespective of changes made to the law, parties to investment contracts may agree on applying certain regulations to the contract that were in force at a specified date.[89] In so doing, the investor need not to concern over the amendments to, or repeal of, legislation by which the underlined contract is interpreted, on the contrary, the law in effect on the date of investment was made governs the parties' relations.[90]

Scholars view stabilization clauses[91] as hedging devices for the mitigation of political risk.[92] As indicated by their name, stabilization clauses are directed at political risks and a direct response to countermanding actions by the host state. They aim to bind the state to a greater extent than a normal contract might do, thereby providing the agreement with greater force.[93] In other words, the state ensures to place the investor in the same position it would have occupied had the law remained unchanged.[94]

Stabilization clauses can take a variety of forms.[95] An *intangibility clause* prevents the host state from unilaterally modifying the contract and may contain a promise not to expropriate the investment. A *consistency clause* signifies the host state's commitment applying domestic law to the investment only insofar as it aligns with the investment contract. Another version is the '*freezing clause*', that fixes the legislation for a certain period thereby exempting the investment from adapting to amendments. The last form is the '*economic equilibrium clause*', that aims to preserve the economic value of the investment through including an obligation to either renegotiate the contract terms if laws change or pay indemnification if the investment is adversely affected by new laws or amendments.[96]

---

[89] *Rubins and Kinsella* points out that stabilization clause is designed the freeze the law of the host state as it was on that date. See Rubins and Kinsella (2005), p. 51.

[90] Rubins and Kinsella (2005), p. 16.

[91] Some scholars employ the term "stand-still clause", See Kunoy (2005), p. 478.

[92] See Mazin (2017), p. 191 and similarly, Osasu (2013), pp. 250–251.

[93] Waelde and Ndi (1996), p. 236.

[94] Rubins and Kinsella (2005), p. 53.

[95] For the sample clauses, please see Wolfgang (1998).

[96] Comeaux and Kinsella (1994), pp. 260, 261. A sample stabilization clause might be as follows "*any amendment or repeal of the Regulations shall not affect the contractual rights of the Company without its consent*". For other examples see Rubins and Kinsella (2005), pp. 52–53. An example of economic equilibrium clause reads "*if the project is not completed within the timeframe for investment recovery, the National Executive, through the Ministry of Popular Power for Energy and Petroleum shall grant to the "Mixed Company", the reduction of royalty and taxes under the Organic Hydrocarbon Law and request that other national authorities grant similar tax incentives*

Amendments brought to the regulatory framework existing at the time investment made can be objectionable.[97] Thus, host states should honor their commitments or avoid unilaterally altering the irretractable rights granted to the foreign investor.[98] Moreover, altering the legislation may have severe ramifications on the part of investors and deprive them of revenues. If possible, the investment can be structured in a manner that can adapt to such modifications.

The downside of the stabilization clauses is that, even if circumstances become unendurable for the host state and necessitate modifications to commitments, these clauses enforce contractual rigidity and rule out the possibility of revisions. The restrictive nature of such clauses may lead to conflicts. Renegotiation clauses, however, can be tremendously beneficial to investors in the long run. In this way, parties may enjoy both the means of a fixed legal regime and adaptability of their contract to recent developments.

Renegotiations can occur in various forms; it can be due to the parties' voluntary decision to renew the contract before its expiration or conditioned upon the lapse of a certain period or the occurrence of specific events.[99] In the latter case, events, whether specified in the contract or not, whether internal or external, that cause a radical change in the benefits of the parties, foist an obligation on the parties to engage in renegotiations.[100] Although such a clause might aim to restore balance, in our opinion, in most cases, its inclusion is unnecessary if the same contract already provides for a dispute resolution mechanism, such as an amicable solution. Additionally, an amicable solution should not serve as a barrier to arbitration. The reason is that prevailing events may have created circumstances unbearable for a party, prompting it to either fail to meet its obligations or cancel the contract entirely. In such cases, renegotiations or attempts at an amicable solution might be futile. A court or tribunal must not circumvent from hearing a dispute solely because the claimant deliberately omitted the 'renegotiation' or 'amicable solution' clause.

Similar thorny questions within the same scope must also be addressed; *Does a stabilization clause eliminate the host government's right to unilaterally alter an investor's right by changing the municipal law? To what extent is a state entitled to dismantle the legal framework constructed to attract foreign investors.*[101] Even if one were to argue that states will find themselves squeezed between their promises

---

that may be necessary to make the project financially viable." For the other examples see Solimene (2014), p. 8, and finally, see Salacuse (2013), pp. 153, 154.

[97] See *Parkerings v. Lithuania*, para. 332. Available at https://www.italaw.com/sites/default/files/case-documents/ita0619.pdf accessed 03.09.2024.

[98] In *Texaco Overseas* it was held that "*a State cannot invoke its sovereignty to disregard commitments freely undertaken through the exercise of this same sovereignty*". Please visit: https://www.trans-lex.org/261700/_/texaco-overseas-petroleum-company-v-the-government-of-the-libyan-arab-republic-yca-1979-at-177-et-seq-/ accessed 03.09.2024.

[99] Wolfgang (1998), p. 890.

[100] For detail, see Salacuse (2013), p. 276 et seq.

[101] See *El Paso v. Argentina* case, para. 517. Available at https://www.italaw.com/sites/default/files/case-documents/ita0270.pdf accessed 03.09.2024. Also see Waelde and Ndi (1996), p. 245.

on one side and the needs of their nationals on the other.[102] Stabilization clauses do not hinder the host state's right to pass new laws or alter existing ones; in other words, states do not contract away their rights to enact or amend the laws. In essence, these rights are an inherent part of its sovereignty and powers in its eminent domain and represent the exercise of the host state's absolute legislative prerogatives. States cannot bind themselves to refrain from using these powers[103] and or derogate from their sovereignty; on the contrary, in our opinion, the principle of sovereignty nullifies the applicability of, or diminishes reliance on, such clauses.[104]

7.7.2 The Prominence of Bilateral Treaties

Investing in countries with which the investor's country has a BIT will be for the benefit of investor.[105] Through BITs, host states undertake providing foreign investors with 'international standards of treatment' and refrain from taking hasty actions concerning foreign investments. Consequently, foreign investors must consider the BIT a 'building block' for their investments and, in a sense, conduct a security check to verify that a BIT is in force between the host state and their home state. In a similar vein, a number of political risk insurers provide insurance coverage contingent on the adoption of BITs.[106] The reason is that BITs serve to preserve the subrogatory right of the insurer, and host states, through the subrogation clauses contained in the BITs, recognize such a right pertained to the opposing party's insurer. Conversely, it is worth mentioning that the absence of a BIT represents a downside; BITs can be employed as a means of 'threat' or 'political persuasion' at best.[107] This is because the home state may threaten the host-state with abrogating the BIT if its investor is likely to incur a political risk.

---

[102] See *Total v. Argentina* para. 115. Available at https://www.italaw.com/sites/default/files/case-documents/ita0868.pdf accessed 03.09.2024.

[103] The tribunal in *Cavalum v. Spain* held that it would be inconceivable that a state would make a general commitment never to change its legislation whatever the circumstances, and it would be unreasonable for an investor to rely on such a freeze, especially upon changing needs, or in a time of a crisis. See para. 427, https://jusmundi.com/en/document/decision/en-cavalum-sgps-s-a-v-kingdom-of-spain-decision-on-jurisdiction-liability-and-directions-on-quantum-monday-31st-august-2020 accessed 03.09.2024. Also see Levashova (2022), p. 116.

[104] Salacuse (2013), p. 149.

[105] For instance, *Tan* states that some insurance agencies from Belgium, Germany and the Netherlands seek the existence of an investment treaty between the host state and the country of investor. Violating BITs will have negative ramifications for the rating of the host state. See Tan (2015), p. 183.

[106] Poulsen (2010), p. 15 and similarly see Dolzer and Schreuer (2012), pp. 230–231.

[107] According to scholars, BITs provide a platform for embassy officials to discourage the host government for investments from taking action prejudicial to investments of their country's nationals. see Hay (1997), p. 154.

BITs may list stability side by side with FET,[108] or arbitration tribunals may link stability with FET.[109] Therefore, FET treatment is believed to embrace an obligation to provide sustainability in the essential characteristics of the legal regime.[110] BITS may also require a host country to provide assurance against substantial changes in the investment regime that would be detrimental to foreign investors. Scholars opine that international arbitration and stabilization clauses preventing unilateral changes in the legal regime provide the needed protection to investors.[111] In the absence of a stabilization clause freezing the legal regime,[112] an alteration of the law may be asserted as a violation of the FET standard. However, in the wording of *EDF Limited v. Romania* tribunal "*investor may not rely on a bilateral investment treaty as a kind of insurance policy against the risk of any changes in the host State's legal and economic framework. Such expectation would be neither legitimate nor reasonable.*[113]" What we can deduct from the tribunal's ruling is that changes to regulatory regime relied upon by the investor must not take place in a drastic fashion. Developing countries are pitted against each other due to the mobility and low risk-taking profile of international capital. If a developing country wishes to vacuum foreign investment and transform itself into an investor-friendly country, it must avoid altering the substance of the law as it applies to foreign investment. If need be, it can make amendments in a manner that does not have a material impact on carrying out the business.

Cases

AMCO: AMCO Asia Corporation and others v. Republic of Indonesia, (ICSID Case No. ARB/81/1), Award

Ampal v. Egypt: Ampal-American Israel Corporation and others v. Arab Republic of Egypt, (ICSID Case No. ARB/12/11), Decision on Liability and Heads of Loss, 21 February 2017)

AMT v. Zaire*:* American Manufacturing & Trading, Inc. (AMT) (USA) v. Republic of Zaire, (ICSID Case No. ARB/93/1), Award

[108] Kriebaum et al. (2022), p. 206.

[109] See *BP Group v. Argentina* case, para. 307. Available at https://www.italaw.com/sites/default/files/case-documents/ita0081.pdf accessed 03.09.2024.

[110] See *EISER v. Spain* (para. 382–383) Available at https://www.italaw.com/sites/default/files/case-documents/italaw9050.pdf accessed 03.09.2024.

[111] Haque and Burdescu (2004), p. 252.

[112] According to *Enron v. Argentina* tribunal (para. 261), the stabilization requirement does not mean the freezing of the legal system or the disappearance of the regulatory power of the state.

[113] See para. 217.

Azurix v. Argentina: Azurix Corp. v. The Argentine Republic, (ICSID Case No. ARB/01/12), Decision on the Application for Annulment of the Argentine Republic

Bayindir v. Pakistan: Bayindir İnsaat Turizm Ticaret Ve Sanayi A.Ş. v. Islamic Republic of Pakistan, (ICSID Case No. ARB/03/29), Decision on Jurisdiction

Biloune v. Ghana: Antoine Biloune and Marine Drive Complex Ltd. v. Ghana Investments Centre and the Government of Ghana, (Ad hoc Arbitration), Award on Jurisdiction and Liability - 27 Oct 1989

BP Group v. Argentina: BP Group Plc. v. The Republic of Argentina, (UNCITRAL Arbitration), Final Award

Cavalum v. Spain: Cavalum SGPS, S.A. v. Spain, ICSID Case No. ARB/15/34, Decision on Jurisdiction, Liability and Directions on Quantum

CMS v. Argentina: Cms Gas Transmission v. The Argentine Republic, (ICSID Case No. ARB/01/8), Award

EDF v. Argentina: EDF International S.A., SAUR International S.A. and León Participaciones Argentinas S.A. v. The Argentine Republic, (ICSID Case No. ARB/03/23), Award

EDF Limited v. Romania: EDF (Services) Limited v. Romania, (ICSID Case No. ARB/05/13), Award

EISER v. Spain: Eiser Infrastructure Limited and Energia Solar Luxembourg s.à r.i. v. Kingdom of Spain, (ICSID Case No Arb/13/36), Award

Electrabel v. Hungary: Electrabel S.A. v. Republic of Hungary, (ICSID Case No. ARB/07/19), Decision on Jurisdiction, Applicable Law and Liability

El Paso v. Argentina: EL PASO Energy International Company v. The Argentine Republic, (ICSID Case No. ARB/03/15), Award

ELSI: SpA Elettronica Sicula S.p.A. (ELSI) (United States of America v. Italy, International Court of Justice

ENRON v. Argentina: Enron Corporation Ponderosa Assets, L.P v. The Argentine Republic, (ICSID Case No. ARB/01/3), Award

Genin Alex Genin, Eastern Credit Limited, INC. and A.S. Baltoil v. Republic of Estonia, (ICSID Case No. ARB/99/2), Award

Glamis Gold Ltd. : Glamis Gold, Ltd. v. United States of America, (ICSID case), Award

Impregilo v. Pakistan: Impregilo S.p.A. v. Islamic Republic of Pakistan, (ICSID CASE No. ARB/03/3), Decision on Jurisdiction

Inceysa v. El Salvador: Inceysa Vallisoletana, S.L. v. Republic of El Salvador (ICSID Case No ARB/03/26), Award

İçkale v. Turkmenistan: İçkale İnşaat Limited Şirketi v. Turkmenistan, (ICSID Case No. Arb/10/24), Award

Maffezini v. Spain: Emilio Agustín Maffezini v. The Kingdom of Spain, (ICSID Case No. ARB/97/7), Award

Metalclad v. Mexico: Metalclad Corp. V. United Mexican States, ICSID Case No. Arb(AF)/97/l

MTD Equity v. Chile: MTD Equity Sdn. Bhd. and MTD Chile S.A. v. Republic of Chile, (ICSID Case No. ARB/01/7), Award

Occidental: Occidental Exploration and Production Co v. Ecuador, (UNCITRAL Arbitration, London Court of International Arbitration), Administered Case No. UN 3467

Parkerings v. Lithuania: Parkerings-COMPAGNIET AS v. Republic of Lithuania, (ICSID Case No. ARB/05/8), Award

Plama v. Bulgaria: Plama Consortium Limited v. Republic of Bulgaria, (ICSID Case No. ARB/03/24), Award

Salini v. Jordan: Salini Costruttori s.p.a. and Italstrade s.p.a v. The Hashemite Kingdom of Jordan, (ICSID Case No. Arb/02/13), Award

Suez v. Argentina: Suez, Sociedad General de Aguas de Barcelona S.A., and InterAguas Servicios Integrales del Agua S.A. v. The Argentine Republic, (ICSID Case No. ARB/03/17), Decision on Jurisdiction

SGS v. Pakistan: Société Générale de Surveillance (SGS) vs. Pakistan, (ICSID Case No. ARB/01/13), Decision of the tribunal on objections to jurisdiction

SGS v. Philippines: Société Générale de Surveillance (SGS) v. Philippines, (ICSID Case No. ARB/02/6) Decision of the Tribunal on Objections to Jurisdiction

Tecmed v. Mexico: Tecnicas Medioambientales Tecmed S.A. v. The United Mexican States, (ICSID Case No. ARB (AF)/00/2), Award

Telenor v. Hungary: Telenor Mobile Communications v. The Republic of Hungary, (ICSID Case No. ARB/04/15), Award

Texaco Overseas: Texaco Overseas Petroleum Company/California Asiatic Oil Co. v. The Government of the Libyan Arab Republic, YCA 1979, at 177 et seq.

Total v. Argentina: Total S.A. v. Argentine Republic, (ICSID Case No. ARB/04/1), Decision on Liability

Online Database

http://www.digitalcommons.law.scu.edu
https://www.jusmundi.com
https://www.icj-cij.org
https://investmentpolicy.unctad.org
https://www.italaw.com
http://www.lawsturkey.com
https://www.legal.un.org
https://www.trans-lex.org

References

Abba K, Wälde T (2008) Capital transfer restrictions under modern investment treaties. In: Reinisch A (ed) Standards of investment protection. Oxford University Press. https://doi.org/10.1093/acprof:oso/9780199547432.003.0010

Bjorklund AK (2008) National treatment. In: Reinisch A (ed) Standards of investment protection. Oxford University Press. https://doi.org/10.1093/acprof:oso/9780199547432.003.0003

Born G (2021) International arbitration: law and practice, 3rd edn. Kluwer Law International

Caron DD, Shirlow E (2015) Chapter 29: most favored-nation treatment: substantive protection. In: Kinnear M, Fischer GR et al (eds) Building international investment law: the first 50 years of ICSID. Kluwer Law International, pp 399–414

Comeaux PE, Kinsella N (1994) Reducing political risk in developing countries: bilateral investment treaties, stabilization clauses, and MIGA & (and) OPIC investment insurance. N Y Law School J Int Comp Law 15(1):1–48

Dolzer R (2014) Fair and equitable treatment: today's contours. Santa Clara J Int Law 12:7. http://digitalcommons.law.scu.edu/scujil/vol12/iss1/2

Dolzer R, Schreuer C (2012) Principles of international investment law, 2nd edn. Oxford University Press, Oxford

Dumberry P (2017) The importation of the FET standard through MFN clauses: an empirical study of BITs. ICSID Rev 32(1):116–137

Giuditta CM (2008) Full protection and security. In: Reinisch A (ed) Standards of investment protection. Oxford University Press. https://doi.org/10.1093/acprof:oso/9780199547432.003.0007

Golcuklu I (2018) Umbrella clauses in the ICSID arbitration. Public Priv Int Law Bull 37(2): 352–375

Haque I, Burdescu R (2004) Monterrey consensus on financing for development: response sought from international economic law. Boston Coll Int Comp Law Rev 27(2)

Hartwell G et al (2005) Assessing damages are arbitrators good at it; should they be assisted by experts; should they be entitled to decide ex aequo et bono: some war stories. J World Invest Trade 6(1):7–22

Hay R (1997) Protecting assets from political risk. Priv Client Bus 3:152–164

Hyder AA, Attanasio DL (2021) International investment protection of global banking and finance: legal principles and arbitral practice. Kluwer Law International

Konrad S (2013) Investment treaties and international centre for settlement investment disputes: what investment insurers need to know. In: Verheyen G, Quintrell E (eds) Old risks, new solutions, or is it the other way around?

Kriebaum U, Dolzer R, Schreuer C (2022) Principles of international investment law, 3rd edn. Oxford University Press, Oxford

Kunoy B (2005) Developments in indirect expropriation case law in ICSID transnational arbitration. J World Invest Trade 6(3):467–492

Levashova Y (2022) Chapter 6: The legitimate expectations of investors under the fair and equitable treatment in times of pandemic and aftermath. In: Levashova Y, Lorfing PA (eds) Balancing the protection of foreign investors and states responses in the post-pandemic. World Kluwer Law International

Mazin A (2017) Dealing with political risk in PPP infrastructure projects: legal recommendations based on recent cases. J Article Int Bus Law J 3:189–202

Newcombe A, Paradell L (2009) Law and practice of investment treaties: standards of treatment. Kluwer Law International

Osasu O (2013) Legitimate expectations and political risk: lessons from investment arbitration for energy investors. Int Energy Law Rev 6:249–262

Paparinskis M (2013) International minimum standard and the law of treaties. The international minimum standard and fair and equitable treatment, Oxford Monographs. In: International law. Oxford University Press

Potočnik M (2019) Arbitrating brands: international investment treaties and trademarks. Edward Elgar Publishing Limited, Cheltenham, Gloucestershire

Poulsen L (2010) The importance of BITs for foreign direct investment and political risk insurance: revisiting the evidence. In: Sauvant KP (ed) Yearbook on international investment law & policy. Oxford University Press, New York

Ratner SR (2008) Regulatory takings in institutional context: beyond the fear of fragmented international law. Am J Int Law 102(3):475–528

Reed LF, Consedine S (2015) Chapter 20: Fair and equitable treatment: legitimate expectations and transparency. In: Kinnear M, Fischer GR et al (eds) Building international investment law: the first 50 years of ICSID. Kluwer Law International, pp 283–294

Reinisch A (2015) Chapter 28: National treatment. In: Kinnear M, Fischer GR et al (eds) Building international investment law: the first 50 years of ICSID. Kluwer Law International, pp 389–398

Rubins N, Kinsella NS (2005) International investment, political risk and dispute resolution "a practitioner's guide". Oxford University Press

Salacuse JW (2013) The three laws of international investment: national, contractual, and international frameworks for foreign capital. Oxford University Press

Salacuse JW (2016) The law of investment treaties, 3rd edn. Oxford University Press, Oxford

Salacuse JW, Sullivan NP (2005) Do BITs really work?: An evaluation of bilateral investment treaties and their grand bargain. Harv Int Law J 46(1):67–130

Schill SW (2009) The multilateralization of international investment law. Cambridge University Press (Cambridge International Trade and Economic Law), Cambridge. https://doi.org/10.1017/CBO9780511605451

Sharpe JK (2015) Chapter 19: The minimum standard of treatment, Glamis Gold, and Neer's Enduring Influence. In: Kinnear M, Fischer GR et al (eds) Building international investment law: the first 50 years of ICSID. Kluwer Law International, pp 269–282

Solimene F (2014) Political risk in the oil and gas industry and legal tools for mitigation. Int Energy Law Rev 2:81–90

Sprankling JG (2014) The international law of property, 1st edn. Oxford University Press, Oxford

Stefano CD (2020) Attribution in international law and arbitration, 1st edn. Oxford University Press, Oxford

Sureda AR (2015) Chapter 27: The Umbrella Clause. In: Kinnear M, Fischer GR et al (eds) Building international investment law: the first 50 years of ICSID. Kluwer Law International, pp 375–388

Tan C (2015) Risky business: political risk insurance and the law and governance of natural resources. Int J Law Context [Online] 11(2):174–194

Tudor I (2008) The fair and equitable treatment standard in the international law of foreign investment. Oxford University Press, Oxford

Waelde TW, Ndi G (1996) Stabilizing international investment commitments: international law versus contract interpretation. Tex Int Law J 31(2):215–268

Weiler T (2003) The treatment of SPS measures under NAFTA Chapter 11: preliminary answers to an open-ended question. Boston Coll Int Comp Law Rev 26(2):229

Wolfgang P (1998) Stabilization clauses in state contracts. Int Bus Law J 8:875–891

Yackee JW (2014) Political risk and international investment law. Duke J Comp Int Law 24(3)

Ziegler AR (2008) Most-Favoured-Nation (MFN) Treatment. In: Reinisch A (ed) Standards of investment protection. Oxford University Press. https://doi.org/10.1093/acprof:oso/9780199547432.003.0004

Chapter 8
Political Risks

8.1 In General

Investors assume two basic risks in their investments: commercial and political. Commercial risks are those deriving from the ordinary commercial activities affecting the enterprise.[1] In essence, whether commercial or political, when a risk occurs, the loss the foreign investor incurs is a loss of economic, and therefore commercial, nature. Host states possess the power to regulate and introduce measures, and political risks can arise from regulatory actions or inactions by the host state. By way of example, a host state may place limits on capital inflow or outflow, ban convertibility, or terminate a concession agreement concluded with a foreign investor. Political risk can encompass the possibility of government actions which either deny or restrict the right of an investor/owner (i) to use or benefit from his/her assets; or (ii) reduce the value of the firm.[2]

Some authors classify risks based on their form and employ abbreviations which are reminiscent of underwriting jargon, formed by combination of the initial letters of each risk. To illustrate, CF refers to insurance against contract frustration or repudiation by government obligors,[3] while CEN[4] refers to confiscation, expropriation, nationalization; in CEND, the letter "D" stands for deprivation.[5] Both abbreviations combine risks of similar or identical nature. Simply put, risks serving for the

[1] Salacuse (2016), p. 41.

[2] See Peinhardt and Allee (2016), p. 206. In *Tokios Tokelės v. Ukraine* the tribunal explained that "diminution *of 5% of the investment's value will not be enough for a finding of expropriation, while a diminution of 95% would likely be sufficient.*" See para. 120. Available at https://www.italaw.com/sites/default/files/case-documents/ita0866.pdf accessed 04.09.2024.

[3] See George and Searle (2013), p. 28.

[4] See Spagnoletti and O'Callaghan (2011), p. 3, fn 3.

[5] See Wagner (2012), p. 102, also see Jensen and Young (2008), p. 529.

Ö. Tosun, *The Law of Political Risk Insurance*, AIDA Europe Research Series on Insurance Law and Regulation 12, https://doi.org/10.1007/978-3-031-74675-8_8

same legal consequence for which various jurisdictions employ different terms are consolidated under a single heading.

Rubins and Kinsella categorize risks as outright expropriation, regulatory interference, currency risk, civil unrest, breach of state contracts, corruption,[6] and trade restrictions.[7] According to *Waelde and Ndi,* seeking a coverage against future tax risks is not unthinkable.[8] And finally, kidnapping and ransom can also be the elements of the political risks if the goal is to overawe the investor.[9] Among others, corruption is often ignored segment of political risk.[10] In our opinion, bribery is not a politically driven action targeting foreign investment. A real persons' appetite for money should not be attributable to the state, therefore should not be deemed a political risk. Trade restrictions share a blurry line with expropriation in terms of their consequences. For instance, banning the export of products[11] is one form of such risk, which may also constitute expropriation.

8.2 Expropriation

8.2.1 In General

Sovereignty acts as the 'event horizon[12]' of international investment; once exercised, none of an investor's acquired rights can escape its grasp. The concept of expropriation[13] can be debated; while some deem it unlawful relying due to deprivation inherent in its nature, where the asset is taken without the consent of its owner, expropriation remains as a core sovereign right.[14] This dilemma, therefore has

[6]The Black's Law Dictionary defines as "The act of doing something with an intent to give some advantage inconsistent with official duty and the rights of others."

[7]Rubins and Kinsella (2005), p. 6.

[8]Waelde and Ndi (1996), p. 222, fn 27.

[9]Please visit: https://www.lloyds.com/conducting-business/risk-locator/business-guidance/political-risk#Political%20violence accessed 04.09.2024.

[10]Rubins and Kinsella (2005), p. 22.

[11]See *Myers v. Canada*, available at https://www.italaw.com/sites/default/files/case-documents/ita0747.pdf accessed 04.09.2024. Also see Aldrich (1994), p. 600.

[12]The event horizon (the black hole's surface) captures any light passing through it and whatever passes into the event horizon is doomed to stay inside it. Hence, when a foreign investor decides to enter the horizon area (jurisdiction of the sovereign) its investment will inevitably be affected by the sovereign's acts even if the foreign investor is entitled to arbitrate and challenge the action or decision that tantamounts to expropriation. For event horizon please visit: https://universe.nasa.gov/black-holes/anatomy/ accessed 04.09.2024.

[13]See Williams (1993), p. 66. According to *Rubins and Kinsella* expropriation is the taking by a host state of property owned by a foreign investor and located in the host state. See Rubins and Kinsella (2005), p. 6.

[14]The authority of states to expropriate their nationals' assets finds its basis in their constitutions. As an illustration, Article 46 and 47 of the Turkish constitution specifically address expropriation and

garnered significant attention. Use and enjoyment, control and possession, disposal and alienation are the essential characteristics of an ownership and expropriation claims arise as any one of these ownership attributes is affected.[15] Sovereigns, driven by social or political objectives, may apply a seizure that deprives foreign investors of legal title to,[16] control over, or at least fruits of the asset, which eventually ripens into an expropriation. However much the Sovereign claims that its bona fide efforts are to uphold the public interest,[17] as one scholar aptly puts it, *'the allurement of the bird in hand will be very hard to resist*[18]'. Hence, an increase in the investment's value after the passage of time may lure or encourage the sovereign to take illegal actions to extract benefits from that investment.

In referring to the host state's seizure, terms such as 'expropriation', 'nationalization' 'requisition[19]', 'dispossession', 'deprivation', 'sequestration', or 'confiscation[20]' are used interchangeably.[21] Although these terms are alike in meaning, some jurisdictions provide distinct definitions. By way of illustration, in Turkey, '*nationalization*' requires a specific enactment of law and applies to the seizure of an entire industry, whereas 'expropriation' requires an administrative decision and refers to

---

nationalization, respectively. Furthermore, while not explicitly outlined in a single convention, the grounding for expropriating foreign assets rests on customary international law. Art. 4 of the United Nations General Assembly resolution 1803 (XVII) of 14 December 1962, Permanent Sovereignty over Natural Resources address expropriation right of the host state in the following definition "*Nationalization, expropriation or requisitioning shall be based on grounds or reasons of public utility, security or the national interest which are recognized as overriding the purely individual or private interests, both domestic or foreign. In such case, the owner shall be paid appropriate compensation, in accordance with the rules in force in the State taking such measures in the exercise of its sovereignty and in accordance with international law. In any case where the question of compensation gives rise to a controversy, the national jurisdiction of the State taking such measures shall be exhausted. However, upon agreement by sovereign States and other parties concerned, settlement of the dispute should be made through arbitration or international adjudication*" Please visit: https://www.ohchr.org/sites/default/files/resources.pdf accessed 04.09.2024. In the forthcoming pages, we will delve extensively into the conditions of illegality of such acts. For the English version of Constitution of the Republic of Turkey, please visit: https://www.anayasa.gov.tr/media/7258/anayasa_eng.pdf accessed 04.09.2024.

[15] *Mamidoil v. Albania*, available at https://www.italaw.com/sites/default/files/case-documents/italaw4228.pdf accessed 04.09.2024.

[16] In some cases, expropriation may occur through, the government's transferring ownership to another legal person or natural person. See *AMCO* case, available at https://jusmundi.com/en/document/decision/en-amco-asia-corporation-and-others-v-republic-of-indonesia-award-tuesday-20th-november-1984 accessed 04.09.2024.

[17] Some scholars suggest that the intent of the measure is not a determining factor, whereas the tribunal in *Tecmed v. Mexico* (paras. 117, 118) focused not only on the effects of the measure. See. Kunoy (2005), p. 471.

[18] Christie (1962), p. 328.

[19] Expropriations of property during wartime or national emergency, see Newcombe and Paradell (2009), p. 324.

[20] It is a seizure of property without compensation to punish the owner for who he is or what he has done. See Rubins and Kinsella (2005), p. 10

[21] Kunoy (2005), pp. 473–474 and see Verwey and Schrijver (1984), p. 4.

the seizure of a particular asset.[22] Notwithstanding the variety in terminology, the result is uniform. All measures tantamount to compulsory taking and transfer of foreign investor's proprietary rights.[23] Aside from these variations in meanings, considering that expropriation is a generic term and a wider concept, hence subsumes nationalization,[24] and finally, since a variety of meanings can be ascribed to the term 'taking', we will adopt the same approach that some BITS do[25] and will principally employ the term of 'expropriation' for any form of taking throughout this book.[26]

8.2.2 Expropriation of Metaverse Property and Domain Name

Expropriation is associated with taking of a physical asset; however, it may extend to things in the virtual realm that do not appeal to sense of touch.[27] The question at hand is whether investments made in metaverse can be protected against expropriation by political risk insurance, or in fact whether an expropriation can take place in the meta realm. Based on the structure of the metaverse, the answers to these questions may vary. The rules of the centralized metaverse are similar to those of conventional banking. Individuals can only act within the constraints of the entity that provides the metaverse. As the entity holds full ownership over the virtual assets, expropriation risks befalling on individuals appear to be impossible within such a structure. When it comes to a decentralized metaverse, the more decentralized the metaverse is, the more rights pertaining to ownership the individual can acquire. Users are able to manage digital assets themselves in the decentralized metaverse, often in the form of (non-)fungible tokens[28] on a public blockchain.[29] Hence, upon

---

[22] Salacuse (2013), pp. 138, 139. Also see Tosun (2020), p. 144.

[23] BITs may employ a language as "*measures having similar effect*" or "*measures tantamount to expropriation*". This language does not create an additional type of interference that would merit compensation. Also see Potočnik (2019), p. 140.

[24] Rajput (2018), p. 22.

[25] For example, in the China –UK BIT (1986) and similarly in the China – Turkey BIT (2015), the term "*expropriation*" is preferred. Please visit: https://investmentpolicy.unctad.org/international-investment-agreements/treaty-files/793/download and https://investmentpolicy.unctad.org/international-investment-agreements/treaty-files/6085/download both accessed 04.09.2024.

[26] For related sample insurance policy provision, see Kantor (2015), p. 176.

[27] Also see Chaisse and Bauer (2019), p. 585.

[28] NFTs are pieces of digital content linked to the blockchain, the digital database underpinning cryptocurrencies such as Bitcoin and Ethereum. See Lau (2022), p. 78.

[29] See Goldberg and Schär (2023), p. 3.

the assumption that the metaverse is not a ‘no man’s land[30]’ and the host state has overcome the jurisdiction problem, the risk of expropriation can arise.

Domain names[31] are a form of virtual asset[32] and are akin to a piece of real estate.[33] Virtual property comprises three attributes of the real-world assets, namely; rivalrousness, persistence, and interconnectivity. The owner of an internet address holds a rivalrous code so that only it can post content to that address. Codes are also persistent; they do not fade after each use or run on a single computer. Accessing an e-mail account from different computers can exemplify persistence. Finally, even it is proprietary, third parties can enjoy the internet address without vitiating the owner’s interest in it.[34]

The virtual assets we come across most might be domain names, email addresses, or bank accounts. A property right exists in a domain name. The registrant's (the person who registers the domain name) has an interest that can be precisely defined; it has exclusive control over the domain (includes the ability to sell the domain). Finally, similar to registration of a plot of land at the title office, the registration of a domain name has a constitutive effect. The registrant has an exclusive right, can stake claim on the domain accordingly. The transfer of the domain is carried out in reliance on the registration record. Put it another way, the transferor must be the registered the name holder for the domain name in order to initiate a transfer request.[35]

Some may raise the question of ‘under whose sovereignty do domain names or the internet reside?’ The control over the root server for the DNS system by the U.S. represented a claim to own the internet.[36] In essence, the internet was once considered to be U.S. property.[37] If we were to regard all virtual assets as situated within the U.S., the U.S. could have been the only perpetrator of seizing domains. However, the U.S. handed over the control to ICANN.[38] ICANN is a U.S.-based non-profit organization composed of stakeholders, including government

[30] In *Lau’s* view, due to multi-territorial/non-territorial nature of the metaverse, identifying the law that governs the metaverse transaction can be problematic. For detail see Lau (2022), p. 80, similarly, see Lapatoura (2022), p. 201.

[31] A unique name that forms the basis of the uniform resource locators (URLs) that people use to find resources on the Internet, see ICANN Acronyms and Terms. Available at https://www.icann.org/en/icann-acronyms-and-terms?nav-letter=d&page=1 accessed 04.09.2024.

[32] Sprankling (2014), p. 91.

[33] Fairfield (2005), p. 1055.

[34] Fairfield (2005), pp. 1054, 1055.

[35] Chein (2006), p. 1075.

[36] https://www.usnews.com/news/articles/2014/03/17/the-us-gives-the-internet-to-the-world accessed 04.09.2024.

[37] https://www.bbc.com/news/technology-37527719 accessed 04.09.2024.

[38] https://www.businessinsider.com/the-us-government-no-longer-controls-the-internet-2016-10 accessed 04.09.2024. The handover of managing the DNS system was challenged at the U.S. courts, however it was rejected by the court. For detail, please visit: https://www.bbc.com/news/technology-37526598 accessed 04.09.2024.

organizations. ICANN manages the domain name system (DNS) through a hierarchical structure under its command[39] and exercises control over the Internet Assigned Numbers Authority (IANA), the body that manages and coordinates the web's DNS.[40] Unless ICANN is still believed to operate with the oversight of the U.S. government, countries retain authority over domains, including their country code.[41]

In the *France.com* case, the French State claimed the ownership of and expropriated the domain 'France.com[42]'. The French court discussed whether the domain name could constitute, for the French State, 'an element of identity' akin to the family name of a natural person. The decision of the French court did not quell concerns about expansion of the government's power of eminent domain. By contrast, the court created a conundrum regarding the scope of eminent domain. In the court's view, the word 'French[43]' in the domain could result in the risk of confusion in the public's mind and might generate a perception that the products or services promoted in the domain were either issued from the French State or benefitted from its reputation.[44] As we will see in this chapter, one of the factors providing legitimacy to an expropriatory conduct hinges on whether the conduct serves a 'public purpose'. However, according to scholars, the nature of domain names falls short of applying such a test.[45]

The corporation 'France.com' filed an action before the Virginia courts of the United States against the French entities and based its allegation on the exemption to

---

[39] Novák (2020).

[40] IANA coordinates the DNS, for detail, please visit: https://www.iana.org/ accessed 04.09.2024.

[41] ICANN has adopted 'the principles and guidelines for the delegation and administration of country code top level domains (The Principles)'. The main principle is that ccTLD (country code Top Level Domain) policy should be set locally and the Internet naming system is a public resource in the sense that its functions must be administered in the public or common interest. Art. 4.1.1 of the Principle states that "*Ultimate public policy authority over the relevant ccTLD rests with the relevant government or public authority*" and 4.2.1 reads "*The relevant government or public authority is strongly encouraged to ensure that the ccTLD is being administered in the public interest, within the framework of its national public policy and relevant laws and regulations.*" Principles are available at https://gac.icann.org/principles-and-guidelines/public/principles-cctlds.pdf accessed 04.09.2024.

[42] https://www.theverge.com/2018/4/30/17302000/france-website-domain-name-lawsuit-french-government accessed 04.09.2024. Another expropriation of a domain name took place in Spain. "sareb.es" was expropriated by the Spanish Domain Names Authority Red.es. For detail please visit: https://www.lexology.com/library/detail.aspx?g=dd858796-c732-44bd-bb5f-65095f472af1 accessed 04.09.2024. Similarly, for instance, Information and Communication Technologies Authority of Turkey is conferred power to cancel the allocation of domain names.

[43] Please also visit: https://arstechnica.com/tech-policy/2018/04/france-seizes-france-com-from-man-whos-had-it-since-94-so-he-sues/ accessed 04.09.2024.

[44] See the judgment of 22.09.2017 of the Court of Appeal of Paris. Available at https://www.documentcloud.org/documents/4446106-Copy-20of-20the-20-Translation-20-Jugement-20of.html accessed 04.09.2024. One may need to note that disputes over domain name system (DNS) can be resolved by Uniform Domain-Name Dispute-Resolution Policy established by the ICANN.

[45] Also see Crusto (2022), p. 698.

the sovereign immunity. The Court of fourth Circuit ruled on and reversed the district court's decision, in which the district court denied the defendants' motion to dismiss that asserted entitlement to FSIA immunity.[46] The appeal court did not apply the commercial activity and expropriation exceptions to FSIA immunity.[47] In so holding, the court held that "*the French State's actions in obtaining the website in a judicial proceeding constitute a "seizure" or an "expropriation" for purposes of the FSIA's "expropriation" exception to immunity. But even if those actions did constitute an "expropriation" under the FSIA, they clearly do not constitute a "commercial activity." Rather, it is well established that a "seizure" by a foreign government constitutes a sovereign activity*".[48] Although, the suffix '.com' stands for 'commercial' and distinct from '.gov[49]', and seizure of a domain with a commercial suffix may support the argument that the French State has engaged in a commercial activity, the Court of fourth Circuit however disagreed. In the view of the court, doing so would negate France's sovereign immunity. Even if one were to suppose that the company infringed on France's exclusive personal rights and its sovereignty by using the name 'France' for its interest, the ruling of the French court over an expropriation by the country from which it received its adjudicatory power has cast a pall on the independence of the court and caused the risk of denial of justice accordingly.

In the context of PRI, even if the insurance policy provides coverage against the expropriation of domain names, the valuation of the domain name and the subrogation will be more problematic. The monetary worth of a thing is formed by the societal perception. Therefore, the valuation of a virtual property might significantly differ from that of tangible assets. Not all virtual properties can be redeemable in money. Because people predisposed to value only physical beings will assign value only to virtual things that represent or have been associated with a tangible asset.[50]

---

[46] For the court's order, please visit: https://www.state.gov/wp-content/uploads/2020/09/21.c.-France.com-order-of-dismissal-of-Le-Drian.pdf and also visit: https://jolt.law.harvard.edu/digest/france-com-inc-v-the-french-republic-fourth-circuit-holds-france-immune-from-trademark-infringement-claims and https://cases.justia.com/federal/district-courts/virginia/vaedce/1:2018cv00460/386659/1/0.pdf?ts=1525111549 all accessed 04.09.2024.

[47] In the following chapters, we will discuss the concept of sovereign immunity and Foreign Sovereign Immunities Act of the USA (FSIA) in detail.

[48] See the decision of the United States Court of Appeals for the Fourth Circuit. Available at https://cases.justia.com/federal/appellate-courts/ca4/20-1016/20-1016-2021-03-25.pdf?ts=1616697062 accessed 04.09.2024.

[49] The root level names can be in two different forms. Geographic roots indicate the country of registration as in ".us" of the United States or ".cn" of the China. Non-geographic roots, on the other hand, fall in five categories. ".edu" is short for education, ".gov" represents government and ".net" denotes internet networking facilitator, ".com" stands for commercial, and finally ".org" is the abbreviation of non-profit organization. The excessive demand to a single domain renders the ".com" domain overcrowded and generates collision problems. The solution is to bifurcate the ".com" domain and allocate new root level names. For detail, see Yee (1997).

[50] According to chattel theory, property affects the internet through real world chattel property rights in physical computers. By way of illustration, if someone hacked your personal computer to get to

8.2.3 Creeping Expropriation

Governments treat investors' property rights with some degree of care; however, such mindfulness may not necessarily stem from governments' respect for investors' rights. As of today, governments are less inclined towards or show little interest in engaging in direct expropriation.[51] The main potential drawback is that the negative perception associated with a physical takeover via explicit actions may promptly reduce the government's reputation. To avoid this and in order not to receive a political backlash in the international arena,[52] governments, without a manifest or discernible intention,[53] may gain benefits flowing from expropriation. Governments, in doing so, may use their regulatory powers that may not amount to an actual taking as the regulation enters into force; however, the effects thereof unfold over time. Besides, in such cases, losses attributed to series of events may go uncompensated. Thus, a particular weight must be accorded to forms of indirect expropriation.

Substantial deprivation and economic severity of the host state's measures are the most significant criterion in indirect expropriation analysis.[54] However, the less intrusive or depriving the act, the less it will lend itself to the expropriation analysis. An array of adjectives is used to describe forms of indirect expropriation, such as 'de facto[55]', 'disguised', 'constructive',[56] 'consequential' or 'regulatory' or 'virtual'.[57] The boundaries of creeping expropriation are not blurred,[58] on the contrary, case law[59] as well as international agreements[60] define or illustrate its meaning. In

---

your email, you would have a chattel exclusion right, See Fairfield (2005), p. 1075, also see Chein (2006), p. 1074, fn 98.

[51] Yackee (2014), p. 487. According to *Salacuse*, governments dissatisfied with the original bargains made with foreign investors rarely send their troops to seize a factory or occupy a mine. See Salacuse (2013), p. 140.

[52] Burnett and Bret (2017), p. 41.

[53] Also see Reinisch (2008), p. 172.

[54] Potočnik (2019), pp. 146–148.

[55] Measures adopted by a state, whether regulatory or not, give rise to indirect de facto expropriation if they are irreversible and permanent. See *Tecmed v. Mexico*. Similarly see *Dilaver v. Turkey*, detail of the case is available in Guide on Article 1 of Protocol No. 1 to the European Convention on Human Rights, p. 22.

[56] Marboe (2017), pp. 65–66.

[57] Newcombe and Paradell (2009), pp. 325–326, similarly see Newcombe (2005), p. 8 and Kunoy (2005), p. 474 and Salacuse (2013), p. 315.

[58] See Hoffmann (2008), p. 154.

[59] In *Generation Ukraine* case (para. 20.22), the tribunal defined creeping expropriation as "*a form of indirect expropriation with a distinctive temporal quality in the sense that it encapsulates the situation whereby a series of acts attributable to the State over a period of time culminate in the expropriatory taking of such property.*" Also in *Siemens v. Argentina, (Award, para. 263),* the tribunal described "creeping expropriation" in the following terms "*By definition, creeping expropriation refers to a process, to steps that eventually have the effect of an expropriation. If the process stops before it reaches that point, then expropriation would not occur. This does not necessarily mean that no adverse effects would have occurred. Obviously, each step must have an*

contrast to other political risks, this type of expropriation is one of its kind. In our opinion, creeping expropriation distinguishes between overt and covert forms of expropriation. It can manifest itself in ways that neither insurers nor insureds can expect. The phrase 'creeping' captures a broad spectrum of intentional[61] regulatory acts,[62] omissions,[63] combinations of the decisions and events[64] attributable to the host government, allowing the investor to retain nominal ownership of the investment,[65] however, diminishing the value of the property[66] and cumulatively

---

adverse effect but by itself may not be significant or considered an illegal act. The last step in a creeping expropriation that tilts the balance is similar to the straw that breaks the camel's back. The preceding straws may not have had a perceptible effect but are part of the process that led to the break." Available at https://jusmundi.com/en/document/decision/en-siemens-a-g-v-the-argentine-republic-award-wednesday-17th-january-2007 accessed 04.09.2024. Also see Dolzer and Schreuer (2012), p. 126.

[60]The OECD Draft Convention on the Protection of Foreign Property of 1967 ("OECD Convention") indicates a "creeping nationalisation". According to the document, interference by the host government may amount to indirect deprivation; its extent and duration are important. However, even if it is temporary, at some stage, owner may not be able to resume enjoyment of his property. Also visit: https://www.oecd-ilibrary.org/docserver/780155872321.pdf?expires=1725442612&id=id&accname=guest&checksum=D6A475D6BC75F140580D66B2048328D4 accessed 04.09.2024.

[61]In *Tippets*, the tribunal stressed the effects of the actions rather than the intention and stated that "*While assumption of control over property by a government does not automatically and immediately justify a conclusion that the property has been taken by the government, thus requiring compensation under international law, such a conclusion is warranted whenever events demonstrate that the owner was deprived of fundamental rights of ownership and it appears that this deprivation is not merely ephemeral. The intent of the government is less important than the effects of the measures on the owner, and the form of the measures of control or interference is less important than the reality of their impact.*" Available at http://translex.uni-koeln.de/231000/_/iran-us-claims-tribunal-tippetts-abbett-mccarthy-stratton-v-tams-affa-6-iran-us-ctr-at-219-et-seq/ accessed 04.09.2024. Also see Hoffmann (2008), p. 158, similarly, Ratner (2008), p. 506 and Aldrich (1994), p. 603.

[62]Case law is believed to rely on a combination of actions and omissions. See Hoffmann (2008), p. 161, also see Salacuse (2013), p. 139.

[63]As *Newcombe* states, expropriation need not take place as a positive act of the host country. Omissions such as not issuing a license/permit that is vital for the operation could be expropriatory. See Newcombe and Paradell (2009), pp. 337–338. In *Olguín v. Paraguay, (para. 84)* the tribunal found omissions insufficient to deem indirect expropriation. In the tribunal's word "*For an expropriation to occur, there must be actions that can be considered reasonably appropriate for producing the effect of depriving the affected party of the property it owns, in such a way that whoever performs those actions will acquire, directly or indirectly, control, or at least the fruits of the expropriated property. Expropriation therefore requires a teleologically driven action for it to occur; omissions, however egregious they may be, are not sufficient for it to take place.*" Available at https://www.italaw.com/sites/default/files/case-documents/ita0587.pdf accessed 04.09.2024.

[64]See *Tradex v. Albania*, available at https://www.italaw.com/sites/default/files/case-documents/ita0871.pdf accessed 04.09.2024. See Wagner (2012), p. 104.

[65]In *Middle East Cement v. Egypt*, the tribunal stated the following "*When measures are taken by a State the effect of which is to deprive the investor of the use and benefit of his investment even though he may retain nominal ownership of the respective rights being the investment, the measures are often referred to as a 'creeping' or 'indirect' expropriation or, as in the BIT, as measures "the*

preventing the owner from substantially enjoying the benefits of the investment[67] or losing the attributes of ownership.[68]

The pitfall in this type of risk is that, in the end of a list of a governments' series of actions[69] or omissions, none of which separately constitute an expropriation, the investor may still be restrained from enjoying the investment (reasonably expected economic benefit[70]) however, they may have an economic impact on the investment such that the investment may not operate profitably.[71] Through onerous regulations[72] or taxation[73] upon the investor or the project, the host government gradually attains a result that formal expropriation achieves immediately.[74]

---

effect of which is tantamount to expropriation." See para. 107. Available at https://www.italaw.com/sites/default/files/case-documents/ita0531.pdf accessed 04.09.2024.

[66]Born (2021), p. 513.

[67]For the detailed explanation of substantial deprivation, see Newcombe and Paradell (2009), pp. 344–345. Some policies cover the risk of depriving the owner of its ability to manage, use, or control its property in a meaningful way. See Soopramanien (2017), p. 599. Also see Kantor (2015), p. 179 and see Burnett and Bret (2017), p. 41, finally, see Rubins and Kinsella (2005), p. 12.

[68]In *LG&E Energy v. Argentina* (para. 199), the tribunal did not agree that the investor was deprived of ownership and held that "*it cannot be said that Claimants lost control over their shares in the licensees, even though the value of the shares may have fluctuated during the economic crisis, or that they were unable to direct the day-to-day operations of the licensees in a manner different than before the measures were implemented.*" Available at https://www.italaw.com/sites/default/files/case-documents/ita0460.pdf accessed 04.09.2024.

[69]Governments opt to take a series of actions that have the cumulative effect of destroying the value of the investment. See Norton (2004), pp. 96–97. ILC art. 15 deals with series of actions of states and provides "*1. The breach of an international obligation by a State through a series of actions or omissions defined in aggregate as wrongful occurs when the action or omission occurs which, taken with the other actions or omissions, is sufficient to constitute the wrongful act. 2. In such a case, the breach extends over the entire period starting with the first of the actions or omissions of the series and lasts for as long as these actions or omissions are repeated and remain not in conformity with the international obligation.*"

[70]See *Metalclad v. Mexico,* available at https://www.italaw.com/sites/default/files/case-documents/ita0510.pdf accessed 04.09.2024.

[71]One of the tests the tribunal in *POPE & TALBOT v. Canada* applied was whether the regulation made it impossible for the firm to operate at a profit, the tribunal came to conclusion that the interference did not tantamount to expropriation. See p. 35 fn 80. The case is available at https://www.italaw.com/sites/default/files/case-documents/ita0674.pdf accessed 04.09.2024. Also see Introduction to regulatory expropriations in international law and case Summaries. New York University Environmental Law Journal, p. 3.

[72]A discriminatory regulation, such as imposing a levy, may remarkably diminish the profits gained from the investment or may render the investment impractical to operate. As a result of a dramatic reduction in the value of the investment, the investor may wish to transfer its rights at a bargain price.

[73]In *Yukos* expropriation however, Russia relied on Yukos noncompliance with tax law by failing to pay taxes deemed expropriatory. Kantor (2015), pp. 183–184.

[74]Salacuse (2016), p. 73.

A variety of interference attributable to the host country[75] may give rise to creeping expropriation, including the appointment of new management to the investment[76] or cancelling or refusing to renew a license[77] or a permit,[78] adopting fiscal measures such as imposing additional tax,[79] increasing royalties,[80] introducing export quota limits,[81] harassing the key personnel[82] of the investment, conducting

[75] Harvard Draft Convention on the International Responsibility of States for Injuries to Aliens defines in detail the indirect expropriation According to Article 10/3- (a) A "taking of property" includes not only an outright taking of property but also any such unreasonable interference with the use, enjoyment, or disposal of property as to justify an inference that the owner thereof will not be able to use, enjoy, or dispose of the property within a reasonable period of time after the inception of such interference. (b) A "taking of the use of property" includes not only an outright taking of use but also any unreasonable interference with the use or enjoyment of property for a limited period of time. Please visit: https://legal.un.org/ilc/documentation/english/a_cn4_217.pdf accessed 04.09.2024. For other draft international regulations, see Newcombe and Paradell (2009), pp. 328–331.

[76] In *Sedco v. NIOC* case, the seizure of control by appointment of temporary managers was considered to ripen into an outright taking of title. Available at https://jusmundi.com/en/document/decision/en-sedco-inc-v-national-iranian-oil-company-and-the-islamic-republic-of-iran-award-award-no-419-128-129-2-thursday-30th-march-1989 accessed 04.09.2024, similarly, see *Starrett Housing v. Iran.*

[77] In *Middle East Cement v. Egypt*, the tribunal had no difficulty in finding that revocation of free-zone license and prohibition of import was indirect taking. Also see Dolzer and Schreuer (2012), p. 109. Also see Burnett and Bret (2017), pp. 41–44

[78] In *Metalclad v. Mexico (para. 107),* the tribunal found that "the *absence of a timely, orderly or substantive basis for the denial by the Municipality of the local construction permit, amount to an indirect expropriation*".

[79] In *Telenor v. Hungary*, (para. 70) a special levy on all telecommunication service providers were introduced, however, according to the tribunal, "the *determinative factors were the intensity and duration of the economic deprivation suffered by the investor as the result of them" and in the levy was not intensive amount to call expropriation.* Available at https://www.italaw.com/sites/default/files/case-documents/ita0858.pdf accessed 04.09.2024. Also see Burnett and Bret (2017), pp. 48–49.

[80] In *Revere Copper v. OPIC* case, the Government of Jamaica substantially increased the royalties. The case is available at https://jusmundi.com/en/document/decision/en-revere-copper-and-brass-inc-v-overseas-private-investment-corporation-award-thursday-24th-august-1978 accessed 04.09.2024.

[81] This form is deemed "bluntest instrument" for limitation of investor's playing ground. See Burnett and Bret (2017), pp. 51–52.

[82] An investor's technical or managerial personnel may carry out a crucial role in the establishment, maintenance, management or enjoyment of the investment. On the other hand, governments, in order to create more jobs and protect national security, may require investors to impose limits on the use of human resources from the home country. Such limitation may constitute a political risk. Personnel of the investor should be permitted to enter and reside within the host country. Art. 11 of the ECT employs a term of "key personnel" and states: "(1) *A Contracting Party shall, subject to its laws and regulations relating to the entry, stay and work of natural persons, examine in good faith requests by Investors of another Contracting Party, and key personnel who are employed by such Investors or by Investments of such Investors, to enter and remain temporarily in its Area to engage in activities connected with the making or the development, management, maintenance, use, enjoyment or disposal of relevant Investments, including the provision of advice or key technical*

legal proceedings, prosecuting, arresting, deporting,[83] or blocking access to the investment.[84]

Some scholars divide this type of expropriation into three categories. *Factor market policies* encompass restrictions on the firm's factor inputs, minimum wage laws and hiring restrictions are typical examples of interference with employment practices. *Product market policies* such as increasing value added taxes and export taxes influence the sale of the investor's output. Finally, the third category is the other *restrictions on the investment's ownership and control.*[85] For creeping expropriation, the deprivation of ownership should be significant, substantial[86] and be justified with whether it has a severe economic impact on the investment.[87] However, it may be difficult to link a perceived expropriation action with its economic impact. A decline in profit may not be entirely attributable to recently imposed restriction.[88] Hence, the definition of creeping expropriation should be broad enough to encompass every form of sovereign conduct,[89] and the presence of indirect expropriation should be determined on a case-by-case basis.[90]

A case-by case fact finding approach has also been adopted by several treaties.[91] The need for such a technique stems from two facts; first, the occurrence of a series

services. (2) A Contracting Party shall permit Investors of another Contracting Party which have Investments in its Area, and Investments of such Investors, to employ any key person of the Investor's or the Investment's choice regardless of nationality and citizenship provided that such key person has been permitted to enter, stay and work in the Area of the former Contracting Party and that the employment concerned conforms to the terms, conditions and time limits of the permission granted to such key person." Charter does not identify the term "key personnel" therefore provides an ample room for controversy as to its meaning which, on a case-by-case basis should be interpreted.

[83] In *Biwater Gauff v. Tanzania*, deportation of the senior staff was one of the series actions of the host state the occurrence of which amounted to an indirect expropriation, available at https://www.italaw.com/sites/default/files/case-documents/ita0095.pdf accessed 04.09.2024. Also see *Biloune v. Ghana case.*

[84] Newcombe and Paradell (2009), pp. 327–328.

[85] Allen and Viscusi (1976), p. 159.

[86] Also see Hoffmann (2008), p. 158.

[87] In *Generation Ukraine, (para. 20.32)* in the tribunal's wording "*the conduct of the Kyiv City State Administration does not come close to creating a persistent or irreparable obstacle to the Claimant's use, enjoyment or disposal of its investment*". Also see Sprankling (2014), p. 279.

[88] Allen and Viscusi (1976), p. 159.

[89] See *Waste Management* case, para. 145, available at https://www.italaw.com/sites/default/files/case-documents/ita0900.pdf accessed 04.09.2024.

[90] For instance, in *POPE & TALBOT v. Canada* case, diminished profits of the claimant due to the Export Control Regime did not rise to an expropriation (creeping or otherwise). For a similar conclusion, see *PSEG v. Turkey.*

[91] Annex B of the 2012 U.S. Model Bilateral Investment Treaty (BIT) requires a case-by-case, fact-based inquiry that considers, among other factors: (i) the economic impact of the government action, although the fact that an action or series of actions by a Party has an adverse effect on the economic value of an investment, standing alone, does not establish that an indirect expropriation has occurred; (ii) the extent to which the government action interferes with distinct, reasonable

of incremental actions rather than a singular act. Decision-making in a series of incremental actions requires the observance of each event. Second, the polycentric decision making of international law: simply put, arbitration tribunals are not constrained by decisions of prior tribunals and inconsistent interpretations pose legal impediments before a cohesive body of case law.[92]

What matters in this kind of expropriation is the purpose that the regulation serves, whether the means employed are proportionate[93] and reasonable to the ends pursued, and whether there are less restrictive alternatives available.[94] It should be noted that a government's ordinary exercise of regulatory power (police power)[95] differs from this disguised, regulatory, or sneaky taking.[96] In addition, non-discriminatory, non-arbitrary and transparent legal measures designed and applied to protect legitimate public welfare objectives, such as health, safety, and

---

investment-backed expectations; and (iii) the character of the government action. Treaty is available at https://ustr.gov/sites/default/files/BIT%20text%20for%20ACIEP%20Meeting.pdf accessed 04.09.2024. Similarly, see article 5(2) of the China-Turkey BIT 2015, article 6(4)(b) of the Hungary - Oman BIT (2022) and Annex II of the ACIA. Hungary - Oman BIT is available at https://investmentpolicy.unctad.org/international-investment-agreements/treaty-files/6443/download accessed 04.09.2024. Finally, for the comparison of Annexes of ACIA and the US. Model BIT see Cotula (2015), pp. 284–285. Scholars opine that *Railroad Development Corp* case, provided the basis for the first arbitral award that applied the expropriation annex. Annex 10-Cof the relevant BIT (Central American Free Trade Agreement 'CAFTA' was almost identical with the Annex B of the US Model BIT. The tribunal concluded that "*the effect on Claimants' investment does not rise to the level of an indirect expropriation.*" Para. 152. Also see Cotula (2015), p. 283.

[92]Also see Sprankling (2014), p. 278.

[93]Also see Sprankling (2014), pp. 284–285.

[94]Salacuse (2016), p. 421.

[95]Dolzer and Schreuer (2012), p. 121. Police power will be discussed in depth under the heading of 'Expropriation in The Era of Climate Change'.

[96]In *Philip Morris v. Uruguay*, Uruguay introduced several measures including the adoption of a single presentation requirement "the SPR" precluding tobacco manufacturers from marketing more than one variant of cigarette per brand family, and the increase in the size of graphic health warnings appearing on cigarette packages. According to claimant, the SPR banned some variants of those manufactured and diminished the value of the remaining variants; both measures impacted the value of the company and resulted in deprivation of intellectual property rights. Sovereigns exercise their prerogatives through regulatory means some of which are effective and crucial for the maintenance of public order, health or morality. The question is whether a compensation can be due as far as measures of similar nature are concerned. In the tribunal's view, a partial loss of the profits cannot confer an expropriatory character on the measure, and the measures in question were taken bona fide, non-discriminatory and proportionate and thus satisfied these conditions. Therefore, the tribunal came to the conclusion that the measures were a valid exercise of police powers. See paras. 9–12, 286, 295, 305, 306, 307. Available at https://www.italaw.com/sites/default/files/case-documents/italaw7417.pdf accessed 04.09.2024. According to one author, sovereigns presumably pursue public interest in their measures, however, this does not necessarily mean that virtually all non-discriminatory measures enacted under due process must be characterized as non-compensable regulations. By contrast, this radical approach must be abandoned and there must be a nuance between non-compensable regulations and compensable expropriations. Attention should be paid to the degree of the impact in defining the character of the measure. See Radi (2018), pp. 78–79.

environment, do not constitute indirect expropriation.[97] Takings that are temporary or do not depriving investors of the economic use of the property or the proprietary rights do not fall within the scope of this political risk.[98] *Gilbert* exemplifies a case where the host state confiscated instruments of a music group since the promoter did not sign certain required documents to permit local customs authorities to authorize the re-export of the group's musical instruments. The insured believed that compensation for temporary deprivation was available and took the dispute to arbitration which could have been resolved prior to issuance of the policy if temporary deprivation was a real concern for the insured at the outset.[99]

In *Revere Copper (insured) v. OPIC*, the insured believed that its operations had failed due to the imposition of a 7.5 percent levy on aluminum by the Jamaican government. In the mind of the insured, the passage of the levy led to a creeping expropriation through abrogating fundamental rights secured for the investor, which it relied upon in making the investment. According to OPIC, it was simply a form of commercial failure rather than expropriation. After OPIC's refusal to the request for compensation, the insured took the case to arbitral proceedings. The tribunal assessed the relevant provisions of the insurance contract[100] and identified the nature

---

[97] Art. 6 of the Bilateral Agreement for the Promotion and Protection of Investments between the Government of the United Kingdom of Great Britain and Northern Ireland and Republic of Colombia (2010) enunciates as follows; "*For the purposes of this Agreement, it is understood that: (a) indirect expropriation results from a measure or series of measures of a Contracting Party having an equivalent effect to direct expropriation without formal transfer of title or outright seizure; (b) the determination of whether a measure or series of measures of a Contracting Party constitute indirect expropriation requires a case-by case, fact based inquiry into various factors including, but not limited to the scope of the measure or series of measures and their interference with the reasonable and distinguishable expectations concerning the investment; (c) non-discriminatory measures that the Contracting Parties take for reasons of public purpose or social interest (which shall have a meaning compatible with that of "public purpose") including for reasons of public health, safety, and environmental protection, which are taken in good faith, which are not arbitrary, and which are not disproportionate in light of their purpose, shall not constitute indirect expropriation*". Please visit: https://investmentpolicy.unctad.org/international-investment-agreements/treaty-files/3253/download 04.09.2024. For a similar article see Art. 6 of the Turkey - Bangladesh BIT(2012) https://investmentpolicy.unctad.org/international-investment-agreements/treaty-files/274/download accessed 04.09.2024.

[98] Many international tribunals recognized only "substantial" or "significant" deprivations as expropriations. See Appleton (2002), pp. 45, 46.

[99] Gilbert (1986), p. 412.

[100] Section 1.15 of the contract reads as: "The term '*Expropriatory Action' means any action which is taken, authorized, ratified or condoned by the Government of the Project Country, commencing during the Guaranty Period, with or without compensation therefor, and which for a period of one year directly results in preventing:….. (b) the Investor from effectively exercising its fundamental rights with respect to the Foreign Enterprise either as shareholder or as creditor, as the case may be, acquired as a result of the Investment; provided, however, that rights acquired solely as a result of any undertaking or agreement with the Government of the Project Country shall not be considered fundamental rights merely because they are acquired from such undertaking or agreement; or "(c) the Investor from disposing of the Securities or any rights accruing therefrom; or "(d) the Foreign Enterprise from exercising effective control over the use or disposition of a*

of the investment contract. The tribunal believed that the impact of the levy was of considerable significance and concluded that the levy constituted a repudiation by the government of its commitments, resulting in the investor being deprived of the ability to exercise effective control over its investment.[101]

8.2.4 *Legality of Expropriation*

8.2.4.1 In General

International law may not stand in the way of a legal taking by the government; however, it may place some limitations on exercising such rights. Throughout the twentieth century, whether the mere non-payment of compensation would affect the lawfulness of expropriation was highly debated.[102] In the 1970s, countries were less inclined to provide compensation. By way of example, in 1973, General Assembly of the United Nations adopted 'Resolution on Permanent Sovereignty over Natural Resources ('Resolution 3171')' which among other things, stated "*the application of the principle of nationalization carried out by States, as an expression of their sovereignty in order to safeguard their natural resources, implies that each State is entitled to determine the amount of possible compensation and the mode of payment, and that any dispute which might arise should be settled in accordance with the national legislation of each State carrying out such measures*".

The notion of 'possible compensation' as well as settlement of the dispute in accordance with municipal law was abandoning the investor at the mercy of the host state. The language employed did not soften in the Resolution 3281 adopted in the following year.[103] Over the years, opinions on this issue have changed, and as of today, it is less disputed. Hence, an investor that has not received compensation in

substantial portion of its property or from constructing the Project or operating the same.... The abrogation, impairment, repudiation or breach by the Government of the Project Country of any undertaking, agreement or contract relating to the Project shall be considered an Expropriatory Action only if it constitutes Expropriatory Action only if it constitutes Expropriatory Action in accordance with the criteria set forth in this section." For the summary of the case, see Kantor et al. (2011), pp. 740–793.

[101] The tribunal held that: "*The effects of the Jamaican Government's actions in repudiating its long-term commitments to RJA have substantially the same impact on effective control over use and operation as if the properties were themselves conceded by a concession contract that was repudiated.*" See Kantor et al. (2011), p. 766.

[102] Marboe (2017), pp. 56–65, 143.

[103] Art. 2(2)(c) of the Resolution stated that "*each state has the right to nationalize, expropriate or transfer ownership of foreign property, in which case appropriate compensation should be paid by the State adopting such measures, taking into account its relevant laws and regulations and all circumstances that the State considers pertinent. In any case where the question of compensation gives rise to a controversy, it shall be settled under the domestic law of the nationalizing State and by its tribunals, unless it is freely and mutually agreed by all States concerned that other peaceful means be sought on the basis of the sovereign equality of States and in accordance with the*

itself is likely to render the expropriation concerned unlawful. The presence of a 'compensation offer' by the host state whether in good faith or not, should not result in otherwise either.

8.2.4.2 Significance of Legality

Scholars provide an inspirational example as to the legality of expropriation, according to which expropriation only applies to the 'nuclear warheads' of government regulation, in the end of which, waste can be laid to the investment without compensation.[104] Some scholars' propositions stand for the idea that a mere 'deprivation' or 'taking,' does not, by itself, constitute expropriation. According to the same scholars, a two-fold analysis must be conducted. In the first stage, the nature or magnitude of the interference must be identified to understand whether the acts of the state constitute a taking. If the findings justify a taking, in the second stage, it is determined whether the taking rises to the level of an expropriation.[105] Needless to say, when expropriation is identified, its legality will rest upon whether the taking was for a public purpose,[106] nondiscriminatory,[107] accompanied by adequate,[108]

---

principle of free choice of means" Please visit: https://investmentpolicy.unctad.org/international-investment-agreements/treaty-files/2778/download accessed 04.09.2024.

[104] Weiler (2003), p. 253.

[105] Paulsson and Douglas (2004), pp. 148, 149 also see Salacuse (2013), p. 315.

[106] Art. 4 of General Assembly resolution 1803 (XVII) of 14 December 1962, "Permanent sovereignty over natural resources states" Nationalization, *expropriation or requisitioning shall be based on grounds or reasons of public utility, security or the national interest which are recognized as overriding purely individual or private interests, both domestic and foreign.*" See https://www.ohchr.org/Documents/ProfessionalInterest/resources.pdf accessed 04.09.2024. In case law, the meaning given to public purpose varies. For instance, in *BP v. Libya*, (para. 111) in the words of arbitrator "*expropriation was made for purely extraneous political reasons and was arbitrary and discriminatory in character.*" available at https://jusmundi.com/en/document/decision/en-bp-exploration-company-libya-limited-v-government-of-the-libyan-arab-republic-award-wednesday-10th-october-1973 accessed 04.09.2024. And In *ADC v. Hungary*, the tribunal required state to demonstrate the genuine interest in its action. Therefore, the burden of proof de facto reversed. Available at https://www.italaw.com/sites/default/files/case-documents/ita0006.pdf accessed 04.09.2024. Also see Newcombe and Paradell (2009), pp. 370–373 and similarly, Reinisch (2008), p. 186 and Hoffmann (2008), p. 153.

[107] Nationalization of an industry owned (where the ownership relies on a historic pattern) by a national or ethnic group may not be discriminatory. See Newcombe and Paradell (2009), pp. 373–374.

[108] A payment that is equal to the 'fair market value' of the property taken. See Merrill (2002), p. 112. According to *Salacuse*, this term is difficult to define, and adequacy exists in the eye of the beholder, please see Salacuse (2016), p. 557. In case law, some tribunals, to satisfy the legal requirement, sought an offer of appropriate payment rather than actual payment. See Reinisch (2008), pp. 199–200, See Sabahi (2011), p. 92.

prompt[109] and effective[110] compensation[111] and made in accordance with due process of law.[112] Treaties provide almost identical conditions,[113] and expropriation is considered lawful if it complies with those conditions. Tendencies of the developing countries, however, are to the contrary. According to a theory which is founded on a quasi-national equity, nationals and foreigners should receive the same treatment and compensation should thus be determined by reference to the domestic laws of the host state.[114]

---

[109] The payment must be without undue delay. Some scholars also opine that the word 'prompt' may also denote a payment that also includes interest from the time of the taking to the time of payment. See Merrill (2002), p. 112.

[110] Payment must be made in a currency freely exchangeable into such a currency and eligible for repatriation. See Merrill (2002), p. 112. If the government makes payment in bonds, bonds must have a market value when issued equal to the required compensation award. See Hu (1979), p. 64.

[111] This formulation is called 'Hull formula' and was derived from the correspondence between U.S. Secretary of State Cordell Hull and Mexican Minister of Foreign Affairs Eduardo Hay. Secretary Hull laid out a principle that the host state owes adequate, effective, and prompt compensation to the foreign investor upon the occurrence of the expropriation of its asset. See Salacuse (2016), p. 77, see Reinisch (2008), p. 196, and Sabahi (2011), p. 61, also see Simmons (2012), p. 205 and Newcombe and Paradell (2009), p. 396, see Appleton (2002), p. 39 see Merrill (2002), p. 112, Marzal (2021), p. 264 and finally, see Salacuse (2013), p. 317.

[112] Scholars opine that expropriation must be exercised in a manner pursuant to conditions laid down by the international law and the notion of 'due process' implies the legality of the measure. In order to ensure due process, the measure in question must be based upon domestic law, taken in accordance with procedures prescribed in the Constitution or (relevant) laws, subject to the possibility of appeal, and not applied in an arbitrary manner. See Verwey and Schrijver (1984), p. 9. Other scholars opine that due process is the expression of the minimum standard under customary international law and the requirement of fair and equal treatment. See Dolzer and Schreuer (2012), p. 100. The criteria of due process are satisfied if the process is in conformation with municipal law which does not depart from international standards and also the case can be reviewed by independent and impartial adjudicators. See Potočnik (2019), pp. 154–155. In *ADC v. Hungary*, (para. 376), the tribunal determined that due process of law, in the expropriation context, demands an actual and substantive legal procedure for a foreign investor to raise its claims against the depriving actions already taken or about to be taken against it. Some basic legal mechanisms, such as reasonable advance notice, a fair hearing and an unbiased and impartial adjudicator to assess the actions in dispute, are expected to be readily available and accessible to the investor to make the legal procedure meaningful. In general, the legal procedure must be of a nature to grant an affected investor a reasonable chance within a reasonable time to claim its legitimate rights and have its claims heard. If no legal procedure of such nature exists at all, the argument that "the actions are taken under due process of law" rings hollow. Also see Newcombe and Paradell (2009), pp. 375–376, similarly Salacuse and Sullivan (2005), p. 87, Also see Reinisch (2008), p. 194 and finally, see Sprankling (2014), p. 267.

[113] For instance, art. 13(1) of the Energy Charter Treaty states that "*Investments of Investors of a Contracting Party in the Area of any other Contracting Party shall not be nationalised, expropriated or subjected to a measure or measures having effect equivalent to nationalisation or expropriation (hereinafter referred to as "Expropriation") except where such Expropriation is: (a) for a purpose which is in the public interest; (b) not discriminatory; (c) carried out under due process of law; and (d) accompanied by the payment of prompt, adequate and effective compensation.*"

[114] Ochoa (2008), p. 127.

That being said, Khachvani suggests that an expropriation lacking compensation can be lawful, the scholar supports this opinion with the hierarchy in the norms. According to the scholar, the obligation to pay compensation in accordance with a treaty is a primary norm, whereas the duty to pay compensation as a modality of reparation is a secondary norm, distinct from the former, and applies when a breach of a primary obligation is established. While the act of taking itself is legitimate, (for instance when exercised to protect public health or welfare), the illegality may stem from one of the constituent acts comprising the taking (for instance mere lack of prompt, adequate and effective compensation) and reparation must establish a situation wiping out the consequences of the irregularity in that particular illegal act.[115]

The legality of expropriation may be an irrelevant factor in influencing the amount of the compensation. According to scholars, the distinction between whether expropriation is legal or illegal may be of relevance for certain reasons. Apart from states' reluctance to take actions that are deemed illegal, in terms of PRI, prior to making claims, insurance policies may require the taking be illegal under international law. The illegality may also provide alternative means of reparation such as the right to demand restitution of property.[116] Besides, an illegal taking hampers the furtherance of public welfare and may have severe financial as well as political consequences. The host state, by committing an illegal taking, may expose itself to investment arbitration commenced whether by the foreign investor or PRI provider as its successor. Taxpayers of the state will not be pleased once they ascertain that the amount the state is obliged to pay, as per the arbitral award, could have been lesser if the expropriation were legal.

Some may believe that in the event of an expropriation, prior to commencing arbitration or seeking diplomatic assistance or intervention, an investor must first exhaust local remedies and claim that expropriation was illegal.[117] In the presence of PRI, a three-party settlement with the host government is possible.[118] The initial approach may rely on the assumption that mitigating the loss is the insured's obligation. However, the sovereign risks, by their nature, are neither predictable nor reversible. To put the matter another way, particularly, an illegal taking is not determined in the blink of an eye; governments do bear in mind investor's nationality, the effects on bilateral relations, reputation loss, and the economic consequences of the taking. Rather than payment of compensation, governments may also wish to allocate the money for the welfare of nationals, by doing so economic consequences of the illegal taking spread over time, at least until an arbitration award is rendered in the investor's favor.

Compensation distinguishes expropriation from other form of taking, such as confiscation and forfeiture, which are legal seizures exercised under criminal law

---

[115] Khachvani (2017), pp. 385–403 also see Burgstaller and Ketcheson (2017), pp. 197, 202.

[116] Rubins and Kinsella (2005), p. 8.

[117] Allen and Viscusi (1976), p. 154.

[118] HELLER (1978), p. 232.

where compensation is not due if the taking is legal.[119] Governments may wish to benefit from a list of acts,[120] at the end of which the taking occurs and whereby the value of the asset gradually decreases. The legality of the state conduct complained of has a direct effect on the scope of investor's claim. In lawful expropriation, up until 2006, as a solidified norm, the valuation date taken into consideration by arbitration tribunals was the date of expropriation. However, international guidelines[121] and scholars,[122] point out that the appraisal of the investment can be made just before the occurrence of the taking. The influence on valuation begins as public receives knowledge of the regulatory/expropriatory legal act/measure,[123] and after the taking, a reduction in the value of the asset is highly likely. To prevent such an end, appreciation can be made according to the value of the asset on the eve of the day on which the taking was carried out. For instance, if the taking occurred via a decree, the value on the eve of the day on which the decree was issued. Besides, such measures, in most cases are not rapidly introduced. Impending measures are open to public access during the drafting phase; hence, in such a case the valuation date should be the date of whichever is earlier.[124]

In unlawful expropriation however, *ADC v. Hungary*[125] sets a threshold for the reference date. With this case, the valuation date was shifted to the date of award[126]

---

[119] Burnett and Bret (2017), p. 40.

[120] The tribunal in the *Yukos* (para. 1761) held that "*in the event of an expropriation through a series of actions, the date of the expropriation is the date on which the incriminated actions first lead to a deprivation of the investor's property that crossed the threshold and became tantamount to an expropriation*". Available at https://www.italaw.com/sites/default/files/case-documents/italaw3279.pdf accessed 04.09.2024.

[121] Art. 4(3) of The World Bank Guidelines on the Treatment of Foreign Direct Investment is as follows "*Compensation will be deemed "adequate" if it is based on the fair market value of the taken asset as such value is determined immediately before the time at which the taking occurred or the decision to take the asset became publicly known.*" The Energy Charter Treaty also introduced a definition of "valuation date" which bears in mind the value of investment either before the expropriation or it has become publicly known.

[122] For detail, see Burgstaller and Ketcheson (2017), pp. 201–203.

[123] See Marboe (2017), pp. 135–136.

[124] See *Mobil Cerro v. Venezuela* case, available at https://www.italaw.com/sites/default/files/case-documents/italaw4011.pdf accessed 04.09.2024.

[125] See *ADC v. Hungary* and *Siemens v. Argentina*, para. 352. And see Marboe (2017), pp. 84–85.

[126] In this case, (paras. 496, 497) the tribunal held that "*The present case is almost unique among decided cases concerning the expropriation by States of foreign owned property, since the value of the investment after the date of expropriation (1 January 2002) has risen very considerably while other arbitrations that apply the Chorzów Factory standard all invariably involve scenarios where there has been a decline in the value of the investment after regulatory interference. It is for this reason that application of the restitution standard by various arbitration tribunals has led to use of the date of the expropriation as the date for the valuation of damages. However, in the present, sui generis, type of case the application of the Chorzów Factory standard requires that the date of valuation should be the date of the Award and not the date of expropriation, since this is what is necessary to put the Claimants in the same position as if the expropriation had not been committed. This kind of approach is not without support. The PCIJ in the Chorzów Factory case stated that*

aiming to prevent unjust enrichment, ensure proper restitution, and safeguard awarded damage from exchange rate fluctuations.[127] Scholars argue that, although the amount investor would have received for a lawful expropriation serves as a floor, the investor may also benefit from any increase in the value of its investment following the expropriation date, assuming there is an increase.[128]

8.2.5 The Effect of Climate Change and Pandemic on Sovereignty

8.2.5.1 Environmental Concerns

8.2.5.1.1 Introduction to Environmental Law

The property of an alien is not a 'holy land' and neither are property rights absolute. Ownership of an immovable asset in a foreign country may entail certain responsibilities or sacrifices towards the society of the country in question, most of which become due when environment and public health are concerned.[129] In the twenty-first century, the acceleration in human-generated (anthropogenic)environmental pollution stands as a scientific fact. Despite nature being home to millions of species,[130] the activities of one species (us) have been causing irreparable and undeniable harm on environment.

In response to the fears of doomsday scenarios, states-the regulatory device of humanity- have introduced environmental laws with the goal of preserving biological diversity, prevention of global warming, combating desertification, deforestation and protecting water sources and agricultural fields. In the contemporary environmental agenda, the most addressed and debated topic is climate change. Scholars point out that international climate change law begins with article 2 of the UNFCCC.[131] Nevertheless, the fight against climate change has spawned the emergence of a binding multilateral treaty.

---

damages are "not necessarily limited to the value of the undertaking at the moment of dispossession" (Page 47 of the Judgment)." Available at https://www.italaw.com/sites/default/files/case-documents/ita0006.pdf accessed 04.09.2024. Also see Sabahi (2011), pp. 12, 62 and similarly, Newcombe and Paradell (2009), pp. 382–383.

[127] Saldarriaga and Kantor (2009), p. 200.

[128] Burgstaller and Ketcheson (2017), p. 208.

[129] Newcombe (2005), p. 22.

[130] It is estimated that 8.7 million species of plants and animals exist. For detail please visit: https://education.nationalgeographic.org/resource/biodiversity accessed 04.09.2024.

[131] Related part of the article is as follows "*The ultimate objective of this Convention and any related legal instruments that the Conference of the Parties may adopt is to achieve, in accordance with the relevant provisions of the Convention, stabilization of greenhouse gas concentrations in the atmosphere at a level that would prevent dangerous anthropogenic interference with the climate*

Whereas the Paris Agreement[132] stands as the first legally binding international treaty that aims to combat climate change, Kyoto Protocol[133] and other regulations were mostly constructed in the form of soft law[134] and carried a hortatory tone.[135] The Paris Agreement was adopted on 12 December 2015 at the twenty-first session of the Conference of the Parties ('COP 21' in short)[136] to the UNFCCC.[137] The

---

system." The Convention is available at https://unfccc.int/resource/docs/convkp/conveng.pdf accessed 04.09.2024. Also see Firger (2013), p. 176.

[132]It entered into force in 2016, and as of today 194 Parties (193 states plus the European Union) have joined the Paris Agreement. The main goal of the Agreement is specified in article 2(a) of the Agreement which is as follows; "*Holding the increase in the global average temperature to well below 2 °C above pre-industrial levels and pursuing efforts to limit the temperature increase to 1.5 °C above pre-industrial levels…*" Agreement is available at https://unfccc.int/files/meetings/paris_nov_2015/application/pdf/paris_agreement_english_.pdf Also see https://www.un.org/en/climatechange/paris-agreement both accessed 04.09.2024.

[133]The parties to Kyoto protocol were expected to commit transitioning their economies to limit and reduce greenhouse gases by adopting regulations on mitigation. Kyoto Protocol Reference Manual is available at https://unfccc.int/sites/default/files/08_unfccc_kp_ref_manual.pdf Protocol is available at https://unfccc.int/sites/default/files/resource/docs/cop3/l07a01.pdf#page=24 Also visit: https://unfccc.int/kyoto_protocol all accessed 04.09.2024. Prior to the birth of the Kyoto protocol in 1997, several regulatory attempts were carried out. The Rio Declaration (Rio Declaration on Environment and Development) was adopted in 1992 and the Global Pact for the Environment, as indicated by its name, aimed to become a legally binding international treaty that enshrines the general principles of environmental law, was presented at the United Nations General Assembly in 2017. However, in the presence of the only hard law such as the Paris Agreement, we opt not to explore texts that embody elements of soft law. For detail and on the Rio Declaration and the Global Pact for the Environment, please see Marisi (2020), p. 40 et seq.

[134]Soft law is nonbinding in character and does not include coercive mechanisms. For the advantages and disadvantages of environmental soft law, see Marisi (2020), p. 35 et seq.

[135]The 1972 United Nations Conference on the Environment in Stockholm (Stockholm Conference) is recognized as the birth of international environment law. It is the first world conference to make the environment a major issue. The Vienna Convention for the Protection of Ozone Layer, on the other hand, was signed in 1985 and entered into force in 1988. It provides the necessary framework to protection of layer. Finally, the United Nations Convention on the Law of the Sea was opened for signature in 1982 and came into force in 1994. It lays down a comprehensive regime of law including marine pollution. Please visit respectively, https://www.un.org/en/conferences/environment/stockholm1972 and https://treaties.un.org/pages/ViewDetails.aspx?src=IND&mtdsg_no=XXVII-2&chapter=27&clang=_en and https://www.un.org/depts/los/convention_agreements/convention_overview_convention.htm all accessed 04.09.2024. For detail see Dupuy (2013), pp. 12, 17. In addition, attempts of western states through OECD initiative failed in 1998, for detail, see Di Benedetto (2013), p. 9, fn 2.

[136]Please visit: https://treaties.un.org/Pages/ViewDetails.aspx?src=IND&mtdsg_no=XXVII-7-d&chapter=27&clang=_en accessed 04.09.2024.

[137]As the name implies, the UN Framework Convention on Climate Change (UNFCCC) sets out the basic legal framework in combating with climate change. The Convention entered into force in 1994 and is mainly geared towards "*stabilization of greenhouse gas concentrations in the atmosphere at a level that would prevent dangerous anthropogenic interference with the climate system.*" For the full text of the Convention, please visit: https://unfccc.int/resource/docs/convkp/conveng.pdf, also see https://treaties.un.org/pages/ViewDetailsIII.aspx?src=TREATY&mtdsg_no=XXVII-7&chapter=27&Temp=mtdsg3&clang=_en both accessed 04.09.2024.

Agreement set a goal of limiting global warming to well below 2 Celsius(°C) and pursuing to limit the temperature increase to 1.5 °C. Despite this, the Emissions Gap Report (EGR) 2021[138] projects a rise of 2.7 °C in the global temperature by the end of this century, while another study paints a bleaker picture and predicts an increase of 6 °C by 2050.[139] Although estimations as to how nasty the consequences vary, the urgency of the precautions remains unwavering. Hence, the potential danger requires more than cajoling those who still underestimate the turmoil that lies ahead.

Multilateral agreements adopt environment-centric or environment-friendly provisions. To illustrate, under article 19 of the Energy Charter Treaty, in order to minimize the occurring of the harmful environmental impacts, each Contracting Party, in its policies and actions, shall strive to take precautionary measures to prevent or minimize environmental degradation. There is an increasing drive in inclusion of environmental and climate obligations in the treaties; however, treaty drafting techniques are not coherent, therefore, environmental protection in bilateral treaties has taken several forms.

Treaties may employ a preambular reference, some treaties contented themselves with promoting the protection of the environment only in their preambles.[140] Other treaties, whether in their preambles or not, may impose concrete obligations with regard to environmental protection upon the parties.[141] Some treaties are designed to include exception clauses and grant states greater and exclusive authority over their regulatory power and allow them to escape international responsibilities,[142] while other treaties may carve out certain control measures and reduce the scope of parties' international commitments.[143] Finally, some BITs may guide arbitrators in their

[138] The report is available at https://www.unep.org/resources/emissions-gap-report-2021 accessed 04.09.2024.

[139] See Spier (2013), p. 123.

[140] See Wendy and Lawry-White (2019), p. 12.

[141] The preamble of the Rwanda - United States of America BIT (2008) is as follows: "Desiring to achieve these objectives in a manner consistent with the protection of health, safety, and the environment, and the promotion of internationally recognized labor rights". Available at https://investmentpolicy.unctad.org/international-investment-agreements/treaties/bit/2870/rwanda%2D%2D-united-states-of-america-bit-2008- accessed 04.09.2024. Scholars state that the third form of the preambular language is "non-derogation" where the objectives of the treaty are to be achieved without relaxing regulatory standards in fields such as the environment, health or safety. For detail, see Gehring and Kent (2013), p. 204.

[142] Exception clauses can be sector-specific or general. For instance, article 4(1)(a) of the China-Turkey BIT (2015) is as follows "*Nothing in this Agreement shall be construed to prevent a Contracting Party from adopting, maintaining, or enforcing any non-discriminatory and necessary measures: (a) designed and applied for the protection of human, animal or plant life or health, or the environment…*". A similar approach has been adopted by Georgia - Japan BIT (2021) under article 11(4). Available at https://investmentpolicy.unctad.org/international-investment-agreements/treaty-files/6078/download. For a similar wording, also see article 5 and 6 of the Belarus-Turkey BIT (2018). Available at https://investmentpolicy.unctad.org/international-investment-agreements/treaty-files/5981/download both accessed 04.09.2024.

[143] A BIT may exclude certain measures concerning environmental protection and may categorize them as "non-expropriatory". In so doing, it may reduce the scope of the claims and, accordingly,

potential adjudication.[144] With regard to the latter, in *Douglas*' opinion, such provisions may provide an allowance to tribunals in recourse to treaties concluded by contracting parties which address environmental law. However, the power of the tribunal may be called into question if such explicit provisions are not included.[145] The enforcement of a treaty provision will be successful to the extent that it provides a precise meaning and content. The provision must be phrased in a way that draws a clear line of demarcation and eliminates potential legal uncertainty. This will allow arbitrators in a dispute to adopt a clear position and render decisions by making explicit references to that provision.[146]

Recent BITs tend to engage in interaction with international agreements aimed at promoting environmental protection.[147] The protection afforded in the Paris agreement is of a kind that may accelerate the harmonization of municipal laws and international law on as wide a basis as possible. The Paris agreement has already begun to carve out the scope of some BITs, and parties thereto undertake to implement its provisions. For instance, the provisions with regard to environment protection of the Italy–August 2022 Model BIT have been drafted by incorporating the provisions of the Paris Agreement.[148] In a similar vein, the Belgium-Luxembourg Model BIT provides a reference to the UNFCCC,[149] whereas some treaties designed -only to protect the environment purposefully avoids such

limit the discretion of arbitrators. Also see Alschner and Tuerk (2013), pp. 220, 223. On the other hand, a BIT may incorporate environmental protection into the concept of an 'investment', in so doing, only investments that fall within that category can benefit from the provisions of the BIT in question. Also see Wendy and Lawry-White (2019), p. 13.

[144] Article 8 (6) of the Czech Republic-Netherlands BIT (1991) reads as; "*The arbitral tribunal shall decide on the basis of the law, taking into account in particular though not exclusively: · the law in force of the Contracting Party concerned; · the provisions of this Agreement, and other relevant Agreements between the Contracting Parties; · the provisions of special agreements relating to the investment; · the general principles of international law*". Available at https://investmentpolicy.unctad.org/international-investment-agreements/treaty-files/968/download accessed 04.09.2024.

[145] Douglas (2013), pp. 425, 426.

[146] For detail, please see Marisi (2020), chapter four.

[147] In scholars' view, such interaction can create a chilling effect on states' willingness to pursue and enforce policies that align with the objectives of other agreement. For detail, see Gehring and Kent (2013), p. 213.

[148] Art. 21(2/a) of the treaty is as follows; "*Each Party shall effectively implement the UNFCCC and the Paris Agreement adopted thereunder, including its commitments with regard to its Nationally Determined Contributions*...." The Treaty is available at https://investmentpolicy.unctad.org/international-investment-agreements/treaty-files/6438/download accessed 04.09.2024.

[149] Article 17(2) of the BIT reads as "*the Contracting Parties recognise the importance of pursuing the objectives of the UNFCCC in order to address the threat of climate change*." For the text, please visit: https://jusmundi.com/en/document/pdf/treaty/en-agreement-between-the-belgium-luxembourg-economic-union-on-the-one-hand-and-on-the-other-hand-on-the-reciprocal-promotion-and-protection-of-investments-bleu-model-bit-2019-thursday-28th-march-2019 accessed 04.09.2024.

Model Green Investment Treaty does not provide a specific reference to UNFCC. In doing so, the Treaty aims at encompassing climate-related treaties that are not under the UNFCCC. See Magraw et al. (2019), p. 104.

reference.[150] The drafters of these treaties might have wished to ensure the compliance and adaptation of the investments to amendments to these agreements. And finally, as readers got familiar with the concept of 'distributed ledger' from the chapter dealing with blockchain, some model treaties aim at creation of a distributed ledger to meet measurement, transparency, reporting, verification and monetization requirements of the Paris Agreement.[151]

The *negative externality* is one of the pivotal facts of today's foreign investment perception, imposing costs not just on the society of the host state,[152] but also on the nationals of the neighboring states.[153] The pollution complained of need not necessarily involve environmental decline in the vicinity of the populated area. Even if the polluting enterprise creates a buffer or sanitary zone (e.g., between its plant and the residential area), depending on the width of the zone as well as the absence of a purification equipment (e.g., filtration for the plant's chimney), the pollution concerned may have impact on the nationals of the neighboring states. Given the '*polluter pays*' principle[154] combined with the responsibility of the states, despite the foreign investor gives origin to pollution,[155] the host state's responsibility not only towards its nationals but also towards anyone who has suffered therefrom shall remain.[156] As one scholar noted earlier on this topic; "*A State owes at all times a duty*

[150] The Green Investment Protocol involves a provision that refers to future agreements. Article 2(2)(c) of the Protocol is as follows: "*…any future mechanism or technology created to achieve the aims of the Paris Agreement.*" See Henin et al. (2019), p. 48.

[151] The proposed distributed ledger serves as a tool to verify or match the actual data (for instance performance of the investment) with the data saved on the ledger throughout the course of the investment. See Elrifai et al. (2019), p. 84 et seq. Some model treaties, on the other hand, require investors to conduct environmental impact assessment to conform to ISO 37001 Anti-Bribery Management System. Although scholars suggest that assessment of corruption is relevant to the concept of sustainable development, they have not provided a specific instance where corruption can be directly linked to climate-change. Magraw et al. (2019), p. 119. et seq.

[152] Also see Ghaleigh (2013), p. 424.

[153] Although a state-state dispute, in *Pulp mills* case (Para. 101), the court highlighted the state's obligation and held that "*A State is thus obliged to use all the means at its disposal in order to avoid activities which take place in its territory, or in any area under its jurisdiction, causing significant damage to the environment of another State.*" available at https://www.icj-cij.org/public/files/case-related/135/135-20100420-JUD-01-00-EN.pdf accessed 04.09.2024.

[154] In the opinion of *Marisi*, states have liabilities for environmental damage engendered by private or public parties, therefore, public regulators can act in 'sub-rogation' against polluters. For the principle and the discussion see Marisi (2020), p. 49 et seq. Also see article 16 of the Rio Declaration. Available at https://www.un.org/en/development/desa/population/migration/generalassembly/docs/globalcompact/A_CONF.151_26_Vol.I_Declaration.pdf accessed 04.09.2024.

[155] Investor's title to the investment cannot include the right to put the asset to noxious use and he must not take the absence of any regulation as a sign of the state's active stance in his favor. See Khachvani (2020), pp. 162, 169.

[156] "No harm rule" has been adopted at Stockholm Conference. The principle 21 of the Stockholm Declaration (Declaration of the United Nations Conference on the Human Environment) is as follows; "*States have, in accordance with the Charter of the United Nations and the principles of international law, the sovereign right to exploit their own resources pursuant to their own*

to protect other States against injurious acts by individuals from within its jurisdiction".[157] To illustrate; *Trail Smelter* case stands as a pioneer in setting out the 'polluter pays' principle,[158] in that case, Canada was held liable for the conduct of the Trail Smelter, a Canadian corporation that caused damaged in the State of Washington.[159]

The ILC principles[160] provide prompt and adequate compensation for victims of transboundary damage[161] and entitle states to take responsive measures.[162] The commentary to the ILC principles does not indicate a specific statement that prohibits the affected state (neighboring state) from advancing compensation to its nationals by liquidating the assets of the foreign investor in its jurisdiction whose conduct caused a 'foreign loss event'.[163] Hence, foreign investor whose conduct carries limited or significant adverse environmental risks and who possess assets in neighboring states might need an insurance coverage against the actions of both neighboring states and the host state.

---

environmental policies, and the responibility to ensure that activities within their jurisdiction or control do not cause damage to the environment of other States or of areas beyond the limits of national jurisdiction." See Report of the United Nations Conference on the Human Environment, Stockholm, 5–16 June 1972. Document is available at https://digitallibrary.un.org/record/523249?ln=en For a similar provision see article 194(2) of the United Nations Convention on the Law of the Sea, document is available at https://www.un.org/depts/los/convention_agreements/texts/unclos/unclos_e.pdf both accessed 04.09.2024. Also see Spier (2013), p. 128. For a sample case in which the tribunal emphasized "no harm rule", see Wendy and Lawry-White (2019), p. 8.

[157] For the pronouncement of Professor Eagleton, see page 1963 of the case, available at https://legal.un.org/riaa/cases/vol_III/1905-1982.pdf accessed 04.09.2024.

[158] See Wendy and Lawry-White (2019), p. 7.

[159] The tribunal's findings were that "*the gases emerging from the stacks of the Trail Smelter find their way into (the upper air currents and are carried by these currents in a fairly continuous stream down the valley so long as the prevailing wind at that level is in that direction.... the concentration of sulphur dioxide falls off very rapidly from Trail to a point about 16 miles downstream from the Smelter, or 6 miles from the boundary line*". See pp. 1923, 1924.

[160] Draft principles on the allocation of loss in the case of transboundary harm arising out of hazardous activities (2006), text is available at https://legal.un.org/ilc/texts/instruments/english/draft_articles/9_10_2006.pdf accessed 04.09.2024.

[161] The article 4(1) provides for "*Each State should take all necessary measures to ensure that prompt and adequate compensation is available for victims of transboundary damage caused by hazardous activities located within its territory or otherwise under its jurisdiction or control.*" and article 4(3) is as follows "*These measures should also include the requirement on the operator or, where appropriate, other person or entity, to establish and maintain financial security such as insurance, bonds or other financial guarantees to cover claims of compensation.*" Also see Convention on Long-Range Transboundary Air Pollution, certified true copy of the Convention is available at https://treaties.un.org/doc/Treaties/1979/11/19791113%2004-16%20PM/Ch_XXVII_01p.pdf accessed 04.09.2024.

[162] Article 5 (d) of the ILC's principles reads as "*the States affected or likely to be affected by the transboundary damage shall take all feasible measures to mitigate and if possible, to eliminate the effects of such damage.*"

[163] ILC Commentary explains it as the activities causing significant transboundary harm. See para. 29, p. 81. Available at https://legal.un.org/ilc/reports/2006/english/chp5.pdf accessed 04.09.2024.

8.2.5.1.2 The Exercise of Police Power

To effectively combat global warming, the enduring cooperation of states that is not ephemeral is of an essential need. In our opinion, case law provides the backdrop against which the international environmental laws can be incorporated into municipal laws,[164] thus international law must seep into the municipal laws and states must reform their regulations.[165] Despite the predominant view to the contrary,[166] governments, imbued with the instinct of safeguarding their nationals, must be in a position to impose tax, stringent standards, fines and restrictive licensing on foreign investments whose conduct is pollutant.[167]

Host states' interest to tackle climate change and reach the goal of becoming climate-neutral by 2050[168] must not yield to foreign investors' ownership rights. Respecting the investor's legitimate expectations while also not derogating from states' right to regulate, and simultaneously achieving the objectives of the Paris Agreement is not an easy task for states.[169] These two objectives do not stand as alternatives; in fact, if one were to suppose that the Paris Agreement must prevail

---

[164]The tribunal in *Chemtura v. Canada,* for the first time, applied the police power doctrine to shield environmental measure. The tribunal found the use of "police power" rational when human health is at stake, and held that "*the measures challenged by the Claimant constituted a valid exercise of the Respondent's police powers. As discussed in detail in connection with Article 1105 of NAFTA, the PMRA Pest Management Regulatory Agency (of Canada) took measures within its mandate, in a non-discriminatory manner, motivated by the increasing awareness of the dangers presented by lindane for human health and the environment. A measure adopted under such circumstances is a valid exercise of the State's police powers and, as a result, does not constitute an expropriation*". See para. 266, available at https://www.italaw.com/sites/default/files/case-documents/ita0149_0.pdf accessed 04.09.2024. Also see Viñuales (2013), p. 303.

[165]See Maljean-Dubois and Richard (2013), p. 75.

[166]According to *Gehring and Hepburn*, if the government places a cap on the use of carbon that may be emitted by a given sector is evidently a form of "control". Whereas environment and human health are the subjects in which governments are responsive in protecting their nations, a nexus may not be laid between the aim pursued and the desired outcome of regulatory actions. Sooner or later, measures of a restrictive nature can distort the financial viability of the foreign investment in question. See Gehring and Hepburn (2013), pp. 400, 405. Similarly, see Gehring and Kent (2013), p. 206.

[167]Proulx and Simma (2012), p. 270.

[168]The European Parliament has endorsed the EU objective of achieving net-zero greenhouse gas emissions by 2050 in its resolution of 14 March 2019 on climate change. For the detail see Proposal for a REGULATION OF THE EUROPEAN PARLIAMENT AND OF THE COUNCIL establishing the framework for achieving climate neutrality and amending Regulation (EU) 2018/1999 (European Climate Law) Available at https://www.europarl.europa.eu/meetdocs/2014_2019/plmrep/AUTRES_INSTITUTIONS/COMM/COM/2020/09-10/COM_COM20200080_EN.pdf accessed 04.09.2024. In reaching the target set out in the EU Climate Law, the Parliament and Council secured an agreement concerning zero-emission road mobility (new passenger cars and light commercial vehicles) by 2035, please visit: https://www.europarl.europa.eu/news/pt/press-room/20221024IPR45734/deal-confirms-zero-emissions-target-for-new-cars-and-vans-in-2035 accessed 04.09.2024.

[169]Also, see Wendy and Lawry-White (2019), pp. 4–6.

over domestic laws, the threat of climate change will necessitate a thorough examination of the 'legitimacy' of investors' expectations. The regulatory risk induced by international environmental law must not be divided between the investor and the host state; investors' omission or negligence in considering such regulations at the time of making their investment or not adjusting their expectations according to environmental constraints should be considered part of business risk.

States are vested with powers to regulate their domestic affairs in a bona-fide, non-discriminatory manner and within the public interest. Their actions are justified by so-called '*police power*[170]'. Therefore, it might be crucial to draw a bright and easily distinguishable line between the investor's expectations and regulatory powers of the host state. By doing so, host states ensure that investors are free from coercion or harassment by their own regulatory authorities.[171] While not every regulatory restraint is akin to expropriation, some tribunals hold, a blanket exception for regulatory measures could potentially create a gaping loophole in international protections against expropriation.[172] In fact, those rights vested in states may come with certain boundaries. States must implement their policies and exercise domestic laws in a manner that complies with their international environmental obligations. Such domestic laws, according to the scholars, must not be treated on the same footing as a purely domestic measure and their legitimacy is strengthened in a decisive manner to the extent that a link between international environment law and domestic measure is established.[173] However, some tribunals seem to be reluctant in giving international environmental law a larger room and have taken a strict approach and focused only on the legal character of the measure. The tribunal in *Santa Elena v. Costa Rica* found it irrelevant to observe the international source of the obligation that was imposed on the state to protect the environment.[174]

---

[170]In the Black's Law Dictionary, police power is defined as "*the inherent and plenary power of a sovereign to make all laws necessary and proper to preserve the public security, order, health, morality, and justice. - It is a fundamental power essential to government, and it cannot be surrendered by the legislature or irrevocably transferred away from government.*" on the police powers doctrine, see Khachvani (2020), pp. 154–173, see Viñuales (2013), pp. 301–309 and Salacuse (2013), pp. 315, 316.

[171]For the discussion of whether Russian government's forcing foreign investors to accept to participate in the government-arranged restructuring in 1999, see Abba and Wälde (2008), p. 237.

For cases involving coercion and harassment, also see *Saluka v. Czech Republic*, available at https://www.italaw.com/sites/default/files/case-documents/ita0740.pdf and similarly, see *Aconquija v. Argentina available at* https://www.italaw.com/sites/default/files/case-documents/ita0206.pdf both accessed 04.09.2024.

[172]See *POPE & TALBOT v. Canada* case para. 99.

[173]Viñuales (2013), pp. 277, 287.

[174]The tribunal rejected the defendant's argument by noting "*the purpose of protecting the environment for which the Property was taken does not alter the legal character of the taking for which adequate compensation must be paid. The international source of the obligation to protect the environment makes no difference*". (para. 71), Available at https://www.italaw.com/sites/default/files/case-documents/italaw6340.pdf accessed 04.09.2024. Scholars find this conclusion controversial on the grounds that within the context of human rights, the environmental justification of a measure is recognized as a legal basis to reduce the compensation. See Viñuales (2013), p. 281.

The basic principle of international law[175] is that a state should not invoke its domestic laws as a reason to avoid international obligations and shield an illegitimate end (not in the public interest) it pursues,[176] such acts may call for compensation.[177] Scholars might be divided on the question of how to determine when a regulation that renders investment economically unviable or substantially deprives the investor of the use or benefit of his investment is exempt from compensation.[178] International law has not pinned down the scope of police power and drawn a clear line between compensable and non-compensable regulations. The uncertainty is evident from divergent findings of different tribunals dealing with this issue. The tribunal in *Saluka v. Czech Republic*, although concluded that a state's exercise of its regulatory power is non-compensable, has left room open for further discussions. In the tribunal's view, international law had to identify "*in a comprehensive and definitive fashion precisely what regulations are considered 'permissible' and 'commonly accepted'.*[179]"

Any means of regulation can be transformed into the use of police power that is inherent in a sovereign. However, regardless of the deleterious impact on foreign investment,[180] the end pursued must be to serve for the protection of environment.[181] If one were to take a view through the lens of nationals of the host state, the violation of foreign investors' proprietary rights might be rational to the extent not doing so violates the fundamental rights of those nationals. Besides, if the regulation concerns environment and public health, the use of police power will be less likely to be contested under international law.[182] Despite the presence of the awards to the contrary,[183] the protection of environment and human health are one of the categories of police power regulation recognized by international authorities that might justify non-compensation where there is a deprivation. In several decisions, courts gave weight to the precedence of the considerations in relation to environment over

[175] Art. 32 of the ILC articles is as follows: "*The responsible State may not rely on the provisions of its internal law as justification for failure to comply with its obligations under this part.*"

[176] Daniel and Michael (2013), p. 234. Verwey and Schrijver (1984), p. 9.

[177] In *Metalclad* however, the tribunal did not find it necessary to ascertain the intent behind the adoption of the environmental regulation (Ecological Decree), in the tribunal's mind, "*the implementation of the Ecological Decree would, in and of itself, constitute an act tantamount to expropriation*". See para. 111, available at https://www.italaw.com/sites/default/files/case-documents/ita0510.pdf accessed 04.09.2024.

[178] *Kachavani* highlights that not all regulatory changes must be encumbered with the duty of compensation. In the scholar's view, such an approach will constitute a burden on the state's sovereignty. See Khachvani (2020), pp. 155, 158.

[179] In *Saluka v. Czech Republic* (paras. 262, 263).

[180] Rubins and Kinsella (2005), p. 13.

[181] For instance, article 15(1) of the Georgia - Japan BIT (2021) reads as; "... *nothing in this Agreement shall be construed so as to prevent the former Contracting Party from adopting or enforcing measures: (a) necessary to protect human, animal or plant life or health...*"

[182] Daza-Clark (2016), p. 64.

[183] See *Santa Elena v. Costa Rica.*

fundamental rights such as the right of property.[184] Scholars also add that due to the absence of international expropriation law cases which could have provided express guidance, such justification cannot be made.[185]

Regulatory acts may not only aim at protecting the environment; by contrast, in order for attracting investments, host states may tend to lower their restrictive regulations[186] or adopt 'freezing clauses' in contracts concluded with the foreign investors, by which state undertakes not to alter the regulations to the detriment of investors.[187] However, scholars view that new cap-and-trade regulations can be inconsistent with the stabilization clause in question.[188] Condoning damage to the environment cannot be justified by the protection of the investor's rights, nor can it be defended by concessions granted to foreign investors that allegedly increase the nation's prosperity. Besides, it is inappropriate to weaken or reduce the protections afforded in municipal environmental laws.[189]

Scholars, in reliance on the *Metalclad* case[190] are of the view that international investment protection law can threaten the sovereign's right to implement strict environmental regulations. On the other hand, same scholars propose that investors engaged in carbon-intensive investments, must not be entitled to claim that

---

[184] In one of the most-cited case in the environment context (*Turgut and Others v. TURKEY* -para. 90-)

the ECHR, in its reasoning, explained the delicacy of protecting the environment. In the court's view, the justification of non-compensation could have been made on exceptional circumstances. The court held that "*the environment, is a cause whose defense arouses the constant and sustained interest of the public, and consequently the public authorities. Financial imperatives and even certain fundamental rights, such as ownership, should not be afforded priority over environmental protection considerations, in particular when the State has legislated in this regard)*" Available at https://hudoc.echr.coe.int/eng#{%22itemid%22:[%22001-87441%22]} accessed 04.09.2024. For decisions of similar nature, see *G.I.E.M. S.R.L. v. ITALY,* available at https://hudoc.echr.coe.int/eng#{%22itemid%22:[%22001-184525%22]} and *Hamer v. Belgium,* available at https://hudoc.echr.coe.int/eng#{%22itemid%22:[%22001-83537%22]} all accessed 04.09.2024.

[185] Newcombe and Paradell (2009), pp. 358–361. similarly see Newcombe (2005), p. 26.

[186] *Di Benedetto* argues that developing countries will not be willing to lose foreign investments carried out within their jurisdictions while establishing environmental protection standards. See Di Benedetto (2013), p. 20.

[187] Di Benedetto (2013), p. 15. Also see the chapter dealing with stabilization clause.

[188] Daniel and Michael (2013), p. 254.

[189] Treaties may contain a "non-waiver" clause in principle, for instance, article 12 of the U.S. Model Bilateral Investment Treaty (2012) provides the following: "*each Party shall ensure that it does not waive or otherwise derogate from or offer to waive or otherwise derogate from its environmental laws in a manner that weakens or reduces the protections afforded in those laws, or fail to effectively enforce those laws through a sustained or recurring course of action or inaction, as an encouragement for the establishment, acquisition, expansion, or retention of an investment in its territory*. However, same treaty adopts an exclusion, which turns out to be a dilemma before the goal of protecting environment.

[190] The case concerns the indirect expropriation of Hazardous Waste Landfill by the Mexican government. According to scholars, the regulation has amounted to an illegitimate expropriation despite it aimed to protect the environment, see Boute (2009), p. 366.

implementation of domestic climate change policies affects the profitability of their investments, thus they must lower their expectations to a reasonable degree.[191]

Regulations aimed to protect the environment are as legitimate as any other regulation by which governments address human health or public welfare, and propriety rights do not necessarily stand as an obstacle in the way of these regulations. A BIT can be adopted in a way that the treatment that the investment receives will vary upon its potential to harm the environment.[192] If the investment is classified according to a classification clause the BIT contains, the foreign investor can learn; the category into which his potential investment falls, thereby understanding whether his investment is sustainable and the treatment to which he will be entitled.[193] Host states will want to bring their BITs and environmental commitments into line with each other. However, an attempt to create such harmony may cast disputes. Unilaterally disengaging from a BIT and withdrawing therefrom could impair investors' legitimate expectations. Moreover, one might argue that, if the BIT contains a sunset clause,[194] the host state cannot derogate from rights vested in the investor, at least for the time being that the BIT remains in force.[195]

The presence of a foreign investment that is in conformity with the municipal laws on the one hand and yet it operates in a manner detrimental to the environment

---

[191] See Boute (2009), pp. 369–370.

[192] Also see Aaken and Broude (2022).

[193] Article 3.1 of the Treaty on Sustainable Investment for Climate Change Mitigation and Adaptation provides as follows: "*1. An investor of a Party or its investment in a host State Party may request to the host State Party a determination of whether such investment qualifies, or whether a proposed investment of that investor would qualify, as a Sustainable Investment, Unsustainable Investment or non-classified investment in the host State Party for purposes of the application of this Treaty. 2. The host State Party shall issue a decision-making the requested determination within [sixty] days from the date of receipt of a request by an investor or investment. 3. To make its determination, the host State Party shall consider: a) the relevant characteristics of the investment or proposed investment; b) the definitions contained in Article 1.1: Definitions; c) the content of the host State Party's Schedules to Annexes I and II; and d) other factors it may deem relevant.*" Also see Brauch et al. (2019).

[194] BITs may encompass clauses defining the commencement and expiration dates. Sunset clauses embedded in BITs ensure that investments made before the termination of the BIT will be protected by the BIT for a specific period which may range from 5 to 20 years. This allows investors the chance to accommodate their investments to the new situation. To put it differently, after this period, the investor will not have access to the BIT and will be prevented from making claims against states. In *Gavazzi v. Romania*, the claimant submitted an arbitration request to ICSID after the Agreement between the Government of the Italian Republic and the Government of Romania on the Mutual Promotion and Protection of Investments had expired. The case is available at https://www.italaw.com/sites/default/files/case-documents/italaw9506.pdf accessed 04.09.2024. See Salacuse (2013), p. 370. In the view of *Kouroutakis,* the name given to the clause is not coincidental; just as the sun sets, the duration of laws expires, and a sunset clause serves to render a treaty of a temporary nature within limited lifespan, in contrast to permanent laws and treaties. See Kouroutakis (2022).

[195] For instance, according to article 12(2) of the China-Turkey BIT 2015 "*Either Contracting Party may, by giving one year's written notice to the other Contracting Party, terminate this Agreement at the end of the initial ten-year period or at any time thereafter.*"

on the other may give rise to chaotic results. A succeeding government will likely seek a contrasting legislative end by subsequent amendments that could frustrate the foreign investor who, in fact, has been operating the investment in a way that is injurious to public health. The new regulations may render the investment economically worthless,[196] prompting the investor bringing claims to challenge the legality of the measure that had an adverse impact on its activities.[197] In order to achieve environmental goals without causing countries that lack sufficient financial means or infrastructure to abandon their promises, international jurisprudence must lower its expectations (as was done in Kyoto Protocol[198] and in WTO's SPS Agreement[199]) and take very much into account the needs of developing countries.[200]

8.2.5.1.3 Disputes Arising Out of Environmental Matters

8.2.5.1.3.1 Counterclaims by the Host States

The interaction between environmental law and foreign investment seems to occur not seldom.[201] As global warming or climate change escalates, adjudicators have begun to hear more disputes in regards of this phenomenon. Conventionally, investment claims are brought by foreign investors who challenge the given measures that adversely affect their investments. However, environmental damage emanating from the activities of the foreign investor does not only lead to imposition of quasi-expropriatory measures. Accordingly, a state prone to safeguard its nationals may seek a remedial mechanism (preferably compensation) for the loss it and/or its nationals have suffered. In a simpler way, any of the foreign investor, host state or its national may become the claimant in the dispute.

---

[196] A legitimate environmental measure causing a decrease in the value of the foreign investment will not create a right to compensation. See Wagner (1999), p. 538.

[197] Viñuales (2013), p. 276.

[198] It was only binding for developed countries and placed a heavier burden due to their responsibility for the high levels of greenhouse gas emissions. Annex I of the Convention specified the developed country parties, and other Parties to the Convention have committed themselves to limiting anthropogenic emissions and enhancing their greenhouse gas (GHG) sinks and reservoirs. Paris Agreement on the other hand obliges all parties and only differentiate developed countries, imposing financial obligations on them. The Kyoto Protocol remains in force but superseded by the Paris Agreement which became the principal regulatory instrument governing the global response to climate change. For detail, see Bodansky (2021).

[199] Under article 10 of the agreement, WTO adopts a special and differential treatment for the developing countries. We will address the agreement in detail.

[200] Some scholars opine to the contrary. According to their view, the cost of reducing the emissions can be lower in emerging countries than in industrialized ones. Furthermore, since the infrastructure of an emerging market is not yet established, construction thereof could be carried out with huge emission savings. See Luterbacher (2013), p. 62.

[201] Also see Drabek and Mavroidis (2013), p. 241.

The term 'investor-state dispute' implies an adjudication in which the party entitled to seek compensation is the investor. However, host states may also assert a counterclaim in the same dispute. Provisional rules may provide the basis for submitting counterclaims. By way of illustration, article 47 of the ICSID Convention, as well as rule 48(1) of the ICSID Arbitration Rules,[202] confer an express power upon arbitrators to hear counterclaims.[203] In fact, both provisions, by employing the following language "*counterclaims arising directly out of the subject-matter of the dispute*", constrain the scope of the disputes that can be submitted to arbitration. Some treaties on the other hand, do not include a similar limitation upon the counterclaim[204] or include obligations on investors.[205] Similarly, tribunals have discussed whether international law obligations can be attached to the non-state individual, the tribunal in *Urbaser S.A. v. Argentina* noted that corporate social

---

[202]The article reads as "*Unless the parties agree otherwise, a party may file an incidental or additional claim or a counterclaim ("ancillary claim") arising directly out of the subject-matter of the dispute, provided that such ancillary claim is within the scope of the consent of the parties and the jurisdiction of the Centre.*"

[203]The article is as follows "*Except as the parties otherwise agree, the Tribunal shall, if requested by a party, determine any incidental or additional claims or counterclaims arising directly out of the subject-matter of the dispute provided that they are within the scope of the consent of the parties and are otherwise within the jurisdiction of the Centre.*"

[204]Although not in force, article 5 of the Basel Protocol on Liability and Compensation for Damage Resulting from Transboundary Movements of Hazardous Wastes and their Disposal grants the host state, without any limitation, the right to claim compensation. Article is as follows "Without *prejudice to Article 4, any person shall be liable for damage caused or contributed to by his lack of compliance with the provisions implementing the Convention or by his wrongful intentional, reckless or negligent acts or omissions.*" Protocol is available at https://treaties.un.org/doc/Treaties/1999/12/19991210%2012-52%20PM/Ch_XXVII_03_bp.pdf accessed 04.09.2024. For instance, article 35.2 of the Model Green Investment Treaty obliges investors to put in place a compliance program before commencing an investment, and article 36 requires the investor to comply with domestic law and international safeguards. According to article 37.1 of the Treaty, a Party may initiate a counterclaim against the investor or investment for a breach of the obligations set out in these articles (article 35–36). See Magraw et al. (2019), pp. 100, 101, 124. Similarly, Article 14 of the Green Investment Protocol obliges the investor to comply with the environmental laws, regulations and standards in force in the host state. The Protocol also enables the host state to assert counterclaim by virtue of the article 18. According to the article, by submitting its claim to arbitration, the investor is deemed to have consented to the tribunal's jurisdiction over counterclaims provided that the investor's alleged breach relates to the Green Investment defined under the Protocol. See Henin et al. (2019), pp. 64, 67.

[205]Article 7(1) of the Netherlands Model Investment Agreement (2019) reads as "*Investors and their investments shall comply with domestic laws and regulations of the host state, including laws and regulations on human rights, environmental protection and labor laws.*" Article 6(2) of the same BIT is as follows "*Each Contracting Party shall ensure that its investment laws and policies provide for and encourage high levels of environmental and labor protection and shall strive to continue to improve those laws and policies and their underlying levels of protection.* Available at https://investmentpolicy.unctad.org/international-investment-agreements/treaty-files/5832/download similarly see art. 11 of the Norway Model BIT, available at https://investmentpolicy.unctad.org/international-investment-agreements/treaty-files/2873/download both accessed 04.09.2024.

responsibility,[206] as a standard, is embodied in the international law and entails commitments to comply with human rights.[207]

Dumberry reminds that the tribunals have jurisdiction over a claim brought by an investor. It does not imply jurisdiction over a counterclaim submitted by the respondent state. BITs deal with the state's responsibilities and rights of investors. A state cannot make a counter claim on the grounds that one of its rights contained in BIT has been breached, since no such right exists.[208] Bilateral treaties contain 'one-way' commitments[209] of the states towards each other's' nationals. In investor-state disputes, foreign investors base their dispute upon the failure by the state of its commitments. According to this strict approach, host states should be unable to bring counterclaims based upon the same instrument (violating the treaty obligation).[210] However, in *Perenco v. Ecuador*, the counterclaims Ecuador raised for alleged environmental harm and infrastructure damages[211] were not rejected in the tribunal's interim decision. The tribunal found that the claimant was strictly liable for environmental damage.[212] Conversely, in *Roussalis v. Romania*, the tribunal did not recognize its jurisdiction over the counterclaim. Tribunal believed "*the BIT does not provide for counterclaims to be introduced by the host state in relation to obligations of the investor' because the 'meaning of 'dispute' is the issuance of compliance by the State with the BIT*[213]". *Douglas* opposes this approach, in the scholar's view, if

---

[206] Corporate responsibility requires companies to comply with the international environmental norms and act in a manner that respects human rights, while also preventing, mitigating and where necessary remediating adverse human rights impacts. See Morgera (2013), p. 332 et seq. and also see Gehring and Kent (2013), p. 209 et seq. The case is available at https://www.italaw.com/sites/default/files/case-documents/italaw8136_1.pdf accessed 04.09.2024.

[207] Despite the tribunal has accepted the investors obligation to respect human right to water, it has rejected the counterclaim. See paras. 1195, 1211–1221. Also see Wendy and Lawry-White (2019), p. 18.

[208] Readers must note that, the scholar provides this view within the concept of satisfaction. See Dumberry (2012), p. 235. Also see Born (2021), p. 499.

[209] Some scholars define international investment agreements as a "double-edged sword" on the grounds that they may promote investment in green technologies while being used to challenge regulatory efforts aimed at reducing greenhouse gases. See Alschner and Tuerk (2013), p. 221.

[210] Douglas (2013), p. 431.

[211] Ecuador argued that its law established strict liability for environmental damage, and within the "polluter pays principle" proving the occurrence of the damage was sufficient. Perenco based its defense on the fact that, Ecuador must prove Perence's negligence in its operations in addition to the presence of harm, and that the 2008 Ecuadorian Constitution that contains the strict liability standard cannot be applied retrospectively to the investor's pre-2008 operations. The tribunal however, opted to employ a strong rebuttable presumption that a regulatory exceedance is evidence of the investor's fault. Agreeing to the contrary would make it too onerous for the host state to prove the investor's failure in its duty of care in cases where regulatory exceedances occurred. The case is available at https://www.italaw.com/sites/default/files/case-documents/italaw6315.pdf accessed 04.09.2024. For detail, see Harrison (2016), pp. 479–488.

[212] See para. 611(4).

[213] The relevant part of the article 9 of the Greece - Romania BIT (1997) is as follows: "*Disputes between an investor of a Contracting Party and the other Contracting Party concerning an*

the dispute submitted by the investor is related to the investment in which the investor breached his contractual undertakings to comply with environmental standards, and if the counterclaim is based upon this breach, arbitrators should hear counterclaims.[214]

8.2.5.1.3.2 Recent Disputes

International courts attach significance to the human effect on the environment. According to the International Court of Justice, "*the environment is not an abstraction but represents the living space, the quality of life and the very health of human beings, including generations unborn.*[215]" With growing environmental awareness and the application of the Paris Agreement on a wide basis, courts or tribunals will be compelled, inclined or encouraged to adopt a preemptive or punitive approach. Adjudicators' focus will shift from simply determining the importance of the environment to taking proactive measures or imposing penalties on foreign investors or host states, or both. As a matter of fact, in *Urgenda* case, Dutch citizens alleged that the Dutch government had failed in its duty to prevent climate change.[216] The Dutch Supreme Court elaborated the Paris Agreement and reached the conclusion that "*the country must do its part.... cannot escape its own share of the responsibility to take measures by arguing that compared to the rest of the world...Dutch government must take more effective action*".[217] By contrast, in *R v. Heathrow Airport Ltd,* the Supreme Court overturned the decision of the Court of Appeal that blocked the construction of the third runaway at Heathrow airport on the

---

obligation of the latter under this Agreement, in relation to an investment of the former." See para. 868, 869 of the award. Available at https://www.italaw.com/sites/default/files/case-documents/ita0723.pdf accessed 04.09.2024.

[214] Douglas (2013), p. 435.

[215] See 'Legality of the Threat or Use of Nuclear Weapons, Advisory Opinion' (1996) ICJReports, p. 241, para. 29, available at https://www.icj-cij.org/public/files/case-related/95/095-19960708-ADV-01-00-EN.pdf accessed 07.09.2024. The tribunal in *Gabčíkovo-Nagymaros Project* noted the following "*Throughout the ages, mankind has, for economic and other reasons, constantly interfered with nature. In the past, this was often done without consideration of the effects upon the environment. Owing to new scientific insights and to a growing awareness of the risks for mankind - for present and future generations - of pursuit of such interventions at an unconsidered and unabated pace, new norms and standards have been developed, set forth in a great number of instruments during the last two decades. Such new norms have to be taken into consideration, and such new standards given proper weight, not only when States contemplate new activities but also when continuing with activities begun in the past. This need to reconcile economic development with protection of the environment is aptly expressed in the concept of sustainable development.*" See *Gabčíkovo-Nagymaros Project*, para. 53 and 140, the case is available at https://www.icj-cij.org/public/files/case-related/92/092-19970925-JUD-01-00-EN.pdf accessed 04.09.2024.

[216] For the details of the case, please visit: https://www.urgenda.nl/en/themas/climate-case/ accessed 04.09.2024.

[217] The decision is available at https://www.urgenda.nl/wp-content/uploads/ENG-Dutch-Supreme-Court-Urgenda-v-Netherlands-20-12-2019.pdf accessed 04.09.2024.

grounds that the government failed to conform its commitments to prevent global warming.[218]

As provided for in article 4(2)[219] of the Paris Agreement, treaties empower or oblige parties to implement certain measures. This may give rise to the vexing question of whether host states may interfere with the foreign investors' ownership and, if so, to what extent. Basically, for reasons of public health and relying on international treaties, states are entitled to do so. In the attainment of a disguised expropriation, states may exceed the legitimate use of their regulatory prerogatives and label an investment as environmentally polluting.[220] It is crucial that the environmental risk is so authentic that the sovereign cannot be easily accused of disguising an ulterior motive.

In 2021, nations adopted Glasgow Climate Pact COP26, in which they were called to scale up the deployment and dissemination of clean power generation and energy efficiency measures by phasing down of unabated coal power and phasing out inefficient fossil fuel subsidies.[221] Environmental concerns must be in the host states' forefront. To put the matter in another way, the environmental justification of a measure may stand as a ground for reducing compensation; therefore, it should carry greater weight,[222] and municipal laws or their interpretation must not be lax or run afoul of the internationally recognized environmental principles.

As a result of growing awareness, the issue of environment began to come to the fore, and adjudicators began to take bold stances on disputes where the climate and its effect on investment are discussed. Of these disputes, the one arising from efforts to mitigate the reliance on coal is of particular importance. RWE, a German energy company, commenced arbitration proceedings against the Dutch government due to the coal phase-out that would require the company to close its power plant by the end

[218]In the view of the divisional court, the Paris Agreement did not impose an obligation on any individual state to implement its global objective in any particular way. According to the Court of Appeal, formal ratification of the Paris Agreement showed that the Government's commitment to the Paris Agreement was part of "Government policy". The Court of Appeal assessed whether the infrastructure plans were consistent with the Paris Agreement. However, the Supreme Court disagreed with the Court of Appeal. In the view of the Supreme Court "the words 'Government policy' were ordinary words which should be applied in their ordinary sense to the facts of a given situation" and in the Supreme Court's final belief, the UK government did not neglect its commitments. See paras. 103, 104, 107. The decision is available at https://www.supremecourt.uk/cases/docs/uksc-2020-0042-judgment.pdf Also please visit: https://www.whitecase.com/insight-alert/supreme-court-overturns-block-heathrows-expansion#article-content, https://www.nytimes.com/2020/02/27/world/europe/heathrow-airport-third-runway-uk.html also visit: https://www.theguardian.com/environment/2020/feb/27/heathrow-third-runway-ruled-illegal-over-climate-change all accessed 04.09.2024.

[219]The article is as follows; "*Parties shall pursue domestic mitigation measures, with the aim of achieving the objectives of such contributions.*"

[220]Newcombe (2005), p. 2.

[221]See: 36th para. of Section IV Mitigation, available at https://unfccc.int/sites/default/files/resource/cma2021_10_add1_adv.pdf accessed 04.09.2024.

[222]Viñuales (2013), pp. 281, 292.

of the decade. However, the Netherlands invoked before German courts, the issue of inadmissibility of the claim, which the Higher Regional Court of Cologne agreed with. The court took the view that such arbitral proceedings were prohibited.[223] However, while the position of the arbitral tribunal was to the contrary,[224] in its response to the claimant's request for provisional measures, it adopted a seemingly 'fair shake for all' approach. In another German energy company's (*Uniper*) case, the company disclosed its intention to vindicate its rights against Netherlands since the law regarding the coal phase-out does not include a compensation but will halve the value of the plant, and amount to expropriation. The German Federal government decided to acquire %99 of the company, which led the company to drop its claims.[225]

8.2.5.1.3.3 The Concept of Necessity

The question to be raised is: on whom to place the consequences of environmental harm? According to the *Newcombe,* within the context of police power, states may protect the citizens from pollutant acts associated with the use of property[226] and will not assume a burden to compensate. *Wagner* draws on environmental protection and argues that the parties responsible for harming the environment must also bear the cost of protecting it.[227] As per its nature, those who are in conscious defiance of the preservation of environment must be held accountable for deleterious consequences of their conduct.[228] In a simplified way, society

---

[223] For the reasonings of the court please visit: http://arbitrationblog.kluwerarbitration.com/2021/07/11/rwe-and-uniper-can-german-courts-assess-the-jurisdiction-of-icsid-arbitral-tribunals/ and http://arbitrationblog.kluwerarbitration.com/2022/11/03/rwe-and-uniper-german-courts-rule-on-the-admissibility-of-ect-based-icsid-arbitrations-in-intra-eu-investor-state-disputes/ both accessed 04.09.2024.

[224] The tribunal could not find that the German proceedings infringed on its exclusive authority to determine its own competence under the ICSID Convention, the Claimants' substantive rights, or the procedural integrity of this arbitration. See *RWE* case, para 88. Available at https://www.italaw.com/sites/default/files/case-documents/italaw170585.pdf accessed 04.09.2024.

[225] Please visit: https://www.euractiv.com/section/energy/news/energy-charter-treaty-strikes-again-as-uniper-sues-netherlands-over-coal-phase-out/ and https://www.euractiv.com/section/energy/news/not-approprite-uniper-seeks-compensation-for-dutch-coal-phase-out/ and finally please visit: https://www.bmwk.de/Redaktion/DE/Pressemitteilungen/2022/09/20220921-bundesregierung-verstandigt-sich-auf-anpassung-des-stabilisierungspakets-fur-uniper.html all accessed 04.09.2024.

[226] Newcombe (2005), p. 33.

[227] According to the 'polluter pays principle', the cost of environmental harm is shifted from society at large to the person causing the harm. See Wagner (1999), pp. 466, 470, 529.

[228] OECD Guidelines for Multinational Enterprises sets out the necessary actions that enterprises must take. According to the Guidelines, "*Enterprises should, within the framework of laws, regulations and administrative practices in the countries in which they operate, and in consideration of relevant international agreements, principles, objectives, and standards, take due account of the need to protect the environment, public health and safety, and generally to conduct their activities in a manner contributing to the wider goal of sustainable development.*" For the detail of the principles, see pp. 42–46, available at https://www.oecd-ilibrary.org/docserver/81f92357-en.

should not pay a price greater than the benefit they may accrue. In this regard, the necessity is conducive to the preclusion of wrongfulness.[229]

The WTO Agreement on the Application of Sanitary and Phytosanitary Measures (SPS Agreement) applies to measures with regard to food, animal or plant borne pests and diseases that may pose health risks to humans, animals or plants. According to article 2(2) of the SPS Agreement, measures taken by WTO members can only be applied to the extent necessary to protect human, animal or plant life or health. Members must base their measures on scientific principles and should not maintain them without sufficient scientific evidence.[230] According to *Weiler*, the SPS' necessity principle requires two main things; first, the measure must be applied in a manner consistent with the stated objectives and second, there must be no alternative means to address the risk that would be less harmful to the ownership interests at stake.[231]

Scholars are of the opinion that an international arbitral tribunal is not an appropriate body to weigh competing scientific claims and determine whether the risk is enough to justify the measure in question, or whether the measure is supported by the 'correct' or 'best', or 'most accepted' science.[232] Understanding the imminence of the threat, the magnitude of the harm and ascertaining those accountable may entail a local assessment (as in the case of an emerging site inspection that investigates the link between contamination of water source and the operation of a chemical facility). The ECHR, for instance, requires the adverse effects of environmental pollution or nuisance to attain a minimum level of severity.[233] In the same court's view, the pollution in question does not necessarily have to endanger people's health,[234] the pollution, without causing any quantifiable harm to human health, may worsen the quality of human lives and make them vulnerable to various illnesses.[235]

---

pdf?expires=1725454482&id=id&accname=guest&checksum=7669DF4DA9001108ADDC96CF97324E81 accessed 04.09.2024.

[229] See *Enron v. Argentina* para. 339. Also see *Sempra v. Argentina*, para. 388. https://www.italaw.com/sites/default/files/case-documents/ita0770.pdf accessed 04.09.2024.

[230] Article is as follows "*Members shall ensure that any sanitary or phytosanitary measure is applied only to the extent necessary to protect human, animal or plant life or health, is based on scientific principles and is not maintained without sufficient scientific evidence*" Full text can be found at https://www.wto.org/english/docs_e/legal_e/15-sps.pdf accessed 04.09.2024.

[231] Weiler (2003), p. 256.

[232] Wagner (1999), p. 534.

[233] See *Erol ÇİÇEK v. TURKEY* (para. 29) available at https://hudoc.echr.coe.int/eng#{%22itemid%22:[%22001-201673%22]} accessed 04.09.2024.

[234] In *Taşkın v. Turkey* (paras. 117, 132) the court ruled that "pollutant conduct must not infringe the effective enjoyment of the right to life and the right to live in a healthy environment". Available at https://hudoc.echr.coe.int/eng#{%22languageisocode%22:[%22ENG%22],%22appno%22:[%2246117/99%22],%22documentcollectionid2%22:[%22CHAMBER%22],%22itemid%22:[%22001-67401%22]} accessed 04.09.2024.

[235] See *Jugheli v. Georgia* (para 71) available at https://hudoc.echr.coe.int/eng#{%22itemid%22:[%22001-175153%22]} accessed 04.09.2024.

It must not be interpreted as an intrusion into state sovereignty when international adjudicators hear the scientific facts and decide whether the adopted protective measures were based on scientific assessments. However, one may need to note that, as provided for in article 5 of the SPS Agreement, if the scientific evidence is insufficient, states may adopt measures on the basis of available pertinent information. Nonetheless, the vague meaning of the term 'sufficiency' will assist states in adopting arbitrary measures.

The conditions of the necessity principle are crystallized under article 25 of the ILC.[236] According to the article, the host state may invoke the 'necessity' provided that the conditions of the various manifestations of necessity are met[237] and it has not contributed to the situation giving rise to a state of necessity. Insofar, the long-lasting debates on the invocation of necessity have been held in the context of economic crisis. ILC articles emphasize the '*essential interest*' of the state and '*graveness*' and '*imminence*' of the peril. Measures of an economic nature are designed to cope with the urgent financial needs of the state and may not be justified by necessity within the meaning of the ILC. An economic crisis is believed not to be a catastrophic event where the states are armed with other options.[238] However, for instance, the political violence risk could be argued in terms of the essential security interest. In some scholars' view, an economic crisis could lead to civil unrest if the nationals of the state concerned cannot afford heating expenses.[239]

On the other hand, the commentary to the ILC explicitly extends the notion of necessity to safeguarding the environment.[240] The concept of 'necessity' is of particular relevance and is not invoked only by states in their defense. Courts may find a state 'wrongful' if it fails to adopt the necessary measures.[241] Claims relying

---

[236] Article 25 of the ILC dealing with necessity reads as "*Necessity may not be invoked by a State as a ground for precluding the wrongfulness of an act not in conformity with an international obligation of that State unless the act: (a) is the only way for the State to safeguard an essential interest against a grave and imminent peril; and (b) does not seriously impair an essential interest of the State or States towards which the obligation exists, or of the international community as a whole. 2. In any case, necessity may not be invoked by a State as a ground for precluding wrongfulness if: (a) the international obligation in question excludes the possibility of invoking necessity; or (b) the State has contributed to the situation of necessity.*"

[237] Heard and Laryea (2021), p. 625.

[238] In *CMS v. Argentina* (para. 356) the tribunal held that "*the crisis in and of itself might not be characterized as catastrophic and while there was therefore not a situation of force majeure that left no other option open*".

[239] Also see Heard and Laryea (2021), p. 639.

[240] According to the article 14 of the Commentary to the article 25 of the ILC, "*necessity has been invoked to protect a wide variety of interests, including safeguarding the environment, preserving the very existence of the State and its people in time of public emergency, or ensuring the safety of a civilian population*". Please visit: https://legal.un.org/ilc/texts/instruments/english/commentaries/9_6_2001.pdf Also see *Impregilo v. Argentina*, p. 75 et seq. https://www.italaw.com/sites/default/files/case-documents/ita0418.pdf both accessed 04.09.2024.

[241] In *Greenpeace E.V. v. Germany*, the applicant alleged the lack of effective measures to curb diesel-vehicle emissions. In the ECHR's view, the applicant had failed to prove that state, by refusing to take a measure to install particulate filters, exceeded its discretionary power and failed to

on necessity must not be accepted on an exceptional basis[242] under the auspices of measures for the preservation of the environment.

In our opinion, measures for the preservation of the environment entail exceptional treatment. While the economic crisis leads to an imminent and distinguishable financial collapse in the pockets of a vast majority of the nationals, the impact of global warming unfolds over time. Therefore, at first glance, some may find the adoption of measures concerning the environment far from satisfying key components, such as its 'imminence'. However, global warming, backed by scientific facts like July 2023 setting all-time records as the world's hottest month on record,[243] will likely result in irreversible deterioration on a global scale.

The concept of compensation in expropriation serves to provide satisfaction to the owner in return for the deprivation. According to the majority's viewpoint, the payment of compensation is the essential element that attributes legality to expropriations. However, such actions by states cannot be simplified as mere 'dispossession.' On the contrary, they aim to put an end to activities that harm people and ensure that they do not favor proprietary rights over public interest or allow acts that present danger. Accepting otherwise implies that an investor operating a facility that poses a threat to human health might be rewarded through compensation. One could argue for a distinction between the state's obligation to provide compensation and the rectification of investors' actions. In our view, acts posing a threat to human health take on a criminal nature, and the states' response functions similarly to administrative forfeiture that does not require prosecution and compensation. Nevertheless, in such a case, the investor's intent or degree of negligence, as well as whether confiscating the asset leads to more severe consequences as opposed to those of the crime (the investor's harming human health), must be considered irrelevant. Hence, if a coal-powered power station is confiscated, PRI underwriters or lawyers should no longer ponder the measure's legality.

strike a fair balance between the interests of the individual and of the community as a whole. Available at https://hudoc.echr.coe.int/eng#{%22itemid%22:[%22001-92809%22]} accessed 04.09.2024.

[242] The tribunal in *LG&E v. Argentina* (paras. 245–250) by referring to ILC held that "the *possibility of alleging the state of necessity is closely bound by the requirement that there should be a serious and imminent threat and no means to avoid it. Such circumstances, in principle, have been left to the State's subjective appreciation, a conclusion accepted by the International Law Commission.*" and the tribunal further stated that "*the State must have exhausted all possible legal means before being forced to act as it does*".

[243] Please visit: https://www.theguardian.com/environment/2023/aug/08/july-2023-worlds-hottest-month-climate-crisis-scientists-confirm and https://www.euronews.com/green/2023/08/08/july-breaks-record-for-earths-hottest-ever-month both accessed 04.09.2024.

8.2.5.1.4 PRI Providers and Sustainable Development

Climate change has galvanized PRI providers and financial institutions in supporting foreign investments conducive to sustainable development. Investments that have significant adverse impact on the environment are eligible neither for an operating license under the jurisdiction of the host state nor for international loans. To eschew such end, foreign investors must structure their activities in consideration of relevant international principles[244] and must ensure that they will conduct operations in a manner that is socially and environmentally responsible.

Non-governmental organizations (NGOs)[245] or international organizations/institutions[246] endowed with international legal personality[247] contribute to protecting

[244] Principles for Responsible Investment is a network supported by the United Nations and aims to understand the investment implications of environmental, social and governance issues, and coincidently, it is referred to as PRI in short. Please see the PRI brochure, available at https://www.unpri.org/about-us/about-the-pri#How_is_the_PRI_funded accessed 04.09.2024.

[245] By way of amici curiae participation, NGOs may provide scientific information. The term, *amicus curiae* denotes "'friend of the court'. The wider connotation of this term can be fleshed out as "*a] person who is not a party to a lawsuit but who petitions the court or is requested by the court to file a brief in the action because that person has a strong interest in the subject matter*". Tribunals, in reaching their decision, may obtain assistance of third parties provided that the submission does not go beyond the neutral assessment on the facts and NGOs do not take a politically driven or biased position. Institutional rules also confer tribunals with a discretion to allow such submission. Article 37(2) of the ICSID Rules provides that a person or entity (non-disputing party) may file a written submission with the tribunal regarding a matter within the scope of the dispute. Tribunals may proceed with the *amici* submission if they are satisfied that "(a) the non-disputing party's submission assist the tribunal in the determination of a factual or legal issue related to the proceeding by bringing a perspective, particular knowledge or insight that is different from that of the disputing parties; (b) the non-disputing party's submission will address a matter within the scope of the dispute; (c) the non-disputing party has a significant interest in the proceedings. In *Pac Rim v. El Salvador*, according to the Canadian claimant, El Salvador denied its pending applications for the environmental permits, and the exploitation concession for the project was an exercise of a *defacto* ban on all metallic mining. The Center for International Environmental Law ("CIEL") submitted an application as non-disputing party pursuant to mentioned article of ICSID and its submission stated that "*in a country like El Salvador, who suffers from high pollution density and scarcity of water resources, the application of legal requirements and administrative processes are indispensable tools for the State to safeguard the rights threatened by extractive industries*." See part 3, page 5 et seq. Available at https://www.italaw.com/sites/default/files/case-documents/italaw7640_0.pdf A submission of a similar nature was made by non-disputing party (DHUMA) in *Bear Creek v. Peru,* which arose out of the revocation of the claimant's mining concession. DHUMA highlighted the probability of the project to contaminate the environment and threaten the existence and culture of indigenous communities. See para. 230, p. 57. Available at https://www.italaw.com/sites/default/files/case-documents/italaw9381.pdf both accessed 04.09.2024. For another amicus submission, see *Suez v. Argentina,* also see See Baltag (2020), pp. 305–309. And see Yu (2020), pp. 224, 229.

[246] Scholars believe that international organizations/institutions are vehicles through which states operate. For the discussion see Daugirdas (2016), pp. 325–381.

[247] The International Court of Justice came to the following conclusion "*international organizations are subjects of international law, and, as such, are bound by any obligations incumbent upon them under general rules of international law.*" See Interpretation of the Agreement of 25 March 1951

the environment by adopting international principles and requiring the prospective debtors to conduct an appropriate environmental and social assessment ('ESA' in short) prior to funding. ESA is a key component and a prerequisite for most fundings. It may explore the effects of the investment at an international level and monitor/screen the transboundary effects of the proposed investment.[248]

ESA assists in investigating the characteristics of the investment and the possibility of any potential damage. Once the latter is identified, the assessment proceeds to the estimation of the probable impacts of the damage and the appraisal of the weight of those impacts.[249] After this initial review, a preliminary assessment is published, and in the final stage, depending on the content of the preliminary assessment, the final assessment may reveal changes in the negotiation positions of the parties. If the final assessment has been rendered in the investor's favor, ESA may serve to attain a triple win for trade, environment and development.[250] ESA helps the host state, its nationals, and even the investor itself to fully understand the pros and cons of the proposed investment. For the sake of clarity and predictability, a mechanism where the public proactively takes part in the deliberations or has access to information can be put in place. By doing so, complaints against the proposed business activity will be heard;[251] if need be, an appeal procedure can be invoked, and ultimately, good governance will be sustained.[252] Of course, the host state will have the upper hand by having the wind of its people at her back in its decision-making and the investor, will necessarily need to mitigate economic expectations, accordingly, considering the potential impact of its investment on the environment.

Between the WHO and Egypt, Advisory Opinion, 1980, International Court of Justice, available at https://www.icj-cij.org/public/files/case-related/65/065-19801220-ADV-01-00-EN.pdf accessed 04.09.2024. Also see Langer (2013), p. 158.

[248] For detail, please see Gehring and Kent (2013), p. 193.

[249] Marisi (2020), p. 93 et seq.

[250] Athanasakou (2013), p. 255.

[251] For instance, the UN Global Compact requires companies to address environmental risks and mandates participants/signatories to align their actions with the commitments they have undertaken with regard to the Global Compact Ten Principles (the seventh principle pertains to environmental concerns). If a complaint is raised, the Global Compact Office requires the company to provide written comments, and offers guidance and assistance to the participating company concerned in taking actions to remedy the situation. Although in its preamble, it states that "*The United Nations Global Compact initiative is not designed, nor does it have the mandate or resources, to monitor or measure Participants'/Signatories' performance*", the Office is equipped with the authority to share with parties the information about the specific instance procedures of the OECD Guidelines for Multinational Enterprises for cooperation. It can also refer the matter to one or more of the UN entities for its assistance or action or to the Global Compact Board to draw on its business members' expertise. If the abuse is admitted by an authorized company representative or is the subject of a finding of guilt by a competent court of other body, the Office is entitled to delist the company from the UN Global Compact. See Morgera (2013), p. 338 et seq. Please visit: https://d306pr3pise04h.cloudfront.net/docs/about_the_gc%2FIntegrity_measures%2FIntegrity_Measures_Note_EN.pdf accessed 04.09.2024.

[252] Also see Morgera (2013), pp. 326, 337.

By requiring ESA, international financial institutions respect court decisions[253] and international treaties.[254] The International Finance Corporation (IFC) is the largest international institution focused on the private sector in emerging markets.[255] It adopts the Equator Principles[256] and incorporates the due diligence principle, that it also applies in its activities.[257] The IFC does not finance investment activities that do not meet the requirements of its performance standards.[258] More importantly, the World Bank[259] Group has implemented a bold action plan and, as per its Climate Change Action Plan, has decided to make its financing operations consistent with the

[253] The International Court of Justice stressed that carrying out an environmental impact assessment is a requirement under international law. See *Pulp mills* case (Paras. 203–229).

[254] Environmental assessment has been integrated to various regulations. Article 4 (1)(f) of the UNFCCC, article 17 of the Rio Declaration and article 19 of the Energy Charter Treaty provides for environmental assessment. Also, see Daugirdas (2016), pp. 340–342.

[255] Please visit: https://www.ifc.org/en/about accessed 04.09.2024.

[256] The Equator Principles are risk management framework that provides the minimum standards in identifying, assessing and managing environmental and social risks when financing Projects. Its name represents the draftsmanship's' intention for adoption by institutions from every corner of the world and as many as possible. Although its membership comprises as many as 130 institutions, the Principles seem to be far from achieving its goal due to participation of financial institutions from only 39 countries. The principles, in its preamble, explicitly declares its support for the objectives of the Paris Agreement. The Equator Principles as the name implies, consists of 10 principles namely: 1- Review & Categorization (The Equator Principle adopts a categorization based on that of the IFC), 2- Environmental and Social Assessment, 3- Applicable Environmental and Social Assessment Standards (to evaluate the Project's compliance with relevant host country laws, regulations, and permits that pertain to environmental and social issues), 4-Environmental and Social Management (E&S) System & Equator Principles Action Plan (client/investor is required to develop and/or maintain an E&S Management System) 5- Stakeholder Engagement (clients/investors are required to conduct an informed consultation and participation process and make appropriate assessment documentation readily available to the affected communities in order to comply with the rights and protections for Indigenous People who are deemed to be vulnerable segments of affected communities), 6-Grievance Mechanism (clients/investors are required to establish an effective grievance mechanisms to receive and facilitate resolution of concerns), 7-Independent Review (an independent environmental and social consultant will carry out an independent review of the assessment process to detect any deviation from the applicable standards and assist in financial institution in determining whether the Project complies with the principles), 8-Covenants (This remedial action aims to ensure clients/investor comply with all relevant host country environmental and social laws, regulations and permits in all material respects), 9-Independent Monitoring & Reporting (an independent environmental and social consultant will provide monitoring and reporting)10- Reporting & Transparency. For detail, please visit: https://equator-principles.com/about-the-equator-principles/#. Also see Green Bond Principles, available at https://www.icmagroup.org/sustainable-finance/the-principles-guidelines-and-handbooks/green-bond-principles-gbp/ both accessed 04.09.2024.

[257] See Langer (2013), p. 164, similarly, see Marisi (2020), p. 94 et seq.

[258] See para. 22 of the IFC's Policy on Environmental and Social Sustainability. For detail, also see Morgera (2013), p. 326 et seq.

[259] In *Salacuse*'s view, the rules or the decisions of the international organizations such as the World Bank, ICSID, IMF or ICC may have an impact on international investment. Salacuse (2013), pp. 46–47.

goals of the Paris Agreement.[260] On the other hand, some model treaties stipulate that investments must comply with the standards adopted by the IFC.[261] Hence, a project must not only conform to municipal laws of the host state but also to the principles or standards adopted or introduced by pioneering financial institutions.

The transition towards a green economy, therefore, a green investment[262] matter for the PRI providers as they do for the international financial institutions and lenders. Insurers provide coverage upon the fulfillment of the principles they have adopted.[263] To illustrate, OPIC(DFC), as a result of its monitoring, discovered that one of the investments it was covering posed substantial adverse environmental impacts on environment and canceled the relevant insurance policy.[264] MIGA has adopted Performance Standards on Environmental and Social Sustainability[265] in line with its Policy on Environmental and Social Sustainability.[266] MIGA's 'do no harm' principle requires investments not to conduct activities with adverse impacts on the environment. The source of an ESA can be a financial institution/insurer, investor or a third party. MIGA accepts presentation of an ESA for the project for which insurance is sought and which is composed by a development finance institution (such as ECAs) or World Bank Group entities. The purpose of this

[260] Please visit: https://www.worldbank.org/en/publication/paris-alignment accessed 04.09.2024.

[261] See art. 6.1 of Multilateral treaty for the encouragement of investment in climate change mitigation and adaptation, available at https://thinktank30.de/wp-content/uploads/2018/08/Think-Tank-30-Model-MIT.pdf accessed 04.09.2024. Also see Elrifai et al. (2019).

[262] The green economy denotes "one that results in improved human well-being and social equity, while significantly reducing environmental risks and ecological scarcities." And a green investment must be low in carbon, resource efficient and socially inclusive. For the definition of the United Nations Environment Programme please visit: https://www.unep.org/pt-br/node/23750 accessed 04.09.2024. Finally, article 2 of the Green Investment Protocol is as follows: "1. *A Green Investment means an investment that contributes to achieving the aims set out in Article 2.1 of the Paris Agreement, taking into account the Contracting Parties' international obligations, including their human rights obligations. 2. A Green Investment shall include any Investment that: (a) qualifies as eligible to participate in the mechanism to contribute to the mitigation of greenhouse gas emissions and support sustainable development, in accordance with Article 6(4) of the Paris Agreement; or (b) has been made in pursuit of Article 6(1) of the Kyoto Protocol and has received the necessary approvals or qualifies as eligible to participate in the clean development mechanism as defined in Article 12 of the Kyoto Protocol; or (c) constitutes any future mechanism or technology created to achieve the aims of the Paris Agreement.*" See Henin et al. (2019), p. 48.

[263] According to the commentary to MIGA Convention, non-discriminatory environmental measures are not covered. See art. 14 of the commentary, p. 9, similarly see art. 10(5) of the Harvard Draft Convention.

[264] For detail, see Tan (2015), p. 189.

[265] For the full text, please visit: https://www.miga.org/sites/default/files/archive/Documents/MIGA_Performance_Standards_October_2013.pdf accessed 04.09.2024.

[266] By adhering to the policy, MIGA seeks to (i) enhance the predictability, transparency, and accountability of its actions and decision making (ii) help its clients to manage their environmental and social risks and impacts and (iii) enhance positive development outcomes on the ground. Please visit: https://www.miga.org/sites/default/files/archive/Documents/Policy_Environmental_Social_Sustainability.pdf accessed 04.09.2024.

book is not to engage in an analysis of the principles adopted by those organizations. The growth of the population poses a high risk for the preservation of the environment. While developed countries have managed to minimize the problems associated with the environment, developing ones, however, struggle in such efforts. The development of a country must be sustainable and not detrimental to the environment.[267] Accordingly, investments must be subordinated to the protection of nature, and developed countries must provide the necessary financial means to developing countries on terms that are not burdensome. The Paris Agreement adopts a mechanism in which developed countries take the lead in combating climate change.[268] In accordance with the Santiago network[269] that was established at COP 25 to contribute to the effective implementation of the functions of the Warsaw International Mechanism for Loss and Damage,[270] developed countries undertake to compensate developing countries for the damages they have sustained.[271]

Climate change necessitates a reclassification in investments. For instance, the IFC established a process of environmental and social categorization whereby it assesses the magnitude of risks and impacts associated with the proposed business activity.[272] Sustainable and green investments are financially sound and pose fewer

[267] Sustainable development is defined as "*development that does not take place at the expense of future generations*". See Salacuse (2013), p. 59.

[268] Article 9(1) of the Paris Agreement provides "*Developed country Parties shall provide financial resources to assist developing country Parties with respect to both mitigation and adaptation in continuation of their existing obligations under the Convention.*"

[269] The Santiago network was established for averting, minimizing and addressing loss and damage associated with the adverse effects of climate change, to catalyze the technical assistance of relevant organizations, bodies, networks and experts for the implementation of relevant approaches at the local, national and regional levels, in developing countries that are particularly vulnerable to the adverse effects of climate change. See Decision 2/CMA.2, para. 43. Available at https://unfccc.int/sites/default/files/resource/cma2_auv_6_WIM.pdf also visit: https://unfccc.int/santiago-network/ about both accessed 04.09.2024.

[270] Warsaw international mechanism for loss and damage associated with climate change impacts was created to address loss and damage associated with impacts of climate change at COP 19. The Paris Agreement recognizes the document through its article 8(2) and (3), please visit: https://unfccc.int/topics/adaptation-and-resilience/workstreams/loss-and-damage/warsaw-international-mechanism and for the Decision 2/CP.19 under which the mechanism was established, please visit: https://unfccc.int/resource/docs/2013/cop19/eng/10a01.pdf both accessed 04.09.2024.

[271] Parties to Glasgow Climate Pact (COP 26) decided the Santiago network to be provided with funds for its operations and for the provision of technical assistance. See paras. 67 and 70 of the document, available at https://unfccc.int/sites/default/files/resource/cma3_auv_2_cover%20decision.pdf and same approached remained at COP 27, see para. 25 of the Decision -/CP.27 available at https://unfccc.int/sites/default/files/resource/cop27_auv_2_cover%20decision.pdf both accessed 04.09.2024.

[272] The IFC's classification comprises 4 categories. Category A represents business activities with the potential for significant adverse environmental or social risks and/or impacts that are diverse, irreversible, or unprecedented. Category B involves business activities with potentially limited adverse environmental or social risks, which are mostly reversible. As expected, business activities falling under category C are those with minimal or no adverse environmental or social risks and/or impacts. The final category encompasses business activities involving investments in financial

risks to insurers. Hence, PRI providers must value environmental sustainability over other criteria. Just as the necessity exception provides host states the means to protect their interest in the eventuality of any of the situation provided for in the regulations of ILC or WTO,[273] so too will investments that deviate from the determinations in the environmental assessment provide insurers with a means to terminate insurance coverage. This implies that foreign investments must adapt to the constraints adopted as a result of international principles. Failure to do so may result in PRI providers facing compensation claims to a much higher amount. PRI providers must be prepared for the economic threats lying ahead. If the transformation of the investment into an environment-friendly one is not fruitful due to inputs being higher than outputs, expropriation, as a last resort, must be considered. However, the vast number of such insured investments may put PRI providers in economic difficulties. The question then will be how the equilibrium between the protection of environment and foreign investment activity that provides both job opportunities and prevents migration can be sustained.

8.2.5.2 Expropriation in the Era of Pandemic

Sovereigns act in the interests of national security and defend public welfare; however, environmental disasters or pandemics, however, pose threats to the preservation of the public good. As of today, it may look like a scene from an apocalyptic movie, however, the Covid-19[274] outbreak has claimed and taken millions of lives worldwide and shaken the global economy. Despite medical advancements, the pandemic has revealed in several respects that humanity is still vulnerable and slow in responding to pandemics.

To cope with the outcomes of the Covid-19 pandemic, governments have adopted several measures. First and foremost were lockdowns/travel bans which had severe impact not only on individuals, but also on merchants depending on mobility. To fight economic consequences of the pandemic, states have instituted price controls on essential supplies and halted tariffs on services and utilities.[275] With regard to the former measure, one may need to note that business interruption does not necessarily require tangible or structural damage. On-site production can be vital for specific

intermediaries (FI) which are further subdivided into several categories based on the content of the portfolio held by the FI. For detail, please see para. 40 of the IFC's Policy on Environmental and Social Sustainability, available at https://www.ifc.org/content/dam/ifc/doc/2023/ifc-policy-on-environmental-and-social-sustainability-2012-en.pdf accessed 04.09.2024.

[273] Heard and Laryea (2021), p. 624.

[274] Coronavirus disease 2019, for detail see https://www.who.int/emergencies/diseases/novel-coronavirus-2019/technical-guidance/naming-the-coronavirus-disease-(covid-2019)-and-the-virus-that-causes-it accessed 04.09.2024.

[275] For example, the Australian government announced that the Foreign Investment Review Board (FIRB) would review all FDIs, which sought to purchase distressed Australian assets. See Heard and Laryea (2021), p. 617. Also see Stephens-Chu (2022), pp. 171–190.

sectors. Certain companies, for their continuity, may rely on employees or key individuals working within the premises of the corporation.[276] Another measure introduced by governments came in the form of hospital expropriation[277] and restriction of the exportation of medical equipment.[278]

Property can be confiscated during an epidemic of an infectious disease.[279] The *Booker v. Scottish Minister* case pertains to the outbreak of VHS (Viral haemorrhagic septicaemia) confirmed at the claimant's farm which led to the slaughter and destruction of the fish without compensation. In the view of the court, the right to property was one of the fundamental rights, could be considered in relation to their social function and thus, restrictions could be imposed on the exercise of those rights.[280] In the *Bischoff* case, a carriage was detained by the police upon a false information that it was carrying two passengers afflicted with smallpox. Despite the police's offer to return the carriage, the claimant was not satisfied, believing that he suffered damage at the time of detention. The umpire, however, took a position justifying the legitimacy of measures, holding that "*an epidemic of an infectious disease there can be no liability for the reasonable exercise of police power, even though a mistake is made.*[281]" What is evident is that differing measures across various jurisdictions compelled some foreign investors to resort to investment arbitration.[282] Enforcement of measures on a global scale obscures the extent of their

[276] Also see Gürses (2021), pp. 71–83.

[277] In 2020, Spain nationalised its hospitals and healthcare providers to help fight against COVID-19. Please visit: https://www.globalarbitrationnews.com/2021/03/30/part-ii-of-a-trilogy-investor-claims-in-response-to-the-states-protective-measures-during-the-covid-19-pandemic/ accessed 04.09.2024.

[278] For example, the Indian and Australian governments imposed certain limitations on the export of goods, such as personal protective equipment and hand sanitizers, essential for combating COVID-19. For similar measures, please see Ziadé and Hoebeke (2022), p. 164. Also see Asteriti (2022), pp. 21–22. Scholars classified measures into four categories, namely, containment and closure, economic response, health systems and miscellaneous, and made a distinction according to the motivation of the measure. While primary measures were the ones aimed at slowing down the spread of COVID-19, secondary measures were directed at mitigating the effects of the primary measures on the economy. The final distinction was made based upon the party whose action is essential. Positive measures required expenditure, and negative ones necessitated behavioral changes from the public. Nationalisation and export/import bans are positive secondary measures. See Asteriti (2022), pp. 13–15.

[279] In 1984 Brazilian authorities destroyed several lots of watermelons due to an outbreak of cholera. See Newcombe and Paradell (2009), p. 361, similarly see Newcombe (2005), p. 26.

[280] The court also concluded that "*fish farm carries commercial risks can expect, as farmers, that a fish disease may break out at any moment and cause them loss. Such risk is inherent in the business of raising and selling livestock and is the consequence of a natural occurrence*." See paras. 67, 68 and 83 available at https://curia.europa.eu/juris/showPdf.jsf;jsessionid=20E7F320FF7163A9AC7B0DA9EE41E8CE?text=&docid=48497&pageIndex=0&doclang=EN&mode=lst&dir=&occ=first&part=1&cid=22031418 accessed 04.09.2024.

[281] Please visit: https://legal.un.org/riaa/cases/vol_X/420-421.pdf accessed 04.09.2024.

[282] In *ADP v. Chile*, claimants brought an ICSID claim on the basis of the Chilean government's alleged refusal to renegotiate the terms of the concession and failure to compensate claimants for

impact upon a specific investor and whether these measures exhibited discrimination towards them.[283] Host states must not be stymied on the question of whether necessity argument can be invoked during pandemics.

Scholars propose that the sovereign's necessity defense might have undergone a transformation due to the conditions brought about by the global response to the pandemic.[284] As regards the invocation of the necessity defense, host states could invoke the Covid-19 outbreak to justify their failure to fulfill international obligations towards foreign investors. The measures must indicate that they are the only means in preventing the spread of the pandemic and dealing with its impact. However, host states will need to justify these measures by emphasizing their role in preserving public health. In fact, treaties that exclude measures taken for public health may provide a sufficient basis for such a defense.[285] Besides, as far as human health and well-being are concerned, interference by the international organizations such as the World Health Organization (WHO) is conceivable. The WHO took active role during the pandemic, its recommendations had an indirect regulatory impact on foreign investors[286] and governments exercised their regulatory powers based on the scientific insights addressed by the WHO.

Tackling a virus which knows no borders was almost about to grip the entire globe. The margin of a state's appreciation in its regulatory actions must justify the proportionality and relevance of the aim pursued.[287] Thus, the legitimacy of the measures taken under international investment law will be in question as long as the benefits of these measures to society outweigh the consequences on foreign investment. Thus, PRI providers must mould themselves to such unprecedented events in the years to come.

8.3 Political Force Majeure/Violence

8.3.1 Conceptual Difference Between Regular Contracts and Investor-State Contracts

The concept of force majeure finds its origin in the Roman law term 'vis maior', whose function is to set a limit on the strict liability.[288] Force majeure events cover a

economic losses in the context of the COVID-19 pandemic. Please visit: https://www.italaw.com/cases/9727 accessed 07.09.2024. Also see Ziadé and Hoebeke (2022), pp. 163–164.

[283] The tribunal in *Plama v. Bulgaria* noted that a rule cannot be said to be discriminatory when it has been adopted by many countries around the world. See *Plama v. Bulgaria* para. 269 and see Stephens-Chu (2022), pp. 187, 188.

[284] See Heard and Laryea (2021), p. 631.

[285] Also see Cristani (2022), pp. 71, 72.

[286] Also see Asteriti (2022), pp. 10, 11.

[287] For the detailed analysis of proportionality see Levashova (2022), pp. 122, 125.

[288] McKendrick (1995), p. 21.

variety of circumstances spanning from acts of God[289] (natural disasters, *floods and hurricanes,* quarantines) to acts of community/human origin (riots, *strikes*, war).[290] As the examples clearly set forth, force majeure necessitates an event that is unpredictable, irresistible and external.[291] An event of force majeure attributes impossibility to the parties' obligations;[292] however, an event of a foreseeable kind or one that is resistible, and that reasonable person would be able to control or surmount, given the circumstances, does not provide a basis for the obligors to withdraw from their performance.

An impediment beyond the obligor's control or one that renders performance unreasonably and excessively onerous[293] is termed force majeure exemption.[294] These exemptions excuse the obligor from the obligation to provide a specific

---

[289] Some scholars define as "*such an operation of the forces of nature as reasonable foresight and ability could not foresee or reasonably provide against.*" McKendrick (1995), p. 142.

[290] In ICC's interpretation, those events are a) war (whether declared or not), hostilities, invasion, act of foreign enemies, extensive military mobilization; b) civil war, riot, rebellion and revolution, military or usurped power, insurrection, act of terrorism, sabotage or piracy; c) currency and trade restriction, embargo, sanction; d) act of authority whether lawful or unlawful, compliance with any law or governmental order, expropriation, seizure of works, requisition, nationalisation; e) plague, epidemic, natural disaster or extreme natural event; f) explosion, fire, destruction of equipment, prolonged break-down of transport, telecommunication, information system or energy; g) general labour disturbance such as boycott, strike and lock-out, go-slow, occupation of factories and premises. Please visit: https://iccwbo.org/news-publications/icc-rules-guidelines/icc-force-majeure-and-hardship-clauses/ accessed 04.09.2024.

[291] ICC defines force majeure as "*the occurrence of an event or circumstance ("Force Majeure Event") that prevents or impedes a party from performing one or more of its contractual obligations under the contract, if and to the extent that the party affected by the impediment ("the Affected Party") proves: a) that such impediment is beyond its reasonable control; and b) that it could not reasonably have been foreseen at the time of the conclusion of the contract; and c) that the effects of the impediment could not reasonably have been avoided or overcome by the Affected Party*". Please visit: https://iccwbo.org/content/uploads/sites/3/2020/03/icc-forcemajeure-hardship-clauses-march2020.pdf accessed 04.09.2024. The Black's Law Dictionary defines force majeure as 'an event or effect that can be neither anticipated nor controlled.'

[292] McKendrick (1995), pp. 24–25.

[293] Brunner (2008), p. 221, in *Sempra v. Argentina*, (para. 246), the tribunal emphasized the subtlety of the term "impossibility." According to the tribunal, in times of political or economic crises, the state's obligation must revive and thus, such situations cannot render the performance materially impossible.

[294] The first three paragraphs of article 79 of United Nations Convention on Contracts for the International Sale of Goods are as follows: (1) A party is not liable for a failure to perform any of his obligations if he proves that the failure was due to an impediment beyond his control and that he could not reasonably be expected to have taken the impediment into account at the time of the conclusion of the contract or to have avoided or overcome it, or its consequences. (2) If the party's failure is due to the failure by a third person whom he has engaged to perform the whole or a part of the contract, that party is exempt from liability only if: (a) he is exempt under the preceding paragraph; and (b) the person whom he has so engaged would be so exempt if the provisions of that paragraph were applied to him. (3) The exemption provided by this article has effect for the period during which the impediment exists. Please visit: https://uncitral.un.org/sites/uncitral.un.org/files/media-documents/uncitral/en/19-09951_e_ebook.pdf accessed 04.09.2024.

performance.[295] Upon the occurrence of such events, depending on the wording of the clause, parties may be granted an extension of time, a variation of the contract in certain events or a refund of moneys paid.[296] In most cases, owing to a force majeure event, performance of the contract is either impeded or prevented, relieving parties from the responsibilities they assumed and permitting contract cancellation.[297]

In contracts between foreign investors and states, the language of force majeure events can be tailored to the parties' preferences. Unexpected regulations, legislation, and refusals of licenses or permits can be described as instances of force majeure in contracts between private parties and State agencies or subdivisions.[298]

Article 23 of ILC articles points a way-out for states to be relieved from their wrongful acts under numerous conditions.[299] The tribunal in Iran-United States Claims, defined force majeure as "social *and economic forces beyond the power of the state to control through the exercise of due diligence*". In the tribunal's view, injuries caused by the operation of such forces were not attributable to the state for the purposes of its responding for damages.[300] If the situation provides to the state, the element of no choice[301] and for so long as it subsists, the wrongfulness of the

---

[295] Hardship exemption on the other hand, can arise through an increase in the cost of performance or a decrease in the value of the performance by the other party. Unlike force majeure events, hardship exemption allows courts to restore equilibrium or terminate the contract. Brunner (2008), p. 221.

[296] McKendrick (1995), p. 9.

[297] In civil law, jurisdictions as Turkey, parties, prior to cancellation of the contract, may recourse to courts for the adaptation of their performance to the recent circumstances. For instance, art. 138 of Turkish Code of Obligations provides: "If an extraordinary situation, which was unforeseen and not expected to be foreseen by the parties at the time the contract was made, arises due to a reason not attributable to the debtor, and this situation changes the circumstances existing at the time the contract was made to such an extent that demanding performance from the debtor would be contrary to the principles of good faith, and if the debtor has not yet performed their obligation or has performed while reserving the rights arising from the excessive difficulty of performance, the debtor has the right to request the court to adapt the contract to the new conditions, or, if this is not possible, to withdraw from the contract." Please note that this is an unofficial translation.

[298] Rubins and Kinsella (2005), p. 57.

[299] The article reads as follows; "*The wrongfulness of an act of a State not in conformity with an international obligation of that State is precluded if the act is due to force majeure, that is the occurrence of an irresistible force or of an unforeseen event, beyond the control of the State, making it materially impossible in the circumstances to perform the obligation*". Please visit: https://legal.un.org/ilc/texts/instruments/english/commentaries/9_6_2001.pdf accessed 04.09.2024.

[300] See *Gould Marketing v. Iran*. Available at https://www.trans-lex.org/230700/_/iran-us-claims-tribunal-gould-marketing-inc-v-ministry-of-national-defence-3-iran-us-ctr-at-147-et-seq/ accessed 04.09.2024.

[301] In *Aucoven v. Venezuela*, the tribunal did not accept Venezuela's excuse of impossibility deriving from civil unrest of significant magnitude. In the view of the tribunal, there was an apparent public resistance that had the potential to jeopardize the future of the concession. Nonetheless, one of the tribunal's findings was that the local officials quelled the protests. See paras. 106–129. The case is available at https://jusmundi.com/en/document/decision/en-autopista-concesionada-de-venezuela-c-a-v-bolivarian-republic-of-venezuela-award-tuesday-23rd-september-2003 accessed 04.09.2024.

state's action will be precluded.[302] For instance, while expropriation risk requires deliberate action(s), by the sovereign, the same sovereign power may have little or no control, influence or whatsoever in the occurrence of events composing political force majeure.[303]

8.3.2 Political Force Majeure Events

A force majeure event included in a PRI contract may not void the contract; instead, given that one of the risks covered by PRI contracts is 'political force majeure/ political violence', it may entitle the insured party to compensation. Political violence or political force majeure subsumes a wide spectrum of fierce or vicious events. Events of a political nature can be determined by the presence of a motive to overthrow the government. However, some political force majeure events may aim at solely breaking the law and instilling fear and therefore may not fit in the traditional definition.

Political force majeure events can be classified based on the means employed. By way of example, armed forces or military equipment are the components of war, civil war, terrorism and coup d'état. On the other hand, riots, insurrection, strikes, lockouts, civil strife and civil disturbance[304] can be used interchangeably and are civilian-induced actions. The probability of the latter group of risks is higher in comparison to the first group; as a result, PRI providers offer stand-alone war or terrorism coverage.[305]

The full protection and security standard holds significance if foreign investment has been affected by one of the political force majeure events.[306] It is the host state's duty to prevent the risk occurrence and protect the physical integrity of the investment against interference by the use of force.[307] The wrongdoings may stem from either the host state's action(s) taken under sovereign authority with a view to prevent, hinder or suppress the attack that is committed in the course of a disturbance

[302] See commentary to ILC, at page 76, art. 2, 3.

[303] Torrado (2005), pp. 309, 310.

[304] Some scholars opine that 'civil disturbance' subsumes these disorders. See Rubins and Kinsella (2005), p. 19.

[305] For instance, OPIC began to offer stand-alone terrorism coverage after September 11, 2001, attacks. See Salacuse (2013), p. 258.

[306] If one were to wonder whether the standard imposes strict liability upon the host state, the assessment will be addressed in the subsequent chapters of this book.

[307] According to the tribunal in *AMT v. Zaire*, the state of Zaire was responsible to ensure the protection and security of the investment. Article IV paragraph 1(b) of the relevant BIT imposed an obligation on Zaire to compensate nationals or companies of the other party who suffer damages due to revolution, state of national emergency, revolt, insurrection, riot or act of violence in the territory of other party. See paras. 6.12–6.14. Also see *Saluka v. Czech Republic* paras. 483, 484.

to the public peace[308] or the host state's response(s) to events[309] which might be in the form of precautionary or preparatory measures. The host state must provide due diligence to insulate the investment from negative effects of violent act,[310] immediately crush it, and provide an effective remedy to the foreign investor.[311]

In addition to physical harm, business interruption (BI)[312] and loss of profit are the binary effects of these risks.[313] With regard to the latter, the coverage may comprise the loss deriving from the investor's inability to conduct operations that are essential to the investment's financial viability. As of today, the operations of most companies depend on digital means. Preventing a terrorist attack may not always be possible to foresee and monitor,[314] and terrorism can take the form of malicious cyber acts, which may lead to business interruption as well as physical damage to the investment.[315] The kinds of losses will vary depending on the nature of the company's business.[316]

---

[308] For the definition of 'war damage' in War Damage Act, 1943. Please visit: https://vlex.co.uk/vid/war-damage-act-1943-861282086 accessed 04.09.2024.

[309] See Parsons (Great Britain) v. United States, available at https://jusmundi.com/en/document/decision/en-parsons-great-britain-v-united-states-award-monday-30th-november-1925 accessed 04.09.2024. In *Sea-Land Service v. Iran* (para. 48) the tribunal held that "*Sea-Land relies on two other instances of interference, not ascribed to PSO itself but to other governmental agencies, which took place in early 1979. The first of these was the imposition by customs officials of restrictions on the types of cargo which could be unloaded at Bandar Abbas, limiting them to foodstuffs and medicine. The Tribunal considers this to be a reasonable and legitimate measure during a time of civil unrest.*" Available at https://jusmundi.com/en/document/decision/en-sea-land-service-inc-v-the-government-of-the-islamic-republic-of-iran-ports-and-shipping-organization-award-award-no-135-33-1-friday-22nd-june-1984 accessed 04.09.2024.

[310] In *AAPL v. Sri Lanka, (Award, para. 72)* the tribunal held that *"A State on whose territory an insurrection occurs is not responsible for loss or damage sustained by foreign investors unless it can be shown that the Government of that state failed to provide the standard of protection required, either by treaty, or under general customary law, as the case may be; and (ii) - Failure to provide the standard of protection required entails the state's international responsibility for losses suffered, regardless of whether the damages occurred during an insurgents' offensive act or resulting from governmental counter-insurgency activities."* Available at https://jusmundi.com/en/document/decision/en-asian-agricultural-products-ltd-aapl-v-republic-of-sri-lanka-award-wednesday-27th-june-1990 accessed 04.09.2024. Also see Sprankling (2014), pp. 271–272.

[311] Oppenheim et al. (2008), p. 552.

[312] BI policies operate on the basis that the assured can recover financial losses caused by the relevant insured peril for an indemnity period as laid down by the policy. See Gürses (2021), p. 72.

[313] Wagner (2012), p. 108.

[314] Merkin and Kullmann (2006).

[315] Cyber risk is defined as "*risks emanating from the use of electronic data and its transmission*" See OECD (2017), p. 20. For the documented examples of physical damage, see Ibid, p. 35. Available at https://www.oecd-ilibrary.org/docserver/3e164d0c-en.pdf?expires=1725478287&id=id&accname=guest&checksum=AF51D69E3B77FBE98DAE9446055B256A accessed 04.09.2024.

[316] For instance, a cyber-attack on a textile manufacturer may lead to disruption of financial systems or the malfunctioning of machinery. In companies operating in e-commerce, social networking,

In response to the evolution in the form of terrorist attacks, cyber-security insurance can serve as coverage against cyberterrorist attacks, thereby insureds may avoid absorbing losses from such attacks.[317] Some might argue that insurance schemes, whether government-subsidized or government-provided, are entirely counterintuitive or, at best, cumbersome in fulfilling the modern needs of the insurance market. However, as will be discussed in the following chapters, the Pool Re of UK provides coverage against remote digital interference alongside BI risk.[318] In our view, grey areas persist in such coverage. A PRI provider may seek that the location of the risk-occurrence be within the host state's territory. Coverage might not be extended to cyber-related losses deriving from attacks on a foreign investment's servers located in a country other than the host state.

A special attention should be paid to strikes, lockouts and any means of labor-based actions.[319] In ILO's definition, strike is '*a temporary work stoppage effected by one or more groups of workers with a view to enforcing or resisting demands or expressing grievances, or supporting other workers in their demands or grievances.*' and a lockout is '*a total or partial temporary closure of one or more places of employment, or the hindering of the normal work activities of employees, by one or more employers with a view to enforcing or resisting demands or expressing grievances, or supporting other employers in their demands or grievances.*[320]' As the definitions suggest, strikes and lockouts are the reactions of the parties to unfair terms or practice of employment. Then the following question requires an answer: Should PRI cover the losses caused by the actions of those whom, whether contractual or not, the investor does not have even an employment relation with.

Strikes and lockouts are rights granted to parties primarily through constitutions, and they must be exercised within the limits provided therein. To put it differently, strikes resulting from an investor's failure to fulfill its obligations under the employment contract, and which occur while employees are exercising constitutional rights, cannot be considered insurable risks. This risk can be covered only to the extent that they lose their legal character and involve elements of violence in their occurrence.

---

digital streaming, cloud computing or online advertising, such attacks could result in network or service disruption, data/software loss or extortion perpetrated by digital means.

[317] For detail as to companies providing stand-alone insurance against cyber threats, see OECD (2020), Insurance Coverage for Cyber Terrorism in Australia, pp. 14–15. Available at https://www.oecd-ilibrary.org/docserver/3e164d0c-en.pdf?expires=1725478287&id=id&accname=guest&checksum=AF51D69E3B77FBE98DAE9446055B256A accessed 04.09.2024 and also see OECD (2017), p. 34.

[318] Also visit: https://www.poolre.co.uk/cover/ accessed 04.09.2024.

[319] In some scholar's view, lockouts and labour disturbances are forms of industrial actions. See McKendrick (1995), p. 142. Public insurers may require a labor disturbance not to be a pay dispute. Wagner (2012), p. 108.

[320] See International Labour Office Resolution concerning statistics of strikes, lockouts and other action due to labour stoppages, adopted by the Fifteenth International Conference of Labour Statisticians (January 1993). Available at https://www.ilo.org/wcmsp5/groups/public/%2D%2D-dgreports/%2D%2D-stat/documents/normativeinstrument/wcms_087544.pdf accessed 04.09.2024. For a variety of definitions also see McKendrick (1995), pp. 88, 89.

What inspires the action or how the event is defined or characterized under international law is irrelevant.[321] According to the 'doctrine of effect', the insurer should focus on the outcomes. For instance, war is defined as "the state in which we prosecute our right by force",[322] or as express by *Hall*, "*When differences between states reach a point at which both parties resort to force, or one of them does acts of violence, which the other chooses to look upon as a breach of the peace, the relation of war is set up, in which the combatants may use regulated violence against each other, until one of the two has been brought to accept such terms as his enemy is willing to grant.*[323]" An action involving military equipment between two sovereign nations may constitute a formal state of war. This does not necessarily mean that the coverage should be limited to losses deriving from the means of war. Otherwise, a loss incurred from a fire lit by a soldier's cigarette butt during a military conflict could not be a covered peril.

Insureds or underwriters might not need to distinguish war risks or risks alike from the description of political force majeure events. Each event may connote a disturbance more or less extensive than the other, and each term may carry a depth besides the level of violence. The policy wording should not grant a broad discretion to the underwriter at the time of claim determination, and the intention of the perpetrators or the form of the conduct must not be a bar before indemnification. By way of illustration, if the policy covers war and similar events, the underwriter must not reject the claim merely due to a lack of a formal declaration of war. In a similar vein, in the case of terrorism, neither the perpetrators nor those attempting to suppress it might represent a sovereign power, but acts should still be attributable. Moreover, the violence used may not have political ends to overthrow the lawfully constituted government and seize its powers; instead, the acts they commit might solely endanger lives, harm individuals or cause damage to property.[324] Additionally, the number of actors involved in the event may not be sufficient for the underwriter's criteria. However, the underwriters must refrain from exploiting the ambiguities in the definitions.

It is worth noting that single-risk coverage might not be as beneficial as it initially appears for the investor. Despite paying a lesser premium, investors could remain vulnerable to excluded risks. By way of example, in the *Sea-Land Service v. Iran*

---

[321] For instance, art.2 of Geneva Convention states the following "*In addition to the provisions which shall be implemented in peacetime, the present Convention shall apply to all cases of declared war or of any other armed conflict which may arise between two or more of the High Contracting Parties, even if the state of war is not recognized by one of them.*"

[322] de Vattel (1852), p. 291. International law prohibits governments from destructing property; however, defines certain exemptions. According to the article 23(g) of the Regulations Concerning the Laws and Customs of War on Land (Hague Regulations), governments are prohibited from destroying or seizing the enemy's property, unless such destruction or seizure is imperatively demanded by the necessities of war.

[323] Hall (1880), p. 51.

[324] For the definitions of terrorism in different jurisdictions, see Merkin and Kullmann (2006), pp. 6–8.

expropriation claim, Sea-Land alleged confusion and a lack of continuity in Iranian government operations. The claimant relied on the argument that the immigration or health officials were inexplicably absent to perform their duties and even the officials were to carry out their duties, it was only after a considerable delay. In Sea-Land's assertion "*The disruptive effect on the flow of containers was immediate, and this in turn is said to have affected Sea-Land's worldwide service, leading to its suspension of inbound services in November 1978 and its eventual termination of all operations on 1 August 1979.*" However, the tribunal found this argument unsatisfactory. In reaching that conclusion, the tribunal attached substantial weight to the evidence, which was insufficient to justify a finding of expropriation, by contrast, these events tend to indicate a state of upheaval.[325]

Finally, in the *Nord Resources Corp*, the insured formed a joint venture company (SRL), to develop a rutile project in Sierra Leone. However, a fight erupted between government troops and rebel forces in the vicinity of SRL's mine site, resulting in the temporary suspension of operations, and the loss of possession and control over the mine site. In the view of OPIC, the substantial evidence satisfied the causation test,[326] finding that the damage, as defined under the insurance contract[327] was caused by political violence.[328]

[325] In *Sea-Land Service v. Iran*, (IUSCT Case No. 33, Award, 22 June 1984, paras. between 42–47).

[326] According to the section 1.07 of the contract, "*[A]n act shall be considered to be the direct cause of a Loss if there is an unbroken chain of causes and effects from the act to the Loss, without the intervention of any force operating actively from an independent source, and the Loss would not have occurred but for the act. An action taken to combat or defend against an actual or anticipated act of war, revolution, insurrection, civil strife, terrorism or sabotage can constitute an element in a chain of causes and effects.*"

[327] Damage was defined under Section 1.07 of the Contract as follows: "*Damage means (a) injury to, (b) disappearance of, or (c) seizure and retention of Covered Property (any of which events, for the purposes of this Section, shall be referred to as a 'Loss') directly caused by an act of (1) war (whether or not formally declared), (2) revolution or insurrection, or (3) civil strife, terrorism or sabotage. An act of revolution or insurrection is an act committed by an organized group having as its principal objective either the violent overthrow of the established political authorities or the ouster of such authorities from a specific geographic area. An act of civil strife, terrorism or sabotage is a violent act undertaken by an individual or group with the primary intent of achieving a political objective. For purposes of this Section, a Loss caused by an individual or a group acting primarily to achieve demands of labor or students shall be excluded from coverage.*"

[328] For the summary of the case, see Kantor et al. (2011), pp. 671–679 and please visit: https://www.dfc.gov/sites/default/files/2019-08/claim_nord.pdf accessed 04.09.2024.

8.4 Transfer Restrictions and Inconvertibility

8.4.1 Transfer Restrictions in General

States hold exclusive sovereignty over the entry and exit of capital from their territory.[329] In simpler terms, states are entitled to regulate matters pertaining to the movement of the capital.[330] The imposition of a ban on the entry of capital falls outside the scope of the transfer restriction risk;[331] thus, focus should be placed on the prohibition of the exit of capital from the host country's territory.[332] The institution of capital controls inevitably leads to severe consequences. It mainly distorts the perception of a free-market and discourages foreign nationals from investing in the host country. In addition, transfer restrictions thwart importers from engaging in a commonly used mechanism in trade insurance, which is to import goods at a reduced cost in exchange for an upfront payment.

For the establishment, operation and extension of the investment, investors may need to make payments for raw materials, machinery, craftsmanship, maintenance and consulting service. Reimbursing investment credits, paying interests, dividends, profits and sometimes repatriating the capital once invested under the sovereignty of the host country also requires money transfers.[333] Granting investors to freely transfer so-called 'investment related funds' is essential but poses certain risks especially if those funds are to be transferred out of the host country. Transferring large outflows of funds may cause depreciation in the host country's currency, affect

---

[329] Capital controls can be justified on five grounds; 1- to manage and correct a balance of payments crisis through limiting volatile short-term capital flows 2- to preserve domestic savings (domestic savings are used to finance domestic investment) 3- to generate government revenues (to maintain the authorities' ability to tax domestic financial activities, income and wealth) 4- to avoid capital flows that can make the structural reform programs unsustainable and 5- to achieve foreign policy goals. See Mathieson and Rojas-Suárez (1992), pp. 6–10. Also, see Salacuse (2013), pp. 80–85.

[330] Article VI, Section 3 of the IMF articles grants discretion to the Sovereigns to impose capital control. The article entitled "Controls of Capital Transfers," reads as follows; "*Members may exercise such controls as are necessary to regulate international capital movements, but no member may exercise these controls in a manner which will restrict payments for current transactions or which will unduly delay transfers of funds in settlement of commitments, except as provided in Article VII, Section 3(b) and in Article XIV, Section 2.*" However, Section 2 (a) of Article VIII requires the approval of the Fund to impose restrictions. See Articles of Agreement of the International Monetary Fund, can be found at https://www.imf.org/external/pubs/ft/aa/pdf/aa.pdf accessed 04.09.2024.

[331] A measure of this kind may constitute an indirect expropriation if the investment requires a capital import for its furtherance.

[332] See Salacuse (2013), p. 76.

[333] For instance, the US-Turkey BIT includes a non-exclusive list of what may be transferred freely. Such as (a) returns; (b) compensation pursuant to Article III; (c) payments arising out of an investment dispute; (d) principal and interest payments arising under loan agreements, and; (e) proceeds from the sale or liquidation of all or any part of an investment. Please visit: https://tcc.export.gov/Trade_Agreements/All_Trade_Agreements/exp_005487.asp accessed 04.09.2024. Also see Abba and Wälde (2008), p. 214.

macroeconomic management, and exchange and interest rate policies, and reduce the volume of exports.

8.4.2 Active-Passive Blockage

The active blockage of repatriation for an indefinite period results in significant economic harm and must be lifted as the benefit is acquired. A restriction for an irrational duration, on the other hand, constitutes a passive blockage.[334] It is worth noting that if restrictive regulations were already in force at the time of the investment being made, in other words, if the investor knew or could have known about the existence of such measures, PRI policies will not cover such a degree of negligence on the part of the insured.

Given that this risk encompasses deprivation of ownership rights, in some cases, either independently or alongside transfer restriction risk, expropriation may be in question. In a case in the U.S., the U.S. court ruled that the question of whether a state's exchange controls impose an expropriation, or instead constitute a lawful act of regulation that a foreign court must respect, turns on whether the IMF has approved the controls.[335]

Host countries would not usually want to curtail their discretion to adopt measures or enact legislation for the purpose of controlling monetary transactions.[336] Governments or their instrumentalities may grant investors the illusion of liberty to transfer funds; on its face, investors appear to have this freedom, while in reality, governments continue to hinder their ability to do so. Arbitrary and discriminatory discretion not justified by economic necessity[337] could qualify such actions as political risks. Hence, an impediment before a minor scale of capital outflow is almost a default political risk. It is worthy to note that, some investments might yield returns in the form of raw materials. For example, in commodity-backed finance, the investor might be under an obligation to make payments in kind.[338] In a broad sense,

[334] Also, see Salacuse (2013), p. 254.

[335] See Stephan (2007), p. 228.

[336] Salacuse (2016), p. 344. Salacuse and Sullivan (2005), p. 85. For the occurrence of risk, regulations do not necessarily encompass payments only made out of the territory; measures constraining cash flows made within the territory would also constitute a quasi-expropriation.

[337] As readers will recall, the host state's wish to derogate from its international obligations may rely upon 'necessity' as stated under art. 25 of ILC. See Abba and Wälde (2008), p. 218. According to aforementioned article, necessity should be "the *only way for the State to safeguard an essential interest against a grave and imminent peril*" However, in *LG&E Energy v. Argentina*, the tribunal came at different conclusion and opined that regulations of Argentina were not the only means but the legitimate means to respond economic crisis. See paras. 239, 240.

[338] In 1995, in Sudan, Chinese companies entered into a joint venture for oil exploration, exploitation, and refining. They secured loans from China Eximbank, which were repaid with oil. Please see Bräutigam and Gallagher (2014), p. 347.

preventing investors from transferring any asset with monetary value, (including crypto assets) should be within the scope of this risk.

A review of the BIT, between the home and the host country, along with investor-state arbitration cases, can provide a clearer grasp of the scope and subrogation rights.[339] Some BITs indicate the extent of restrictions and the power vested with the host country to regulate.[340] In some BITs, such scope may extend even to International Monetary Fund regulations, which could serve as a basis for limitations.[341] Alongside BITs, investors might be protected via investment contracts, where specific provisions may protect investors against the host country's passing laws limiting the conversion of the currency.[342]

Exporters or investors may resort to offering bribes and persuading host countries' officials to exceed their discretionary power by granting approval/license[343] not only to bypass capital controls, but also for money laundering and terrorism financing, activities against which countries, both developing and developed, have adopted regulations to combat.[344] It is worth noting that investors may encounter requirements aimed at combating corruption or money laundering as barriers before completing a transaction, especially if the merits of the transfer fall within the scope of regulations. However, it is important to consider that governments may restrict capital outflows from investors due to alleged bribes received by their officials from the investors. Such restrictions may not necessarily constitute a political risk within the context of transfer restriction.[345]

---

[339] See Ginsburg (2013), pp. 955–956.

[340] By way of example, the Finland-Brazil BIT provides unrestricted transfer, while China-Kuwait BIT states a transfer allowance subject to domestic law. See Abba and Wälde (2008), pp. 215–216.

[341] Art. 6 of the France-Uganda BIT states the following restriction: "*In case of a serious balance of payments difficulties and external financial difficulties or the threat thereof, each contracting party may temporarily restrict transfers, provided that this restriction: i) shall be promptly notified to the other party; ii) shall be consistent with the articles of agreement with the International Monetary Fund; iii) shall not exceed in any case six mo*nths; iv) would be imposed in an equitable, non-discriminatory and in good faith basis." Please visit: https://investmentpolicy.unctad.org/international-investment-agreements/treaty-files/1289/download Also see Art. 7 of the Comprehensive Economic Cooperation Agreement between The Republic of India and the Republic of Singapore , Please visit: https://investmentpolicy.unctad.org/international-investment-agreements/treaty-files/2707/download both accessed 04.09.2024.

[342] Rubins and Kinsella (2005), p. 65.

[343] See Salacuse (2013), p. 86.

[344] For UK, see 'sanctions and Anti-Money Laundering Act 2018' please visit: https://www.legislation.gov.uk/ukpga/2018/13/part/1 accessed 04.09.2024 and for Turkey Law on preventing terrorism financing, please visit: https://www.mevzuat.gov.tr/MevzuatMetin/1.5.6415.pdf accessed 04.09.2024. In international arena, UN and EU employed similar approaches. Please see 'International Convention for the Suppression of the Financing of Terrorism', 'Anti-money laundering (AMLD V) Directive (EU) 2018/843' and 'REGULATION (EU) 2015/847' It is worthy to note that the recent proposed amendment of EU seeks to track even crypto assets. Please visit: https://treaties.un.org/doc/db/terrorism/english-18-11.pdf and https://eur-lex.europa.eu/legal-content/EN/TXT/?uri=celex%3A32018L0843 accessed 04 09.2024.

[345] Also see Salacuse (2013), p. 256.

In 2003, Venezuelan authorities announced the creation of an Exchange Administration Board, knowns as the Comisión de Administracion de Divisas ("CADIVI")[346] which was vested with power to regulate the purchase and sale of foreign currency. The regime imposed currency controls, requiring the purchase of currency at a fixed rate subject to the authorization of CADIVI. Investors acquired foreign currency from either CADIVI, however, there was always the possibility of obtaining USD in Venezuela through the parallel foreign currency market. In the Caterpillar case, the length of CADIVI's approval process lasted for more than 9 months.[347] In OPIC's view, this justified that, despite the insured's extensive efforts, the authority was unable to convert local currency.[348]

In *Continental v. Argentina*, the tribunal conducted an analysis of the transfer restrictions that Continental had raised as a complaint. In the tribunal's view, the type of transfer did not correspond to any of the categories permitted in the BIT's provision[349] addressing transfer restrictions. Although the tribunal concluded that Argentina did not commit a breach with respect to the transfer restriction, it also drew a conclusion in light of the gamut of measures taken in response to a complete

[346] In *OI European v. Venezuela* (para. 624) the establishment of CAVIDI was interpreted by the tribunal in the following wording "*The introduction of exchange control systems is part of the economic and financial sovereignty of the States and does not constitute an 'undue restriction' Venezuela instituted a dual system in which the foreign investor could freely opt between repatriating its profits through CADIVI or opt for the parallel marke*t." Available at https://www.italaw.com/sites/default/files/case-documents/italaw7100.pdf accessed 04.09.2024. For other cases, see Hyder and Attanasio (2021), pp. 68–80.

[347] Section 2.01 of the Contracts set forth the following requirements for inconvertibility coverage: "(1) the Insured or the foreign enterprise is unable legally to convert local currency. (2) held by or for the account of the foreign enterprise for conversion into U.S. dollars to discharge a scheduled payment (or part thereof) into United States dollars (3) through any customary legal channels for transactions of the type contemplated in the loan agreement on any business day (4) during the 60 successive days following a scheduled payment date. ..." OPIC finds that each of these requirements has been met.

[348] Please visit: https://www.dfc.gov/sites/default/files/2019-08/caterpillarfinancialservices082106.pdf accessed 04.09.2024.

[349] Article V of the Argentina-US BIT reads: 1. Each Party shall permit all transfers related to an investment to be made freely and without delay into and out of its territory. Such transfers include: (a) returns; (b) compensation pursuant to Article IV; (c) payments arising out of an investment dispute; (d) payments made under a contract, including amortization of principal and accrued interest payments made pursuant to a loan agreement directly related to an investment; (e) proceeds from the sale or liquidation of all or any part of an investment; and (f) additional contributions to capital for the maintenance or development of an investment. 2. Except as provided in Article IV paragraph 1, transfers shall be made in a freely usable currency at the prevailing market rate of exchange on the date of transfer with respect to spot transactions in the currency to be transferred. The free transfer shall take place in accordance with the procedures established by each Party; such procedures shall not impair the rights set forth in this Treaty. 3. Notwithstanding the provisions of paragraphs1 and 2, either Party may maintain laws and regulations (a) requiring reports of currency transfer; and (b) imposing income taxes by such means as a withholding tax applicable to dividends or other transfers. Furthermore, either Party may protect the rights of creditors, or ensure the satisfaction of judgments in adjudicatory proceedings, through the equitable, nondiscriminatory and good faith application of its law.

break-down of the economy. The tribunal positioned itself within the context of findings justifying the necessity of the measures; thus, it did not distinctly differentiate the claims from one another.[350] In our opinion, the plea of necessity must be associated with preserving the public order, alongside fundamental human rights such as the right to adequate housing, food or health care. The margin of the state's discretion is formed by the magnitude of the events and the severity of their consequences. In simpler terms, to the extent that the consequences are severe, the scope of the necessity should be excused.

8.4.3 *Inconvertibility*

Host countries may restrain investors from converting the local currency, or transferring funds in the convertible currency in which the capital was originally invested. Restrictions may also come in the form of conversion at a rate lower than the nominal value of the local currency to the detriment of investors.[351] Thus, this risk is of a particular concern for investments that do not generate foreign exchange directly through payments of exports.[352] Fewer countries maintain restrictions on currency conversion, and cases of inconvertibility comprise a smaller portion of PRI claims.[353] However, some scholars suggest that it is the riskiest and most purchased form of investment insurance[354] . Investors expect a steady rate of return from their investments. Besides numerous other factors, the interaction between local and international currency may affect such a return. One may need to note that this risk encapsulates the inconvertibility of the host country's currency into an effective one; in a simplified language, the host country cannot escape responsibility if it allows conversion to a currency that is of no use.

8.4.4 *The Risks of Devaluation and Inflation*

The value of the local currency at the time of conversion might differ from the value when the investment was made. In relatively less developed and economically unstable countries, devaluation or high inflation are facts, thus, currency alterations

[350] See paras. 197, 205, 237 and 245, the case is available at https://www.italaw.com/sites/default/files/case-documents/ita0228.pdf accessed 04.09.2024, also see; Turyn and Pérez-Aznar (2010), pp. 51–78.

[351] Rubins and Kinsella (2005), p. 17.

[352] Shihata (1987), p. 680.

[353] Peinhardt and Allee (2016), p. 210. This may explain why some BITs, whether intentionally or not, exclude this risk. However, if an investor anticipates the likelihood of such a risk, PRI would be an accurate solution.

[354] Wagner (2012), p. 106.

detrimental to investors are the corollary of investing in developing markets. Therefore, some may believe that devaluation is a commercial/business-originated risk.[355] In fact, except for DFC[356] PRI providers are hesitant to assume the burden of what might be obvious or inevitable, instead of expecting investors to predict and shoulder the consequences of doing business in such an environment.

Just as devaluation and inflation present risks to the inhabitants of the host state so, too, do they to the foreign investor. If PRI is presumed to serve as a coverage against material reduction in investor's legitimate expectations (including the value of the investment and profits generated therefrom), inflation or devaluation should remain among covered risks. For instance, in cases of devaluations hitting rates somewhere between %33 to %50, circumscribed devaluation coverage could be considered, enabling investors to receive compensation for the decrease in value.[357]

The veracity of investors' claims is tied to the malicious conduct of the host governments. In order to vacuum foreign investments, governments offer competitive and cheaper investment costs, but they may also cloak their intentions in a regulatory veil. Decisions that appear to be rational in the first place may eventually be expropriatory. To illustrate; investments are appraised in reserve currencies such as the US dollar or Euro, with the valid exchange rate at the time of calculation applied. In other words, the value of the local currency determines the value of the foreign investment. If the government causes a decrease in the value of the local currency [for instance, by lowering the policy (interest) rates] the investment will have a lower worth in the reserve currency. Such a sharp loss in value might prompt the investor to exit the foreign market and hand over the assets in exchange for a considerably lesser amount than the investor could have received had the host country avoided such a devaluation. Should the new buyer of the asset be the host country or its affiliated company, a seemingly voluntary transfer of the asset's proprietary rights can be read as an indirect expropriation. One may note that governments may also tend to curb capital flight before a devaluation takes place. The same government might manipulate the official exchange rate of the local currency, therefore, the currency exchange rate and the reference date of such rate,[358] which could be subtle nuances at the outset, might create an enormous disparity in computing the amount of compensation.[359]

---

[355] Also see Williams (1993), p. 78.

[356] In 2001, the DFC issued a devaluation guarantee for a project in Brazil. The DFC provided a standby foreign exchange liquidity facility, which could be drawn upon by the project company if it failed to make its dollar debt payments as a consequence of devaluation. See Hansen (2004), p. 85.

[357] See Martin (1967), p. 296. MIGA does not provide coverage for such risk. See art. 11 (b) of MIGA convention, available at https://www.miga.org/sites/default/files/archive/Documents/MIGA%20Convention%20February%202016.pdf accessed 04.09.2024.

[358] PRI policies prefer the host government's official exchange rate; however, the foreign exchange market rate may better reflect the present value of the currency calculated by independent market players.

[359] *Ginsburg* provides several sample PRI policy wordings and evaluates their soundness. According to the author, governments impose restrictions ahead of devaluing their local currency.

The language of BITs may empower governments to retain rights to take a wide array of measures of financial nature. For instance, the BIT between Japan and Vietnam contains an exception clause and identifies the incidents in which the host country is conferred to impose restrictions.[360] However, the same BIT, among other limitations on transfer restrictions, does not grant regulatory authority solely at the discretion of the host country. It requires that the measures in question be consistent with the provisions of the IMF Agreement.[361] Parties to such BITs will have several options in times of economic instability, unlike parties to other BITs that lack such exceptions.[362]

8.4.5 Restriction of Crypto Currency

8.4.5.1 The Nature of the Blockchain

The basis of the blockchain dates back to 2008 when a person or a group of people under the pseudonym *Satoshi Nakamoto* developed a peer-to-peer method of

---

Investors, upon learning a devaluation, might attempt to convert and transfer their funds denominated in the local currency. If the refence date is set as the day 181 (the first day following the waiting period), the amount of money investors will receive could be lesser. However, investors can safeguard themselves from the devaluation if the compensation is determined based on the exchange rate that predates the devaluation. See: Ginsburg (2013), pp. 959, 960.

[360]The BIT between Japan and Vietnam (2003) empowers parties to impose exchange controls. Article 16 of the BIT describes following events as circumstances that may entitle the host state to take measures: 'Serious balance-of-payments and external financial difficulties, movements of capital cause, or threaten to cause serious difficulties for macroeconomic managements, in particular monetary and exchange rate policies.' Available at https://investmentpolicy.unctad.org/international-investment-agreements/treaty-files/1738/download accessed 04.09.2024. For a similar wording, see Article 16 of the Georgia - Japan BIT (2021) and article 7(4) of the China - Turkey BIT.

[361]Article 16(2) of the BIT between Japan and Vietnam (2003) provides the scope and the process of the transfer restrictions in the following language: 'Measures referred to in paragraph 1 above: (a) shall be consistent with the Articles of Agreement of the International Monetary Fund so long as the Contracting Party taking the measures is a party to the said Articles; (b) shall not exceed those necessary to deal with the circumstances set out in paragraph 1 above; (c) shall be temporary and shall be eliminated as soon as conditions permit; and (d) shall be promptly notified to the other Contracting Party.' Similarly see article 7(5) of the China–Turkey BIT.

[362]Arbitration tribunals however, opined differently in Argentine's economic crises. The tribunal in LG&E *Energy v. Argentina* (para. 231) held that "*the conditions as of December 2001 constituted the highest degree of public disorder and threatened Argentina's essential security interests. This was not merely a period of "economic problems" or "business cycle fluctuation" as Claimants described (Claimants' Post-Hearing Brief, 14). Extremely severe crises in the economic, political and social sectors reached their apex and converged in December 2001, threatening total collapse of the Government and the Argentine State.*". Although the tribunal in *Enron v. Argentina (para. 306–307)* acknowledged that there was a severe crisis, the same tribunal ruled that *"there was no convincing evidence that the events were out of control or had become unmanageable"*. For detail see Ginsburg (2013), pp. 963–966.

exchanging electronic currency.[363] The blockchain system is a mutually distributed ledger;[364] therefore, it is not owned by one person and nor dominated. Some model treaties require investments to be registered on the distributed ledger in order to be protected by the treaty.[365] Copies of the transactions are stored in units of blocks. The blocks form a chain of data as ownership changes hands, and confirm the exact time and sequence of transactions, and they link securely together to prevent any block from being tampered with, duplicated, or revised.[366]

Crypto (digital) currency, on the other hand is "*a digital currency in which encryption techniques are used to regulate the generation of units of currency and verify the transfer of funds, operating independently of a central bank*[367]". The cryptographic validation system does not require third parties to validate or approve the transaction;[368] hence, one may presume that blockchain aims to be detached from centralized governance and that the nature of the blockchain is a decentralized platform where transactions of the digital currencies can be tracked and traded only on their networks.

The current financial system, with its coins or banknotes has not been dethroned and the days to recognize tokens or digital currencies as the main mediums of exchange are yet to come. The digital currency system is still reliant on the means of current financial system; in other words, the digital currency owner must convert its crypto to an effective currency in order to make expenditure. This will beg the question of whether host governments can retain digital currencies from being converted or transferred.

One may need to note that, by contrast to its nature, digital currencies can operate in a centralized manner similar to that of a stock exchange. The buyers and sellers (parties) may not have a personal key to, or full control over their assets on centralized exchanges. Additionally, exchange service providers (intermediaries) must conform to the measures of the jurisdiction in which they are domiciled. Needless to say, parties trading on this system and those willing to convert or transfer their digital currencies will be prone to government interference.

The commercial nature of crypto assets, whether they exhibit certain characteristics of a commodity, and possess investment attributes is subject to disputes. In

---

[363] See Hirsh and Alman (2019), p. 14, also see Cong and He (2019), p. 1760.

[364] Mainelli and Von Gunten (2014), p. 6.

[365] See articles 5, 6 of the Model Treaty in Elrifai et al. (2019), p. 80.

[366] Scholars state that the blockchain may represent a book where each page is a different document or set of information. The pages are numbered in order and attempts to add or modify a page within the book is traceable. The book may have an unlimited number of pages, but only the end of the book may be changed without impacting the previous pages. See Hirsh and Alman (2019), p. 14, also see Cong and He (2019), p. 1760, finally please visit: https://www.ibm.com/topics/what-is-blockchain accessed 04.09.2024.

[367] Mainelli and Von Gunten (2014), p. 18.

[368] Figueiredo (2017), p. 10.

SEC v. Ripple case[369] SEC alleged that; Ripple conducted an unregistered securities offering to investors in the U.S. and worldwide through the sale of digital assets known as XRP[370] and that the sale of XRP funded Ripple's operations and enriched its executives.[371] In its response, Ripple argued that XRP is not a stock, by contrast, it is a medium of exchange and traded through exchanges both inside and outside of the U.S. Hence SEC has no jurisdiction over the XRP, and it can only be registered with the Commodity Futures Trading Commission (CTFC).[372] Although in early July 2023, the judge of the case ruled that the XRP token at issue was not, in and of itself, a security,[373] the SEC was preparing itself to seek an appeal.[374] Hence, the final outcome will be of utmost importance. If resolved in SEC's favor, SEC may require companies to regulate their crypto tokens as securities and to register with the SEC as broker dealers.[375]

In decentralized exchange systems, however, as the name implies, parties conduct transactions without the supervision of an authority or the service of an intermediary. The one who possesses the encrypted personal key to digital currency can make the transaction. Additionally, the owner of the digital currency can store the data in regards to his/her ownership within a device called '*cold wallet*'. A cold wallet can take the form of a USB stick, therefore, and may not be distinguished from any other USB device keeping irrelevant data. Despite the fact that the cold wallet owner needs to enlist the services of the banks or financial institutions alike to convert his/her digital currency to an effective one,[376] the owner can transfer the data/currency abroad without logging into the system. And, as the data is transferred to a jurisdiction other than that of the host country, the investor will not struggle with the conversion. Hence, cryptocurrency, even when perceived as an investment, stands as a host country's weakest spot in terms of its exercise of sovereignty over it, due to decentralized platforms and instruments like cold wallets which are almost

[369]Ripple is registered American company which enables SEC to purse a legal action against Ripple. Please visit: https://www.nasdaq.com/articles/the-ripple-xrp-lawsuit:-what-you-need-to-know accessed 04.09.2024.

[370]Please visit: https://www.sec.gov/news/press-release/2020-338 accessed 04.09.2024.

[371]Please visit: https://capital.com/ripple-token-xrp-sec-lawsuit-cbdc accessed 04.09.2024.

[372]Please visit: https://www.culawreview.org/journal/sec-v-ripple-the-regulation-of-cryptocurrencies-as-securities also see https://www.cnbc.com/2022/04/14/ripples-court-battle-with-sec-has-gone-exceedingly-well-ceo-says.html both accessed 04.09.2024.

[373]Please visit: https://www.nysd.uscourts.gov/sites/default/files/2023-07/SEC%20vs%20Ripple%207-13-23.pdf accessed 04.09.2024.

[374]Please visit: https://www.bloomberg.com/news/newsletters/2023-08-17/what-s-next-in-sec-v-ripple-xrp-crypto-lawsuit accessed 04.09.2024.

[375]In August 2024, the Southern District of New York ordered a penalty of $125,000,000 against Ripple, finding that Ripple's sales of XRP on digital asset exchanges were "not investment contracts" and therefore not classified as "securities." The calculation of the penalty was based on the institutional sales of XRP to hedge funds and other institutional buyers. This decision is expected to be appealed. Please visit: https://www.jdsupra.com/legalnews/sdny-issues-final-ruling-on-sec-v-ripple-8028715/ accessed 30.08.2024.

[376]Hirsh and Alman (2019), p. 15.

intractable in nature. In a simpler language, since the nature of these assets and the transactions they involve haven't been definitively decided, and because it's possible to conduct transactions beyond the governments' sight, restrictive measures may have a lesser impact than anticipated.

8.4.5.2 Peer-to-Peer PRI

Peer to peer (P2P) insurance is not a brand-new concept; in terms of the creation of the pool, it is similar to the basis of the tontine[377] where a group of individuals pools their resources together.[378] The terms 'risk-sharing', 'social insurance' or 'crowdsourcing' may also serve the same purpose. In P2P, each participant contributes to the pool and if one of the participants incurs a loss, compensation is provided from the pool. If the risk is not materialized, participants get their shares back. In theory, the participants can be both the insureds with the same interest and the insurers covering the same type of risk simultaneously. The concept requires transparency[379] and reliability; therefore, the composition of the group must be on a multilateral contractual basis, or peers must have a high level of trust in each other.

The P2P communication system and insurance ('the insurtech') can be a trend, but it can also instill fear of the new at the same time. In conventional practice, some investors may experience difficulties in meeting eligibility criteria that PRI providers require. In addition, long waiting periods after the materialization of the risk may cast irreparable harm to the investor. The concept we refer to as 'P2P PRI' or 'electronic PRI (e-PRI)' may not have been percolated in law studies, however, may put an end to such concerns.

However, P2P PRI may have several drawbacks. *First*, if all participants are expected to be foreign investors, the adoption of this concept may have a limited scale and if several participants incur losses at the same time, the pool might be insufficient to compensate each participant. A solution can be found by deviating from the orthodox P2P practice and allowing for the concept of '*one insured and contribution of a wider range of insurers*'. These insurers will be comprised of anonymous non-foreign investor participants who would benefit solely from the valuation of the funds in the pool. In such a mechanism, the pool would operate like investment funds do, and unless a risk occurs, the profit generated at the end of the policy period will be distributed amongst the participants. Finally, tangible assets or even investments can be tokenized on blockchain. In other words, a token can represent the digitized real-world asset and provide its owner with the associated rights. The proportion of the tokens acquired among all tokens available will indicate

---

[377] Tontine is the principle of distributing the assets composed of contributions among the survivors at a determined date. *Merkin and Steele* define as "*A form of mutual insurance under which the sums are payable to the last surviving member.*" See Merkin and Steele (2013), p. 41 fn 19.

[378] Denuit et al. (2022), p. 616.

[379] Marano (2019), p. 305.

the extent of the entitlement.[380] While the number of insured parties will remain constant, extending the distribution of profits to the insured will result in a 'win-win' scenario for those who hold shares in the investment through their digital currencies.

The second drawback pertains to the position of the peers. PRI contracts are bilateral, specific and therefore detailed in scope. Peers of the P2P PRI will be benefit-driven and will mostly sign smart contracts[381] lacking the fundamentals of the political risks to be assumed. Hence, in the first place, professionals must institute the legal foundation and prepare the terms and conditions of the mechanism. *Third*, the blockchain market is volatile, and crypto transactions have permeated across limited industries. Unless the crypto amount of the insurance policy is fixed at a rate recognized by all industries or tied to the price of one of the real-world reserve currencies, the investor may suffer the value loss in digital currency. *Finally*, due to large number of anonymous insurers and the absence of a treaty between insurers and the host government, insurers may be frustrated in recouping their receivables at the time of subrogation. Hence the system, by default, must operate on a 'no-subrogation' basis.

8.4.5.3 Peer-to-Peer Funding of Political Risk-Based Disputes

In exchange for a return contingent on success, profit-seeking third parties may provide funds to the disputing parties for the payment of legal fees, orders, awards, or judgments rendered against that party, or both.[382] The stage on which parties fight for money and justice becomes the 'litigation asset' of the funding party.[383] Parties may also have access to funds in the form of litigation expense insurance, for instance 'Before-The-Event' (BTE) and 'After-The-Event' (ATE) insurance.[384]

Third party funding in investor-state disputes may be a strong fit for the funder and the funded; however, as of today the reach of disputes funded by blockchain is limited. Digital currencies may be linked to a project and function similar to stock markets. The value of the currency depends on the promotion of the project, and the currency is purchased in anticipation of the profit that relies upon the efforts of others. While drafting this book, a Turkish businessman was preparing to file a lawsuit worth USD 68 billion against several private companies and the Savings Deposit Insurance Fund (TMSF) of Turkey on the basis of an alleged colossal abuse

---

[380]For an illustration of tokenizing please visit: https://brickken.com/asset-tokenization/#:~:text=Asset%20tokenization%20is%20how%20any,take%20the%20form%20of%20tokens accessed 04.09.2024.

[381]Smart contracts are digital contracts allowing terms contingent on decentralized consensus that are tamper-proof and typically self-enforcing through automated execution. See Cong and He (2019), pp. 1761, 1762.

[382]Nieuwveld and Sahani (2017), p. 1.

[383]Von Goeler (2016), p. 4.

[384]Nieuwveld and Sahani (2017), pp. 259–266.

of power and seizure by the TMSF.[385] According to the news, the Turkish businessman had agreed with a cryptocurrency, however, details of the deal are not publicly available. It appears that coin owners will contribute to the case funding, and if the court rules in the claimant's favor, funders will receive a share of the amount to be collected.[386] Third-party funding can be problematic in arbitration, the presence of a third-party funder may create a conflict of interest with the arbitrators. For instance, in *Sehil Inşaat v. Turkmenistan*,[387] tribunal ordered the disclosure of the identity of the third-party. However, in a decentralized blockchain where digital currency owners/case funders are anonymous in nature, execution of such a ruling is unlikely.

8.5 Breach/Repudiation of Contract and Denial of Justice

8.5.1 Breach/Repudiation of Contract

Parties' needs, consent, and bargaining power[388] form the terms of a contract. *Barnhizer* opines that the '*power'* often substitutes for the derivative concept of 'authority' the ability of the state, through its agents, to coerce individual actors within the polity into obeying the sovereign's commands.[389] The power of each party to bargain can be grievously impaired by reason of their immediate needs. In the realm of foreign investment, concession or license agreements cannot be based on the assumption that parties thereto negotiate with equal bargaining power. The weaker party always has more than a little to say as to the scope of the contract. The imbalance, as well as the disparity, may result in imposition of unfavorable conditions on him/her. Weakness of a party in such agreements does not derive from one's race, gender, poverty or lack of education or business sophistication.[390] On the contrary, to the extent the contract deals with national resources or infrastructure and depending on foreign investors' demands, the state would wish to lead negotiations, and it might be of investor's benefit to remain alert to the possibility that the

[385] For detail, please visit: https://www.ft.com/content/9debb4e0-c23a-4dd9-83f2-017659b0d6a2 accessed 04.09.2024.

[386] Please visit: https://halktv.com.tr/gundem/cem-uzan-68-milyar-dolarlik-davasinin-nftsini-satisa-cikardi-694550h accessed 04.09.2024.

[387] See para. 8 available at https://www.italaw.com/sites/default/files/case-documents/italaw4350.pdf accessed 04.09.2024.

[388] Bargaining power is described as "*the power to fool and bluff the ability to set the best price for yourself and fool the other man into thinking this was your maximum offer*". Schelling (1956), p. 282.

[389] See Barnhizer (2005), p. 157.

[390] See Barnhizer (2005), p. S200.

host state may contravene or renege on its obligations, abrogating the contract and compelling a change in the terms.[391]

The moment a contract is made, the parties are vested with some rights. Terminating the contract is one of the contractual rights and, depending on whether it has retroactive effects or not, one may employ 'to rescind', while the other may employ 'to denounce'. Parties may face with uncontemplated turn of events that render their obligations radically different from that which were contracted for.[392] The political risk in question, however, does not derive from a party's enjoying its contractual rights. By contrast, the action or the declaration of consent to terminate the contract is against the terms thereof.

A breach, repudiation or frustration[393] of a contract is undesirable but is one of the probable consequences of commercial life, and therefore it might be a political risk of most concerned to investors.[394] According to scholars it is the alpha and omega of political risk.[395] Governments can repudiate a contract just like any private contractor, even if it was made with a foreign national.[396] A violation that could have been committed by any other contractual party does not necessarily give rise to the occurrence of the risk.[397] As a result, a government's mere repudiation of a contract is not inherently a political risk.[398]

This risk is relevant to the FET standard, which some multilateral agreements address.[399] If the government acted in a commercial and non-discriminatory manner,

---

[391] Rubins and Kinsella (2005), p. 20, also see Spagnoletti and O'Callaghan (2011), p. 4.

[392] MacMillan (2021), p. 63.

[393] When the contract is frustrated, the contract is immediately and automatically brought to an end, hence, after the event, the wishes of the parties become irrelevant and, they cannot negotiate. McKendrick (1995), p. 44.

[394] MIGA's political survey indicates that 'Breach of Contract' is the political risk that is most concern to the participants. See MIGA (2009), p. 30.

[395] Mazin (2017), p. 189.

[396] Newcombe and Paradell (2009), p. 352.

[397] Dolzer and Schreuer (2012), p. 153.

[398] See *Suez v. Argentina*.

[399] Art. 12 of the Harvard Convention is as follows; 1. The violation through an arbitrary action of the State of a contract or concession to which the central government of that State and an alien are parties is wrongful. In determining whether the action of the State is arbitrary, it is relevant to consider whether the action constitutes: (a) a clear and discriminatory departure from the proper law of the contract or concession as that law existed at the time of the alleged violation; (b) a clear and discriminatory departure from the law of the State which is a party to the contract or concession as that law existed at the time of the making of the contract or concession, if that law is the proper law of the contract or concession; (c) an unreasonable departure from the principles recognized by the principal legal systems of the world as applicable to governmental contracts or concessions of the same nature or category; or (d) a violation by the State of a treaty, 2. If the violation by the State of a contract or concession to which the central government of a State and an alien are parties also involves the taking of property, the provisions of art.10 shall apply to such taking. 3. The exaction from an alien of a benefit not within the terms of a contract or concession to which the central government of a State and an alien are parties or of a waiver of any term of such a contract or concession is wrongful if such benefit or waiver was secured through the use of any clear threat by

exercised its contractual rights, and lawfully concluded the contract, then any allegation has to be settled according to the terms of the contract. The motivation behind the action is essential; simple breaches of payment obligations, for instance, do not necessarily entail an abuse of government power.[400] The distinction between the use of sovereign power and a commercial act will define the occurrence of the risk. However, scholars make a distinction based on the scope or size of the agreement that is breached. They underline that the breach of concession agreements or investment agreements can be akin to expropriation since it effectively deprives investors of their rights.[401]

Within the legal context, the consequences attached to the contractual breach, repudiation of the contract, or forced negotiation of the contract vary. Within the PRI coverage however, these events primarily address two main perils related to arbitration. Therefore, scholars stress that the notion of 'breach of contract' can be misleading, as this risk covers losses deriving from the inability to obtain or enforce an arbitral award following a breach of contract.[402] In simpler language, this risk comes to the insurer's table, when a state denies either the investor's ability to recourse to arbitration or the enforcement of the award rendered in the investor's favor. In some scholars' view, contract frustration insurance may protect against losses from an embargo, or license cancellation, war, political violence, insurrection, actions by armed forces, strikes, or riots.[403] In our opinion, the scope of stand-alone coverage must not exceed its intended purpose; the risks above must be the subject of a general PRI policy.

In some cases, a breach of contract or non-payment by the government is deemed a sovereign action amounting to an indirect expropriation.[404] Therefore, one could

---

the central government of the State to repudiate, cancel or modify any right of the alien under such contract or concession. 4. The annulment or modification by a State, to the detriment of an alien, of any contract or concession to which the alien and a person or body other than the central government of a State are parties is wrongful if it constitutes: (a) a clear and discriminatory departure from the proper law of the contract or concession; (b) an unreasonable departure from the principles recognized by the principal legal systems of the world as applicable to such contracts or concessions; or (c) a violation by the State of a treaty.

[400] See *Société Générale v. Paraguay*, available at https://www.italaw.com/sites/default/files/case-documents/italaw1525.pdf accessed 04.09.2024. For instance, in *Siemens v. Argentina* (para. 253) the tribunal concluded that "*…for the State to incur international responsibility it must act as such, it must use its public authority. The actions of the State have to be based on its "superior governmental power". It is not a matter of being disappointed in the performance of the State in the execution of a contract but rather of interference in the contract execution through governmental action*".

[401] Salacuse (2013), p. 319.

[402] Wagner (2012), p. 109 and see Mazin (2017), p. 190.

[403] Pasich and Thayer (2011), p. 27.

[404] See *Alpha v. Ukraine*, available at https://www.italaw.com/sites/default/files/case-documents/ita0026.pdf accessed 04.09.2024. Also see Kantor (2015), p. 184. By contrast in *Azinian*, the claimant (investor) based his expropriation claim on the annulment of the investment contract by the host state, the tribunal was of the opinion that there must be a basis to equate ordinary breach of

argue that this type of risk is a variation of or akin to an expropriation,[405] and the basis of this view may lie in the government's police power. In the *Panderosa Assets* case, Enron Corp (the insured) acquired indirect (35 percent) equity interest in Transportadora de Gas del Sur ('TGS'). The Government of Argentina granted TGS a gas transportation license with a term of thirty-five years, enabling TGS to generate revenues for transporting gas through tariffs set by the Government. However, the enactment of the Public Emergency Law brought about changes to the tariffs, prompting the insured to file a compensation request with OPIC. In OPIC's view, both TGS and the government conducted themselves in a manner as if the license was essentially a contract, and its material modification constituted a repudiation. This case stands apart due to two noteworthy factors: firstly, the discussions encompassed whether the enactment could also be viewed as an instance of expropriation alongside the risk of contract repudiation; secondly, OPIC's conclusion was influenced by an investment arbitration case (ENRON v. Argentina)[406]

The underlying dispute or ambiguity in these types of risks is whether government repudiates the contract without good faith and with political motives and acts in sovereign capacity, not merely as a commercial party.[407] The distinction between

contract to expropriation. See para. 90, available at https://www.italaw.com/sites/default/files/case-documents/ita0057.pdf accessed 04.09.2024.

[405] According to the tribunal in *Waste Management* "*The mere non-performance of a contractual obligation is not to be equated with a taking of property, nor (unless accompanied by other elements) is it tantamount to expropriation. Any private party can fail to perform its contracts, whereas nationalization and expropriation are inherently governmental acts, as envisaged by the use of the term "measure" in NAFTA art. 1110(1). It is true that, having regard to the inclusive definition of "measure", one could envisage conduct tantamount to an expropriation which consisted of acts and omissions not specifically or exclusively governmental. All the same, the normal response by an investor faced with a breach of contract by its governmental counter-party (the breach not taking the form of an exercise of governmental prerogative, such as a legislative decree) is to sue in the appropriate court to remedy the breach. It is only where such access is legally or practically foreclosed that the breach could amount to a definitive denial of the right (i.e., the effective taking of the chose in action) and the protection of art. 1110 be called into play*" See para. 174.

[406] For the summary of the case, see Kantor et al. (2011), pp. 929–946, also visit: https://www.dfc.gov/sites/default/files/2019-08/ponderosa_assets_l.p._202005.pdf accessed 05.09.2024.

[407] OPIC, while determining in 'Marine shipping' claim, made the following statement: "*First, with respect to the Insured's general harassment theory, this claim is based on fee and price disputes between the Insured and various Egyptian entities, including the Canal Company, the Port Authority, and MSC's various contract partners. The disputes with the Canal Company appear to have involved disagreements over the price offered to purchase MSC's assets. The fee disputes with the Port Authority involved fees assessed on MSC for dredging the quay and a berthing fee. The disputes with MSC's contract partners involved MSC's claim that it was being underpaid, under the terms of its agreements with these entities, and MSC's dissatisfaction with proposed new Contract terms. Even as alleged by MSC, each of these fee and price disputes was commercial in nature. The GOE entities involved were parastatal corporations acting for commercial reasons in a commercial capacity rather than from governmental motives. Nothing MSC has submitted demonstrates that these entities acted in bad faith or in violation of their contractual commitments to MSC. Even assuming that this had occurred, a state does not commit a violation of international law by*

sovereign motivation or commercial capacity can be a difficult one to make and the latter may serve as an escape hatch allowing governments or vice versa insurers more leeway in denying investors' claims.[408] In *Bank of America*, the insurance contract excluded '*expropriatory action taken by a foreign authority in its capacity or through its power*'. The insured argued that the motivation of the state agency in defaulting on payments and MSEB's rescission of the contract was governmental rather than commercial. OPIC did not agree with the insured; in its belief, the insured's interpretation would have the phrase 'in its capacity' read to mean, 'motivated by', however, the power to rescind the contract, laid uniquely with MSEB[409] and it acted in its capacity.[410] It is worth mentioning that motivation and capacity cannot be used interchangeably, and the action couched in the clause seems to capture only the element of authority.

8.5.1.1 Non-Honoring of Sovereign Financial Obligations

Sovereigns borrow funds from creditors for many reasons, including to perform their spending commitments, to finance projects and to cope with liquidity shocks which, for one reason or another cannot be filled by tax revenues.[411] The main distinction between privately issued loan and sovereign debt lies basically in the legal personality of the latter. The debtor's being a sovereign facilitates the disbursement of a cheaper loan; at the same time, it exposes a significant risk. Unless the loan agreement requires otherwise, sovereigns borrow on an unsecured basis without posting collaterals.[412] However, when the sovereign's debt falls due and is not paid, the liquidation of the collaterals within its territory can be hindered by the immunity of the sovereign and the attachment of the sovereign assets requires certain conditions. We shall assess this topic in depth in the subsequent chapters.

The undisciplined behavior of the sovereign can put the repayment of the borrowing in jeopardy. The sovereign may pursue irrational financial policies and

---

engaging in commercial actions of this character. That is especially true when the state affords the foreign national a dispute settlement procedure. (See generally Restatement (Third) Foreign Relations Law §712 Comment h, Reporters' Note 8.) MSC filed actions, and later at least one appeal, in Egyptian courts regarding some of these matters, and it appears that judgments were found in favor of the GOE entities. There has been no claim that MSC suffered a denial of justice in the proceedings in Egyptians courts. Accordingly, there is no basis for concluding that the alleged instances of harassment constituted violations of international or local law." Please visit: https://www.dfc.gov/sites/default/files/2019-08/claim_marine_shipping.pdf accessed 05.09.2024.

[408] Khachaturian (2006), p. 1058.

[409] The Maharashtra State Electricity Board ("MSEB"), the enterprise owned by the State of Maharashtra was the sole purchaser of the power to be produced by DPC.

[410] See Kantor et al. (2011), p. 843 and please visit: https://www.dfc.gov/sites/default/files/2019-08/bankofamerica-september30-2003.pdf accessed 05.09.2024.

[411] Salacuse (2013), p. 126 and Martinez et al. (2022).

[412] Sovereign debt is considered as a safe and high-quality asset for banks to meet the liquidity requirements. See Hesse and Miyajima (2022), p. 6.

abet the creditor's predicament through its reckless actions. Financial distress of the sovereign may also result from global events, such as a deterioration in international markets. Although acute financial distress can prevent the sovereign from making timely payments,[413] financial necessity alone is not a sufficient basis to dishonor the debt obligation.[414] In theory, a sovereign's assets are inexhaustible, however, for a variety reasons, the value of the sovereign's liabilities may exceed its assets. In simplified terms, a country's debts can accumulate to a point where they outweigh its available assets. And finally, political stability or external factors such as deterioration in global markets and even climate change can render debt management complex. Thus, it will be in the interest of all parties to loan agreement to restructure unsustainable debts.

Scholars believe that evolution of capital markets has exacerbated collective action difficulties.[415] In times of economic distress, sovereign debts may be unsustainable, and debt repayment may be hampered. Thus, rather than 'all or nothing', creditors of the same debtor may agree upon 'Collective Action Clauses' to modify payment terms of the debt whereby creditors may either obtain a belated repayment in full or a portion of the debt via reducing the value of the principal. In response to the global financial crisis, the UNCTAD adopted the Principles on Promoting Responsible Sovereign Lending and Borrowing (the UNCTAD Principles) in 2012. According to these principles, when the sovereign debt is not honored, it is under responsibility to move in a timely fashion to communicate with its creditors and commence a debt rearrangement.[416]

The IMF envisaged restructuring sovereign debts through amending its Articles of Agreement. The Argentinian economic crisis 2001 unveiled the need for the Sovereign Debt Restructuring Mechanism (SDRM),[417] The SDRM engineered a restructuring process accompanied by an automatic stay on creditor enforcement. This stay prevents creditors from exercising their rights and stops the debtor from dissipating assets by making payments to other creditors. However, this process could give rise to crucial shortcomings. Firstly, postponing the requirement for the recalcitrant debtor to address its arrears might shift leverage from creditors to debtors. Consequently, this could potentially encourage debtors to default. Secondly, the nature of debt restructuring as a last-resort measure could lead to reckless lending practices. The SDRM also allowed for the cramdown of dissenting creditors

[413] Article 9 of the UNCTAD Principles indicates a debt restructuring mechanism in the event of economic necessity.

[414] Also see Draft convention on the responsibility of States for injuries caused in their territory to the person or property of aliens, prepared by the Deutsche Gesellschaft fur Volkerrecht (German International Law Association) in 1930 https://legal.un.org/ilc/documentation/english/a_cn4_217.pdf accessed 05.09.2024.

[415] Hagan (2008), p. 199. Please visit; https://www.elibrary.imf.org/view/book/9781589065079/9781589065079.xml?BookTabs=booktoc accessed 05.09.2024.

[416] See the implications in article 15 of UNCTAD Principles, available at https://unctad.org/system/files/official-document/gdsddf2012misc1_en.pdf accessed 05.09.2024.

[417] Michalowski and Bohoslavsky (2009), pp. 107, 108, see Hagan (2008), pp. 195–196.

and envisioned a priority system for new financing. Regarding the latter, if the sovereign defaults, existing creditors would have to transfer any received amounts from the sovereign to the priority creditor until the priority creditor is fully satisfied. Lastly, the SDRM established a dispute resolution forum that holds exclusive jurisdiction over all disputes that may arise during the restructuring proceedings.[418] However, attempts for SDRM have failed. For the allocation and cancellation of special drawing rights, as stated in article 28,[419] the needed eighty-five percent majority of the total voting power could not be reached.[420]

In a debt restructuring mechanism, a supermajority of the creditors or bondholders outvotes the minority, so that dissenting minority or, to some extent 'free riders' cannot abuse the forbearance exercised by the majority in reaching an agreement. This prevents so-called 'rogue creditors' from demanding repayment on the original terms. However, this entitlement provided to the majority to mute the minority's voice is applied in circumstances where holders are issued the same bond.[421] Sovereign debts can also be restructured through a 'debt for equity swap'. Foreign investors may purchase the debt obligations of the host country on very favorable terms and present them to the central bank of the indebted country, and then convert the obligation at or near its face value in local currency in order to finance investments approved by the host country.[422]

The PRI providers may offer protection against the failure of a government entity or any agent acting on its behalf to honor its payment obligations.[423] Payment obligation may derive from either a finance or an unconditional guarantee contract.[424] In other words, the sovereign must pre-acknowledge that it is not entitled to raise objections or defenses against the claim that the obligation is due and payable. If the PRI Policy does not require an arbitral award prior to filing a claim with the provider, banks may attain capital relief, potentially reducing the loan cost for the sovereign entity.[425] Thus, this coverage can be a booster for financial institutions seeking to shield themselves from nonpayment by downgraded countries as a result of economic recession.

---

[418] For detail see Hagan (2008), pp. 242–263. Fiebelman (2007), p. 747.

[419] Please visit: https://www.imf.org/external/pubs/ft/aa/index.htm accessed 05.09.2024.

[420] Hagan (2008), pp. 195–196.

[421] Krueger (2002), pp. 14–15, also see Krueger (2001). Similarly, see Choi et al. (2012), pp. 141–142. Also see Fiebelman (2007), p. 750.

[422] A debt equity swap is a scheme through which the debt of a country is exchanged for local currency equity in a local company. For detail see Asiedu-Akrofi (1989). Also see Salacuse (2013), pp. 133–136.

[423] See Thurber and Shah (2013), p. 45.

[424] Sovereigns extend funds, either in the form of cash or non-cash, to their suppliers or exporters, using the loans that have been advanced to them. Irrespective of the outcome of the contract that the sovereign funds or guarantees, it assumes the obligation to repay its lenders. For detail, also see Thurber and Shah (2013), pp. 45–57.

[425] Baroudi (2017), p. 409.

In project finance, lending can be exercised on a non-recourse basis, where the sponsors or shareholders of SPV are not held responsible for repayment of the loan.[426] Lenders predicate the loan amount on the expected cash flow of the project, and, in the case of a concession agreement, may require insurance to secure repayments committed by the government. The lenders will also wish to be as little dependent on the SPV as possible to recover their losses, especially if the lender occupies the position of a 'loss payee'. The insurer will be discharged from its payment obligations under the policy by directing the money to the lender.[427] Funding developing markets carries greater risk, given the multiplicity of the challenges they experience.[428]

International loan agreements can often contain several 'boilerplate' clauses. A *pari-passu clause* ensures equal ranking among different creditors,[429] a *negative pledge clause* on the other hand, constrains the debtor from collateralizing its assets and prevents it from granting security to other creditors without the permission of the current creditor or without prioritizing the current creditor's assets.[430] *Acceleration clause* and *cross-default clause* are of particular relevance to the sovereign's failure to meet its obligations under the loan agreement. An *acceleration* clause empowers the creditor to accelerate all future payments and collect outstanding amounts.[431] Finally, a default in one loan agreement can be linked to another through a *cross-default* clause. If the sovereign defaults on one debt, it can trigger an event of default on other debts, even if it was otherwise current on the first debt.[432] A *'cross-default' clause* functions similar to a pari-passu clause; it grants an equal treatment so that the lender of one loan can place himself in the same position of another, whose loan has been defaulted upon by the same sovereign. In other words, lenders of different agreements have approximately equal opportunities to proceed against the sovereign's assets.[433]

The list of coverages in PRI contracts is not exhaustive, mostly for reasons including the premium costs and propensity of the sovereign toward a particular risk. Coverage can be tailored to specific investments. As their names suggest,

---

[426] See Salacuse (2013), pp. 220, 225, 226.

[427] Cohen (1997), p. 36.

[428] See Nehru and Thomas (2008), p. 21, available at http://www.worldbank.org (in the search dropdown menu choose "Documents" and search for "odious debts nehru"; then follow the document title hyperlink that corresponds to "Report No" "WPS4676"; links to the report are available in the Downloads section) See Michalowski and Bohoslavsky (2009), p. 62, fn 12.

[429] Guzman and Stiglitz (2016), p. 5. For a broad discussion please see Olivares-Caminal (2013).

[430] Choi et al. (2012), p. 144.

[431] See Brown (2015), pp. 729–730, also see Choi et al. (2012), p. 140 and Salacuse (2013), p. 243.

[432] For instance, article 4 of the UNCTAD Principles is as follows: "*Lending beyond a borrower's reasonable capacity to repay not only risks a default on the loan in question, it adversely affects the position of all other creditors of that sovereign debtor.*"

[433] Syndicate loan agreements incorporate sharing clauses, whereby if one lender gains access to the defaulting borrower's assets, it shares those assets with other participants in the loan agreement. See Wallman (1985), p. 478 and 479 fn 29.

clauses addressing defaults serve to initiate a claim for insurance indemnification. The terms of the policy designed to provide coverage against a sovereign's non-honoring its financial obligations and the loan agreement may not always be in harmony. In this case, particular attention must be given to the wording of PRI policies covering loan (or guarantee) agreements with acceleration clauses. Despite the fact that the creditor (the insured party) is entitled to all outstanding debts under the loan agreement, the policy can adopt otherwise, enabling the insurer to compensate on due dates of payments as scheduled in the underlying loan agreement.

When it comes to indemnification, the insured may experience a substantial waiting period. In this particular type of risk, the waiting period can be as long as 180 days, commencing from the time of filing the occurrence of the alleged risk. However, the perceived unfairness of this duration can be misleading. Waiting periods found in PRI policies are longer than those in conventional insurance policies, but still speedier compared to the time required for dispute resolution in court or through arbitration.

8.5.1.2 Odious Debt

8.5.1.2.1 State Succession and Classification of Debts

As a general principle of heritage law, the rights and obligations of the predecessor are assigned in their entirety. Simply put, unless a real-person heir agrees to possess the heritage, it will not be responsible for the debts it inherited from its predecessor. With respect to sovereign debt,[434] public international law imposes an opposing system; under the doctrine of succession,[435] the government cannot cleanse itself

[434] Although the Vienna Convention on Succession of States in respect of State Property, Archives and Debts ('the Vienna Convention of 1983') was regarded as "an example of the less successful codification efforts undertaken within the United Nations", it defined the meaning of 'State debt' under article 33 as "*any financial obligation of a predecessor State arising in conformity with international law towards another State, an international organization or any other subject of international law*". Also see King (2007), p. 613. For the Convention, please visit: https://legal.un.org/ilc/texts/instruments/english/conventions/3_3_1983.pdf accessed 05.09.2024.

[435] The International Law Commission has attempted to codify state succession. The Commission drafted rules concerning the fate of the state's debt under various scenarios. For instance, as outlined in article 37, when a part of a state's territory is transferred, either party (successor and predecessor) must settle the matter by agreement. In the absence of such an agreement, debts are passed in an equitable proportion. According to article 38, unless parties' agreement states otherwise, the debt of the predecessor will not pass to newly independent successor state. It is worth noting that article 39 is the only provision in which the Commission envisaged an automatic passing of the debt. To be specific, as per article 39, if two or more states unite to form one successor state, the debts of the predecessor states pass to the successor state. Articles 40 and 41 address the separation and dissolution of states, in which the legal personality of the borrowing state is likely to remain intact. Under article 40, in cases of the separation of a part or parts of a state's territory, and according to article 41, when a state dissolves and ceases to exist, and the parts of the territory of the predecessor

from the debt previously incurred.[436] On the contrary, it automatically and unconditionally accepts debts contracted by its predecessor.[437] However, the concept of odious debt is an exception to the general principle.[438] To put it another way, an odious debt when substantiated by valid grounds, transforms into a means of defense to evade payment, setting it apart from political risks associated with non-honoring payment obligations by the sovereign.

Some hold the opinion that debt is not valid if it is essentially imposed by force. The debt of Third World is categorized as odious debt, and if the principles of odious debt were to be applied, a significant portion of the debt could disappear.[439] If the odious debt doctrine were strictly applied, sovereign debt might be seen as congenital, adhesive, and ineradicable.[440] In this chapter, we will canvass possible responses to the following questions: To what extent should the successor government bear its predecessor's debt? Should the nationals of a state be held liable for the government's malicious acts, which took the form of imprudent borrowing, simply because they were born within its territory or due solely to their citizenship?

Scholars offer two terms to differentiate the debts. **Virtuous debts** are those for which people benefitting from them are expected to repay.[441] According to *Buchheit et al.*, debts incurred to construct durable infrastructure and to wage defensive wars are virtuous. Same scholars went on to provide a specific example of a bridge as a virtuous debt, stating that taxpayers will inherit the burden of repaying the debt while simultaneously enjoying the benefit of driving over the bridge.[442] Weakened legal systems lack accountability, and the costs or fees associated with infrastructure[443] or

---

state form two or more successor states, in both instances, debts will pass in equitable proportions in the absence of an agreement.

[436] Ochoa (2008), p. 125.

[437] Buchheit et al. (2007), p. 1205, Brown (2015), p. 745, similarly, Feinerman (2007), pp. 193, 194, similarly see Megliani (2020), pp. 1654, 1655.

[438] Yianni and Tinkler (2006), p. 751.

[439] See Barsamian (2000).

[440] Buchheit et al. (2007), p. 1208.

[441] Ochoa (2008), p. 112.

[442] Illustrations of similar cases have become evident in the Turkish context, where a bridge, construction and disposal of which was not expected to impact people's lives may have become the basis of an odious debt claim. In the following paragraphs we will discuss the Turkish case.

[443] Most of the infrastructure contracts are known by their acronyms. In BT (Build and Transfer), the developer constructs the facility and hands it over to the government upon completion. In BLT (Build-Lease and Transfer) the facility is handed over to government for a fixed period in accordance with a lease agreement, with ownership transferring at the lease's end. In BOT (Build operate and transfer) the developer undertakes the maintenance of the facility and operates the facility over a fixed term. In BOO (Build-Own and Operate) unlike BOT, developer has no contractual obligation to transfer property rights after a certain period. In BOOT (Build-Own-Operate-Transfer) the developer is authorized to construct, operate and maintain the project. The project is vested in the developer for a specified period at the end of which, it is handed over to government. In BTO (Build -Transfer-and-Operate), the developer constructs the facility on a turn-key basis, title of the facility is vested in government, however developer is entitled to operate it

superstructure projects, intended to benefit the nationals of the state, might not undergo proper auditing. Some projects may not be a blessing for the nationals and in that case, the benefit a project conveys to public will determine whether or not a debt is odious.[444] If the project is impractical or irrational in monetary terms, or if the benefit the nation derives from the project is highly disputed, no matter if it was contracted by the 'voted leader' and the intended use of proceeds has been for the needs of the state; the debt of the project should be branded 'odious'. For instance, if the construction cost of a bridge or its toll could have been lesser, we may all question the validity of the project and, therefore, the validity of the debt.

The second category of debts is **profligate debts**, where governments see no harm in pledging the full faith and credit of their countries for non-virtuous purposes,[445] such as otiose and ill-advised projects that ignore the needs and well-being of the nation and are established to boost the prosperity of a selected few. The international law community recognizes three types of debts that may lift the onus of payment in a contract. Thus, the state does not question the existence of the debt; rather the validity and fairness thereof are disputed. Scholars developed a variety of classifications. While some scholars attached no importance to the identification of odious debt, others opined to the contrary. To be specific; in *Sack*'s view, debts could be categorized as regime debts,[446] subjugation debts[447] and war debts.[448] *Yianni and*

---

once it is commissioned. In CAO (Contract-Add-and-Operate) the developer expands an existing infrastructure facility that is rented from the government and is entitled to operate the expanded facility. DOT (Develop- Operate-and-Transfer) means a contractual arrangement whereby favorable conditions external to an anew infrastructure project which is to be built by the developer are integrated into the arrangement by giving that entity the right to develop adjoining property, and thus, enjoy some of the benefits the investment creates such as higher property or rent values. In ROT (Rehabilitate-Operate-and-Transfer) the developer refurbishes, operates and maintains an existing facility prior to handing it over to government. And finally in ROO (Rehabilitate-Own-and-Operate), similar to ROT, but without a time limitation for operation, the developer enjoys the rights of ownership. For detail and expropriation of a BOT project by Iranian government see Rubins and Kinsella (2005), pp. 34–38. Other variations can be listed as build, lease and transfer (BLT); contract, add and operate (CAO). See Salacuse (2013), pp. 219–220.

[444] Buchheit et al. (2007), p. 1212, and similarly, Paulus (2007), p. 6.

[445] Buchheit et al. (2007), pp. 1210–1211.

[446] When a despotic regime contracts a debt, not for the needs and in the interest of the state, but to strengthen its own despotic regime. See Nehru and Thomas (2008), p. 5, also See Michalowski and Bohoslavsky (2009), p. 62, fn 12, Howse (2007), p. 2.

[447] When the government contracts debts to subjugate the population of part of its territory. See Nehru and Thomas (2008), p. 5.

[448] War debts are those contracted during a war by the previous sovereign to cover the costs of a war. See Paulus (2007), p. 6 and Buchheit et al. (2007), pp. 1212–1214. War debts are also defined as "*debts arising out of transactions which helped or are presumed to have helped the defeated country in waging or preparing war against the successor state or its allies.*" See King (2007), p. 629, also see Howse (2007), p. 3. And according to *Nehru and Thomas*, war debts are concerned when the government of a state contracts debts with a view to waging war against another state, see Nehru and Thomas (2008), p. 5. Scholars provide British refusal to take on war debts of the Boer Republics after annexation in 1900, as an example of war debt as being odious. See Yianni and

Tinkler also identified debts in three pillars. According to authors, hostile debts,[449] war debts and dictator debts[450] formed the basis of odious debt.[451] *Buchheit et al.*, in a similar way, did not treat 'odious debt' as a standalone category under which debts of similar kind could be grouped. By contrast, some authors were of the opinion that odious debt was a form of profligate debts, along with war debts and hostile debts.[452] *King* however, introduced a four-category for odious debts. He included war debts, subjugation debts,[453] illegal occupation debts, and fraudulent, illegal, or corruption debts.[454] The scholars' 'subjugation debts' and 'fraudulent, illegal, or corruption debts' correspond with *Yianni and Tinkler's* 'hostile debts' and 'dictator debts' respectively.[455]

The International Law Commission has put effort to regulate the doctrine of odious debt. The Commission established various forms of debts and made a distinction between 'state debts' and 'other state debts'. Odious debts were classified as a subcategory of 'other state debts' along with war debts, subjugation debts, and regime debts.[456] Although the Commission's articles have never entered into force, a specific article addressed the concept of odious debt and defined it as follows: *"(a) all debts contracted by the predecessor State with a view to attaining objectives contrary to the major interests of the successor State or of the transferred territory; (b) all debts contracted by the predecessor State with an aim and for a purpose not in conformity with international law and, in particular, the principles of international law embodied in the Charter of the United Nations.*[457]" The concept of odiousness in a debt should have consequential effects. Thus, in the subsequent

Tinkler (2006), p. 760, also see Fiebelman (2007), p. 739; Nehru and Thomas (2008), p. 5; Ochoa (2008), p. 114.

[449] Hostile debts are debts used "aggressively against the interests of a population" such as suppressing citizens of the state, Brown (2015), p. 734, also see Feinerman (2007), p. 195, fn 9, for another definition see Howse (2007), p. 19. Buchheit et al. (2007), p. 1214.

[450] Authors define dictator debts as proceeds spent on personal items, used to fight unjust wars or distributed in a discriminatory fashion. See Yianni and Tinkler (2006), pp. 761–762.

[451] Yianni and Tinkler (2006), pp. 757–762.

[452] Buchheit et al. (2007), pp. 1211–1220.

[453] According to *King*, subjugation debts would presently include those whose purpose is known to the creditor to assist the subjection of the population of a state by a despotic leader, the repression of an independence movement, or the economic or political colonization of a territory. See King (2007), pp. 650–651.

[454] King (2007), pp. 650–659. Some scholars divided debts into three groups: criminal debts, unfair debts and ineffective debts. See Nehru and Thomas (2008), pp. 17–23.

[455] Brown (2015), p. 735.

[456] See Draft articles on Succession of States in respect of State Property, Archives and Debts with commentaries, (ILC Articles on Succession) section 13, p. 74, available at https://legal.un.org/ilc/texts/instruments/english/commentaries/3_3_1981.pdf accessed 05.09.2024.

[457] This definition was brought by Mohammed Bedjaoui, see ILC Articles on Succession, article C, p. 79. Also see King (2007), pp. 627, 628.

provision of the draft, the Commission formulated the rule of non-transferability of the debt to the successor state.[458]

8.5.1.2.2 Odious Debt, the Meaning and Components

Odious debts simply denote the debts that are contracted and spent against the interests of the population of a state, without their consent, and with the creditor being fully aware.[459] In 1927 Alexander Sack articulated the concept of odious debt as debts of the despotic power to strengthen its regime and to repress the population that fight against it.[460] According to author, the vagueness of the term could provide a means for the nation to default on their sovereign debts. To avoid such an end, claims should be resolved by tribunals and successor government should prove that; debt in question were odious, was in contradiction to the interests of the people,[461] the creditors, at the moment of paying out the loan, were aware of its odious purpose and the proceeds were not spent in the needs of the state.[462]

---

[458] ILC explained its reasoning in the following words "*The Commission, having discussed articles C and D, recognized the importance of the issues raised in connection with the question of "odious" debts, but was of the opinion initially that the rules formulated for each type of succession of States might well settle the issues raised by the question and might dispose of the need to draft general provisions on it. In completing the second reading of the draft, the Commission confirmed that initial view*." See ILC Articles on Succession, article D, p. 79.

[459] Buchheit et al. (2007), pp. 1216–1219.

[460] According to *King*, Sack's definition was the most comprehensive definition of odious debt which was as follows; "*When a despotic regime contracts a debt, not for the needs or in the interests of the state, but rather to strengthen itself, to suppress a popular insurrection, etc., this debt is odious for the population of the entire state. This debt does not bind the nation; it is a debt of the regime, a personal debt contracted by the power that contracted it, and consequently it falls with the demise of that power. The reason why these "odious" debts cannot be considered to burden the territory of the state is that they do not fulfill one of the conditions determining the regularity of State debts, namely that State debts must be incurred, and the proceeds used, for the needs and in the interests of the state. Odious debts, contracted and utilised, for purposes which, to the lenders' knowledge, are contrary to the needs and the interests of the nation, are not binding on it-when it succeeds in overthrowing the government that contracted them-unless the debt is within the limits of real advantages that these debts might have afforded. The lenders have committed a hostile act against the people, they cannot expect a nation, which has freed itself of a despotic regime, to assume these odious debts, which are the personal debts of the ruler. Even if one despotic regime is overthrown by another, which is as despotic and which does not follow the will of the people, the odious debts contracted by the fallen regime remain personal debts and are not binding on the new regime*". See King (2007), p. 624, also see Howse (2007), p. 2; Ochoa (2008), p. 116.

[461] According to *Paulus*, in case schools or hospitals constructed with money borrowed remain prerogative of the rich or of the family of the ruler, then the following questions may be raised who are the "people" and who should represent them? Paulus (2005), p. 94.

[462] Buchheit et al. (2007), p. 1218, fn 50, (citing Alexander N. Sack, Les effets des transformations des États sur leurs dettes publiques et autres obligations financières [The effects of state transformations on their public debts and other financial obligations]157–84 (1927)), similarly, see Gentile (2010), p. 157, see Paulus (2005), p. 85, and also see Brown (2015), p. 733; Yianni and

Feinerman states that carelessness or profligacy on the part of creditors cannot serve as grounds for debt cancellation under the doctrine[463] of odious debts.[464] According to *King*, following four issues require resolution; (a) the intensity or the hostility of the harm/lack of benefit, (b) whether the proceeds of the debt must be non-beneficial in both purpose and in effect, (c) whether and when general purpose loans might be deemed non-beneficial; and finally, (d) how to assess the absence of benefit.[465]

Some scholars allege that an objective 'should have known' criteria could have a more sound application.[466] Some scholars on the other hand, offer a fourth limb in addition to those advanced by Sack: that for odiousness of the debt, it must have been taken out without the consent of the population.[467] In our opinion, the 'should have known' criteria sit on the opposite end of the spectrum from the latter one. The criteria that rely on the assumption of the past may not be objective and fair. However, creditors are not real-person consumers and lending money to sovereigns requires a certain degree of expertise. Therefore, although the reasons will be provided in the following pages, our solution is debt-centric and leaves the creditors empty-handed. In our belief, creditors should always remain vigilant and be the party shouldering the burden.

Speaking of the latter criteria brought by the scholars; *King* proposes assessing both the legitimacy of regimes and whether the proceeds were used in a beneficial way.[468] Besides, in the scholar's view, the elections may not mirror the platonic idea of 'consent' and for the justification, some may ascertain the propriety of the electoral process. If considerable doubts do not exist, the odious debt doctrine will not apply, and the validity of the debtor's payment obligation arising from the

---

Tinkler (2006), p. 750; Megliani (2020), p. 1653; Fiebelman (2007), p. 739; Michalowski and Bohoslavsky (2009), pp. 60, 61.

[463] *Buchheit* et al. allege that odious debts do not now have, nor is it likely to achieve, the consensus necessary for it to claim the title of "doctrine." See Buchheit et al. (2007), p. 1230, similarly, see Lewis (2007), p. 300.

[464] Feinerman (2007), p. 204.

[465] In the scholar's view, the type of odious debt will determine the intensity of the harm needed. In terms of the second parameter, the proceeds of the debt must be non-beneficial in both purpose and in effect. Concerning the third parameter, much will hinge on the facts known to the creditor prior to lending. As a principle, lending to non-democratic regimes must be for specific non-odious purposes. Finally, last parameter begs the question of who will define the absence of benefit and which standard will be employed. See King (2007), p. 631. Scholar also states that *care of the poor, relief of unemployment, promotion of agriculture and industry, establishment of a state school, a gristmill for public use, and establishment of railroads* are identified as actions of public benefit nature under American public law, see King Ibid, pp. 653–655.

[466] Brown (2015), p. 734.

[467] Paulus (2005), p. 85, fn 14, (citing, Ashfaq Khalfan, Jeff King and Bryan Thomas, Advancing the Odious Debt Doctrine (Mar. 11, 2003) (unpublished working paper), available at https://dette-developpement.org/IMG/pdf/odious_debt_7288.pdf accessed 05.09.2024. Similarly, see Yianni and Tinkler (2006), p. 756 and Ochoa (2008), p. 117.

[468] King (2007), p. 658.

lending contract at issue will not be questioned.[469] Odiousness may partly be concerned, and there will be a continuing obligation with respect to the portion of the funds that were used for legitimate purposes to benefit the population.[470]

8.5.1.2.3 Case Study and Judicial Consideration

The odious debt doctrine has not established a unified and consistent 'debt relief' regime under customary international law.[471] On the contrary, it has gained little momentum. The fact is that there is no extensive and virtually uniform state practice;[472] the case law on this issue may be scarce, which makes it challenging to create unanimity among practitioners and support the doctrine. As will be discussed below, despite the fact that the most recent quasi-application of the odious debt doctrine occurred almost a century ago, these examples may covert this concept into law.

The doctrine originated from arguments made by the U.S. in 1898 during peace negotiations between Spain and the United States.[473] In this *Cuba case*, Spain had contracted bonded debt with Cuba; however, Cuba had no say[474] in the creation of this debt, and the proceeds were used to suppress the aspirations of the Cuban people for independence.[475] When Spain ceded its sovereignty over Cuba to the United States, as the new sovereign power, it proposed to transfer 'all charges and obligations of every kind' and thus requested from United States, the repayment of Cuban's debts.[476] Spain based this allegation on the theory that in case a debt exists at the time of the transfer of a territory, the allocation of the responsibility for the debt must

---

[469] King, Ibid, p. 661.

[470] Art.53 (Treaties conflicting with a peremptory norm of general international law ("jus cogens") of the Vienna Convention on the Law of Treaties (1969) states that "*A treaty is void if, at the time of its conclusion, it conflicts with a peremptory norm of general international law.*" According to *Michalowski and Bohoslavsky*, genocide, slavery, torture, apartheid, crimes against humanity, the use of force form part of ius cogens. Due to the tortures and forced disappearances in the period of 1976–1983, loans made to the Argentinean military regime could be invalid to the extent to which they contributed to the regime's ius cogens violations. Michalowski and Bohoslavsky (2009), pp. 66, 67, 83 and for other instances in which ius cogens was violated and thus the odiousness of the debts arose, see Ibid, pp. 85–87 For partial repudiation, see Howse (2007), p. 12.

[471] See Brown (2015), p. 746, and similarly, see Yianni and Tinkler (2006), pp. 753, 754.

[472] Yianni and Tinkler (2006), p. 755.

[473] Kremer and Jayachandran (2003), p. 5.

[474] Gentile (2010), pp. 154–155 and similarly, see Kremer and Jayachandran (2006), p. 83.

[475] Megliani (2020), p. 1654.

[476] Cuban debt is regarded as the leading example of hostile debt. See Feinerman (2007), p. 195, fn 9, however in some scholar's view, the Spanish debt secured by Cuban revenues were subjugation debt. See Megliani (2020), p. 1660 and similarly, see King (2007), p. 630; Yianni and Tinkler (2006), pp. 757–758; Buchheit et al. (2007), p. 1215. Some scholars identify Cuban case as the classical case of rejection of a subjugation debt, and also for another example of subjugation debt (Indonesian debt), see Nehru and Thomas (2008), p. 6.

be made between the transferor and the transferee, and as the transferee, the United States should assume the debt.[477] In response, the United States claimed that the loans lacked the consent of the Cuban people and were not contracted for the benefit of Cuba. The United States contended that the creditors 'took the obvious chances of their investment on so precarioussecurity[478]'.

The only application of the doctrine in judicial context was *Great Britain v Costa Rica* case.[479] In 1917, Frederico Tinoco, the Costa Rican Secretary of War, staged a coup and overthrew the Costa Rican government. Not surprisingly, he organized elections and was elected as president during his rule. Although he was forcibly removed from office, within his two years in power, he had concluded several contracts, including the sale of an oil exploration concession to a British company and the securing of a line of credit from the Royal Bank of Canada. After his flee, a new election took place, and the Constitutional Congress began to function. The Congress immediately acted and adopted a new law aimed at nullifying the contracts the Tinoco regime had made. Since the shareholders in both entities were British subjects, the government of Great Britain brought a claim against Costa Rica and pressured for the appointment of William Howard Taft, the former president of the United States, as sole arbitrator.[480]

In Taft's view, the credit transaction deviated from the regular course of business.[481] Although countries like the United States and Great Britain did not recognize the Tinoco government, the sole arbitrator viewed the Tinoco government to possess the attributes of 'an actual sovereign government'. Taft's ruling relied on the consideration that the lender was aware of how the proceeds were used,[482] primarily

[477] Buchheit et al. (2007), p. 1214.

[478] Paulus (2007), p. 6 and Buchheit et al. (2007), pp. 1214–1215 and see Paulus (2005), p. 84, also see Gentile (2010), pp. 154–155, similarly, see Brown (2015), pp. 736–737; Fiebelman (2007), p. 739; Stephan (2007), pp. 219, 220; Howse (2007), pp. 10, 11; Ochoa (2008), p. 113; Lewis (2007), p. 313.

[479] Gentile (2010), p. 155.

[480] For detail of the case, please see Salacuse (2013), p. 128.

[481] Taft ruled that "*The whole transaction here was full of irregularities.... .the bank must make out its case of actual furnishing of money to the government for its legitimate use. It has not done so. The bank knew that this money was to be used by the retiring president... The case of the money paid to the brother, the Secretary of War, and the appointed Minister to Italy, is much the same. The government book entry charges him with this as a payment for expenses to be incurred in the establishment of a legation in Italy. It includes the salaries and expenses for four years. To pay salaries for four years in advance is a most unusual and absurd course of business. All the circumstances should have advised the Royal Bank that this second draft, too, was for personal and not for legitimate government purposes... the payment of the money were a mere pretense and abstraction of the money from the public treasury to support a refugee abroad*". See *Great Britain v. Costa Rica*, p. 394. https://www.ilsa.org/Jessup/Jessup12/Tinoco%20Claims%20Arbitration.pdf accessed 05.09.2024 and see Gentile (2010), pp. 154–155, also see Brown (2015), pp. 737–738; Ochoa (2008), p. 115; Lewis (2007), p 312.

[482] Also see Nehru and Thomas (2008), pp. 7, 8

for the personal enrichment of the Tinoco brothers.[483] The most crucial of Taft's findings was that the Tinoco government did not follow the necessary process in concluding the concession agreement. Due to tax exemption granted, the concession agreement required the approval of the country's Chamber of Deputies and Chamber of Senators. However, the concession agreement was only approved by the Chamber of Deputies. Hence, Taft came to the conclusion that the agreement was invalid and not binding on Costa Rica.[484]

This case highlights the absence of an exit strategy for lenders when they are aware of the debtor's odious purpose. It serves as an example of an instance where the odiousness of the debt became salient in the change of government. Odious debt is not a concept of debt repudiation simply because of the succession of states, on the contrary, the odiousness of the debt calls for a distinct treatment and thus impacts the validity of the borrowing. In the view of some scholars, odious debt can constitute a significant defense against a state's failure to afford aliens the minimum standard of treatment in international law, through the non-honor of contractual right.[485] The doctrine offers new governments a legal mechanism to repudiate debts incurred by their predecessors and is a means to facilitate the timely reconstruction of infrastructure.[486]

On the other hand, the doctrine is not a way of cleansing a validated debt that has been properly established. On the flip side, since it may create a perception of discontinuity in statehood. Governments should avoid to exercise odiousness as a shortcut to repudiating contracts on arbitrary grounds. If the new government chooses to repudiate the debt, it may potentially violate the basic legal principle of 'pacta sunt servanda' ('pacts must be respected'), which requires the states to honor their agreements with one another.[487]

Corruption and bribery (the corrupt payment) are crimes, contrary to public policy and can be regarded as a form of statutory loan forgiveness. Their presence might render a loan contract voidable[488] or nullify the consequences attached to the parties' will;[489] nevertheless, the benefits will be subject to government confiscation.

---

[483] He fled with the money borrowed from the Royal Bank of Canada. Frederico Tinoco received $100,000 for expenses related to representation of the Chief of State on his upcoming trip abroad, and Jose Joaquin Tinoco received another $100,000 as Minister of Costa Rica to Italy, for four years' salary and expenses of the Legation in Italy, a position to which he had been appointed by his brother. See Buchheit et al. (2007), pp. 1216–1217, Paulus (2005), pp. 84, 85, similarly, Stephan (2007), p. 220.

[484] Salacuse (2013), p. 129.

[485] Howse (2007), p. 3.

[486] Brown (2015), p. 741.

[487] Howse (2007), p. 4 and similarly, Salacuse (2013), p. 319.

[488] Stephan (2007), p. 223.

[489] For instance, art. 50 of the Vienna Convention on the Law of Treaties (1969) provides for the following: "*If the expression of a state's consent to be bound by a treaty has been procured through the corruption of its representative directly or indirectly by another negotiating State, the State may invoke such corruption as invalidating its consent to be bound by the treaty.*"

One may need to note that the unenforceability of the loan cannot be determined solely upon the debtor's profile; the transaction itself should be tainted by corruption. In the words of *Buchheit et al.*, a loan will not be unenforceable merely because it was contracted by a corrupt regime.[490] Several Conventions are in force in relation to corruption. Among these[491] the United Nations Convention Against Corruption (UNCAC) is the only legally binding universal anti-corruption instrument.[492] On the other hand, the United Nations Office on Drugs and Crime (UNODC) and the World Bank have developed the Stolen Assets Recovery (StAR) initiative. The initiative aimed at supporting countries in implementing Chapter V of the UNCAC and assisting international efforts to deny safe havens for corrupt funds[493] thereby parties to initiative could secure the repatriation of assets stolen by their corrupt former leaders.[494]

As discussed earlier, the 'should have known' criteria are assessed based on the degree of lender's lack of care in monitoring the transaction. What lies beneath the lender's motivation may be irrelevant or unnecessary. In the corrupt[495] or collusive transaction, however, both parties' intentions are explicit: officials of the debtor intend to pocket some of the proceeds and lender acquiesces in this behavior. Both parties either disregard or aim to bend the rule of law, and therefore both share a degree of culpability.

According to *Lewis*, odious debt is problematic for two reasons. First, it places judges in the position of having to answer a fundamental political question: whether

[490] Buchheit et al. (2007), p. 1245.

[491] See OECD Convention on Combating Bribery of Foreign Public Officials in International Business Transactions available at https://www.oecd.org/daf/anti-bribery/ConvCombatBribery_ENG.pdf For Counsel of Europe's "Criminal Law Convention on Corruption" visit: https://www.coe.int/en/web/impact-convention-human-rights/criminal-law-convention-on-corruption#/ and for a comparison of Conventions as well as glossary, see https://www.oecd.org/corruption/acn/41650182.pdf all accessed 05.09.2024.

[492] See https://www.unodc.org/documents/brussels/UN_Convention_Against_Corruption.pdf accessed 05.09.2024.

[493] See the StAR Brochure available at https://star.worldbank.org/star-brochure accessed 05.09.2024.

[494] See Nehru and Thomas (2008), p. 29.

[495] In *World Duty Free v. Kenya* (para. 133), the situation is considered to involve a dictator's debt. Kenya considered that the payment was a bribe given in order to obtain the Agreement on which the claims are based. Conversely, World Duty Free asserted that it was a gift of protocol or a personal donation made to the President to be used for public purposes. The tribunal regarded those payments as a bribe and dismissed the claims on the basis that "*under international public policy, a claimant cannot maintain claims arising under a contract obtained through bribery*" and "*Kenya, was legally entitled to avoid and did avoid legally by its laws*". Available at https://www.italaw.com/sites/default/files/case-documents/italaw15005.pdf accessed 05.09.2024. Although the case satisfied the test of 'absence of nation's consent' and 'consent of the debtor', the project was not against public benefit, and therefore it was not an odious debt. Yianni and Tinkler (2006), pp. 763–766, also see Buchheit et al. (2007), p. 1233, fn 101 and p. 1239, fn 128; Born (2021), p. 517; Bottini (2010), pp. 305–311.

the government is sufficiently 'democratic'. Therefore, the concept of odious debt is judicially challenging to administer. The second issue is that it is narrow in scope, the insidious use of the proceeds is problematic when a portion is used for odious purposes while the remainder is put to good use.[496] According to *Paulus,* one of the cons of odious debt is that employing the doctrine can be fearsome and may lead to problems, the most serious and significant of which is the risk of disrupting international financial flows to developing countries.[497] Although such fears may be misplaced in some cases,[498] when the doctrine is raised, the successor government's access to funds and its reputation may be tarnished. *Buchheit et al.* question if anyone would be willing to lend to a corporate borrower where the debt could be legally repudiated by a successor board of directors or a majority shareholder.[499] In *Feinerman*'s words, "*lenders are not cavalier in making loans to sovereign debtors*", hence, once the doctrine is invoked, and a government repudiates its debts due to the odiousness of the debt, the bridge between the sovereign and international lenders may have been burned.[500] Scholars state that lenders will be under a burden to monitor the actions of their borrowers more closely to ensure that funds lent are to be used for generally accepted purposes; this may increase the cost of borrowing.[501]

The application of the doctrine may be confusing, and upon relying on the Vienna Convention of 1983, some may want to limit its application to state succession. According to such thought, when governments change, the rights and obligations of the nation remain unimpaired.[502] In the *Iran v United States* claims, the doctrine was raised; however, the tribunal[503] was reluctant to stand on the doctrinal debate as to whether it exists in international law. Assuming it did exist, the tribunal found no reason to accept the claims owing to the fact that the doctrine could be invoked in the case of state succession, and in the tribunal's belief, Iran's situation was a case of government succession.[504] The Convention, on the other hand, was silent on the responsibility of the successor government and represented a failed attempt at codification.

---

[496] Lewis (2007), pp. 305, 306.

[497] See Nehru and Thomas (2008), p. 26.

[498] For the cases where states repudiated their debts but maintained financial reliability to future creditors, see Brown (2015), p. 743.

[499] Buchheit et al. (2007), p. 1225.

[500] Feinerman (2007), pp. 205, 206.

[501] Paulus (2005), pp. 88–89, similarly, see Brown (2015), p. 753.

[502] See King (2007), p. 615.

[503] See *U.S. v. Iran.*

[504] The tribunal's reasoning was as follows "*In spite of the change in head of State and the system of government in 1979, Iran remained the same subject of international law as before the Islamic Revolution. For when a government is removed through a revolution, the State, as an international person, remains unchanged and the new Government generally assumes all the previous international rights and obligations of the State.*" See Howse (2007), p. 11. Also see King (2007), pp. 646–649, and similarly, see Megliani (2020), p. 1660; Buchheit et al. (2007), p. 1221, fn 59.

The line between state succession and government succession may be too thin to identify. Besides, the application of the doctrine entails an examination of odiousness, the absence of which may mean that when a governing body is ousted, the proceeds used for odious purposes would remain binding on the successor government. Such debts standing as humpbacks of the country, can perpetuate a never-ending cycle of corruption. As of today, in the case of government succession, a variety of examples lay down at adjudicators' feet to acknowledge and apply the doctrine. Hence, adjudicators need to examine the merits and should not evade hearing the case solely on government succession grounds.

8.5.1.2.4 Institutional Solutions

International institutions have the capacity to provide debt forgiveness or adjustments of every sort for any kind of reason. When a government's stance leans more toward readjustment rather than repudiating the debt, it can signify a compromise that benefits creditors or bondholders with a score of 1 instead of 0. Attempts to excuse debts have been recognized under international law agreements. For instance, in accordance with the treaty of Versailles, debts incurred by Germany and Prussia in the wake of annexing Poland, certain debts did not pass to Poland. In other words, Poland did not assume the debts that were attributable to measures taken by the Prussian or German governments to colonize Poland.[505]

However, Czechoslovakia was not excused from the wartime and pre-war debts incurred by the Austro-Hungarian Empire.[506] Recent examples of such debt restructuring include Iraq's and Argentina's experiences.[507] Saddam Hussein's regime left behind a debt worth USD 125 billion, and according to commentators, these debts were odious, thus new regime was urged to disavow the obligations incurred by its predecessor.[508] In Iraq's debt restructuring, the Paris Club[509] played a

[505] See Megliani (2020), p. 1654, for the other instances of odious-like debt see King (2007), p. 634, see Yianni and Tinkler (2006), p. 759, Fiebelman (2007), p. 740 and Howse (2007), p. 11.

[506] Brown (2015), p. 748.

[507] Brown (2015), pp. 738–739, similarly, see Feinerman (2007), pp. 211, 212, also see Megliani (2020), pp. 1665–1667. For the details of restructurings see https://clubdeparis.org/en/traitements/iraq-21-11-2004/en and https://clubdeparis.org/en/traitements/argentina-29-05-2014/en accessed 05.09.2024.

[508] Fiebelman (2007), p. 733,

[509] The Paris Club is an informal group of official creditors whose role is to find coordinated and sustainable solutions to the payment difficulties experienced by debtor countries. As debtor countries undertake reforms to stabilize and restore their macroeconomic and financial situation, the Paris Club creditors provide an appropriate debt treatment. They also provide debt treatments to debtor countries in the form of rescheduling, which is debt relief by postponement or, in the case of concessional rescheduling, reduction in debt service obligations during a defined period (flow treatment) or as of a set date (stock treatment). Paris Club debt restructurings aim to reschedule the principal rather than reduce the stock of debt, and the decision of restructuring can be tied upon the approval of an IMF financing arrangement. Please visit: https://clubdeparis.org/ accessed

leading role, resulting in an impressive 80% reduction in the debt burden. While the elements of the doctrine did not match with the findings in the Ecuadorian debt restructuring, the president declared two out of three international bonded loans illegal; he also halted coupon payments without formally repudiating the loans.[510] According to some scholars, debt restructuring, and odious debt are not interchangeable and therefore, odious debt cannot be replaced by insolvency tools. While debt restructuring ensures an honest debtor country's ability to repay, odious debt focuses on the legality of the debt and whether the debt is unjust to burden the people of the debtor state.[511]

There were views that a panel of judges operating under the auspices of UNCTAD would have the exclusive power to decide the relevant cases.[512] The UNCTAD Principles do not explicitly mention odious debt; scholars argue that through the following three principles, elements of the doctrine are in some ways embedded in these Principles.[513] According to principle 1, lenders should recognize that government officials responsible for a financial transaction are acting in the name and on behalf of the population. Principle 2 states that lenders should take reasonable steps to ensure that the sovereign understands the risks and benefits of the financial product being offered. Finally, under the 5th principle of the UNCTAD, lenders assume a responsibility to perform their own *ex-ante* investigation into and, when applicable, post-disbursement monitoring of, the likely effects of the project, including its financial, operational, civil, social, cultural, and environmental implications.[514]

Brown, as an *ex-ante* solution discusses the suitability of the UN, G7 and OECD to evaluate acts of the governments and label them as 'odious-debt prone.[515]' If these institutions were to announce whether regimes are odious, the successor government

---

05.09.2024. Also see Feinerman (2007), p. 212, fn 80, Yianni and Tinkler (2006), p. 767, Gentile (2010), p. 163 and finally, see Hagan (2008), p. 219.

[510]Megliani (2020), pp. 1667–1668. According to *Gentile* if the agreements governing Ecuador's sovereign bonds had contained use-of proceeds covenants, investors would have had a basis to assert claims of a "breach of covenant". Besides, in our opinion, such an early warning would have resulted in cutting-off the loan payment or accepting different terms that are to the benefit of the nation. See Gentile (2010), p. 172; Ochoa (2008), pp. 119, 120.

[511]For more, see Michalowski and Bohoslavsky (2009), pp. 107, 108.

[512]Paulus (2005), p. 101.

[513]Megliani (2020), p. 1664.

[514]Please visit: https://unctad.org/system/files/official-document/gdsddf2012misc1_en.pdf accessed 05.09.2024.

[515]Brown (2015), pp. 752–755, also see Feinerman (2007), p. 217. For a similar view also see Kremer and Jayachandran (2003), pp. 14, 15. *Brown* also discusses a "supertrustee" role in the sovereign context. The supertrustee's task would be to continuously monitor the sovereign's compliance with the covenants in the indenture. He/she will be entitled to renegotiate the terms of the bond covenants or to accelerate bond payments, potentially halting the use of additional funds for odious purposes and allowing creditors to recover their investments. However, such a solution would require a contract among bondholders which would need to define the trustee's scope of authority and would be influenced by the Trust Indenture Act. In international bonds, the law

would gain the support of the international community, thereby, avoiding reputational damage from failing to repay odious debt.[516] However, due to the lack of a widely accepted definition of odious debt and the non-binding nature of decisions made by these institutions, such an offer may not gain proponents. In addition, in *King*'s view, such institutions may have disadvantages that outweigh their advantages. First of all, institutions composed of states may not act on the basis of impartial assessments. The UN would have international legitimacy, but it would take years to establish. Regarding G7 or the OECD, according to scholars, the process would be regarded as "*the outcome of a politicized, non-objective, rich-nations' club facilitating the furtherance of a neo-colonial economic agenda as an institution composed of states*".[517] Furthermore, according to some scholars' thinking, the organs or the tribunals vested with the power to determine the odiousness of a situation will require concrete facts to distinguish 'odiousness' from 'non-odiousness[518]'.

Brown also explored the potential of the U.N. Security Council, the World Bank and the IMF as *ex-post* solutions for addressing the odious debt doctrine, and he believes that the IMF and the World Bank are better suited to address the odious debt problem.[519] Speaking of the United Nations, in case a despotic regime poses a threat to peace, in accordance with article 41 of the United Nations Charter, the Security Council may exercise complete or partial interruption of economic relations.[520] According to *Stephan*, this action would call upon member states to refuse to recognize debts contracted by such regimes if the regime odiously uses the proceeds.[521] Additionally, although states must conform carrying out the resolutions, they may not be binding in domestic law.[522] Needless to say, under article 23 and 27, the validity of a measure relies on the concurrence of permanent members of the Council, namely China, France, Russia, the United Kingdom, and the United States.

The World Bank has advocated for debt restructuring[523] and since the World Bank loan contracts are subject to arbitration tribunals, this forum can be more receptive to considering principles of international law such as the doctrine of odious debts.[524] However, the composition of a specific tribunal dedicated to resolving

---

applied to the contracts can vary, and a solution proposed by a recognized international institution may face fewer disputes. For detail, see Brown Ibid, pp. 755–757.

[516] Feinerman (2007), p. 217.

[517] King (2007), p. 659.

[518] See Nehru and Thomas (2008), p. 12.

[519] Brown (2015), p. 748, fn 227.

[520] Please visit: https://www.un.org/en/about-us/un-charter/chapter-7 accessed 05.09.2024.

[521] Stephan (2007), p. 227.

[522] National governments may cite a Security Council resolution as a basis for adopting domestic law, but refusal to carry out a resolution may result only in the issuance of another resolution. See Brown (2015), p. 748, fn 224; Stephan (2007), p. 227.

[523] Michalowski and Bohoslavsky (2009), p. 106.

[524] Feinerman (2007), p. 209.

disputes deriving from debts claimed to be odious has faced criticism. Creating such a tribunal body would give rise to political debates[525] and significant costs.[526] When it comes to IMF, if it were to play a role in the identification of odious debt, it could withhold IMF funds from odious regimes and declare any previous debts unenforceable.[527] In one scholar's view, the dispute resolution forum established in connection with the SDRM mechanism proposed by the IMF could enable the debtor to initiate proceedings and discuss the odiousness of the debt. In the event of failure, the debtor could still be entitled to benefit from the restructuring.[528]

Sovereigns may commit to utilizing funds in the manner as specified in agreements governing sovereign bonds, or the contract may include a definition of odiousness. In our opinion, contractual arrangements or contract-based solutions may alleviate some hesitations as to whether the sovereign is breaching its commitments under the contract.[529] However, provisions such as 'use-of-proceed covenants[530]' are still far from solving the dispute. The decision to cancel further lending may rest upon the odiousness of the borrowing. However, the fate of previously disbursed funds will be vague. If the tribunal detects odiousness in accordance with the contract, that will cause more than just the successor government's relaxation in terms of the compulsory debt payment; it will be entitled to repudiate from the contract.

8.5.1.2.5 Are Turkish Disputes on the Horizon?

It should be well noted that nationals of the state may overlook or tolerate the faults of the governments they voted for. Even if polling shows a dip, the government may apply an attrition policy, leaving its successors with an economic salvage deriving from the 20–25 years of foreign currency securities granted for various projects. In the first place, a fair election may sound like a fresh start for the new government; however, once the successor government fails to address the burdens of the past, it will only be a matter of time before the predecessor attempts to overthrow the successor.

The debts of Turkey have beckoned discussions on sovereign debt. Recent projects undertaken in Turkey have sparked new academic interest in the issue of odious debts. Over the last decade, with the assumption of a robust economy and a stable

---

[525] In *Stephan*'s view, if that is an agency to wielding this authority, it may find itself mired in ideological wars. See Stephan (2007), p. 227.

[526] Fiebelman (2007), p. 744.

[527] Brown (2015), p. 749, also see Feinerman (2007), pp. 209, 215.

[528] The same scholar discusses the applicability of including a provision in BITs addressing odious debt. In the scholar's view, given that BITs aim to safeguard investors, such an inclusion may render investors divested of the return on their funds and, as a result, make parties to BITs less appealing to potential investors. For detail, see Lewis (2007), pp. 335–339.

[529] Fiebelman (2007), pp. 748, 749.

[530] For the opinion, see Gentile (2010), p. 171, and see Stephan (2007), p. 224.

Turkish lira, a high volume of BOOT (Build-Operate-Transfer), infrastructure contracts (city hospitals, bridges, highways, airports), wherein the government assumed a payment guarantee in dollars for up to 20, 25 years were signed. Contracts or guarantees with such long tenors can result in long-term detrimental consequences for the financial stability of the country. Predictably, the Turkish Lira began to plunge a record low against the dollar starting from September 2021. Given the sharp lira depreciation, the validity of the debts began to be questioned and people were concerned as to whether proceeds were misused as one of the periodic financial wrongdoings of the Turkish government. The economic swing has provided a unique occasion for the politicians to mention expropriation of these projects.[531] The first foray into the concept of odious debt came also by same politicians.[532]

The companies constructing, operating these projects, and therefore benefiting from the long-lasting payment promises, have tendered so many public contracts that. According to a World Bank report, five Turkish project companies ranked among top 10 in the world.[533] Moreover, four of them obtained a total of 128 tax exemptions.[534] Among a variety of contracts, in order for exploring the presence of odiousness, we have chosen the Osmangazi bridge where the government provided a traffic/vehicle guarantee to the successful tenderer.

Lewis states that if a tribunal is to decide whether an expenditure is odious, it should look to prevailing international spending practices and determine whether the expenditure is ordinary and necessary.[535] Hence, some may wish to compare the construction and operation costs of a project of an equivalent nature; however, factors such as borrowing and labor costs, as well as financial structure of the project may not match with those of projects abroad. While *Kremer and Jayachandran* present a model and discuss sovereign debt and odious regimes through equations,[536] likewise, *Janus* conducts in a model on preliminary conjectures regarding

[531] Please visit: https://www.reuters.com/markets/currencies/turkish-lira-flat-ahead-cenbank-meeting-2021-12-16/ and https://www.theguardian.com/world/2021/dec/13/turkey-faces-threat-of-financial-crisis-after-lira-plunges-against-dollar and https://anlatilaninotesi.com.tr/20201207/kilicdaroglu-saygin-bir-devlet-vatandaslarina-yalan-soylemez-1043356727.html. For the disputes encompassing government security given to investors, see *the May Case*, available at https://legal.un.org/riaa/cases/vol_XV/47-75.pdf all accessed 05.09.2024 and also see *PSEG v. Turkey*.

[532] Please visit; https://www.sozcu com.tr/2021/ekonomi/aksenerin-bahsettigi-tiksindirici-borc-nedir-6513566/ accessed 05.09.2024

[533] Please visit: https://tr.euronews.com/2018/12/30/turkiye-den-5-insaat-firmasi-dunyada-en-fazla-ihale-alan-ilk-10-firma-arasinda and for a similar report, see https://csnturkiye.com/csn300-2022/ all accessed 05.09.2024.

[534] Please visit: https://www.sozcu.com.tr/2020/gundem/chpli-basarir-5li-yandas-sirkete-128-kez-vergi-ve-harc-indirimi-6181232/ accessed 05.09.2024.

[535] The author further states that according to *peer state standard*, the lender may compare the state's public expenditure practice to that of its peer states and, in doing so, may utilize the variables of geographic location, alternatives, transportation modes available, security concerns, and even GDP figures. See Lewis (2007), pp. 311, 319.

[536] Kremer and Jayachandran (2006), pp. 82–92.

welfare effects of odious borrowing.[537] In the project at hand, however, a combination of simple math and terminology can reveal whether the project serves the nation's interests or not.

The test of odiousness is less challenging when comparing good government to bad government. One could reasonably assume that governments' debts lacking democratic accountability due to suppression of all forms of dissent or engagement in violence against their citizens may qualify as odious.[538] If the regime has no incentive to act in favor of the nation, the proceeds used may presumptively be regarded as odious. For instance, a tyrannical leader using funds to bring the rock band Aerosmith into the country to perform at his daughter's birthday is obviously odious.[539] However, does that mean that 'odiousness' cannot be attributed to 'elected leaders' just because the constitutional requirements(elections) have been satisfied?[540]

Although within the concept of international criminal law, some scholars allege that if the majority of the nation supports the regime, they should be held liable for the crimes committed by the regime.[541] Should the consent of 52% of the population[542] make a debt valid even if the decision to construct generates a %48 of discontent among populace? Even if so, should we require such a rate at the time of election? at the time of an infrastructure construction decision is made? or at the time when the project is delivered? These questions delve into the complex issues surrounding democratic representation, consent, and accountability, and they don't have easy answers. They highlight the challenges in determining the legitimacy and odiousness of debts in various political contexts. Odious debt may not be exclusive to non-democratic regimes, and it should not be restricted solely to cases involving villainy. Despite the fact that the Turkish democracy has been moving forward, albeit gradually, with various challenges and setbacks along the way, the nature and duration of Turkey's debts do not diminish their dubious nature.

As of August 2024, the operational details of the project are as follows; the guaranteed price per vehicle is Turkish Lira equivalent of approximately USD 51,[543] and the toll charged to car drivers is USD 16[544] the difference assumed by the Treasury; thus, fiscal law-wise, a taxpayer-driver pays 1 and the Treasury pays an additional sum of 2 on taxpayer's behalf. Finally, the utmost importance of this

[537] Janus (2012), pp. 305–317.

[538] Stephan (2007), p. 225.

[539] Brown (2015), p. 733.

[540] Megliani (2020), p. 1657.

[541] Merezhko (2018), p. 119.

[542] In the 2023 elections, president Erdogan ended with just over 52% of the vote. Please visit: https://www.bbc.com/news/world-europe-65743031 accessed 05.09.2024.

[543] Please visit: https://www.diken.com.tr/osmangazi-koprusunde-gunluk-garanti-40-milyon-tlye-yaklasti/ accessed 05.09.2024.

[544] Please visit: https://www.kgm.gov.tr/Sayfalar/KGM/SiteTr/Otoyollar/OtoyolKopruUcret/OsmangaziKopruGecisUcret.aspx accessed 25.08.2024.

project is the guaranteed number of vehicles per day, which is 40.000. The subsidy-like guarantee on the part of the Treasury was built on a '40.000 vehicle in any case' basis. Put another way, unless the number of vehicles using the bridge on the same day hits a total of 40.000, the Treasury will not be relieved from its financial obligation and a random taxpayer who may not have even seen the bridge will have paid for this project.[545]

Aside from the dichotomy in terms of guaranteed amount due to lack of transparency, given the extreme depreciation of the Turkish Lira, amounts have begun to change dramatically and instantly, and the Turkish Lira is far from finding its nominal value against the dollar. Thus, the denomination of the price, even in US Dollars, may not provide a sufficient basis for an accurate assessment of the current situation. Therefore, the key to unlocking the door of 'odiousness' is the set of data regarding the affordability of the nation, particularly the ratios between minimum income and tolls due to the fact that the rates between minimum income and the toll have remained almost stable over the years, while the tolls increased, so did the salaries. However, it is worthy to note that the proportion of minimum wage owner in the country is almost %60.[546] Hence, the argument for declaring the debt at hand as 'odious' may derive from the following line of reasoning: A round trip on the bridge costs almost twice as much as the daily earnings of more than half of the population. Moreover, while the minimum wage has swung between 400 and 500 dollars over the last decade, the average pension received by millions is even lower. Hence, the vast majority falls short of being able to benefit from such infrastructure. Whereas the 15 Temmuz Şehitler Bridge serving a similar purpose to the Osmangazi bridge, charged a price for a round-trip toll, which amounts to less than 10% of the toll for the latter.[547] Although some may speculate that thousands still enjoy the latter project, prosperous minorities should not be the reference point in such a situation specifically where the vast majority is still far from reaching it.

An infrastructure is not a piece of art protected by armored glass; by contrast it is meant to be at the nation's disposal. While it may not need to be entirely free, it must be affordable. If the population avoids using the infrastructure, the best case is that the Osmangazi bridge is not nation-friendly. If the debt payments deriving from its

---

[545] *Lewis* proposes a means that can operate between the identification of odious expenditures and debt cancellation. This so-called "*cancellation analysis*" is based on the assumption that the difference between a state's operating cost and tax revenue will determine the amount of recognizable odious expenditures (expenditures eligible for cancellation). On several grounds the method may not be adapted to the Turkish case. First, the tenor of borrowings spans 20 to 25 years. Second the using fees will be adjusted on a regular basis according to the inflation rate and reserve currency. And finally, the number of the projects of similar nature is more than a few. Hence, the difference between operating cost and tax revenue may be calculated per annum but it would provide a basic assumption. For details of the cancellation analysis, see Lewis (2007), pp. 322–329.

[546] Please visit: https://www.bloomberght.com/hangi-ulkede-asgari-ucretli-calisan-orani-ne-kadar-2309803 also visit: https://www.euronews.com/business/2024/02/05/how-do-minimum-wages-compare-across-europe-in-2024 both accessed 05.09.2024.

[547] As of August 2024, the toll of the 15 Temmuz Şehitler Bridge is almost 6% of the Osmangazi bridge. Please visit: https://www.kgm.gov.tr/Sayfalar/KGM/SiteTr/Otoyollar/OtoyolKopruUcret/KopruGecisUcret.aspx accessed 25.08.2024.

construction continue for decades and become unaffordable in the meantime, the project is non-beneficial in both purpose and effect, as seen in *King*'s test. In addition, the real clients of the creditors are the nations who will enjoy those projects, and taxes of whom will conclude the payment.

Regardless of whether funds are extended with the knowledge that the incumbent regime will remain in power long enough to repay the debt,[548] and the lender funded the regime for its odious purposes, the principle of strict liability should be applied to the creditors.[549] Article 11 of the UNCTAD Principles provides the following implication "*If lenders are expected to bear the risk of their sovereign investment decisions, it is necessary that they be given the information required to analyze that risk properly before making the investment.*" Thus, some may find the application of strict liability as 'foisting a heavy burden upon the lender's side'. However, lenders are fully equipped institutions capable of conducting due diligence, distinguishing the provisions of contracts, and assessing and managing the impact of projects on the public whether by means of its construction cost, fees charged for using the project or the securities given. A thorough due diligence can improve governance on both the lender and the sovereign's sides. Thus, prior to disbursement of the loan, lenders should carefully exercise what is known as a 'Know Your Customer' check[550] and, at every stage, apply a high standard of probity and more stringent conditions and controls over the use of proceeds.[551]

Although the capacity of individual bondholders to afford pre-lending due diligence may pose challenges, in the sovereign context, individual bondholders are rare. Apart from that, the odious debt concept is not based on distributing responsibility on a pari passu basis to monitor whether the proceeds are used in an appropriate manner. The concerns of lenders must pale in comparison with the welfare of the society; hence, the consequences should fall on the lender.[552] Those engaging in the construction of infrastructure projects abroad must have assumed that the public's well-being is paramount. These projects may face expropriation, or a new government might avoid repaying the loan, which may trigger the concept of odious debt.

The claim of odiousness in Turkish Project finance is not a punishment of lenders for their so-called irresponsible and reckless lending.[553] At some point, enabling payouts in which the public had no benefit, may unjustly enrich creditors.[554] Lenders should have borne usage fees, and the nation's interest in mind. Even if one were to allege that proceeds were spent for the benefit of Turkey, those alleging odiousness of the debt may raise the question of how many bridges alike might otherwise be

---

548 Buchheit et al. (2007), p. 1215.

549 Megliani (2020), p. 1657.

550 A duty to undertake a certain effort to inquire about their customers and their activities. Michalowski and Bohoslavsky (2009), p. 100.

551 According to *Nehru and Thomas*, lenders may be responsible if they have the leverage to prevent (or at least greatly diminish) the illegal misuse of loans, Nehru and Thomas (2008), p. 18.

552 Stephan (2007), p. 224, fn 32.

553 Nehru and Thomas (2008), p. 15.

554 Masaro (2019), p. 1671.

built with the same amount that will be received by the end of repayment term. While each case has its own attributes, and requires a thorough investigation, and quasi-legal grounds may be sparse, in our thought, if the nation, whether for financial reasons or otherwise, is forced to behave in a way as if what was meant to be built for them does not exist, in other words, if the projects convey no benefit to the nation, odiousness will be an obviousness.

Besides, the dilemma is that even if the government is ousted, these guarantees will haunt Turkey for years. If the repayment terms, that were probably based on over-optimistic or irrational parameters, are not modified, the successor governments may not get the economy back on track. And even if lenders allege that they were deceived and enticed into funding the sovereign's odious plans or believed that advancing funds under those circumstances was not a 'committing a hostile act with the host state[555]', they should still bear the consequences of odious debt. Otherwise, it may mean to force future generations of citizens to repay money borrowed in their name but not for their benefit.[556] In some respects, it punishes many for the deeds of a few, burdening the majority because of the actions of a future minority.[557] And a nation's reckless or ungraciously mannered choice may give rise to cutting off the education of their own children or delaying their own retirements merely because they lacked the discipline to live within their means.[558]

8.5.1.2.6 Concluding Remarks

Paulus is of the opinion that the legal consequences of the 'odious debts' doctrine would not be limited to the nullification of the underlying loan agreement; the lender's right to demand repayment of the loan should also be denied.[559] In civil law systems, the party unjustly enriched is under an obligation to restitute the enrichment. Therefore, some may suppose that the government must repay the loan extended to it. As a well-known phrase suggests "*The party who had committed iniquity shall not have equity.*[560]" Therefore, governments and lenders should not be allowed to profit from their deliberate or neglectful wrongdoings. Restitution of unjust enrichment has a discrete boundary. Illegality of the aim will disqualify the lender's right to restitution of the money transferred under the contract. Simply put, should the asset or the money was given for an unlawful or immoral end, the party is precluded from demanding repayment. However, unless parties found their cause of action upon such illegal or unethical acts and unless it is crystal clear, adjusting the

[555] Ochoa (2008), p. 113.

[556] Buchheit et al. (2007), p. 1203.

[557] Ochoa (2008), p. 113.

[558] Buchheit et al. (2007), p. 1212.

[559] Paulus (2005), pp. 100–102.

[560] English Barrister Richard Francis' expression was quoted from Megliani (2020), p. 1652, fn 71.

terms of the loan agreement with an eye on the nation's interest must always be on the table.

The question might be whether the receivables of the creditors might be subject to PRI coverage. In theory, all risks are insurable if one pays the premium;[561] however, in the occurrence of odious debt, the insurer's right to recourse will not follow a clockwise routine. To exemplify; as discussed above, in odious debt, default by the successor state is not based on an arbitrary and reckless decision, and the lender is not entitled to claim the sum. In subrogation, since the insurer cannot possess a right superior to that of the insured, the insurer thus will be unable to seek reimbursement from the successor government. However, those who gave birth to the odious debt should not go unpunished. The PRI provider, when faced with an odiousness defense while seeking reimbursement from the successor government (assuming that the odiousness of the debt is unearthed after indemnification by the insurer) should be entitled to pursue restitution from the insured parties by asserting a claim of unjust enrichment. In this regard, *Brown* and *Buchheit et al.* offer the very well-known corporate concept of 'veil piercing'.[562] The main difference in the sovereign context is that the citizens of the state bear an unlimited liability and will be responsible for the debts of the government officials who did not act within the range of their rights.[563] However, Employing the doctrine may provide a solution for the lender to recover its claim only from the government officials.

8.5.1.3 Unfair Calling of Guarantees

In the realm of foreign investment, host states that award a project can be concerned about the trustworthiness and ability of the bidder[564] therefore, will not wish to release funds to the bidder until they are provided with a security in respect of the work to be carried out under the project contract. The terminology employed in financial instruments as a means of security may vary from one jurisdiction to another and may not be apposite to the professionals.[565] The same terminological confusion comes to the fore when the parties to the undertaking are concerned. Foreign investors are the bidders and referred to as principals/applicants of the security, while host states, on the other hand, are the beneficiaries of the security.[566]

---

[561] See Williams (1993), p. 70.

[562] In the corporate context, shareholders enjoy limited liability, and if a shareholder abuses the limited liability characteristic of the corporation to harm the lender, courts may disregard the separate entity of the corporation. The lender may look through (to pierce) the limited liability veil of the corporation and claim the receivables from the controlling shareholder who treated the corporation as its alter ego. Buchheit et al. (2007), pp. 1247, 1248.

[563] Brown (2015), p. 745, for detail, see Buchheit et al. (2007), pp. 1247–1251.

[564] Van Der Vaart (1981), p. 38.

[565] According to some scholars, undertakings can be grouped in two categories namely "bonds" and "banker guarantees". See White (1979), pp. 122–123.

[566] Kelly-Louw (2009), p. 712.

The most prominent forms of securities are unconditional advance payment bonds, performance bonds or standby letters of credit. A security can be the subject of this political risk only insofar as it contains the independence and unconditional elements of an undertaking.

Securities offer ex-ante or ex-post protection for the host state. Firstly, the securities serve as a deterrent to the bidder and ensure that the terms of the tender are adhered to. The bond is extinguished if the bidder performs his obligations. Second, securities provide both monetary remedy and punitive measures, the host state can call for the payment from the issuing bank when the bidder defaults on its obligation.[567] Upon the default by the foreign investor, the host state can call on the guarantee by representing a request to the issuing bank, which, unlike a letter of credit, does not establish title to goods. One may need to note that the host state can abuse the proceedings and call on the guarantee merely by asserting the foreign investor's default without justification. Therefore, the fairness of the call must be linked to foreign investor's actual default;[568] regardless of however the host state perceives the call, the foreign investor must consider the call as 'fair' or 'just'.

ISP98,[569] UCP,[570] URCG,[571] URDG[572] and the UNCITRAL Convention[573] are sets of rules that deal with international guarantees and are available to incorporate into the guarantees. ISP98 leaves the determination of whether a call is unfair or not, to applicable jurisdictions.[574] UCP 600 does not contain a provision that bars the unfair calling of standby letter of credit.[575] The URCG rules are more protective for

[567] Along with non-performance, poor performance can constitute an event of default according to the underlying contract. Also see Williams (1995), p. 79.

[568] Scholars state that the greatest number of calls made in bad faith took place during the Iranian revolution. For the cases, see Van Der Vaart (1981), pp. 45–50, also for Iran-United States claims, see Aldrich (1994), pp. 585–610.

[569] The International Standby Practices was developed under the auspices of the Institute of International Banking Law & Practice and endorsed by the United Nations Commission on International Trade Law and the ICC (issued as ICC Publication No. 590) see https://iiblp.org/pages/isp98 05.09.2024.

[570] The ICC Uniform Customs and Practice for Documentary Credits.

[571] The ICC Uniform Rules for Contract Guarantees.

[572] The ICC Uniform Rules for Demand Guarantees provide a uniform international practice in the use of demand guarantees and have been in effect since the 1st of July 2010.

[573] United Nations Convention on Independent Guarantees and the Stand-by Letters of Credit. UNCITRAL was established by the United Nations General Assembly by resolution 2205 (XXI) of 17 December 1966 with the objective of promoting the progressive harmonization and unification of the law of international trade. See A Guide to UNCITRAL Basic facts about the United Nations Commission on International Trade Law and its Annex I, available at https://uncitral.un.org/sites/uncitral.un.org/files/media-documents/uncitral/en/12-57491-guide-to-uncitral-e.pdf accessed 05.09.2024.

[574] See Kelly-Louw (2009), p. 728.

[575] Article 34 of the UCP 600 goes as far as stating that "*a bank assumes no liability or responsibility for the form, sufficiency, accuracy, genuineness, falsification or legal effect of any document*". In a similar vein, the ICC Uniform Rules for Contract Bonds states that the Rules does not contain

the principal and do not provide the guarantee payable without the claim being justified by evidence.[576] According to article 8 (3)(b) of the URCG,[577] a claim can be honored if it is supported by documentation as specified in the guarantee or in the rules.[578] Article 9 gives priority to parties' choice in support to justify the claim. Upon the failure by the parties to specify the documentation to be produced; the same article requires the submission of any of the documents specified in its sub-paragraphs (a) and (b)[579] which contradicts with the nature of on-demand guarantees. Hence, scholars suggest that if the rules are to be applied to on-demand guarantees, parties thereto must exclude article 9.[580]

URDG is silent on the issue of unfair calling and leaves the matter to the courts. However, some of its articles provide a balance between the beneficiary's right to payment and the principal's interest in avoiding the unfair calling. Article 20 (a) and (c)[581] and article 9[582] restrict the outright unfair calling of the beneficiary and oblige

---

provisions dealing with the problem of unfair calling. For detail, see Kelly-Louw (2009), p. 716, similarly, see Kelly-Louw (2010), p. 76.

[576] The creation of URDG was to replace URCG, according to the scholars, one of the main reasons why URCG are not in general use lies in article 8 and article 9 of the URCG. Also see Kelly-Louw (2009), p. 719; Kelly-Louw (2010), p. 81.

[577] Article 8 is as follows: *(l) A claim under a guarantee shall be made in writing or by cable or telegram or telex to be received by the guarantor not later than on the expiry date specified in the guarantee or provided for by these Rules. (2) On receipt of a claim the guarantor shall notify the principal or the instructing party, as the case may be, without delay, of such claim and of any documentation received. (3) A claim shall not be honoured unless: (a) it has been made and received as required by para. I of this Article; and (b) it is supported by such documentation as is specified in the guarantee or in these Rules; And (c) such documentation is presented within the period of time after the receipt of a claim specified in the guarantee, or, failing such a specification, as soon as practicable, or, in the case of documentation of the beneficiary himself, at the latest within six months from the receipt of a claim. In any event, a claim shall not be honoured if the guarantee has ceased to be valid in accordance with its own terms or with these Rules.*

[578] See Kelly-Louw (2010), p. 82.

[579] Article 9 reads as follows: *If a guarantee does not specify the documentation to be produced in support of a claim or merely specifies only a statement of claim by the beneficiary, the beneficiary must submit: (a) in the case of a tender guarantee, his declaration that the principal's tender has been accepted and that the principal has then either failed to sign the contract or has failed to submit a performance guarantee as provided for in the tender, and his declaration of agreement, addressed to the principal, to have any dispute on any claim by the principal for payment to him by the beneficiary of all or part of the amount paid under the guarantee settled by a judicial or arbitral tribunal as specified in the tender documents or, if not so specified or otherwise agreed upon, by arbitration in accordance with the Rules of the ICC Court of Arbitration or with the UNCITRAL Arbitration Rules, at the option of the principal; (b) in the case of a performance guarantee or of a repayment guarantee, either a court decision or an arbitral award justifying the claim, or the approval of the principal in writing to the claim and the amount to be paid.'*

[580] White (1979), p. 130, similarly see Kelly-Louw (2009), p. 721.

[581] Article provides as follows "*(a) Any demand for payment under the Guarantee shall be in writing and shall (in addition to such other documents as may be specified in the Guarantee) be supported by a written statement (whether in the demand itself or in a separate document or documents accompanying the demand and referred to in it) stating: (i) that the Principal is in breach of his obligation(s) under the underlying contract(s) or, in the case of a tender guarantee,*

him to stipulate the type of breach in his claim. Under article 21, the guarantor is under obligation to deliver to principal, the claim and related documents.[583] Once the guarantor informs the principal with regard to the claim, it is up to the sole discretion of the guarantor to hold the payment until the principal (foreign investor) challenges the unfair call and obtains an injunctive relief on the grounds of fraud by the beneficiary.[584] However, the courts must avoid interfering with the machinery of irrevocable obligations assumed by banks.[585] The UNCITRAL Convention, however, entitles the guarantor to withhold the payment.[586] To put the matter in another way, if the host state has adopted the Convention, the foreign investor may either apply to the court for the issuance of a provisional order[587] or claim indemnification

---

the tender conditions; and (ii) the respect in which the Principal is in breach … (c) Paragraph (a) of this Article applies except to the extent that it is expressly excluded by the terms of the Guarantee…."

[582] Article reads as "*all documents specified and presented under a Guarantee, including the demand, shall be examined by the Guarantor with reasonable care to ascertain whether or not they appear on their face to conform with the terms of the Guarantee. Where such documents do not appear so to conform or appear on their face to be inconsistent with one another, they shall be refused.*"

[583] "*[t]he Guarantor shall without delay transmit the Beneficiary's demand and any related documents to the Principal or, where applicable, to the Instructing Party for transmission to the Principal.*"

[584] For detail, please see Kelly-Louw (2009), pp. 724–726.

[585] For the statement of Kerr J., see White (1979), p. 128.

[586] Article 19 of the Convention is as follows: "*(1) If it is manifest and clear that: (a) Any document is not genuine or has been falsified; (b) No payment is due on the basis asserted in the demand and the supporting documents; or (c) Judging by the type and purpose of the undertaking, the demand has no conceivable basis, the guarantor/issuer, acting in good faith, has a right, as against the beneficiary, to withhold payment. (2) For the purposes of subparagraph (c) of paragraph (1) of this article, the following are types of situations in which a demand has no conceivable basis: (a) The contingency or risk against which the undertaking was designed to secure the beneficiary has undoubtedly not materialized; (b) The underlying obligation of the principal/applicant has been declared invalid by a court or arbitral tribunal, unless the undertaking indicates that such contingency falls within the risk to be covered by the undertaking; (c) The underlying obligation has undoubtedly been fulfilled to the satisfaction of the beneficiary; (d) Fulfilment of the underlying obligation has clearly been prevented by willful misconduct of the beneficiary; (e) In the case of a demand under a counter-guarantee, the beneficiary of the counter-guarantee has made payment in bad faith as guarantor/ issuer of the undertaking to which the counter-guarantee relates. (3) In the circumstances set out in subparagraphs (a), (b) and (c) of paragraph (1) of this article, the principal/applicant is entitled to provisional court measures in accordance with article 20.*" Convention is available at https://uncitral.un.org/sites/uncitral.un.org/files/media-documents/uncitral/en/guarantees.pdf accessed 05.09.2024.

[587] Article 20 of the Convention reads as follows; "*(1) Where, on an application by the principal/applicant or the instructing party, it is shown that there is a high probability that, with regard to a demand made, or expected to be made, by the beneficiary, one of the circumstances referred to in subparagraphs (a), (b) and (c) of paragraph (1) of article 19 is present, the court, on the basis of immediately available strong evidence, may: (a) Issue a provisional order to the effect that the beneficiary does not receive payment, including an order that the guarantor/issuer hold the amount of the undertaking, or (b) Issue a provisional order to the effect that the proceeds of the undertaking*

from the guarantor in the case of an abusive or fraudulent drawing, if the payment has already been made.

A conditional guarantee is of no use to the host state. Hence, irrespective of the title given to the security, the substance thereof is more crucial.[588] Furthermore, a guarantor, issuing a conditional guarantee and subsequently approving the host state's call on the guarantee, may find itself embroiled in a dispute with the foreign investor as to whether the host state was honest in its call on the guarantee.[589] Hence, the autonomous structure of the guarantee implies that foreign investor may incur losses resulting from unfair, wrongful, politically motivated,[590] or capricious calls by host states. PRI policies, in this regard, serve to protect foreign investors when the host state calls in bad faith and provides compensation, generally up to %90 percent of the amount drawn by the host state.

ISP98, URCG or URDG are designed to establish uniformity among practitioners; they are regarded as a rule of law. They leave the determination of whether the call is fraudulent or unjust to the national laws. Hence, scholars find it ironic that experts who, in drafting the UCP, agreed on granting courts to make the relevant rules, will not criticize the ruling of the same court that is contrary to the practice of the letter of credit.[591] However, questions of fraud must not be ruled by the judges who are appointed by and inclined towards the benefits of the host state. This forms another political risk to be discussed in the following chapter.

In *St Michaels Enterprises d.o.o.*, the insured posted a bid bond to the Serbian Privatization Agency (the Agency) and was required to post a performance bond to further the project. The insured requested an extension of the deadline for posting a performance bond; however, the Agency rejected this request and called the Bid Bond. Although calling of bonds was among covered perils in the insurance contract,[592] the insurance contract simultaneously contained exclusions.[593] In the insured's opinion, denial of its request was due to corruption which led to wrongful

paid to the beneficiary are blocked, taking into account whether in the absence of such an order the principal/ applicant would be likely to suffer serious harm. (2) The court, when issuing a provisional order referred to in paragraph (1) of this article, may require the person applying therefor to furnish such form of security as the court deems appropriate. (3) The court may not issue a provisional order of the kind referred to in paragraph (1) of this article based on any objection to payment other than those referred to in subparagraphs (a), (b) and (c) of paragraph (1) of article 19, or use of the undertaking for a criminal purpose."

[588] Also see Kelly-Louw (2009), p. 711, fn 3.

[589] Also see White (1979), p. 124.

[590] See Van Der Vaart (1981), p. 54, fn 91. Similarly, see Wallman (1985), p. 476.

[591] Kelly-Louw (2009), p. 718; Kelly-Louw (2010), p. 79.

[592] The Scope of Coverage set forth in Section 2.01 of the OPIC Contract, as modified in Section 6.0 reads as: "*compensation is payable, subject to the exclusion ... , limitations... , and adjustment... , if the bid guaranty or any portion thereof is called by the buyer: (1) in violation of the terms and conditions governing the posting and calling of the bid bond as set forth in the tender rules ...; and (2) the Insured is not in default of its obligations under the tender.*"

[593] Section 6.09 of the contract provides that: "*Notwithstanding any other provision in this policy to the contrary, no compensation shall be payable under this policy if the bid guaranty or any portion*

calling of the Bid Bond. OPIC reached a contrary conclusion and denied the request for compensation. In OPIC's belief, even in the assumption of a corruptive act on the part of the Agency, corruption had no bearing on the analysis of the issue, moreover, the Agency could deny the insured's request for any reason or for no reason; by doing so, the Agency did not exceed its rights.[594]

In *Uniworld Holdings*, OPIC sided with the insured's position. In the case, the insured posted a performance bond to the Serbian Privatization Agency (the Agency) in connection with the purchase of %70 shares in the Joint Stock Tourist Company Putnik AD Beograd, Serbia Montenegro ('Putnik'). The insured committed to making scheduled payments ($44,332,500 over a period of five years) in Putnik certified by an audit company and posting three successive performance bonds. This public tender encountered notable hostility. Despite the audit company confirming the insured's investment in the first year, the Agency called first performance bond on the basis of the insured's failure to; post second performance bond and meet its investment commitments. The insured then took the dispute to arbitration with the ICC, provoking the Agency to terminate the contract. Despite obtaining an award in its favor, following the Agency's failure to honor the award, the insured filed a request for compensation from OPIC. If one were to wonder the insured's motivation behind invocation of the arbitral process while having a coverage from OPIC, the insurance contract imposed on the insured an obligation to exhaust legal remedies.[595] Although the insurance contract provided a prompt notification obligation[596] on the part of the insured, which the insured failed to fulfill, OPIC waived such non-compliance with the notice provisions. In accepting the claim, in OPIC's perspective, the bond served to ensure the insured's performance. After the termi-

---

thereof is called by the buyer due to the Insured's inability to obtain financing for the project in the form or amount represented in the offer at the date of submission."

[594] For the summary of the case, see Kantor et al. (2011), pp. 987–991 and please visit: https://www.dfc.gov/sites/default/files/2019-08/st_michael_enterprises.pdf accessed 05.09.2024.

[595] Section 2.01 of the OPIC Contract provides: "Compensation is payable, subject to the exclusion … and limitations … , if any portion of the guaranty is called, and the Insured has not materially breached the underlying contract and has sought but not received indemnification from the Agency, provided one of the following conditions also pertains … (a) Unsatisfied Holding in Favor of Insured. The Insured has submitted a claim of wrongful calling to the dispute resolution procedure contained in the underlying contract, the procedure yields a holding in favor of the Insured, and notwithstanding the Insured's best efforts to enforce the holding, the Agency fails to pay the Insured the amount awarded within three months of the date of the holding… ."

[596] Section 5.01(9) of the OPIC Contract provides: Compulsory Notice: "The insured shall notify OPIC promptly of any acts or threats to act in a manner which may come within the scope of wrongful calling coverage (Article II) and shall keep OPIC informed as to all relevant developments." Section 4.09 of the OPIC Contract provides: Notices must be in writing and shall be effective when received. Notices may be given to the Insured at the address on the title page (unless changed in writing) …

nation of the contract, the insured had no obligation left and the Bond served no purpose.[597]

8.5.2 *Denial of Justice*

Denial of justice, in its narrowest sense, refers to a restriction and wholly inadequate sense of procedural refusal of court access. In a broad sense, it consists of violations of the rights of an alien resulting from actions or omissions on the part of the executive, legislative, or judicial branches of government.[598] In an intermediate sense, it denotes 'limited to refusal of a state to grant an alien access to its courts or a failure of a court to pronounce a judgement.[599]' On the other hand, case law brought a variety of interpretations and phraseology to denial of justice. In *Mondev*, tribunal addressed denial of justice with the following expressions "*a willful disregard of due process of law, … which shocks, or at least surprises, a sense of judicial propriety*[600]". While tribunal in *Loewen* underlined the discriminatory element of denial of justice,[601] in *Waste Management*, the tribunal sought the presence of arbitrary, unjust or idiosyncratic court decisions.[602]"

[597] For the summary of the case, see Kantor et al. (2011), pp. 999–1005 and please visit: https://www.dfc.gov/sites/default/files/2019-08/uniworld_mod_03212008.pdf accessed 05.09.2024.

[598] Freeman (1970), pp. 85, 97, also see Newcombe and Paradell (2009), p. 238.

[599] For the author, see fn 174 at page 326 of Torrado (2005).

[600] See *Mondev v. U.S.* para. 127 and for almost identical reasoning, see *Chevron case*, para. 244 and See *ELSI* case para. 128.

[601] According to the tribunal "*an unjust judgment would be inspired by ill-will towards foreigners and…. the responsibility of the State under international law and, consequently, of the courts of a State, to provide a fair trial of a case to which a foreign investor is a party. It is the responsibility of the courts of a State to ensure that litigation is free from discrimination against a foreign litigant and that the foreign litigant should not become the victim of sectional or local prejudice.*" *Loewen* para. 54, 87, 119, 122, 123 and 135. Available at https://www.italaw.com/sites/default/files/case-documents/ita0470.pdf accessed 05.09.2024.

[602] In the tribunal's wording "*the minimum standard of treatment of fair and equitable treatment is infringed by conduct attributable to the State and harmful to the claimant if the conduct is arbitrary, grossly unfair, unjust or idiosyncratic, is discriminatory and exposes the claimant to sectional or racial prejudice, or involves a lack of due process leading to an outcome which offends judicial propriety—as might be the case with a manifest failure of natural justice in judicial proceedings or a complete lack of transparency and candour in an administrative process.*" See *Waste Management* case, para. 98. In *ADF v. U.S.*, (para. 190) the tribunal, while rejecting the investor's submission that a federal administrative body had acted ultra vires in its interpretation of the measures in question, held "*…even had the investor made out a prima facie basis for its claim, the Tribunal has no authority to review the legal validity and standing of the US measures… under US internal administrative law. We do not sit as a court with appellate jurisdiction…. The Tribunal would emphasize, too, that even if the US measures were somehow shown or admitted to be ultra vires under the internal law of the United States, that by itself does not necessarily render the measures grossly unfair or inequitable under the customary international law standard of treatment embodied in Article 1105(1)…. [S]omething more than simple illegality or lack of authority*

In so far as the denial of justice is concerned, one may well take issue with the postulation that 'denial' just be linked to judicial system. In some scholars' view, denial of justice denotes misconduct or inaction by the judicial branch of the government.[603] Denial of justice is not the only possible theory of liability for judicial measures.[604] Acts or omissions of the judiciary may amount to or form the basis of judicial expropriation. On a stand-alone basis, several tribunals have drawn a distinction between denial of justice and judicial expropriation.[605] The tribunal in *Eli Lilly,* did mention the possibility that judicial conduct encompassing manifest arbitrariness or blatant unfairness can be distinct from denial of justice, requiring responsibility of the state for expropriation.[606]

One might interpret denial of justice, based on its natural meaning, as including scenarios where a court refuses to provide justice and render a decision or where an alien is prohibited from accessing the courts upon equal terms with citizens. However, denial of justice cannot be confined to the courtroom. A wider interpretation of denial of justice extends it to actions concerning the administration of justice, whether on the part of the courts or other organs of the state.[607] Arbitrary deprivation of an investor's liberty, inhuman treatment, lack of adequate redress of grievances[608] and unreasonable dilatoriness or excessively fast proceedings, unjustifiable obstacles in adjudication, judicial misconduct during the course of the trial or lack of a regular trial in the accustomed manner are typical examples of denial of justice.

To further elaborate the judicial denial of justice, there must, at the very least, be a seemingly a judicial system. This is to say, the state in question should put at the investor's disposal, a judicial organization/administration of justice capable of assuring protection of his/her rights.[609] As the 'separation of powers' dictates, courts are independent organs and immune from directives of the governments. Hence, some might argue that the conduct of courts cannot be imputable to governments.

---

under the domestic law of a State is necessary to render and act or measure inconsistent with the customary international law requirements of Article 1105(1)…". Available at https://www.italaw.com/sites/default/files/case-documents/ita0009.pdf accessed 05.09.2024 and see, *Waste Management* case, para. 130, fn 86.

[603] Paulsson (2005), p. 44 and similarly, Eagleton (1928), p. 540.

[604] The tribunal in *Azinian* case quoted Judge Aréchaga's statement and proceeded to hold that "*The responsibility of the State for acts of judicial authorities may result from three different types of judicial decision. The first is a decision of a municipal court clearly incompatible with a rule of international law. The second is what it known traditionally as a 'denial of justice.' The third occurs when, in certain exceptional and well-defined circumstances, a State is responsible for a judicial decision contrary to municipal law.*" See. para. 98. Similarly, see *Eli Lilly* para 180. https://www.italaw.com/sites/default/files/case-documents/italaw8546.pdf accessed 05.09.2024.

[605] Gharavi (2018), p. 350.

[606] In the tribunal's words it was "*unwilling to shut the door to the possibility that judicial conduct characterized other than as a denial of justice may engage the respondent's (the State) obligations*". See para. 223.

[607] Fitzmaurice (1932), p. 94.

[608] Eagleton (1928), p. 543.

[609] Freeman (1970), p. 116.

However, such a hypothesis would omit the fact that states function through their various organs and, therefore, their judicial and executive organs are not discrete actors.[610]

Some scholars believe that denial of justice is restricted to cases where the alien is the plaintiff, and only a '*manifest injustice*' occurs if the alien is the defendant. Same scholars rely on the ground that original injury, which the alien complains of at the international level, is the positive act of the judicial authority, and the element of local redress does not come into play at all.[611] This view may originate from the concept of 'thwarted redress'. When an investor has been deprived of proper judicial process, whether he is seeking to establish or to preserve his/her legal rights,[612] justice will be denied. An alien may recourse to courts for a declaration that a property belongs to the applicant, rather than seeking to redress for a wrong.[613] Hence, it is idle to explore whether the investor is a plaintiff or defendant. What is crucial is whether the courts complied with their duty to provide legal protection.

The term '*manifest injustice*' is ambiguous, and its substance may not be distinguishable from denial of justice. Unjust and one-sided judgments[614] may stem from a biased, flagrant piece of dishonesty or malicious misapplication of law,[615] or a manifest disregard of the law. Denial of justice will be the case when an award encompasses more than a single procedural irregularity, a wrong in substance, an error of law[616] or an incorrect finding of facts by a national court.[617]

In case of an erroneous application by the court, unless the error led to a breach of a treaty obligation resting upon the state or the result is so manifestly unjust and against the standards of justice recognized by civilized nations, the state cannot be held internationally responsible.[618] Moreover, to establish a state's responsibility, bad faith[619] must be present, and the conclusion of the court could not have been reached by an impartial judicial body or judgment must be of a kind which no honest and competent court could render.[620]

---

[610] Paulsson (2005), p. 39.

[611] For detail, see Paulsson (2005), p. 61 and Eagleton (1928), p. 553.

[612] Paulsson (2005), p. 63.

[613] Fitzmaurice (1932), p. 106.

[614] Also, see Weiler (2003), pp. 247, 248.

[615] *Tudor* states that in addition to manifest injustice, 'gross unfairness', 'flagrant and inexcusable violation' or 'palpable violation' of law may also be required. Tudor (2008), p. 161 and also, see Paulsson (2005), p. 76.

[616] Paulsson (2005), p. 81.

[617] Also see Salacuse (2016), p. 321.

[618] Oppenheim et al. (2008), p. 546.

[619] According to the tribunal in *Chevron* (para. 198) "*[o]nly in cases where the breach of municipal law is exceptionally outrageous or monstrously grave*" will an unjust decision itself suffice as circumstantial evidence of bad faith. Available at https://www.italaw.com/sites/default/files/case-documents/ita0151.pdf accessed 05.09.2024.

[620] Paulsson (2005), pp. 65, 66, 82; Fitzmaurice (1932), p. 110.

The international obligations of the state are indisputable and bind the organs of the state whether they are engaged in enacting, executing, or construing the law.[621] International responsibility may be triggered by legislators' misfeasance or nonfeasance.[622] Legislatures will be derelict in their duty when they fail to make municipal laws conform to international treaties or a legislative body may not give sufficient jurisdiction to the court, preventing investors from being granted a remedy.[623] Whether municipal legislation violates international law, or the judicial authority applies the legislation in a manner contravening international law, either way, the state will be deemed to have breached its duties under international law.

Another fact is that apparent gross deficiencies in the judicial system may not always fall within the scope of this risk. By way of example, abnormalities in delays may not be arbitrary; the larger the state, the greater the number of the cases are brought before judges;[624] hence, countries with high population may struggle in avoiding delays and a reproach cannot be directed against the state. With respect to delays, in a lengthy judicial process, identifying the presence of the denial of justice can be challenging and standards of international law are not as strict as the municipal laws.[625] Governments of the countries with a high caseload may use the amount of work which courts are incumbent upon to their advantage. For instance, in *White Industries v. India*, the tribunal heard a case where the claimant's application for setting aside, and enforcement had been pending for more than nine years. While concluding whether the claimant has been denied justice within a reasonable delay, the tribunal analyzed various factors such as the complexity of the matter, the need for celerity of decision and the behavior of the litigants involved. After an arrear of nine years, the conclusion of the tribunal could be that the judicial machinery is defective,[626] however, in the tribunal's mind, the delay in question did not amount to 'a particularly serious shortcoming' or 'egregious conduct that shocks or at least surprises, a sense of judicial propriety[627]'.

---

[621] Freeman (1970), p. 29.

[622] See Douglas (2014), p. 880.

[623] Freeman (1970), p. 108; Eagleton (1928), p. 547.

[624] Also, see Freeman (1970), p. 121.

[625] See *Toto Costruzioni* para. 155.

[626] See *El Oro v. Mexico*, p. 198, available at https://legal.un.org/riaa/cases/vol_V/191-199_Oro_Mining.pdf accessed 05.09.2024.

[627] See *White Industries v. India*, para. 10.4.23 and 14.3.6. Available at https://www.italaw.com/sites/default/files/case-documents/ita0906.pdf accessed 05.09.2024. One of the arguments put forward was whether the lapse of nine years to enforce the ICC Award constituted a breach of the 'effective means' obligation under the BIT. The claimant in the case was a company constituted under Australian law; therefore, the Australia–India BIT applied to the case. The aforementioned BIT lacked an 'effective means' provision; however, the tribunal applied Article 4(2) of the BIT which provided for most-favoured nation (MFN) treatment, and the tribunal incorporated the effective means provision of the Kuwait–India BIT and awarded compensation for the loss the claimant suffered as a consequence of India's breach of the BIT. Art. 4(5) of Kuwait- India BIT provides that "*Each Contracting State shall in accordance with its applicable laws and regulations provide effective means of asserting claims and enforcing rights with respect to investments and*

The test for denial of justice may set a high threshold. This was the view followed by the tribunal and the tribunal, in its findings echoed the language used by *Chevron*'s tribunal.[628] However, according to the *Azinian* tribunal, a mere finding of undue delay could be sufficient.[629] As is certain, case law has not established a clear norm on this issue, and since interest is awarded on the amount in dispute, even if the delay is unbearable, international tribunals may be keen to await the outcome of the adjudicative process in the jurisdiction concerned.

In *Bank of America*, the insured provided a loan to DPC (an SPV established under Indian law to develop, construct, own, and operate a power generation station in India). The insured alleged that as a result of actions taken by the Indian government, the SPV defaulted on certain scheduled interest payments due under the Loan, and the loan was automatically accelerated as a consequence of a bankruptcy Event of Default caused by the Bombay High Court's appointment of a receiver. One of the issues determined in this claim was whether the risk of denial of justice had occurred. MSEB (the state-owned purchaser of the power) rescinded the PPA contract (power purchase agreement) and DPC initiated arbitration. However, Maharashtra Electricity Regulatory Commission ("MERC") issued an interim order asserting that it had sole and exclusive jurisdiction to adjudicate the dispute between MSEB and DPC. DPC's attempts to overturn MERC's order failed, as affirmed by the decisions from both Bombay High Court and the Supreme Court confirming MERC's jurisdiction. In OPIC's view, blocking DPC's rights to access arbitration by Indian judicial authorities comprised a substantial factor in the scheduled payment defaults. Despite DPC being granted formal appeal rights, these have been rendered ineffective by delays in the Indian courts.[630]

8.5.2.1 A Glimpse into the Harvard Convention

Among other codification attempts, *Harvard Draft Convention on the International Responsibility of States for Injuries to Aliens* (The Harvard Convention) has a

---

ensure to investors of the other Contracting State, the right of access to its courts of justice, administrative tribunals and agencies, and all other bodies exercising adjudicatory authority, and the right to employ persons of their choice, for the purpose of the assertion of claims and the enforcement of rights with respect to their investments." See Mistelis (2013), p. 83.

628 See *Chevron case*, para. 244.

629 According to the tribunal in Azinian "*A denial of justice could be pleaded if the relevant courts refuse to entertain a suit, if they subject it to undue delay, or if they administer justice in a seriously inadequate way…. A governmental authority surely cannot be faulted for acting in a manner validated by its courts unless the courts themselves are disavowed at the international level*". See *Azinian* case para. 97, 102. Also see *Rompetrol v. Romania,* available at https://www.italaw.com/sites/default/files/case-documents/italaw1408.pdf and *Marvin Feldman v. Mexico,* para. 139–140 available at https://www.italaw.com/sites/default/files/case-documents/ita0319.pdf both accessed 05.09.2024.

630 For the summary of the case, see Kantor et al. (2011), pp. 832–852 also, see Salacuse (2013), pp. 233–239.

peculiar difference.[631] The Convention deals with 'denial of justice' within three articles each of which refers to a particular stage of the legal process, implying that the Harvard draftsmen paid necessary attention to this matter. By way of illustration, article 6 sets out the conditions that cast to 'denial of justice' if an alien fails to access a tribunal or administrative authority. Article 6 reads as: "*The denial to an alien of the right to initiate, or to participate in, proceedings in a tribunal or an administrative authority to determine his civil rights or obligations is wrongful: (a) if it is a clear and discriminatory violation of the law of the State denying such access; (b) if it unreasonably departs from those rules of access to tribunals or administrative authorities which are recognized by the principal legal systems of the world; or (c) if it otherwise involves a violation by the State of a treaty.*"

The basic form of denial of justice is the direct prevention of litigants' (investors) access to judicial authority. Article 6(1)(a) of the Convention provides the alien with a rope to pull himself out of the mud; however, article 6(1)(b) leaves us with a murky understanding of whether impediments related to monetary means can compose this risk. States, during the course of adjudication, may require litigants to pay levies or file bonds. Such tariffs or rates should be applied on a non-discriminatory basis. Even if that is the case, an investor may have devoted a remarkable portion of funds to its investment and bearing the invested amount, thus the dispute in mind, the fees required to settle the dispute might be unaffordable. Thus, the question might be that whether judicial fees can form a denial of justice. A state should ensure a 'just application' of municipal laws to aliens; failing to do so will hold it responsible. And a state treating the alien in a non-discriminatory manner is an impeccable circumstance where the state may cloak its intention and it would be 'a dicing for justice' on the part of the alien. In determining the 'existence of denial of justice' for the aliens, tribunals should avoid only comparing the treatment of justice accorded to aliens and nationals. The continuum of investment and the sums devoted thereto distinguish a foreign investment from a party to local litigation. The length[632] of the proceedings or the fees[633] required for litigation may constitute 'unreasonably departure' as the article 6(1)(b) implies.

---

[631] For the codification attempts, see Paulsson (2005), pp. 93–98.

[632] ECHR opines that a court's hearing of disputes in an expedited manner prevents them from being lengthy, offers an undeniable advantage over a remedy that affords only compensation, and does not merely repair the breach. See *Scordino v. Italy*, para. 183. Available at https://hudoc.echr.coe.int/app/conversion/docx/pdf?library=ECHR&id=001-72925&filename=CASE%20OF%20SCORDINO%20v.%20ITALY%20(No.%201).pdf&logEvent=False accessed 05.09.2024.

[633] In *Burdov v. Russia*, the ECHR listed key criteria for the verification of the effectiveness of a compensatory remedy in respect of the excessive length of judicial proceedings and held that the rules regarding legal costs must not place an excessive burden on litigants. See *Burdov v. Russia*, para. 99, available at https://hudoc.echr.coe.int/eng#{%22itemid%22:[%22001-90671%22]} accessed 05.09.2024.

The casuistic-like article 7, on the other hand, proceeds with a wide range of instances[634] that may give rise to the risk at the time of hearing.[635] The critique is that the Drafting Committee appears to dedicate an entire article to an amid-trial phase of the case. In fact, the article provides events all of which imply 'the right to be heard' and 'equal treatment' principles of procedural law.[636]

Finally, Article 8 distinguishes the merits of the case from the state's procedural misconduct and grants the investor the power to claim the occurrence of the risk, provided that the decision or judgment is adverse and other conditions are met.[637] In our opinion, no one would be led astray by the argument that the merits of the awards and the composition of tribunals may also form denial of justice. Providing aliens with appropriate means of justice is the essential pillar upon which denial of justice is built. An award that is manifestly unjust and partial, and judicial appointees of dependent nature (for instance, if the tribunal is comprised of the nationals of the host state) may leave doubts as to proper justice.

[634] According the mentioned article, in determining the fairness of hearing, following procedural actions should be assessed*; (a) specific information in advance of the hearing of any claim or charge against him; (b) adequate time to prepare his case; (c) full opportunity to know the substance and source of any evidence against him and to contest its validity; (d) full opportunity to have compulsory process for obtaining witnesses and evidence; e) full opportunity to have legal representation of his own choice, (f) free or assisted legal representation on the same basis as nationals of the State concerned or on the basis recognized by the principal legal systems of the world, whichever standard is higher; (g) the services of a competent interpreter during the proceedings if he cannot fully understand or speak the language used in the tribunal; tribunal; (h) full opportunity to communicate with a representative of the government of the State entitled to extend its diplomatic protection to him; (i) full opportunity to have such a representative present at any judicial or administrative proceeding in accordance with the rules or procedure of the tribunal or administrative agency; (j) disposition of his case with reasonable dispatch at all stages of the proceedings; or (k) any other procedural right conferred by a treaty or recognized by the principal legal systems of the world.*"

[635] The European Convention on Human Rights provides right to a fair trial under art. 6. For the full text of the Convention, please visit: https://www.echr.coe.int/documents/convention_eng.pdf accessed 05.09.2024.

[636] The right to a fair hearing entails a number of requirements, including the requirement that the procedure before the national tribunals be conducted expeditiously. See *Toto Costruzioni*, para 158 available at https://www.italaw.com/sites/default/files/case-documents/ita0869.pdf accessed 05.09.2024.

[637] The article is as follows; "*A decision or judgment of a tribunal or an administrative authority rendered in a proceeding involving the determination of the civil rights or obligations of an alien or of any criminal charges against him, and either denying him recovery in whole or in part or granting recovery against him or imposing a penalty, whether civil or criminal, upon him is wrongful: (a) if it is a clear and discriminatory violation of the law of the State concerned; (b) if it unreasonably departs from the principles of justice recognized by the principal legal systems of the world; or (c) if it otherwise involves a violation by the State of a treaty.*"

8.5.2.2 A Must 'Exhaustion of Remedies'

Exhaustion of local remedies stands as a rule under international law and a must in PRI practice. In accordance with article 44 of the ILC, unless available and effective local remedies have been exhausted, a claim will not be admissible, and the responsibility of the state cannot be invoked.[638] Although tribunals in investor-state disputes have found the ILC articles to be a stipulation of international law applicable between states or state entities,[639] the ILC is one of the main codifications that sheds light on the interpretation of the rule.[640]

States may give their consent to ICSID arbitration on the condition of exhausting local remedies. They may impose such condition (i) in a bilateral investment treaty that offers submission to ICSID arbitration, (ii) in domestic legislation, or (iii) in a direct investment agreement that contains an ICSID clause.[641] Article 26 of the ICSID Convention reads; "*Consent of the parties to arbitration under this Convention shall, unless otherwise stated, be deemed consent to such arbitration to the exclusion of any other remedy. A Contracting State may require the exhaustion of local administrative or judicial remedies as a condition of its consent to arbitration under this Convention. A State may require the exhaustion of domestic remedies as a prior condition for its consent to ICSID arbitration*".[642] According to the tribunal in *Kilic İnsaat*, this article requires something other than full "exhaustion of local or administrative remedies". It is the requirement of prior submission of the dispute to the local courts for a specified period as a condition precedent to arbitration.[643] This may be the case if the adjudicative body of the state hears the case. In our opinion, although the state may, for several reasons, view such a compromise as 'fit' over sovereignty, at least to some degree the municipal legal system should be tested so that the international community will not be predisposed, on the contrary, will be equipped in advance, and the state will be given a chance to correct her flaws. Thus,

---

[638] According to commentary, 'local remedies' may entail some ambiguities when applied to an international organization. This terminology has been retained as a term of art to provide some indications regarding the kinds of situations where such a requirement is likely to apply. See Report of Drafting Committee on Responsibility of International Organizations, 4 June 2008, Doc A/CN.4/L.725, p. 7. https://legal.un.org/ilc/sessions/60/pdfs/english/2008_dc_chairman_rio_4june2008.pdf accessed 05.09.2024.

[639] See *Wintershall v. Argentina* (para. 126) Available at https://www.italaw.com/sites/default/files/case-documents/ita0907.pdf accessed 05.09.2024.

[640] Besides, commentary to the ILC articles states that the article is formulated in general terms in order to cover any case to which the exhaustion of local remedies rule applies whether under treaty or general international law. See Commentary to ILC articles, p. 121.

[641] See *Lanco v. Argentina* (para. 39) available at https://www.italaw.com/sites/default/files/case-documents/ita0450_0.pdf accessed 05.09.2024.

[642] For a similar regulation, see art. 19 of Harvard Convention and art. 35 of the European Convention on Human Rights.

[643] See *Kiliç İnşaat v. Turkmenistan* (para. 6.2.5), available at https://www.italaw.com/sites/default/files/case-documents/italaw1515_0.pdf accessed 05.09.2024.

one pillar of this principle may be that international adjudicatory bodies will be entitled to operate as a last resort and second-guess the case.

The need for exhausting available remedies stems from the fact that states provide far-reaching avenues of legal remedies within their domestic systems compared to international organizations.[644] In addition, states may espouse the case during the course of adjudication. In contrast thereto, international courts may be less expedited in or incapable of collecting evidence that requires presence in the same jurisdiction. Besides, some BITs require parties to exhaust local remedies in accordance with Calvo doctrine.[645]

Investment treaties might be an exception to the requirement for local remedies. States may enter into treaties that allow aliens to apply to international tribunals without first having to exhaust local remedies. Hence, the wording of the BITs may reveal whether the sovereign is ceding much of its sovereignty. In *Paulsson*'s expression, such a waiver gives aliens assurance that internationally wrongful conduct will not be swept under the rug indefinitely.[646]

Douglas believes that the 'final result' produced by the domestic system for the administration of justice can be the object of a denial of justice, according to the author, the 'finality rule' is the substantive requirement for international responsibility for a denial of justice.[647] Courts of first instance may commit procedural[648] or substantive errors[649] in their choice of legal provisions; such errors can only affect international law insofar as a treaty provision is entered into account, or the possibility of a denial of justice arises.[650] On the other hand, states incorporate corrective/appeal mechanisms so that the wrong complained of might be rectified or at least the magnitude of the risk deriving from the procedural injustice or erroneous decision may be alleviated.

Preconditions of exhaustion of local remedies may illustrate its importance in other forms of political risks. For instance, as per the *Generation Ukraine* tribunal, exhaustion of local remedies is not merely a precondition under international law; it

---

[644] Thallinger (2008), p. 417.

[645] The doctrine provides that remedies of the foreign nationals are local ones, and they must settle their disputes under domestic law in the local court system. According to article 6(2)(a) of the BIT between the U.S. and Ecuador (1993), they must submit the dispute to the courts or administrative tribunals of the Party that is a party to the dispute. Available at https://investmentpolicy.unctad.org/international-investment-agreements/treaty-files/1065/download accessed 05.09.2024. Also see Diaconis (1989), p. 277 and Salacuse (2013), p. 310.

[646] Paulsson (2005), p. 108.

[647] Douglas (2014), p. 873.

[648] *Douglas* states that if the international law focuses on procedural errors, international courts will be disabled from second-guessing the application of domestic law by a domestic judge. See, Douglas (2014), p. 882.

[649] According to *Douglas*, substantive errors do routinely occur at the first level of the institutional hierarchy. See Douglas (2014), p. 895.

[650] See *SS Lotus* case p. 24. Available at https://www.icj-cij.org/public/files/permanent-court-of-international-justice/serie_A/A_10/30_Lotus_Arret.pdf accessed 05.09.2024.

also serves as a means to rectify the host state's conduct. Without it, the legality of the conduct cannot be tested.[651] The *Elsi* tribunal, in a narrow sense, simply clarifies when remedies are deemed to have been exhausted.[652] The commentary of ILC, on the other hand, has left the door open for futile attempts by stating "*The mere existence on paper of remedies under the internal law of a State does not impose a requirement to make use of those remedies in every case. In particular, there is no requirement to use a remedy which offers no possibility of redressing the situation.*[653]"

If the investor scrupulously pursued his/her rights, exerted due efforts and made sure that the available remedy was ineffective,[654] meritorious, or the state cannot, or will not provide the investor with relief, the local remedies will be deemed to have been exhausted.[655] Sometimes, states may seek to opt out of responsibility, and the adjudicative body of the state may disregard to rule upon the merits of a dispute. By doing so, the local remedy, or in other words, access to any means of obtaining redress will be blatantly foreclosed. Even if the lackadaisical attitude of the state gives rise to such an outcome, denial of justice should capture events where there is '*nowhere to go*' within the same jurisdiction. Thus, if the investor is entitled to be redressed but is precluded from doing so by means of an obvious and direct impediment, or is required to contrive an extravagant application, or if the cost of accessing a remedy outweighs obtaining a satisfactory result,[656] the investor should be entitled to claim indemnification from the insurer.

8.5.2.3 FET Standard and Denial of Justice

BITs may not require exhaustion of local remedies; claims for misfeasance or nonfeasance in respect of the prosecutorial authorities are generally formulated as a breach of the obligation to accord full protection and security or fair and equitable

[651] The tribunal held that "*an international tribunal may deem that the failure to seek redress from national authorities disqualifies the international claim, not because there is a requirement of exhaustion of local remedies but because the very reality of conduct tantamount to expropriation is doubtful in the absence of a reasonable - not necessarily exhaustive - effort by the investor to obtain correction.*" See para. 20.30 of the award.

[652] The tribunal held that "*the local remedies rule does not, indeed cannot, require that a claim be presented to the municipal courts in a form, and with arguments, suited to an international tribunal, applying different law to different parties: for an international claim to be admissible, it is sufficient if the essence of the claim has been brought before the competent tribunals and pursued as far as permitted by local law and procedures, and without success.*" See para. 59.

[653] Please visit: https://legal.un.org/ilc/texts/instruments/english/commentaries/9_6_2001.pdf accessed 05.09.2024. See page 121, commentary 5.

[654] As well defined in *Chevron* case, "*A respondent State must prove that remedies exist before a claimant will be required to prove their ineffectiveness or futility or that resort to them has been unsuccessful.*" See para. 329.

[655] Eagleton (1928), pp. 546, 548.

[656] See *Chevron* case para. 281.

treatment in international investment law rather than a denial of justice.[657] However, denial of justice is also a long-recognized element of the FET standard.[658] In other words, the FET standard can be breached by committing a denial of justice. When states fail to accord due process to aliens, they violate the fair and equal treatment obligation.

Due to subjective nature of denial of justice, a case-by-case assessment is imperative. Hence, an alien may depict the picture as dark if he/she experiences obstacles before obtaining proper justice and may be burdened to prove that the treatment accorded to him/her is flawed by arbitrariness. Pleadings in breaching of the FET standard and denial of justice can be based on similar elements such as arbitrariness, inconsistent conduct, discrimination, executive interference and legitimate expectations.[659]

As stated elsewhere, the insured is under an obligation to take all reasonable efforts to prevent risk or mitigate the loss. Policies do require rigid exhaustion of local remedies; To rephrase, for an investor seeking redress from the insurer, it is incumbent upon him to bring the claim before the competent authority and pursue as far as permitted by local law and procedures provided by the state. One may suppose that there is no need to expend too much labor in defining the denial of justice. The words chosen to describe it may partake of the characteristics of injustice in which investor is not granted opportunity to resort to courts and fails to reach a fair justice by state's preventive acts or omissions. In our view, definition of denial of justice in PRI policy should leave no room for ambiguities. Whether judicial or not, all obstructive actions or omissions by the state should fall within the scope of the insurance.

---

[657] Douglas (2014), p. 883.

[658] In *Mondev v. U.S.* (para. 127), the tribunal spelled out the following explanation "*In the end the question is whether, at an international level and having regard to generally accepted standards of the administration of justice, a tribunal can conclude in the light of all the available facts that the impugned decision was clearly improper and discreditable, with the result that the investment has been subjected to unfair and inequitable treatment.*" Available at https://www.italaw.com/sites/default/files/case-documents/ita1076.pdf accessed 05.09.2024. In *Jan de Nul* case (para. 188) the tribunal held that "*the fair and equitable treatment standard encompasses the notion of denial of justice.*" Similarly in *Vivendi v. Argentina,* (para. 7.4.10 and 7.4.11.) the tribunal concluded that "*To the extent that Respondent contends that the fair and equitable treatment obligation constrains government conduct only if and when the state's courts cannot deliver justice, this appears to conflate the legal concepts of fair and equitable treatment on the one hand with the denial of justice on the other. But if this Tribunal were to restrict the claims of unfair and equitable treatment to circumstances in which Claimants have also established a denial of justice, it would eviscerate the fair and equitable treatment standard. Although the standard is commonly understood to include a prohibition on denial of justice, it would be significantly diminished if it were limited to claims for denial of justice.*" Available at https://www.italaw.com/sites/default/files/case-documents/ita0215.pdf accessed 05.09.2024. Similarly, see *Waste Management* case para. 98 and also see Paulsson (2005), pp. 70–71.

[659] See Balcerzak and Hepburn (2020), pp. 481, 486.

8.5.2.4 Arbitration Award Default

As will be recalled, denial of justice (DOJ) represents a wide spectrum of events where arbitrariness or unfairness may be concerned at legislative, executive or juridical level.[660] Arbitration award default (AAD) risk refers to the host state's precluding the arbitration process from yielding a meaningful outcome.[661] Host states may restrict access to arbitration through amendments to national law, denouncing BITs, requesting investors to waive contractual clauses relating to arbitration, or even through threatening to terminate or reject future dealings.[662]

In many cases misconduct of judicial agencies is supported by executive or legislative authorities. Thus, although the point where DOJ and AAD work in tandem is narrow, underwriters may juxtapose or intermingle these slightly different coverages. DOJ may offer coverage when state improperly exercises any of its adjudicative or enforcement power. In AAD coverage, in terms of international responsibility, state conduct extends only to the host state's refusal to arbitrate disputes or honor the arbitral award arising from contracts concluded with the sovereign.[663]

Some may wonder what lies beneath the need for offering two different products to cover risks associated with due process of law. The answer lies within the ICSID Convention. It is worth noting that only Israel, Costa Rica and Guatemala declared the requirement of exhaustion of legal remedies in accordance with Article 26 of the Convention. Unless a special declaration is made, when there is consent to submit a dispute to the Centre, the exhaustion of local remedies shall have been waived.[664] Apart from this fact, at the time of subrogation, the degree of difficulty in collecting the sums paid to the insured can be higher if investor-state, accordingly insurer-state dispute is to be solved by municipal courts. DOJ may cover national judicial misconduct, and obtaining or enforcing the order against the state from where the court obtains its power to adjudicate may be complicated or even time-wasting.

In commercial arbitration, rights embodied in the arbitral awards arise out of the award itself rather than from an investment. And even if the award is less likely to meet the requirements of an investment in the conventional sense, the responsibility of the state will commence when the prevailing party seeks to enforce the award. A caveat can be registered here that AAD does not come into play only if the award is

[660] Soopramanien (2017), p. 601 and see Stefano (2020), pp. 37–38.

[661] Burnett and Bret (2017), p. 59.

[662] Burnett and Bret (2017), p. 55.

[663] Burnett and Bret (2017), pp. 54–55; Roxanna et al. (2009), p. 72. Under art. 11 of MIGA Convention, breach of contract is defined as "*any repudiation or breach by the host government of a contract with the holder of a guarantee, when (a) the holder of a guarantee does not have recourse to a judicial or arbitral forum to determine the claim of repudiation or breach, or (b) a decision by such forum is not rendered within such reasonable period of time as shall be prescribed in the contracts of guarantee pursuant to the Agency's regulations, or (c) such a decision cannot be enforced.*"

[664] Kryvoi (2020), p. 69.

rendered by a commercial arbitration tribunal, even if some were to suppose otherwise. Investment arbitration awards would also fall within the scope of AAD and in the end, due to state conduct, whether through expropriating the investment or preventing the enforcement of any kind of arbitration award, expectations of commercial returns will face the same fate.

Another question that requires an answer is whether this risk can be considered to have occurred if a third-party state refuses to enforce the award. It may not be reasonable to anticipate a favorable reaction at the time of the enforcement of the arbitral award from the same host state with which the foreign investor had a dispute during the operation of the investment. However, in our opinion, this risk must capture instances of a third state maliciously denying enforcement. Under the New York Convention as well as the ICSID Convention, the prevailing party of the arbitral award can seek enforcement in the territory of any member country.[665] The enforceability of the award as well as the availability of the asset will determine this choice.[666] Some third-party states may be under a heavy influence or domination by host states. The relation between the host state and the influenced state may resemble the relation between a satellite and a planet.[667] The satellite state will be under the influence of the host state and probably will act in the same manner and thus, the satellite state may also hinder the enforcement of the award. The foreign investor's right to take over the assets in the amount or proportion ordered in the arbitral award derives from the ratification of one of the abovementioned Conventions by the third-party state. If the wording of the BIT between the third-party state and the home state (state of the foreign investor) permits, a third-party state may well be involved in the occurrence of such political risk by refusing the enforcement of the award.

PRI providers offer protection against sovereigns' refusal to participate in the arbitration, frustration the arbitration from going forward, or failure to pay an arbitral award under several conditions.[668] The basic requirement is that the host state must have ratified the New York Convention. Additionally, while some insurers may stipulate that the insured must either pursue available legal remedies for a certain period or reach a certain stage in the process, some insurers may not consider a mere lack of necessary funds at the time of payment or abuse of process or exhausting colorable claims, by the host state as a loss covered by the insurance policy. Hence, the language and scope of the policy are of considerable importance to provide investors with flexibility to maneuver. In *MidAmerican Energy Holdings Company* (MAEHC or the insured), the insured contracted with two wholly Government of Indonesia-owned natural resources companies for the development of two separate geothermal fields. One of the claims the insured presented was that Indonesian courts

---

[665] See art. 54(1) of the ICSID Convention and art. 3 of New York Convention.

[666] Dolzer and Schreuer (2012), p. 310.

[667] The orbit of the satellite is the curved path determined by the celestial body (planet) it follows, the satellite cannot deviate from this trajectory without additional propulsion.

[668] For OPIC's (DFC's) 'contractors and exporters coverage' scheme, see Hansen (2004), p. 88.

enjoined the enforcement of arbitral awards and the Indonesian government failed to honor two arbitral awards. In OPIC's view, all these actions collectively amounted to the deprivation of an important element of its fundamental rights in the insured investment.[669]

Cases

AAPL v. Sri Lanka: Asian Agricultural Products Ltd (AAPL) v. Republic of Sri Lanka, (ICSID Case No ARB/87/3), Final Award

Aconquija v. Argentina: Compañía de Aguas del Aconquija, S.A. & Compagnie Générale des Eaux, v. The Argentine Republic (ICSID Case No. ARB/97/3), Award

ADC v. Hungary: ADC Affiliate Limited - and - ADC & ADMC Management Limited v. The Republic of Hungary, (ICSID Case No. ARB/03/16), Award

ADF v. U.S.: ADF Group Inc. v. United States of America, (ICSID Case No. ARB (AF)/00/1), Award

ADP v. Chile: ADP International S.A. and Vinci Airports S.A.S. v. The Republic of Chile (ICSID Case No. ARB/21/40)

Alpha v. Ukraine: Alpha Projektholding GMBH v. Ukraine, (ICSID Case No. ARB/07/16), Award

AMCO: AMCO Asia Corporation and others v. Republic of Indonesia, (ICSID Case No. ARB/81/1), Award

AMT v. Zaire: American Manufacturing & Trading, Inc. (AMT) (USA) v. Republic of Zaire, (ICSID Case No. ARB/93/1), Award

Aucoven v. Venezuela: Autopista Concesionada de Venezuela, C.A. v. Bolivarian Republic of Venezuela, (ICSID Case No. ARB/00/5), Award

Azinian: Robert Azinian, Kenneth Davitian, & Ellen Baca v. The United Mexican States, (ICSID Case No. ARB (AF)/97/2), Award

Bank of America: Expropriation Claim of Bank of America, as Trustee India—Contract of Insurance No. F041, OPIC Claim Determination

Bear Creek v. Peru: Bear Creek Mining Corporation v. Republic of Perú (ICSID Case No. ARB/14/21), Award

Bischoff: --

Biloune v. Ghana: Antoine Biloune and Marine Drive Complex Ltd. v. Ghana Investments Centre and the Government of Ghana, (Ad hoc Arbitration), Award on Jurisdiction and Liability - 27 Oct 1989

[669] Despite the Indonesian government have asserted that the insured was involved in "KKN" (corruption, cronyism, and nepotism) and alleged that the projects were awarded to the insured due to corruption. OPIC has received no evidence of any corrupt practices in this case. For the summary of the case, see Kantor et al. (2011), pp. 728–743, see Kantor and Saldarriaga (2009), p. 230 and please visit: https://www.dfc.gov/sites/default/files/2019-08/claim_mid_american.pdf accessed 05.09.2024.

Biwater Gauff v. Tanzania: Biwater Gauff (Tanzania) Ltd. v. United Republic of Tanzania, (ICSID Case No. ARB/05/22), Award

Booker v. Scottish Ministers: Booker Aquaculture Ltd. & Hydro Seafood GSP Ltd. v. Scottish Ministers [2003] ECR-1-7411

BP v. Libya: BP Exploration Company (Libya) Limited v. Government of the Libyan Arab Republic, Award (Merits)

Burdov v. Russia: ECHR, (Application no. 33509/04), JUDGMENT, Final

Chemtura v. Canada: Chemtura Corporation v. Government of Canada, (Ad Hoc NAFTA Arbitration under UNCITRAL Rules), Award

Chevron: Corporation and Texaco Petroleum Company v. The Republic of Ecuador, (UNCITRAL Arbitration, PCA Case No. 34877), Partial Award on the Merits

CMS v. Argentina: Cms Gas Transmission v. The Argentine Republic, (ICSID Case No. ARB/01/8), Award

Continental v. Argentina: Continental Casualty Company v. The Argentine Republic, ICSID Case No. ARB/03/9, Award

Cuba case: --

Dilaver v. Turkey: --

Eli Lilly: Eli Lilly and company v. Government of Canada, (ICSID Case No. UNCT/14/2), Final Award

El Oro v. Mexico: El Oro Mining and Railway Co (Ltd) (Great Britain) v. United Mexican State, v. RIAA191, Great Britain-Mexico Claims Commission, Decision No. 55

ELSI: SpA Elettronica Sicula S.p.A. (ELSI) (United States of America v. Italy, International Court of Justice

ENRON v. Argentina: Enron Corporation Ponderosa Assets, L.P v. The Argentine Republic, (ICSID Case No. ARB/01/3), Award

Erol ÇİÇEK v. TURKEY: ECHR, (Application no. 44837/07), Second Section, Decision

France.com: 1-Société France.com Inc v. G.I.E. ATOUT FRANCE and the French State

2-France.com Inc., v. the French Republic; atout France; the Ministry for Europe and foreign affairs and jean-yves le dnan, in his official capacity as the French Republic's Minister for Europe and Foreign Affairs; Verisign INC. No. 20-1016 (4th Cir. 2021)

Gabčíkovo-NagymarosProject: Gabčíkovo-Nagymaros *Project*, Hungary/Slovakia, (International Court of Justice), Judgment of 25 September 1997

Gavazzi v. Romania*:* Marco Gavazzi and Stefano Gavazzi v. Romania (ICSID Case No. ARB/12/25), Award

Generation Ukraine: Generation Ukraine Inc. v. Ukraine, (ICSID Case No. ARB/00/9), Award

G.I.E.M. S.R.L. v. ITALY: ECHR, (Application no.1828/06 and 2 others), JUDGMENT

Gould Marketing v. Iran: Gould Marketing, Inc. v. Ministry of National Defence, 3 IRAN-U.S. C.T.R., at 147 et seq.

Great Britain v. Costa Rica: Aguilar-Amory and Royal Bank of Canada Claims
Greenpeace E.V. v. Germany: ECHR, Fifth section decision as to the admissibility of application no. 18215/06)
Hamer v. Belgium: ECHR, (Application no. 21861/03), Judgment, 27 November 2007
Jan de Nul: Jan de Nul N.V. Dredging International N.V. v. Arab Republic of Egypt, (ICSID Case No. ARB/04/13), Award
Jugheli v. Georgia: ECHR, (Application no. 38342/05), Judgment, FINAL, 13/10/2017
Impregilo v. Argentina: Impregilo S.p.A. v. Argentine Republic, (ICSID Case No. ARB/07/17), Award
Kiliç İnşaat v. Turkmenistan: Kiliç İnşaat İthalat İhracat Sanayi Ve Ticaret Anonim Şirketi v. Republic of Turkmenistan, (ICSID Case No. ARB/10/1), Award
Lanco v. Argentina: Lanco International Inc. v. The Argentine Republic, ICSID Case No ARB/97/6, Preliminary Decision: Jurisdiction of the Arbitral Tribunal
LG&E Energy v. Argentina: LG &E ENERGY CORP. LG&E CAPITAL CORP. LG&E International Inc. V. Argentine Republic, (ICSID CASE No. ARB/02/1), Decision on Liability
Loewen: the Loewen Group, Inc. and Raymond L. Loewen v. United States of America, (ICSID Case No. ARB(AF)/98/3), Award
Mamidoil v. Albania: Mamidoil Jetoil Greek Petroleum Products Societe s.a. v. Republic of Albania, (ICSID Case No. ARB/11/24), Award
Marine Shipping: Confiscation Claim of Marine Shipping Corporation, Contract of Insurance No. CO15, OPIC Claim Determination
Marvin Feldman v. Mexico: Marvin Roy Feldman Karpa v. The United Mexican States, (ICSID Case No.ARB(AF)/99/1), Award
Metalclad v. Mexico: Metalclad Corp. V. United Mexican States, ICSID Case No. Arb(AF)/97/l
MidAmerican Energy Holdings Company: Expropriation Claim of MidAmerican Energy Holdings Company (formerly CalEnergy Company, Inc.), Contracts of Insurance Nos. E374, E453, E527, and E759, OPIC Claim Determination
Middle East Cement v. Egypt: Middle East Cement Shipping and Handling Co. S.-A. v. Arab Republic of Egypt, ICSID Case No. ARB/99/6, Award
Mobil Cerro v. Venezuela: Venezuela Holdings, b.v. Mobil Cerro Negro Holding, ltd. Mobil Venezolana de Petróleos Holdings, inc. Mobil Cerro Negro, ltd. and Mobil Venezolana de Petróleos, inc. v The Bolivarian Republic of Venezuela, (ICSID Case No. Arb/07/27), Award
Mondev v. U.S.: Mondev International Ltd. v. United States of America, (ICSID Case No. ARB(AF)/99/2), Award
Myers v. Canada: S.D. Myers, Inc. v. Government of Canada, UNCITRAL Rules), Partial Award
Nord Resources Corp: Political Violence Claim of Nord Resources Corporation Sierra Leone—Contract of Insurance No. A628, OPIC Claim Determination
OI European v. Venezuela: OI European Group BV v Bolivarian Republic of Venezuela, (ICSID Case No. Arb/11/25), Award

Olguín v. Paraguay: Eudoro Armando Olguín v. Republic of Paraguay, (ICSID Case No. ARB/98/5), Award

Pac Rim v. El Salvador: Pac Rim Cayman LLC v. The Republic of El Salvador, (ICSID Case No, Arb/09/12), Award

Panderosa Assets: Expropriation Claim of Panderosa Assets, L.P., Contract Type 234 KGT 12-85 (Second Revised), Contract of Insurance No D733, OPIC Claim Determination

Parsons: Parsons (Great Britain) v. United States, (Ad hoc Arbitration), Award

Perenco v. Ecuador: Perenco Ecuador Ltd. v. The Republic of Ecuador (ICSID Case No. ARB/08/6), Interim Decision on the Environmental Counterclaim

Philip Morris v. Uruguay: PHILIP MORRIS BRANDS SÀRL, PHILIP MORRIS PRODUCTS S.A. and ABAL HERMANOS S.A. v. ORIENTAL REPUBLIC OF URUGUAY, (ICSID Case No. ARB/10/7), Award

Plama v. Bulgaria: Plama Consortium Limited v. Republic of Bulgaria, (ICSID Case No. ARB/03/24), Award

POPE & TALBOT v. Canada: POPE & TALBOT INC v. The Government of Canada, (NAFTA Case), Interim Award

PSEG v. Turkey: PSEG Global Inc., the North American Coal Corporation, and Konya Ilgin Electrik Uretim ve Ticaret Limited Sirketi v. The Republic of Turkey, (ICSID Case No. ARB/02/5), Award

Pulp mills: Pulp Mills on the River Uruguay (Argentina v. Uruguay), Judgment, International Court of Justice Reports 2010

R v. Heathrow Airport Ltd: R (on the application of Friends of the Earth Ltd and others) (Respondents) v. Heathrow Airport Ltd (Appellant) JUDGMENT given on 16 December 2020

Railroad Development Corp.: Railroad Development Corporation v. Republic of Guatemala, (ICSID Case No. Arb/07/023), Award

Revere Copper v. OPIC: Revere Copper & Brass v. Overseas Private Investment Corporation, (AAA Case No. 1610013776), Award

Rompetrol v. Romania: Rompetrol Group N.V. v. Romania, (ICSID Case No. ARB/06/3,) Award

Roussalis v. Romania: Spyridon Roussalis v. Romania, (ICSID Case No. ARB/06/1), AWARD

RWE: RWE AG and RWE Eemshaven Holding II BV v. Kingdom of the Netherlands (ICSID Case No. ARB/21/4), Decision on the Claimant's Request for Provisional Measures

Saluka v. Czech Republic*:* Saluka Investments BV v. The Czech Republic, (UNCITRAL Arbitration 1976), Partial Award

Santa Elena v. Costa Rica: Compañía Del Desarrollo De Santa Elena, S.A. v. the Republic of Costa Rica, (ICSID Case No. ARB/96/1), Final Award

Scordino v. Italy: ECHR, (Application no. 36813/97), JUDGMENT, 29 March 2006

Sea-Land Service v. Iran: Sea-Land Service, Inc. v. The Government of the Islamic Republic of Iran, Ports and Shipping Organization, (IUSCT Case No. 33), Award

SEC v. Ripple: The U.S. Securities and Exchange Commission v. Ripple Labs

Sedco v. NIOC: Sedco, Inc. v. National Iranian Oil Company and The Islamic Republic of Iran, (IUSCT Case Nos. 128 and 129), Award

Sehil Inşaat v. Turkmenistan: Muhammet Çap & Sehil Inşaat Endustri ve Ticaret Ltd Sti v. Turkmenistan, ICSID Case No ARB/12/6, Procedural Order No 3

Sempra v. Argentina: Sempra Energy International v. The Argentine Republic, (ICSID Case No. ARB/02/16), Award

Siemens v. Argentina: Siemens A.G. v. The Argentine Republic, (ICSID Case No. ARB/02/8), Award

Société Générale v. Paraguay: SGS Société Générale De Surveillance S.A. v. The Republic of Paraguay, (ICSID Case No. ARB/07/29), Award

SS Lotus: France v. Turkey, Permanent Court of International Justice

Starrett Housing v. Iran: Starrett Housing International, Inc v. The Government of the Islamic Republic of Iran, Bank Markazi, Others, (IUSCT Case no. 24), Final Award, Award No. 314-24-1 and See; Interlocutory Award No ITL 32-24-1

St Michaels Enterprises d.o.o.: Claim of St. Michael Enterprises d.o.o for Wrongful Calling of a Bid Bond, Republic of Serbia, Contract of Insurance No. F360, OPIC Claim Determination

Suez v. Argentina: Suez, Sociedad General de Aguas de Barcelona S.A., and InterAguas Servicios Integrales del Agua S.A. v. The Argentine Republic, (ICSID Case No. ARB/03/17), Decision on Jurisdiction

Taşkın v. Turkey: ECHR, (Application no. 46117/99), Judgment, FINAL, 30/03/2005

Tecmed v. Mexico: Tecnicas Medioambientales Tecmed S.A. v. The United Mexican States, (ICSID Case No. ARB (AF)/00/2), Award

Telenor v. Hungary: Telenor Mobile Communications v. The Republic of Hungary, (ICSlD Case No. ARB/04/15), Award

The May Case: Guatemala v. United States, Award of 16 November 1900, UN Reports of International Arbitral Awards, Vol. XV

Tippets*:* Tippetts, Abbett, Mccarthy, Stratton v. Tams-affa consulting engineers of Iran, The Government of the Islamic Republic of Iran, Civil Aviation Organization, Plan and Budget Organization, Iranian Air Force, ministry of Defense, Bank Melli, Bank Sakhteman, Mercantile Bank of Iran and Holland, Award No. 141-7-2

Tokios Tokelės v. Ukraine*:* Tokios Tokelės v. Ukraine, (ICSID Case No. ARB/02/18), Award

Toto Costruzioni: Toto Costruzioni Generali S.p.A. v. The Republic of Lebanon, (ICSID Case No. ARB/07/12), Decision on Jurisdiction

Tradex v. Albania: Tradex Hellas S.A. v. Republic of Albania, (ICSID Case No. ARB/94/2), Award

Trail Smelter: Trail Smelter Arbitration (US v. Canada), 16 Apr. 1938, 11 Mar. 1941

Turgut and Others v. Turkey: ECHR, (Application no. 1411/03), Judgment, 8 July 2008

Uniper ---

Uniworld Holdings: Claim of Uniworld Holdings, Ltd. for Wrongful Calling of a Performance Bond, Republic of Serbia, Contract of Insurance No. F448, OPIC Claim Determination

Urbaser S.A. v. Argentina: Urbaser S.A. and Consorcio de Aguas Bilbao Bizkaia, Bilbao Biskaia Ur Partzuergoa v. The Argentine Republic, (ICSID Case No. ARB/07/26), Award

Urgenda: The State of the Netherlands (Ministry of economic affairs and climate policy) v. Stichting Urgenda, The decision of the Supreme Court of the Netherlands, civil division, no. 19/00135 date 20 December 2019

U.S. v. Iran: U.S. v. Islamic Republic of Iran, 32 Iran-U.S. Cl. Trib. Rep.

Vivendi v. Argentina: Compañía de Aguas del Aconquija, S.A. & Vivendi Universal S.A., v. Argentine Republic, (ICSID Case No. ARB/97/3), Award

Waste Management: Waste Management Inc. v United Mexican States, (ICISD Case No. ARB(AF)/00/3), Award

White Industries v. India: White Industries Australia Limited v. The Republic of India, UNCITRAL Arbitration, Final award

Wintershall v. Argentina: Wintershall Aktiengesellschaft v. Argentine Republic, (ICSID Case No. ARB/04/14), Award

World Duty Free v. Kenya: World Duty Free Company Limited v. Republic of Kenya, (ICSID Case No. ARB/00/7), Award

Yukos: Yukos universal limited (isle of man) v. The Russian Federation, (PCA Case No. AA 227), Final Award

Online Database

https://www.anlatilaninotesi.com.tr
https://www.arbitrationblog.kluwerarbitration.com
https://www.arstechnica.com
https://www.anayasa.gov.tr
https://www.bbc.com
https://www.bloomberg.com
https://www.bloomberght.com
https://www.brickken.com
https://www.businessinsider.com
https://www.capital.com
https://www.cases.justia.com
https://www.clubdeparis.org
https://www.cnbc.com
https://www.coe.int
https://www.csnturkiye.com
https://www.culawreview.org
https://www.curia.europa.eu
https://www.dette-developpement.org

https://www.dfc.gov
https://www.digitallibrary.un.org
https://www.diken.com.tr
https://www.education.nationalgeographic.org
https://www.elibrary.imf.org
https://www.equator-principles.com
https://www.euractiv.com
https://www.euronews.com
https://www.europarl.europa.eu
https://www.ft.com
https://www.globalarbitrationnews.com
https://www.halktv.com.tr
https://www.hudoc.echr.coe.int
https://www.iana.org/
https://www.ibm.com
https://www.icann.org
https://www.iccwbo.org
https://www.icj-cij.org
https://www.icmagroup.org
https://www.ifc.org
https://www.iiblp.org
https://www.iiiglobal.org
https://www.ilo.org
https://www.ilsa.org
https://www.investmentpolicy.unctad.org
https://www.italaw.com
https://www.jdsupra.com
https://www.jolt.law.harvard.edu
http://www.jstor.org
https://www.jusmundi.com
https://www.kgm.gov.tr
https://www.legal.un.org
https://www.legislation.gov.uk
https://www.lexology.com
https://www.lloyds.com
https://www.mevzuat.gov.tr
https://www.miga.org
https://www.nasdaq.com
https://www.nysd.uscourts.gov
https://www.nytimes.com
ttps://www.oecd.org
https://www.ohchr.org
https://www.poolre.co.uk
https://www.repository.uchastings.edu
https://www.reuters.com

https://www.sec.gov
https://www.sozcu.com.tr
https://www.state.gov
https://www.supremecourt.uk
https://www.tcc.export.gov
https://www.theguardian.com-change
https://www.theverge.com
https://www.thinktank30.de
https://www.tracxn.com
https://www.trans-lex.org
http://www.translex.uni-koeln.de
https://www.treaties.un.org
https://www.tr.euronews.com
https://www.un.org
https://www.uncitral.un.org
https://www.unctad.org
https://www.unep.org
https://www.unfccc.int
https://www.universe.nasa.gov
https://www.unodc.org
https://www.unpri.org
https://www.urgenda.nl
https://www.usnews.com
https://www.ustr.gov
https://www.vlex.co.uk
https://www.whitecase.com
https://www.who.int
https://www.worldbank.org
https://www.wto.org

References

Aaken AV, Broude T (2022) Ways of reforming international investment agreements to make them more compatible with climate change goals. In: Investment Treaties and Climate Change. OECD Public Consultation, 1–9. https://www.oecd.org/investment/investment-policy/OECD-investment-treaties-climate-change-consultation-responses.pdf

Abba K, Wälde T (2008) Capital transfer restrictions under modern investment treaties. In: Reinisch A (ed) Standards of investment protection. Oxford University Press. https://doi.org/10.1093/acprof:oso/9780199547432.003.0010

Aldrich GH (1994) What constitutes compensable taking of property--the decisions of the Iran-United States claims tribunal. Am J Int Law 88(4):585–610

Allen RM, Viscusi WK (1976) Insuring the expropriation risks of multinational firms. Stanford J Int Stud

Alschner W, Tuerk E (2013) The role of international investment agreements in fostering sustainable development. In: Baetens F (ed) Investment law within international law: integrationist perspectives. Cambridge University Press, Cambridge. https://doi.org/10.1017/CBO9781139855921.014

Appleton B (2002) Regulatory takings: the international law perspective. N Y Univ Environ Law J 11(1):35–48

Asiedu-Akrofi D (1989) A comparative analysis of debt equity swap programs in five major debtor countries. Hastings Int Comp Law Rev 12(3)

Asteriti A (2022) Chapter 2: State measures in response to the COVID-19 pandemic: a review. In: Levashova Y, Lorfing PA (eds) Balancing the protection of foreign investors and states responses in the post pandemic world. Kluwer Law International, pp 7–30

Athanasakou KK (2013) Trade-related incentives: the international negotiations over environmental goods and services. In: Dupuy P-M, Viñuales JE (eds) Harnessing foreign investment to promote environmental protection: incentives and safeguards. Cambridge University Press, Cambridge, pp 254–270. https://doi org/10.1017/CBO9781139344289.013

Balcerzak F, Hepburn J (2020) CASE COMMENT Manchester Securities v Poland, Denial of Justice in the European Union. ICSID Rev 35(3):478–491

Baltag C (2020) The role of Amici Curiae in light of recent developments in investment treaty arbitration: legitimizing the system? ICSID Rev 35(1–2):279–310

Barnhizer DD (2005) Inequality of bargaining power. Univ Colo Law Rev 76(1):139

Baroudi MM (2017) Innovation in political risk insurance: experience from the multilateral investment guarantee agency. Global Policy 8:406–413. https://doi.org/10.1111/1758-5899.12480

Barsamian D (2000) Talking 'Anarchy' With Noam Chomsky. The Nation. https://www.thenation.com/article/archive/talking-anarchy-chomsky/

Bodansky D (2021) Paris Agreement. United Nations Audiovisual Library of International Law. https://legal.un.org/avl/pdf/ha/pa/pa_e.pdf

Born G (2021) International arbitration: law and practice, 3rd edn. Kluwer Law International

Bottini G (2010) Part III Chapter 12: legality of investments under ICSID jurisprudence. In: Waibel M, Kaushal A et al (eds) The Backlash against investment arbitration. Kluwer Law International, pp 297–314

Boute A (2009) The potential contribution of international investment protection law to combat climate change. J Energy Nat Resour Law 27(3):333–376. https://doi.org/10.1080/02646811.2009.11435220

Brauch et al (2019) Treaty on sustainable investment for climate change mitigation and adaptation: aligning international investment law with the urgent need for climate change action. J Int Arbitr 36(1):7–36

Bräutigam D, Gallagher KP (2014) Bartering globalization: China's commodity-backed finance in Africa and Latin America. Global Policy 5(3):346–352

Brown VM (2015) Felonious, erroneous, it's all odious: a story of debt gone wrong. Fordham Law Rev 84(2):725–767

Brunner C (2008) Force majeure and hardship under general contract principles: exemption for non-performance in international arbitration. International arbitration law library, vol 18. Kluwer Law International

Buchheit LC et al (2007) The dilemma of odious debts. Duke Law J 56(5):1201–1262

Burgstaller M, Ketcheson J (2017) Should expropriation risk be taken into account in the assessment of damages? ICSID Rev 32(1):193–215

Burnett HG, Bret L (2017) Arbitration of international mining disputes: law and practice. Oxford University Press

Chaisse J, Bauer C (2019) Cybersecurity and the protection of digital assets -- assessing the role of international investment law and arbitration. Vanderbilt J Entertain Technol Law 21(3)

Chein A (2006) Practical look at virtual property. St. John's Law Rev 80(3):1059–1090

Choi SJ et al (2012) The evolution of contractual terms in sovereign bonds. J Leg Anal 4(1):131–179

Christie GG (1962) What constitutes taking of property under international law. Br Yearb Int Law 38:307–338

Cohen D (1997) Project finance: the position of lending banks under political risk insurance policies. Int Insur Law Rev 5(2):35–39

Cong LW, He Z (2019) Blockchain disruption and smart contracts. Rev Financ Stud 32(5): 1754–1797

Cotula L (2015) Expropriation clauses and environmental regulation: diffusion of law in the era of investment treaties. Rev Eur Comp Int Environ Law 24(3):278–288

Cristani F (2022) Chapter 4: how pandemics (may) affect state defences: invoking necessity in COVID-19-related international investment arbitration cases. In: Levashova Y, Lorfing PA (eds) Balancing the protection of foreign investors and states responses in the post-pandemic world. Kluwer Law International, pp 61–74

Crusto MF (2022) Game of thrones: liberty & eminent domain. Univ Miami Law Rev 76(3): 653–741

Daniel MF, Michael BG (2013) Environmental protection. In: Drabek Z, Mavroidis P (eds) Regulation of foreign investment challenges to international harmonization, chapter 7. World Scientific Publishing Co. Pte. Ltd

Daugirdas K (2016) How and why international law binds international organizations. Harv Int Law J 57(2):325–381

Daza-Clark AM (2016) International investment law and water resources management: an appraisal of indirect expropriation. BRILL, Leiden

de Vattel E (1852) The law of nations, or principles of the law of nature applied to the conduct and affairs of nations and sovereigns. T. & J.W. Johnson, Pennsylvania

Denuit M et al (2022) Risk-sharing rules and their properties, with applications to peer-to-peer insurance. J Risk Insur 89(3):615–667

Di Benedetto S (2013) International investment law and the environment. Edward Elgar Publishing, Cheltenham, Gloucestershire

Diaconis JS (1989) Political risk insurance: OPIC's use of a 'fiduciary agent' to facilitate resolution of subrogation claims. Int Lawyer 23(1):271–279

Dolzer R, Schreuer C (2012) Principles of international investment law, 2nd edn. Oxford University Press, Oxford

Douglas Z (2013) The enforcement of environmental norms in investment treaty arbitration. In: Harnessing foreign investment to promote environmental protection incentives and safeguards. Cambridge University Press. https://doi.org/10.1017/CBO9781139344289.019

Douglas Z (2014) International responsibility for domestic adjudication: denial of justice deconstructed. Int Comp Law Q 63(4)

Drabek Z, Mavroidis PC (2013) Regulation of foreign investment: challenges to international harmonization, vol 21. World Scientific Publishing Co. Pte. Ltd, Singapore

Dumberry P (2012) Satisfaction as a form of reparation for moral damages suffered by investors and respondent States in Investor-State arbitration disputes. J Int Dispute Settlement 3(1)

Dupuy P-M (2013) International environmental law: looking at the past to shape the future. In: Dupuy P-M, Viñuales JE (eds) Harnessing foreign investment to promote environmental protection: incentives and safeguards. Cambridge University Press, Cambridge, pp 9–23. https://doi.org/10.1017/CBO9781139344289.003

Eagleton C (1928) Denial of justice in international law. Am J Int Law 22(3)

Elrifai SN et al (2019) A model multilateral treaty for the encouragement of investment in climate change mitigation and adaptation. J Int Arbitr 36(1):71–94. Kluwer Law International BV, The Netherlands

Fairfield J (2005) Virtual property. Boston University Law Review, vol 85, Indiana Legal Studies Research Paper No. 35:1047–1102

Feinerman JV (2007) Odious debt, old and new: the legal intellectual history of an idea. Law Contemp Problems 70(4):193–220

Fiebelman A (2007) Contract, priority, and odious debt. N C Law Rev 85(3):727

Figueiredo RJM (2017) Peer to peer insurance over blockchain. ProQuest Dissertations Publishing
Firger DM (2013) The potential of international climate change law to mobilise low-carbon foreign direct investment. In: Dupuy P-M, Viñuales JE (eds) Harnessing foreign investment to promote environmental protection: incentives and safeguards. Cambridge University Press, Cambridge, pp 176–205. https://doi.org/10.1017/CBO9781139344289.010
Fitzmaurice GG (1932) The meaning of the term 'denial of justice'. Br Yearb Int Law:1393
Freeman AV (1970) International responsibility of states for denial of justice
Gehring MW, Hepburn J (2013) Climate, trade and investment law in the global green economy. In: Ruppel OC, Roschmann C, Ruppel-Schlichting K (eds) Climate change: international law and global governance: Vol. I: legal responses and global responsibility, 1st edn. Nomos Verlagsgesellschaft mbH. http://www.jstor.org/stable/j.ctv941vsk
Gehring MW, Kent A (2013) International investment agreements and the emerging green economy: rising to the challenge. In: Baetens F (ed) Investment law within international law: integrationist perspectives. Cambridge University Press, Cambridge, pp 187–216. https://doi.org/10.1017/CBO9781139855921.013
Gentile CM (2010) The market for odious debt. Law Contemp Problems 73(4)
George T, Searle C (2013) Claims and recoveries in political risk and trade credit insurance: a U.K. legal perspective. In: Verheyen G, Quintrell E (eds) Old risks, new solutions, or is it the other way around. World Bank, Washington, D.C
Ghaleigh NS (2013) Two stories about EU climate change law and policy. In: Ruppel OC, Roschmann C, Ruppel-Schlichting K (eds) Climate change: international law and global governance: Vol. I: legal responses and global responsibility, 1st edn. Nomos Verlagsgesellschaft mbH. http://www.jstor.org/stable/j.ctv941vsk
Gharavi HG (2018) Discord over judicial expropriation. ICSID Rev 33(2):349–357
Gilbert PR (1986) Acquiring and utilizing political risk insurance; a practitioner's perspective. Hastings Int Comp Law Rev 9(3):407–415
Ginsburg R (2013) Political risk insurance and bilateral investment treaties: making the connection. J World Invest Trade 14(6)
Goldberg M, Schär F (2023) Metaverse governance: an empirical analysis of voting within Decentralized Autonomous Organizations. J Bus Res. https://reader.elsevier.com
Gürses Ö (2021) The Supreme Court on business interruption insurance and Covid-19: Financial Conduct Authority v Arch Insurance (UK) Ltd. King's Law J 32(1):71–83
Guzman M, Stiglitz J (2016) Creating a framework for sovereign debt restructuring that works. https://www8.gsb.columbia.edu/faculty/jstiglitz/sites/jstiglitz/files/Ch.1%20-%20Guzman-Stiglitz%20UPDATED.pdf
Hagan S (2008) Designing a legal framework to restructure sovereign debt. In: Current developments in monetary and financial law, vol 4, pp 195–307
Hall WE (1880) International law, by William Edward Hall. Clarendon Press, England
Hansen KW (2004) PRI and the rise (and fall?) of private investment in public infrastructure. In: Moran TH (ed) International political risk management, vol. 2: the brave new world. World Bank Publications, Washington, pp 75–100
Harrison J (2016) Environmental counterclaims in investor-state arbitration. J World Invest Trade 17(3):479–488
Heard J, Laryea ET (2021) Export credit agencies, international investment law and the spectre of unsustainable developing countries' debts. Afr J Int Comp Law 29(4):612–643
Heller JR (1978) Political risk insurance. J Int Law Econ 12(2)
Henin et al (2019) Innovating International Investment Agreements: A Proposed Green Investment Protocol for Climate Change Mitigation and Adaptation. J Int Arbitr 36(1):37–70. Kluwer Law International BV, The Netherlands
Hesse H, Miyajima K (2022) South Africa: the financial sector-sovereign nexus. IMF Working Papers Vol. 2022: Issue 051
Hirsh S, Alman S (2019) Blockchain. American Library Association, Chicago, Illinois

Hoffmann AK (2008) Indirect expropriation. In: Reinisch A (ed) Standards of investment protection. Oxford University Press. https://doi.org/10.1093/acprof:oso/9780199547432.003.0008
Howse R (2007) The concept of odious debt in public international law, United Nations Conference on Trade and Development'. Discussion Papers, no:185. https://unctad.org/system/files/official-document/osgdp20074_en.pdf
Hu HTC (1979) Compensation in expropriations: a preliminary economic analysis. Va J Int Law 20(1):61–95
Hyder AA, Attanasio DL (2021) International investment protection of global banking and finance: legal principles and arbitral practice. Kluwer Law International
Introduction to regulatory expropriations in international law and case Summaries. N Y Univ Environ Law J (2002) 11(1):1–18
Janus T (2012) Odious debt in an imperfect world: odious debt. Rev Dev Econ 16(2):305–317
Jensen NM, Young DJ (2008) A violent future? Political risk insurance markets and violence forecasts. J Confl Resolut 52(4):527–547
Kantor M (2015) Indirect expropriation and political risk insurance for energy projects. J World Energy Law Bus 8(2)
Kantor M, Saldarriaga A (2009) Damages in international commercial arbitration: methods of calculation. Contemporary Issues in International Arbitration and Mediation. The Fordham Papers, BRILL, Leiden, pp 223–260
Kantor M, Nolan MD, Sauvant KP (2011) Reports of overseas private investment corporation determinations, vol 1. Oxford University
Kelly-Louw M (2009) Initiatives of the international chamber of commerce to prevent fraudulent calls on demand guarantees and standby letters of credit. S Afr Merc Law J 21(5):710–733
Kelly-Louw M (2010) International measures to prohibit fraudulent calls on demand guarantees and standby letters of credit. George Mason J Int Commer Law 1:74–120
Khachaturian A (2006) Are we in good hands? The adequacy of American and multilateral political risk insurance programs in fostering international development. Conn Law Rev 38(5):1041
Khachvani D (2017) Compensation for unlawful expropriation: targeting the illegality. ICSID Rev 32(2):385–403
Khachvani D (2020) Non-compensable regulation versus regulatory expropriation: are climate change regulations compensable? ICSID Rev 35(1–2):154–173
King JA (2007) Odious debt: the terms of the debate. N C J Int Law Commer Regul 32(4):605
Kouroutakis A (2022) Sunset clauses in international law and their consequences for EU law. https://www.europarl.europa.eu/RegData/etudes/STUD/2022/703592/IPOL_STU(2022)703592_EN.pdf
Kremer M, Jayachandran S (2003) Odious debt. Brook Rev 21(2):32
Kremer M, Jayachandran S (2006) Odious debt. Am Econ Rev 96(1):82–92
Krueger A (2001) Speech on a new approach to sovereign debt restructuring. Published by International Monetary Fund
Krueger A (2002) Core features of a sovereign debt restructuring mechanism. In: A new approach to sovereign debt restructuring. Published by International Monetary Fund
Kryvoi Y (2020) International Centre for Settlement of Investment Disputes (ICSID), 4th edn. Kluwer Law International
Kunoy B (2005) Developments in indirect expropriation case law in ICSID transnational arbitration. J World Invest Trade 6(3):467–492
Langer MJ (2013) Key instruments of private environmental finance: funds, project finance and market mechanisms. In: Dupuy P-M, Viñuales JE (eds) Harnessing foreign investment to promote environmental protection: incentives and safeguards. Cambridge University Press, Cambridge, pp 131–175. https://doi.org/10.1017/CBO9781139344289.009
Lapatoura I (2022) Fashion beyond physical space: NFTs and intellectual property challenges in the metaverse. Entertain Law Rev 33(6):197–202
Lau PL (2022) The Murky Waters of the Metaverse: addressing some key legal concerns. Commun Law 27(2):77–83

Levashova Y (2022) Chapter 6: the legitimate expectations of investors under the fair and equitable treatment in times of pandemic and aftermath. In: Levashova Y, Lorfing PA (eds) Balancing the protection of foreign investors and states responses in the post-pandemic world. Kluwer Law International

Lewis BN (2007) Restructuring the odious debt exception. Boston Univ Int Law J 25(2):297

Luterbacher U (2013) The political environment of environmental law. In: Dupuy P-M, Viñuales JE (eds) Harnessing foreign investment to promote environmental protection: incentives and safeguards. Cambridge University Press, Cambridge, pp 50–68. https://doi.org/10.1017/CBO9781139344289.005

MacMillan C (2021) Covid-19 and the problem of frustrated contracts. King's Law J 32(1):60–70. https://doi.org/10.1080/09615768.2021.1885328

Magraw D et al (2019) Model Green Investment Treaty: international investment and climate change. J Int Arbitr 36(1):95–134. Kluwer Law International BV, The Netherlands

Mainelli M, Von Gunten C (2014) Chain of a lifetime: how blockchain technology might transform personal insurance. Long Finance, 2014. SSRN: https://papers.ssrn.com/sol3/papers.cfm?abstract_id=3676416

Maljean-Dubois S, Richard V (2013) The applicability of international environmental law to private enterprises. In: Dupuy P-M, Viñuales JE (eds) Harnessing foreign investment to promote environmental protection: incentives and safeguards. Cambridge University Press, Cambridge, pp 69–96. https://doi.org/10.1017/CBO9781139344289.006

Marano P (2019) Navigating InsurTech: the digital intermediaries of insurance products and customer protection in the EU. Maastricht J Eur Comp Law 26(2):294–315

Marboe I (2017) Calculation of compensation and damages in international investment law, 2nd ed. Oxford International Arbitration Series. Oxford University Press

Marisi F (2020) Environmental interests in investment arbitration, International Arbitration Law Library, vol 51. Kluwer Law International

Martin EM (1967) Multilateral investment insurance: the OECD proposal. Harv Int Law J 8(2): 280–338

Martinez L, Francisco R, Zettelmeyer J (2022) Sovereign debt. IMF Working Papers Vol. 2022: Issue 122

Marzal T (2021) Quantum (in)justice: rethinking the calculation of compensation and damages in ISDS. J World Invest Trade 22(2):249–312. https://doi.org/10.1163/22119000-12340209

Masaro MB (2019) Incorporating the fresh start into sovereign debt restructuring through odious debt. Cornell Law Rev 104(6):1644–1777

Mathieson DJ, Rojas-Suárez L (1992) Liberalization of the capital account: experiences and issues. IMF Working Papers Vol. 1992 Issue 046

Mazin A (2017) Dealing with political risk in PPP infrastructure projects: legal recommendations based on recent cases. J Article Int Bus Law J 3:189–202

McKendrick E (1995) Force majeure and frustration of contract, 2nd edn. Lloyd's of London, London

Megliani M (2020) Mozambican illegal debts: testing the odious debt doctrine. Vanderbilt J Transnatl Law 53(5):1637–1686

Merezhko O (2018) International legal aspects of Russia's War against Ukraine in Eastern Ukraine. In: The use of force against Ukraine and international law. T.M.C. Asser Press, The Hague

Merkin R, Kullmann J (2006) The insurance, reinsurance and the impact of terrorism. http://www.aida.org.uk/pdf/questionnaire2.pdf

Merkin RM, Steele J (2013) Insurance and the law of obligations, 1st edn. Oxford University Press, Oxford

Merrill TW (2002) Incomplete compensation for takings. N Y Univ Environ Law J 11(1):110–135

Michalowski S, Bohoslavsky JP (2009) Ius cogens, transitional justice and other trends of the debate on odious debts: a response to the world bank discussion paper on odious debts. Columbia J Transnatl Law 48(1):59–113

MIGA (2009) World investment and political risk. https://openknowledge.worldbank.org/bitstream/handle/10986/2688/520190PUB0flag10Box345548B01PUBLIC1.pdf?sequence=1&isAllowed=y

Mistelis LA (2013) Award as an investment: the value of an arbitral award or the cost of non-enforcement. ICSID Rev 28(1):64–87

Morgera E (2013) From corporate social responsibility to accountability mechanisms. In: Dupuy P-M, Viñuales JE (eds) Harnessing foreign investment to promote environmental protection: incentives and safeguards. Cambridge University Press, Cambridge, pp 321–354. https://doi.org/10.1017/CBO9781139344289.016

Nehru V, Thomas M (2008) The concept of odious debt: some considerations. Policy File. http://www.worldbank.org

Newcombe A (2005) The boundaries of regulatory expropriation in international law. ICSID Rev 20(1):1–57

Newcombe A, Paradell L (2009) Law and practice of investment treaties: standards of treatment. Kluwer Law International

Nieuwveld LB, Sahani VS (2017) Third-party funding in international arbitration, 2nd edn. Kluwer Law International

Norton JJ (2004) An 'environmental' approach to FDI and effective dispute resolution: the exhortations of the Monterrey consensus. In: Norbert Horn and Stefan M. Kröll (eds) Arbitrating foreign investment disputes: procedural and substantive legal aspects, Studies in transnational economic law, vo. 19. Kluwer Law International: 89–109

Novák Z (2020) Limits of arbitral competence: lessons from a Hungarian Domain Name Dispute. Kluwer Arbitration Blog. https://arbitrationblog.kluwerarbitration.com/2020/01/30/limits-of-arbitral-competence-lessons-from-a-hungarian-domain-name-dispute/

Ochoa C (2008) From odious debt to odious finance: avoiding the externalities of a functional odious debt doctrine. Harv Int Law J 49(1):109–159

OECD (2017) Enhancing the role of insurance in cyber risk management. OECD Publishing, Paris

OECD (2020) Insurance Coverage for Cyber Terrorism in Australia

Olivares-Caminal R (2013) The Pari Passu Clause in Sovereign Debt Instruments: Developments in Recent Litigation. BIS Paper No. 72u. https://papers.ssrn.com/sol3/papers.cfm?abstract_id=2473988

Oppenheim L et al (2008) Oppenheim's international law, vol 1, Peace, 9th edn. Longman, London

Pasich K, Thayer SS (2011) Political risk insurance. Risk Manag 58(5):27

Paulsson J (2005) Denial of justice in international law. Cambridge University Press, Cambridge

Paulsson J, Douglas Z (2004) Indirect expropriation in investment treaty arbitrations. In: Horn N, Kröll SM (eds) Arbitrating foreign investment disputes: procedural and substantive legal aspects, studies in transnational economic law, vol 19. Kluwer Law International, pp 145–158

Paulus CG (2005) Odious debts vs. debt trap: a realistic help? Brooklyn J Int Law 31(1):83

Paulus CG (2007) The concept of 'odious debts': a historical survey. Duke Law School Legal Studies Research Paper Series, Research Paper No. 179

Peinhardt C, Allee T (2016) Political risk insurance as dispute resolution. J Int Dispute Settlement 7(1):205–224

Potočnik M (2019) Arbitrating brands: international investment treaties and trademarks. Edward Elgar Publishing Limited, Cheltenham, Gloucestershire

Proulx VJ, Simma B (2012) Transnational terrorism and state accountability: a new theory of prevention. Bloomsbury Publishing, Oxford

Radi Y (2018) CASE COMMENT, Philip Morris v Uruguay regulatory measures in international investment law: to be or not to be compensated? ICSID Rev 33(1):74–80

Rajput A (2018) Regulatory freedom and indirect expropriation in investment arbitration. Kluwer Law International

Ratner SR (2008) Regulatory takings in institutional context: beyond the fear of fragmented international law. Am J Int Law 102(3):475–528

Reinisch A (2008) Legality of expropriations. In: Reinisch A (ed) Standards of investment protection. Oxford University Press. https://doi.org/10.1093/acprof:oso/9780199547432.003.0009

Roxanna F, Kevin WL, Wang S (2009) Sovereign wealth funds, financial crisis, and management of noncommercial risks. In: Understanding political risk management in the 21st century. World Bank, Washington DC, pp 60–81

Rubins N, Kinsella NS (2005) International investment, political risk and dispute resolution "a practitioner's guide". Oxford University Press

Sabahi B (2011) Compensation and restitution in investor-state arbitration: principles and practice. Oxford University Press, Oxford

Salacuse JW (2013) The three laws of international investment: national, contractual, and international frameworks for foreign capital. Oxford University Press

Salacuse JW (2016) The law of investment treaties, 3rd edn. Oxford University Press, Oxford

Salacuse JW, Sullivan NP (2005) Do BITs really work?: An evaluation of bilateral investment treaties and their grand bargain. Harv Int Law J 46(1):67–130

Saldarriaga A, Kantor M (2009) Calculating damages: arbitrators, counsel, and experts can do better than they have in the past. In: Lu KW et al (eds) Investing with confidence: understanding political risk management in the 21st century. World Bank, Washington DC, pp 196–238

Schelling TC (1956) An essay on bargaining. Am Econ Rev 46(3):281–306

Shihata IFI (1987) Factors influencing the flow of foreign investment and the relevance of a multilateral investment guarantee scheme. Int Lawyer 21(3):671–694

Simmons JB (2012) Valuation in investor-state arbitration: toward a more exact science. Berkeley J Int Law 30(1):196–250

Soopramanien RD (2017) Mind the GAP: tailoring the form and substance of political risk insurance in order to bridge the 'enforcement gap' in investment arbitration. Int Lawyer

Spagnoletti B, O'Callaghan T (2011) Going undercover: the paradox of political risk insurance. Asia-Pac J Risk Insur 5(2):1064

Spier J (2013) Legal strategies to come to grips with climate change. In: Ruppel OC, Roschmann C, Ruppel-Schlichting K (eds) Climate change: international law and global governance: Vol. I: legal responses and global responsibility, 1st edn. Nomos Verlagsgesellschaft mbH. http://www.jstor.org/stable/j.ctv941vsk

Sprankling JG (2014) The international law of property, 1st edn. Oxford University Press, Oxford

Stefano CD (2020) Attribution in international law and arbitration, 1st edn. Oxford University Press, Oxford

Stephan PB Jr (2007) The institutionalist implications of an odious debt doctrine. Law Contemp Problems 70(3):212–232

Stephens-Chu G (2022) Chapter 8: discrimination claims by foreign investors in the aftermath of the COVID-19 pandemic. In: Levashova Y, Lorfing PA (eds) Balancing the protection of foreign investors and states responses in the post pandemic world. Kluwer Law International, pp 171–190

Tan C (2015) Risky business: political risk insurance and the law and governance of natural resources. Int J Law Context 11(2):174–119

Thallinger G (2008) The rule of exhaustion of local remedies in the context of the responsibility of international organisations Nordic J Int Law = Acta scandinavica juris gentium 77(4):401–428

The Black's Law Dictionary

Thurber AM, Shah S (2013) Sovereign risks and political risks: new challenges. In: Verheyen G, Quintrell E (eds) Old risks, new solutions, or is it the other way around, pp 45–57

Torrado PM (2005) Political risk insurance and breach of contract coverage: how the intervention of domestic courts may prevent investors from claiming insurance. Pace Int Law Rev 17(2):301

Tosun O (2020) Turk Eximbank Short Term Export Credit Insurance Contract. Oniki Levha, Istanbul

Tudor I (2008) The fair and equitable treatment standard in the international law of foreign investment. Oxford University Press, Oxford

Turyn A, Pérez-Aznar F (2010) Part I Chapter 3: drawing the limits of free transfer provisions. In: Waibel M, Kaushal A et al (eds) The Backlash against investment arbitration. Kluwer Law International, pp 51–78

Van Der Vaart HJ (1981) Standby letters of credit and the problem of bad faith calls. Yale J World Public Order 8(1):36–61

Verwey W, Schrijver N (1984) The taking of foreign property under international law: a new legal perspective? Neth Yearb Int Law 15:3–96

Viñuales JE (2013) The environmental regulation of foreign investment schemes under international law. In: Dupuy P-M, Viñuales JE (eds) Harnessing foreign investment to promote environmental protection: incentives and safeguards. Cambridge University Press, Cambridge, pp 273–320. https://doi.org/10.1017/CBO9781139344289.015

Von Goeler J (2016) Third-party funding in international arbitration and its impact on procedure, International Arbitration Law Library, vol 35. Kluwer Law International

Waelde TW, Ndi G (1996) Stabilizing international investment commitments: international law versus contract interpretation. Tex Int Law J 31(2):215–268

Wagner JM (1999) International investment, expropriation and environmental protection. Golden Gate Univ Law Rev 29(1–3):465

Wagner D (2012) Managing country risk a practitioner's guide to effective cross-border risk analysis. CRC Press, Boca Raton, Fla

Wallman KM (1985) The politics of default: politically motivated sovereign debt default and repudiation. Tex Int Law J 20(3):475–516

Weiler T (2003) The treatment of SPS measures under NAFTA Chapter 11: preliminary answers to an open-ended question. Boston Coll Int Comp Law Rev 26(2):229

Wendy M, Lawry-White M (2019) Arbitral institutions and the enforcement of climate change obligations for the benefit of all stakeholders: the role of ICSID. ICSID Rev 34(1):1–31

White KK (1979) Bankers guarantees and the problem of unfair calling. J Maritime Law Commerce 11(1):121–132

Williams S (1993) Political and other risk insurance: OPIC, MIGA, EXIMBANK and other providers. Pace Int Law Rev 5:59–113

Yackee JW (2014) Political risk and international investment law. Duke J Comp Int Law 24(3):477

Yee K (1997) location.location.location: a snapshot of internet addresses as evolving property. J Inf Law Technol (JILT) (1). http://elj.warwick.ac.uk/jilt/intprop/97_1yee/

Yianni A, Tinkler D (2006) Is there a recognized legal doctrine of odious debts. N C J Int Law 32: 749

Yu C (2020) Amicus Curiae participation in ISDS: a caution against political intervention in treaty interpretation. ICSID Rev 35(1–2):223–235

Ziadé R, Hoebeke BR (2022) Chapter 7: perspectives on expropriation claims in a post-pandemic world. In: Levashova Y, Lorfing PA (eds) Balancing the protection of foreign investors and states responses in the post pandemic world. Kluwer Law International, pp 131–170

Chapter 9
Exclusions

Exclusion clauses limit the extent of the cover and exculpate the insurer from liability for losses.[1] Underwriters mostly select to set out these clauses in a separate section headed 'Exclusions'. The risk appetite of the insured is the main element that determines the scope of the excluded events. In export credit insurance, exporters may wish to obtain coverage against only risky buyers and in response, ECAs have adopted 'whole turnover' mechanism[2] whereby the policy covers the insured's total credit sales as opposed to key buyer or single risk cover.[3] In PRI, the insurer's risk appetite is defined by its legal status, whether it is a public or private insurer. Since PRI provides coverage for single transactions or projects, the types of covered events can vary and may be few. In contrast, PRI providers may tend to reject indemnification for losses, damages, costs or expenses of whatsoever nature directly or indirectly caused by, or in connection with force majeure and events alike. Policies do not cover losses resulting from toxic or hazardous materials, radioactivity, nuclear fuel/waste, discharge of pollutants or contaminants, natural disasters, chemical or biological exposure of any kind and electromagnetic weapons. Simply put, except for acts of God, natural disasters, radioactive, toxic or other means of hazardous contamination and events alike, the unavoidable hindrances or the events which bring a regular contract to an end may fall within the scope of PRI.

The second group of events are the ones caused by the insured's self-inflicted activities. Policies do not provide any coverage against the insured's dishonest acts, the presentation of inaccurate warranties or the failure to fulfill covenants.[4] Policies also do not cover losses arising from the application of host states' laws that were in force at the time coverage began, and which the insured could have been reasonably

[1] Ginsburg (2013), p. 970.

[2] Also see Merkin and Steele (2013), p. 174.

[3] See ICISA's Glossary of TCI Terms, available at https://icisa.org/tci-glossary/#W accessed 05.09.2024.

[4] See Williams (1993), p. 111, similarly Clarke (2013), p. 99.

Ö. Tosun, *The Law of Political Risk Insurance*, AIDA Europe Research Series on Insurance Law and Regulation 12, https://doi.org/10.1007/978-3-031-74675-8_9

aware of with simple research. Furthermore, although money laundering, collusive practices, coercive practices, corrupt practices or fraudulent activities on the part of the insured are contrary to public policy, in policies governed by common law and lacking an explicit exclusion of such circumstances, insurers will be left to mercy of the adjudicators. Besides, as amply discussed elsewhere, the insured is under an obligation to mitigate or, as the case may be, prevent the risk. Hence, the insured is responsible for losses that arise from breaching its contractual obligations and regardless of whether it is negligent or intentional, from its wrongdoings. One may need to note that even if the value of the investment rises over time, the insurer is not responsible for the portion exceeding the amount of the coverage. Besides, regardless of whether vital to the investment or not the insurer is not responsible for the expenditures that contribute to the value of the investment.

While PRI policies generally provide coverage against war, some underwriters may take a different stance. The risk of war between permanent members of the U.N. Security Council is one of the most underestimated exclusions. PRI policies may tend to exclude losses resulting from war between China, France, Russia, the United Kingdom, and the United States. The reason for excluding such specific wars may lie in the disastrous effects of such wars as well as the concern that the economic market may collapse and therefore the means of subrogation could be beyond reach. The exclusion of war between the five major powers should also be of particular concern for the investors who neither reside nor invest in those countries, as it may lead the investor to forgo insurance. Secondly, an underrated exclusion may be currency fluctuations. Inconvertibility or transfer restrictions are most likely to take place after the local currency drastically fluctuates downward. Sometime these risks can be inextricably entwined insomuch as that the underwriter may have difficulty determining whichever caused the loss or calculating the value of the currency and therefore the amount of the loss. Therefore, the wording of the policy covering the loss arising from inconvertibility or transfer restriction, however excluding risks of inflation or devaluation should leave no room for ambiguities.

At first blush, some may suppose that all risks are presumably insurable; however, the insureds buy the coverage against risks the occurrence of which are comparatively higher. As stated at the beginning of this study, PRI is the insurance of the exceptions. Perils covered by PRI are the risks excluded from conventional insurance policies. Thus, although there is a wide disparity in the premiums rates offered by PRI providers, since the perils are identified as 'exceptions' under conventional insurance policies, the premium rates of PRI can be higher than those of a conventional risk insurance. Although the risk of any kind is insurable, PRI may be unaffordable and beyond reach.

Finally, if a PRI policy provides coverage only against expropriation, must the underwriter state that the same policy does not cover losses arising from fire, flood or gradual deterioration? Is it his/her duty to identify every peril that does not fall within the general umbrella of PRI? If so, what will the ending point of the exclusions be? Will the policy be vague if it omits to exclude some events? As far as burden of proof is concerned, the burden will rest upon the insurer, and it will prove that the loss was caused by one of the excluded perils. In our opinion, a policy is sufficiently indicative if it explicitly states only the covered peril(s). Accepting the 'excluded perils' technique can be irrational. It will not be a bona fide action to claim compensation if the loss arose from an event that is neither covered nor excluded. If the covered perils are *'beneficial'* and uncovered ones *'nonbeneficial'* to the insured, by signing the PRI contract, the insured must be presumed to have accepted what is *beneficial* to him/her. In the assumption to the contrary, each event that is non-listed as an exclusion may mean to be covered. Accordingly, in order to define what is covered, we see no reason to specify what is excluded if it has not already been listed.

References

Clarke MA (2013) The law of liability insurance. Informa Law from Routledge, New York

Ginsburg R (2013) Political risk insurance and bilateral investment treaties: making the connection. J World Invest Trade 14(6)

ICISA's Glossary of TCI Terms. https://icisa.org/tci-glossary/#W

Merkin RM, Steele J (2013) Insurance and the law of obligations, 1st edn. Oxford University Press, Oxford

Williams S (1993) Political and other risk insurance: OPIC, MIGA, EXIMBANK and other providers. Pace Int Law Rev 5:59–113

Chapter 10
Means of Reparation

10.1 Terminological Confusion

In referring to the consequences of the peril and in defining the characteristics of the rectification, a range of terminology has been employed. The notions of *damage* and *injury* share certain similarities and, as a result of terminological confusion, may be considered as synonyms. However, there is a slight distinction. According to *Wittich*, *iniuria* (Latin for injury) denotes a certain category of acts contrary to what is prescribed by the law, while *damnum* (Latin for damage) denotes the actual harmful result of the wrongful or illegal act.[1] Injury refers to a wrongful act giving rise to responsibility,[2] it is of a non-material character, is more linked with real persons and corresponds to the illegality of the state's act. Whereas, specifically in political force majeure events, damage may be defined as 'deterioration of the integrity of or destruction of or impairment in quantity of or in functionality of an asset.'

Damage, loss, and harm are often equated. Damage denotes the amount the host state owes to the investor as a remedy for a treaty breach,[3] whereas the term loss fits to describe consequences detrimental to the investor's interest. The process aiming at rectifying the investor's loss, restoring the 'wrong done' is expressed by the terms compensation, indemnification, reparation or restitution which are interchangeably, and mistakenly used. International law on the other hand stresses the distinction. And in the following chapters we will discuss in detail these terms in the light of the ILC articles.

[1] Wittich (2004), pp. 324–326.

[2] Wittich (2004), p. 323.

[3] Marzal (2021), p. 249, fn 1.

Ö. Tosun, *The Law of Political Risk Insurance*, AIDA Europe Research Series on Insurance Law and Regulation 12, https://doi.org/10.1007/978-3-031-74675-8_10

10.2 Satisfaction

The ILC articles are a non-binding set of rules designed to codify states' responsibilities. Within the scheme of the ILC, reparation[4] takes three forms: restitution, compensation, and satisfaction. The first two forms of remedies are more related to PRI and will be discussed in detail. *Satisfaction,* on the other hand, is an exceptional reparation associated with state-state disputes.[5] States may suffer two kinds of moral damages. Those indirect damages are the ones when individuals are hurt, and states are offended through the 'bond of nationality'. Whereas, in direct damage, states themselves suffer damage, regardless of whether nationals are involved.[6]

Satisfaction is considered the proper mean of reparation for non-material injury caused directly to a state as it aims to condemn the responsible state.[7] The link between moral damage and satisfaction lies in the commentary to ILC. It has been noted in the commentary that satisfaction is the remedy for injuries of a symbolic character,[8] arising from the very fact of the breach of the obligation, which are not financially assessable and amount to an affront to the state. *Dumberry* contributes with a specific type of moral damage that investors may suffer, namely "*injury to the credit and reputation of a legal entity.*[9]"

The reading of article 37 reveals that satisfaction is to address moral injuries and is of an afflictive nature. The remedies it indicates are devised to correspond moral injuries such as "an expression of regret and a formal apology".[10] On the other hand, the forms of satisfaction mentioned in the previous ILC text, reminiscent of the

[4]In investment disputes, 'reparation' is the term generally applied to the full panoply of relief that may be obtained from a government. See Reisman et al. (2014), p. 965.

[5]Also see Sabahi (2011), pp. 12, 62.

[6]Pirim (2020), pp. 246–248.

[7]Dumberry (2012), pp. 211, 212.

[8]Also see Wittich (2004), p. 354.

[9]The scholar seems to have been inspired by the observation made by Umpire Parker at the adjudication of a case involving the sinking of the British liner Lusitania by a German submarine during the First World War. Parker's observation on moral damage is as follows: "*That one injured is, under the rules of international law, entitled to be compensated for an injury inflicted resulting in mental suffering, injury to his feelings, humiliation, shame, degradation, loss of social position or injury to his credit or to his reputation, there can be no doubt, and such compensation should be commensurate to the injury. Such damages are very real, and the mere fact that they are difficult to measure or estimate by money standards makes them nonetheless real and affords no reason why the injured person should not be compensated therefor as compensatory damages, but not as a penalty.*" For the quoted observation and Dumberry's view, see Dumberry (2010), pp. 249, 250.

[10]Art. 37 provides for the last remedy of satisfaction; the article reads as: "*1. The State responsible for an internationally wrongful act is under an obligation to give satisfaction for the injury caused by that act insofar as it cannot be made good by restitution or compensation. 2. Satisfaction may consist in an acknowledgement of the breach, an expression of regret, a formal apology or another appropriate modality. 3. Satisfaction shall not be out of proportion to the injury and may not take a form humiliating to the responsible State.*"

principle of individual criminal responsibility,[11] targeted the perpetrators of the incident, and included "nominal, aggravated or punitive damages and disciplinary action against or punishment of individuals responsible for a breach[12]". This remedy is also of subsidiary nature, since the article 37 provides that states must give satisfaction if the damage caused by the wrongful act cannot be made good by restitution.[13]

The ILC Commentary signifies that satisfaction is not intended to be punitive in character, nor does it include punitive damages.[14] *Dumberry* opines that monetary payment, one of a number of forms of 'satisfaction' serves a different function from monetary compensation proper: it provides a symbolic amount of money to remedy a violation to a state's honor and dignity.[15] In our view, whether symbolic or not, any court-led or ordered action resulting in appeasing the feelings of the aggrieved party would suffice to say that satisfaction appears to aim at the wrongdoer through punitive means. Except for pecuniary satisfaction,[16] a mere apology or regret would leave the actual harm unrepaired.

When it comes to pecuniary satisfaction, it was discussed in *Europe Cement v. Turkey*. Counsel for the respondent argued that the case was not brought in good faith and that "*in ordering an amount for moral damages, the tribunal would be providing a form of satisfaction, even if the award were never to be paid*[17]". If the request of the respondent was admitted, even if the amount would not be paid,

---

[11] This principle stems from the idea that "*a person is only culpable to the extent of his own will*". *Sliedregt* opines that the origins of the international concept of individual criminal responsibility lie in its break with the immunity of state officials. The author also highlights the Nuremberg judgment where the tribunal concluded that "*Case Crimes against international law are committed by men, not by abstract entities, and only by punishing individuals who commit such crimes can the provision of international law be enforced.*" See van Sliedregt (2012), pp. 18–19. For the case, see Trial of the Major War Criminals before the International Military Tribunal, vol. I, Nürnberg, p. 223. Available at https://www.uni-marburg.de/de/icwc/dokumentation/dokumente/protokolle-nuernberg/ntvol01.pdf accessed 05.09.2024.

[12] According to art. 45, para 2 of the 1996 Draft ILC Articles 'satisfaction may take the form of one or more of the following: (a) an apology; (b) nominal damages; (c) in cases of gross infringement of the rights of the injured State, damages reflecting the gravity of the infringement; (d) in cases where the internationally wrongful act arose from the serious misconduct of officials or from criminal conduct of officials or private parties, disciplinary action against, or punishment of, those responsible'. See Wittich (2002), p. 901. See Dumberry (2012), p. 213. Also see Pirim (2020), p. 257, fn 99.

[13] Wittich (2004), p. 363.

[14] Please visit: https://legal.un.org/ilc/texts/instruments/english/commentaries/9_6_2001.pdf p. 107, accessed 05.09.2024.

[15] Dumberry (2012), p. 215.

[16] Scholars state that the number of the cases where the state, (as opposed to its nationals) has been remedied by monetary compensation is few. For *Rainbow Warrior* (the only case where pecuniary satisfaction was recognized) See Dumberry (2012), p. 217 and see Dumberry (2010), p. 251.

[17] Counsel for the respondent made an epic statement in the following words "*there comes a time when those who abusively initiate legal proceedings must be held accountable for their conduct.*" See *Europe Cement v. Turkey*, para. 135. Available at https://www.italaw.com/sites/default/files/

satisfaction would take the form of a tribunal's declaration of acknowledging wrongfulness.[18] However, the tribunal did not award monetary compensation and did not find that exceptional circumstances such as physical duress were present in this case to justify moral damages.[19]

As readers may recall, the availability of counterclaims to the host state is a hotly debated topic. While some scholars find no explicit basis,[20] *Parish et al* sit at the opposite end of this approach, arguing that although investors cannot acquire obligations under investment treaties to which they are not parties, within the meaning of the ILC, moral damages might be awarded to a prevailing respondent state in cases where the investor's claim is vexatious, fraudulently or brought in bad faith. And decrease in incoming foreign direct investment will affect the quantum of the award.[21] In support of this view, *Kryvoi* explains states' entitlement to moral damages as the result of facilitating equality between parties,[22] however, *Gultutar* finds *Parish et al's* reasoning inaccurate on the grounds that the ILC explicitly excludes such monetary entitlement for the host state.[23]

Some scholars are of the opinion that even 'denial of justice' (a frequent political risk) may be remedied by satisfaction.[24] In *Pey Casado v. Chile,* Victor Pey Casado owned shares in a local newspaper which was subjected to confiscation. He was unable to secure any remedies in Chilean courts and therefore commenced arbitral proceedings. In its pleadings, the claimants requested compensation for moral damages.[25] In the view of the tribunal, no attempt was made to advance, or to justify, a specific claim that moral damage had been suffered, and Mr. Pey Casado

---

case-documents/ita0311.pdf Similarly see *Cementownia v. Turkey*. Available at https://www.italaw.com/sites/default/files/case-documents/ita0138.pdf accessed 05.09.2024.

[18] See Dumberry (2012), pp. 230–231.

[19] See *Europe Cement v. Turkey*, para. 181.

[20] See Dumberry (2012), p. 235, similarly, see Born (2021), p. 499 and also see the chapter addressing counterclaims in environmental disputes.

[21] Parish et al. (2011), pp. 239–243.

[22] Kryvoi (2012), pp. 218–220.

[23] However, according to author wrongful acts causing harm to another require one to balance the scale therefore states can also be granted opportunity to strike back. The author, in his reasoning, relies on the art. 37, Commentary (3) which provides "*In accordance with paragraph 2 of art. 31, the injury for which a responsible state is obliged to make full reparation embraces 'any damage, whether material or moral, caused by the internationally wrongful act of a State'. Material and moral damage resulting from an internationally wrongful act will normally be financially assessable and hence covered by the remedy of compensation. Satisfaction, on the other hand, is the remedy for those injuries, not financially assessable, which amount to an affront to the state. These injuries are frequently of a symbolic character, arising from the very fact of the breach of the obligation, irrespective of its material consequences for the State concerned.*" See Gultutar (2021), pp. 45–47, 48.

[24] Wittich (2004), p. 338.

[25] Dumberry (2012), pp. 223, 224.

was the victim of a denial of justice.[26] In fact, the award did not completely disregard moral damages; the tribunal was of the opinion that the award rendered in the claimant's favor itself was a substantial and sufficient moral satisfaction.[27]

In some cases, acts of states, resulting in harm to a corporation have been punished. The *Desert Line Projects case* is the first publicly known award where a moral damage claim brought by an investor succeeded.[28] In this case, the government made no payment in respect of completed contracts. Additionally, the Yemeni Ministry of Public Works declared that the claimant had been "overpaid," which incited unpaid subcontractors, one of whom invaded the project site with armed tribes. Consequently, the dispute arising from mere non-payment caused the investor's executives being threatened and suffering stress and anxiety of harassment. Although the parties reached what appears to be an "on its face" settlement, in which only the investor seemed to materially waive its claims, the settlement was imposed on the claimant. As a result, the claimant filed a claim before ICSID, including an allegation of loss of reputation.[29] In the tribunal's view, in exceptional circumstances an investor is entitled to seek moral damages, and the tribunal held that a legal person (as opposed to a natural one) may be awarded moral damages, including loss of reputation, in specific circumstances only.[30] The tribunal founded its reasoning upon the following legal basis "*the physical duress exerted on the executives of the Claimant, was malicious and is therefore constitutive of a fault-based liability. Therefore, the Respondent shall be liable to reparation for the injury suffered by the Claimant*".[31]

In *Von Pezold v. Zimbabwe*, the tribunal discussed whether tribunals have jurisdiction over a dispute concerning claims of moral damages. The tribunal first discussed the concept of 'corporate espousal' that stems from the concept of 'state espousal' and posits that damage to an employee of a corporation can be considered as damage to the corporation itself. In addition, the tribunal underscored the availability of justice to personnel of the party disputing with the state. In the tribunal's view, although the harm suffered by the executives is not harm to the company itself, the staff would not receive a proper relief from domestic courts, which might lack independence in their decision-making, thereby depriving real persons of justice.

---

[26] See para. 243, 256. Available at https://www.italaw.com/sites/default/files/case-documents/italaw7630.pdf accessed 05.09.2024.

[27] See para. 704 of the award https://www.italaw.com/sites/default/files/case-documents/ita0638.pdf accessed 05.09.2024. The term 'satisfaction' in the award was clearly not used in the same sense as when referring to the proper form of reparation for moral damages incurred by states. See Dumberry (2010), p. 262.

[28] Dumberry (2010), pp. 247–248.

[29] *Desert Line v. Yemen* para. 289. Available at https://www.italaw.com/sites/default/files/case-documents/ita0248_0.pdf accessed 05.09.2024. See Dumberry (2010), pp. 257–260.

[30] See *Desert Line v. Yemen* (para. 286–289). For a case where the tribunal awarded compensation for the state's action that caused serious harm to the reputation and honour of a corporation See LAFICO v. Burundi, Award, 4 March 1991.

[31] See *Desert Line v. Yemen* (para. 290).

The tribunal held that "*Awarding Heinrich (real person) moral damages would reflect the harm he specifically suffered. Simply awarding compensation for unlawful expropriation would not be sufficient.*[32]"

Personnel are one of the imperative components of investments and the main source of profit-making. Investments require human power to carry out operations; however, as case law provides, granting awards in personnel's favor cannot be solely attributed to the protection of investments. It must also encompass a nuanced consideration of respecting human rights. States must not be condemned simply because their abusive conduct harms foreign investments. Personnel can be hurt through the 'bond of employment' as much as corporates or employers can be. Hence, the appraisal must be made by placing the basic human rights affected in such situations at the core. In addition, the conclusion of the tribunal in *Von Pezold v. Zimbabwe* was accurate; judges, holding the nationality of the disputing state and receiving rights, salaries, or privileges(immunities) therefrom, may be prone to bias and political pressure. Moreover, although the concept of independence requires a case-by-case analysis, independence cannot be exercised partially, and judges of the states might not deliver what we call a '*divine municipal justice*'. Finally, caution should be exercised in considering an investor's moral claims and in investigating whether the anxiety personnel suffered is work-related and has a substantial impact on the business.[33] Besides, given the scarcity of case law in which moral damage claims have not been disregarded, insurers might be empty-handed as they pursue investors' claims against the host state via subrogation.

In most instances, investors are corporations rather than real persons, and *Gultutar* notes that when moral damages are availed to corporate investors, host states will not have an open-ended liberty to abuse their legal obligations.[34] Theoretically, there is nothing preventing parties to PRI contract from designing a mechanism to secure investor's moral damage claims. Some may suggest that corporations, being legal entities, are incapable of personally experiencing moral harm.[35] As articulated in *Rubber Improvement* case, "*a company cannot be injured in its feelings, it can only be injured in its pockets, its reputation can be injured by a libel, but that injury must sound in money*[36]". In our view, rather than whether the investor is corporate or not, the key factors that might exclude coverage of non-material[37] losses in PRI contracts are the subjective nature of the loss and the discretionary characteristic of the calculating such losses. Otherwise, even losses

[32] See *Von Pezold v. Zimbabwe*, para. 912–920. Available at https://www.italaw.com/sites/default/files/case-documents/italaw7095_0.pdf accessed 05.09.2024

[33] Gultutar (2021), pp. 32–37.

[34] Gultutar (2021), pp. 23–26.

[35] Gultutar (2021), p. 29.

[36] See *Rubber Improvement* case, p. 262. Available at https://lexlaw.co.uk/wp-content/uploads/2020/05/Daily-Telegraph-1964-A.C.-234.pdf accessed 05.09.2024.

[37] Non-material damage is described as "*any damage which is not damage to a person's assets, wealth or income and which is therefore incapable of being quantified in any objective financial or economic manner by reference to a market.*" See Wittich (2004), p. 329.

incurred by individual investors would fall within the scope of PRI coverage. It is thus not surprising that this remedy is of lesser relevance to investors.

10.3 Restitution

Restitution[38] is recognized as the primary remedy in international law[39] and is the first ranked remedy under the ILC.[40] According to article 35 of the ILC articles, the host state is obliged to re-establish the situation which existed before the wrongful act was committed.[41] As one scholar has well encapsulated, in this remedy, the asset is valued as if it were placed back in the hands of the original investors.[42] The Illegality of expropriation may offer the investor the right to demand restitution of the property, rather than only damages in compensation.[43] In addition, in the case of political force majeure risk, if the investment incurs partial damage, the investor may opt to restore the asset to its pre-risk condition and request restitution in kind. Unless otherwise agreed upon by the parties, the cost of repairs should not exceed the value of the investment, and it is incumbent upon the insurer to repair the investment and get it on track. Restitution, while a primary remedy, can also present disadvantages. For instance, if it is material restitution, the investor may not be satisfied when the property or legal situation is restored. Due to economic fluctuations, the asset's value may have depreciated, or the investor may have lost income during the period they were without possession.[44] In the case of juridical restitution, restoration may be

[38] The Black's Law Dictionary defines restitution as "*return or restoration of some specific thing to its rightful owner or status.*"

[39] See Sabahi (2011), p. 61.

[40] See Reinisch (2008), p. 201.

[41] Full text of the article is as follows: "*State responsible for an internationally wrongful act is under an obligation to make restitution, that is, to re-establish the situation which existed before the wrongful act was committed, provided and to the extent that restitution: (a) is not materially impossible; (b) does not involve a burden out of all proportion to the benefit deriving from restitution instead of compensation.* In *Chorzow Factory* case, according to tribunal, "*a reparation must be as far as possible, wipe out all the consequences of the illegal act and reestablish the situation which would, in all probability, have existed if that act had not been committed*". In the same case the expropriating state had the obligation to pay the 'just price of what was expropriated' which is the value of the undertaking at the moment of dispossession, plus interest to the day of payment, See p. 48. Available at https://jusmundi.com/en/document/decision/en-factory-at-chorzow-merits-judgment-thursday-13th-september-1928 accessed 05.09.2024. For similar cases, see *ADC v. Hungary* and *Siemens v. Argentina.* See Salacuse (2016), p. 72, also see Saldarriaga and Kantor (2009), pp. 198–199. Appraising the value of the investment is subjective; the specific benefit of the property to the owner, or expenses related to legal costs in claiming damages from the host state, may be included in the calculation of the damage. For 'subjective-concrete valuation', Marboe (2017), pp. 88–92, 136.

[42] Cohen et al. (2019), p. 577.

[43] Rubins and Kinsella (2005), p. 8.

[44] See Sabahi (2011), p. 65.

either burdensome, detrimental to the public interest, or materially impossible, especially in irreversible situations such as irremediable deterioration.

10.4 Compensation

10.4.1 In General

Compensation is a pecuniary remedy commonly sought and awarded in investor-state arbitration cases to repair the loss sustained.[45] Compensation refers to a payment of damages,[46] or any other act that a court orders to be done by a person who has caused injury to another, which is supposed to make the injured person whole. This form of remedy is addressed under article 36 of the ILC.[47] The one injured by the act of the sovereign has the right, in consequence thereof, to be fully compensated. Although restitution in kind might fit the expectations of the ideal world, returning the investor what was taken from him/her can be insufficient to cover the actual loss or, might be impossible. In PRI practice, however, compensation in its nature is not payment of the wrongdoer's 'debts', the insurer does not act on behalf of or in favor of the wrongdoer. By contrast, compensation is an obligation designated under the insurance contract; the insurer is relieved from its contractual onus for the amount it pays to the insured. Finally, compensation is the prerequisite for the exercise of the rights of subrogation.[48]

Wittich argues that compensation covers also non-monetary damage suffered by individuals as being financially assessable. He bases his opinion on the commentary to article 36[49] since the only type of non-material damage discussed therein is that

[45] See Sabahi (2011), p. 92.

[46] See the Black's Law Dictionary. In the same dictionary, "damage" is defined as; "*Money claimed by, or ordered to be paid to, a person as compensation for loss or injury*". Although, compensation and damages are used interchangeably, in some jurisdictions, there is a distinction. For detail, see Marboe (2017), pp. 12–20.

[47] The article is as follows "*1. The State responsible for an internationally wrongful act is under an obligation to compensate for the damage caused thereby, insofar as such damage is not made good by restitution. 2. The compensation shall cover any financially assessable damage including loss of profits insofar as it is established.*"

[48] Eggers (2016), p. 246.

[49] Art. 4 of the Commentary to the art. 36 of ILC provides as follows; "*As compared with satisfaction, the function of compensation is to address the actual losses incurred as a result of the internationally wrongful act. In other words, the function of article 36 is purely compensatory, as its title indicates. Compensation corresponds to the financially assessable damage suffered by the injured State or its nationals. It is not concerned to punish the responsible State, nor does compensation have an expressive or exemplary character. Thus, compensation generally consists of a monetary payment, though it may sometimes take the form, as agreed, of other forms of value. It is true that monetary payments may be called for by way of satisfaction under article 37, but they perform a function distinct from that of compensation. Monetary compensation is intended to offset,*

done to individuals.[50] The rationale behind compensation within the context of investment law is to re-establish the investor's financial situation to what it would have been if the expropriation had not been committed.[51] Hence, the damage, which is the difference between the hypothetical and the actual financial situation must be compensated in its entirety.[52] Although its validity[53] and enforceability[54] may well be disputed, parties to an investment contract may agree on clauses concerning damages, interest rates, and local remedies in their contracts.[55]

10.4.2 Valuation of Investment

The crux of the expropriation lies in the valuation of the investment. It should come as no surprise that the insurer will have less difficulty in calculating the damage if the insured asset suffers just physical harm. In terms of risks giving rise to deprivation of ownership however, along with the investment's actual value, it is imperative to appraise the loss of future benefits. In such cases, valuation is not as easy as fixing the visible, concrete loss or calculating the replacement cost(value).[56] On the contrary, the projection will rely on various parameters including but not limited to the scope, nature and foreseeability of the investment. For instance, in the case of expropriation of a project spanning ten years with a concession agreement, it will be

---

as far as may be, the damage suffered by the injured State as a result of the breach. Satisfaction is concerned with non-material injury, specifically non-material injury to the State, on which a monetary value can be put only in a highly approximate and notional way." Please visit: https://legal.un.org/ilc/texts/instruments/english/commentaries/9_6_2001.pdf accessed 05.09.2024.

[50] Wittich (2004), p. 360.

[51] This reminds of the negative damage concept in Turkish law. Turkish law specifies two kinds of damages: "positive damage," which is the harm the injured party would not have suffered had the contract been performed, and "negative damage," which arises from reliance on the contract and reflects the difference in assets if the aggrieved party had not entered into the contract. Also see Marboe (2017), pp. 110–111.

[52] Marboe (2017), p. 88.

[53] For instance, in *National Oil Corporation* case, the tribunal noted that, under Libyan law, liquidated damages provisions are valid: however, "damages fixed in advance by such [liquidated damages] clauses are not due 'if the debtor establishes that the creditor has not suffered any loss'[]" whatsoever. (Id. at 31 [discussing Articles 226 and 227 of the Libyan Civil Code].) The tribunal concluded that "the debtor," Sun Oil, failed to establish that NOC had not suffered a loss. Available at https://law.justia.com/cases/federal/district-courts/FSupp/733/800/1517002/ accessed 05.09.2024.

[54] Enforcement of the award may be refused if it is found to be contrary to public policy of the country. See art. V of The New York Arbitration Convention on the Recognition and Enforcement of Foreign Arbitral Awards, New York, 10 June 1958.

[55] Rubins and Kinsella (2005), pp. 59–62.

[56] The amount needed to acquire an asset of the same type as that which was expropriated. See Salacuse (2016), p. 433. The monetary equivalent of replacing an asset or an investment with another asset or investment having the same features. Stan (2015), p. 55.

'*more art than science*[57]' to presume the hypothetical financial situation. Particular and subsequent (post-act) events[58] may have influence on the valuation or have a detrimental effect on the profits. The asset may have undergone depreciation by reason of obsolescence or, by contrast, may have gained potential and an increase in value.[59] Future profit, on the other hand, is uncertain,[60] speculative, or may become contingent, and the value that the investment would create may be lower than in previous years.

Some may argue to calculate the highest value that the investment would have acquired.[61] According to this insured/investment-friendly approach, the insured would have sold the asset when its price was at its peak if the expropriation had not taken place. Besides, today's money is worth more than money in the future since today's money can always be invested.[62] Hence, apart from facts like inflation, even if income stream remains flat over time, its purchasing power lessens each succeeding year. And finally, host states may select a specific investor on the basis of its needs and the competences of the investor. To the extent that the investment is specific, calculating the loss of future income becomes an impractical hypothesis since finding an alternative investor in the market with a similar or identical capacity to operate the business is less likely.

Although international organizations have developed widely accepted loss or value calculation standards,[63] the value of an asset is subjective; it addresses the questions of 'value to whom' and 'under what circumstances'. Some authors believe that there are two fundamental premises of value; *Value in exchange* is "the value of

---

[57]In *Azurix v. Argentina* (para. 298/h) the claimant argued that "*determining damages is not an exact science, and a certain amount of independent judgement is required*". Similarly, see *ADC v. Hungary* para. 521 and Salacuse (2016), p. 432.

[58]For instance, in *ADC v. Hungary*, the airport traffic increased in time, and that led to the appreciation of the value.

[59]See Marboe (2017), pp. 137–138.

[60]In *Delagoa Bay Railway Arbitration*, after unlawfully termination of railway concession, the tribunal calculated the lost profits on Marboe (2017), p. 151.

[61]For a similar case, see *Unglaube v Costa Rica* para. 307. Available at https://www.italaw.com/sites/default/files/case-documents/ita1052.pdf accessed 05.09.2024.

[62]Marboe (2017), pp. 104–105.

[63]The International Valuations Standards Council publishes 'International Valuation Standards' (IVS) the latest edition has been effective since 31st of January 2020. See https://www.rics.org/globalassets/rics-website/media/upholding-professional-standards/sector-standards/valuation/international-valuation-standards-rics2.pdf accessed 05.09.2024. Another international regulation was created by the United Nations Compensation Commission (was created in 1991 as a subsidiary organ of the United Nations Security Council) According to art. 16 of "The Resolution 687 (1991)" Iraq was liable under international law for any direct loss, damage, including environmental damage and the depletion of natural resources, or injury to foreign Governments, nationals and corporations, as a result of Iraq's unlawful invasion and occupation of Kuwait. The UN Governing Council's 9th decision on "Propositions and Conclusion on Compensation for Business Losses: Types of Damages and Their Valuation" was to apply to compensation for the loss of earnings or profits and other Business losses covered by Security Council Resolution 687 (1991). For detail, visit: https://www.un.org/depts/unmovic/documents/687.pdf accessed 05.09.2024.

the business or business interest changing hands, in a real or a hypothetical sale" and *Value to the holder* is "the value of a property that is not being sold but, instead, is being maintained in its present form by its present owner.[64]" The price that the investor would have obtained in the open market,[65] therefore, *value in exchange* is more linked with PRI.

10.4.2.1 Standards of Compensation

The standards of compensation may be based on book value,[66] replacement value, market value[67] (sunk investment costs[68]) investment value/worth,[69] synergetic

---

[64] Marboe (2017), pp. 174–175.

[65] Also see Marzal (2021), p. 271.

[66] The book value of assets is the value of a particular asset as recorded in the financial statements, the book value of an enterprise is equal to the overall value of assets comprising such enterprise, less the total value of liabilities. See Stan (2015). Book value is not a forward-looking method, by contrast it is a backward-valuation method, appreciation is made according to the balance sheet of the investment and does not reflect future income or entrepreneurial skills. Also book value, as the case may be, can be higher than fair market value, in particular, if a depreciation in the market takes place. Sabahi (2011), p. 61; Saldarriaga and Kantor (2009), p. 208; Salacuse (2016), p. 433; Newcombe and Paradell (2009), p. 390, see Marzal (2021), p. 274 and finally, see Stauffer (1996), p. 461.

[67] According to IVS, "market value" is '*the estimated amount for which an asset or liability should exchange on the valuation date between a willing buyer and a willing seller in an arm's length transaction, after proper marketing and where the parties had each acted knowledgeably, prudently and without compulsion.*" Under the same document "estimated amount" was defined as "*a price expressed in terms of money payable for the asset in an arm's length market transaction. Market Value is the most probable price reasonably obtainable in the market on the valuation date in keeping with the market value definition. It is the best price reasonably obtainable by the seller and the most advantageous price reasonably obtainable by the buyer. This estimate specifically excludes an estimated price inflated or deflated by special terms or circumstances such as atypical financing, sale and leaseback arrangements, special considerations or concessions granted by anyone associated with the sale, or any element of value available only to a specific owner or purchaser.*" In *Starrett Housing v. Iran, (Final Award, para. 277)* the market value was defined as follows: "*the price that a willing buyer would pay to a willing seller in circumstances in which each had good information, each desired to maximize his financial gain, and neither was under duress or threat.*" The case is available at https://jusmundi.com/en/document/decision/en-starrett-housing-corporation-starrett-systems-inc-and-others-v-the-government-of-the-islamic-republic-of-iran-bank-markazi-iran-and-others-final-award-award-no-314-24-1-friday-14th-august-1987 accessed 05.09.2024. See Sprankling (2014), p. 267, also see Merrill (2002), p. 116.

[68] Although it is sometimes mistakenly used as a variant of the book value method, it is the calculation of the amount of capital invested in a project, plus a rate of return from the date of investment to the award date. Saldarriaga and Kantor (2009), p. 209 and, see Marboe (2017), pp. 283–284.

[69] IVS defines Investment Value as "*the value of an asset to a particular owner or prospective owner for individual investment or operational objectives. Investment Value is an entity-specific basis of value. Although the value of an asset to the owner may be the same as the amount that could be realised from its sale to another party, this basis of value reflects the benefits received by an*

value,[70] fair value[71] observed market value[72] and fair market value.[73] Not all underwriters or lawyers have the experience or background the valuation techniques require; accordingly discussing the formulations through the lens of an accountant could be of much help for the readers. In order not to endure the readers and to leave the formulation to experts, we suffice with only providing the basis of these methods.

The fair market value concept is the most prominent valuation method. Tribunals in investor-state disputes consider it as the only valid basis for valuation, and regardless of whether an actual market exists for the investment, generic references to valuation are meant to imply fair market value of the asset.[74] Internationally recognized definition of the fair market value reads as follows: "*The price, expressed in terms of cash equivalents, at which property would change hands between a hypothetical willing and able buyer*[75] *and a hypothetical willing and able seller,*[76]

---

entity from holding the asset and, therefore, does not involve a presumed exchange." Investment value is a subjective, concrete concept; therefore, an investor may, for any reason, pay more than the market would reasonably expect. Also, see Marboe (2017), pp. 181–182.

[70] IVS provides the following definition "Synergistic Value is the result of a combination of two or more assets or interests where the combined value is more than the sum of the separate values. If the synergies are only available to one specific buyer, then Synergistic Value will differ from Market Value, as the Synergistic Value will reflect particular attributes of an asset that are only of value to a specific purchaser."

[71] IVS 2007 edition avoided to put the adjective 'fair' in front of 'market value' as this would bear the risk of confusion with 'fair value'. However, 2020 edition separately defines "fair value" "market value" and "fair market value". IVS 2020 edition, by referring to International Financial Reporting Standard define fair value as "the *price that would be received to sell an asset or paid to transfer a liability in an orderly transaction between market participants at the measurement date*". Also see Marboe (2017), p. 180.

[72] Observed market value denotes the price of a transaction where the asset is bought and sold, and it depends on the market's expectations of the future cash flows that the asset will generate. For the definition and formulation of the observed market value, See Dorobantu et al. (2016), pp. 222–224.

[73] Majority of BITs require Fair Market Value (FMV) to calculate damages. See Saldarriaga and Kantor (2009), p. 203. Section 4, article 2.3 of OECD Draft for a Multilateral Agreement on Investment, codifies "fair market value" in case of expropriation please see https://investmentpolicy.unctad.org/international-investment-agreements/treaty-files/2813/download accessed 05.09.2024. For the awards encompassing fair market value, See Marboe (2017), pp. 96–101.

[74] Marzal (2021), pp. 271, 272.

[75] According to IVS a 'willing buyer' refers to one who is motivated, but not compelled to buy. This buyer is neither over-eager nor determined to buy at any price. This buyer is also the one who purchases in accordance with the realities of the current market and with current market expectations, rather than in relation to an imaginary or hypothetical market that cannot be demonstrated or anticipated to exist. The assumed buyer would not pay a higher price than the market requires. The present owner is included among those who constitute "the market".

[76] According to IVS a 'willing seller' is neither an over-eager nor a forced seller prepared to sell at any price, nor one prepared to hold out for a price not considered reasonable in the current market. The willing seller is motivated to sell the asset at market terms for the best price attainable in the open market after proper marketing, whatever that price may be. The factual circumstances of the actual owner are not a part of this consideration because the willing seller is a hypothetical owner."

acting at arm's length in an open and unrestricted market, when neither is under compulsion to buy or sell and when both have reasonable knowledge of the relevant facts.[77]" In calculating the fair market value, 'the highest and best use' principle[78] is applied. As stated elsewhere, the investment's most optimal use is being appraised.[79]

After selecting the basis for valuation, a valuation approach and valuation method should be chosen. The Governing Council of the UN United Nations Compensation Commission highlights two valuation concepts for income-producing properties.[80] The *market approach* provides an indication of value by comparing the asset with identical or comparable (that is, similar) assets for which price information is available.[81] One of the critiques this approach receives pertains to the valuation of small businesses; due to their scarcity, finding a comparator with the same products, same size, same financial condition, and same capital structure can be like finding a 'needle in a haystack'.[82] The *cost approach* provides an indication of value using the economic principle that a buyer will pay no more for an asset than the cost to obtain an asset of equal utility, whether by purchase or by construction, unless undue time, inconvenience, risk or other factors are involved. The approach provides an indication of value by calculating the current replacement or reproduction cost of an asset and making deductions for physical deterioration and all other relevant forms of obsolescence.[83] Finally, the *income approach*, as the name suggests, is the technique to assess the income that investment would create over its life.

[77]An investment can be valued from the perspective of the expropriated owner, host state and independent third person and the perspective of third person refers to "value which is given to the object by the market". See Marboe (2017), p. 27.

[78]For detail see IVS paras. 140.1–140.5.

[79]Dukes (2006), p. 1.

[80]Decision taken by the Governing Council of the United Nations Compensation Commission during the resumed Fourth Session, at the 23rd meeting, held on 6th March 1992. Please visit: https://www.trans-lex.org/800800/_/decision-taken-by-the-governing-council-of-the-united-nations-compensation-commission-s-ac26-1992-9-06-march-1992/ also visit https://digitallibrary.un.org/record/141403?v=pdf#files accessed 05.09.2024.

[81]In the IVS' interpretation "the market approach provides an indication of value by comparing the asset with identical or comparable (that is similar) assets for which price information is available". The characteristics of the investment would be decisive in finding a comparable asset. To avoid such an obstacle, stock price, prior transactions, offerings (although offerings not materialized have less evidentiary weight, however maybe taken into account), partial (when a part of the company is sold) or comparable sales (when a similar company in the market is sold) and finally multiples can be considered. For detail, see Marboe (2017), pp. 188–189, 255–233. For the case law see Stan (2015), pp. 76 et seq.

[82]Dukes (2006), p. 2.

[83]See IVS para. 60.1. The advantage of this methodology is it looks into the past and reduce speculations of future gains. See Marboe (2017), pp. 202–203.

10.4.2.2 Discounted Cash Flow (DCF)

Liquidation,[84] going concern,[85] and discounted cash flow (DCF)[86] are the prominent methodologies used in appraising the value of the investment. Scholars state that 'net book value' and 'going concern value[87]' are the two concepts to ascertain the fair market value of the asset in question. The distinction is that the former is a backward-looking approach where accumulated depreciation, liabilities, depletion and amortization are subtracted from the asset's historical cost (the cost incurred over the course of the asset's useful life), whereas the latter is forward-looking and relies upon an assumption that the business could continue to operate; hence, calculation is based on the future earnings.[88]

DCF is the predominant valuation technique employed by investment bankers;[89] however, it has not gained formal recognition among arbitrators.[90] It serves as an alternative to market-based valuation techniques, which can be distorted, for instance by market aberrations,[91] and is standard practice in the business and financial spheres.[92] DCF is conversion of the investment's anticipated future stream of net cash flows over a specific future period of time[93] to the value of those cash flows as of the valuation date. It relies on determining the present value of future cash flows generated by the investment (revenues minus expenses with certain

---

[84] The price at which assets comprising the investment is sold less liabilities of the investment. Stan (2015), p. 62.

[85] A going concern and liquidation are the fundamental basis on which an investment(companies) may be valued. In going concern, the investment's cash generation capability is used as an indicator, on the contrary, in liquidation, the investment's value is estimated as if it is sold to the highest bidder. See Dukes (2006), pp. 1–3. Saldarriaga and Kantor (2009), p. 207, Salacuse (2016), p. 433 and also see Marboe (2017), pp. 192, 207.

[86] According to the World Bank Guidelines, the conduct of value determination will be deemed reasonable if (i) discounted cash flow value is applied for a going concern with a proven record of profitability (ii) liquidation value is applied for an enterprise which is not a proven going concern and demonstrates lack of profitability. and (iii) for other assets, on the basis of (a) the replacement value or (b) the book value in case such value has been recently assessed or has been determined as of the date of the taking and can therefore be deemed to represent a reasonable replacement value see the World Bank Guidelines on the Treatment of Foreign Direct Investment, Art. IV (Expropriation and Unilateral Alterations or Termination of Contracts), clause IV.

[87] Entities with little to no track record are not going concerns, see Simmons (2012), p. 231.

[88] Same scholars suggest that several mechanics can serve as alternatives to fair market value. Payment can be fixed based on the benefits received by the taker from acquiring the asset or the loss sustained by the owner. See Merrill (2002), pp. 113, 114, 119.

[89] Kantor (2008), p. 132; Pearl and Rosenbaum (2013), p. 13; Simmons (2012), p. 225.

[90] Stan (2015), p. 129.

[91] Pearl and Rosenbaum (2013), p. 135.

[92] Simmons (2012), p. 224.

[93] Which is in general 5 years, See Kantor (2008), p. 182; Sabahi (2011), fn 205; Pearl and Rosenbaum (2013), p. 137. In *CME v. Czech Republic*, the forecast period was of 10 (ten) years. Also, as an example case of law DCF calculation. Available at https://www.italaw.com/sites/default/files/case-documents/ita0180.pdf accessed 05.09.2024.

adjustments and after paying taxes[94]), and a rate[95] (which takes account of the cost of capital and risk) is used[96] to discount the investment's projected cash flow. In other words, to find the present value of the cash flows, the projected cash flows are discounted back to the present value by applying a discount rate.[97] In determining the discount rate,[98] one of the 'build-up[99]' or WACC[100] (Weighted Average Cost of Capital) procedures are applied.[101] Bankers also employ a formula known as

[94] Pearl and Rosenbaum (2013), p. 137.

[95] Discount rate is the rate of return used to convert a future monetary sum into present value. Kantor (2008), p. 141.

[96] Sabahi (2011), pp. 119–120; Salacuse (2016), p. 43. For an illustration of a project generating cash flow over a period of 6 years, see Stauffer (1996), pp. 464–468.

[97] Kantor (2008), p. 140 and Stan (2015), p. 127.

[98] In assessing the country risk premium, some tribunals have considered the sovereign bond yield of the host state. See Domínguez (2016), p. 109. In investor-state disputes, while the claimant investors propose lower discount rates, the respondent sates often propose higher rates to lower the valuation amount. Tribunals are not bound by either of these proposals, by contrast, they on some occasions, find these proposals "*an air of unreality*," and make their own allocations. Also see Saldarriaga and Kantor (2009), p. 237.

[99] In debt investment, the 'base rate' (the base rate includes the cost of the debt plus the incremental cost of partially employing equity funds) and the 'risk-free rate' (which is for USD cash flow forecasts, the risk-free component of a discount rate is generally a comparable US Treasury debt security of a similar tenor so that inflation factor is added) are used in calculation. Smaller companies tend to assume higher risks than large companies do. Equity investment is riskier than the debt investment, due to volatility of equity market. An 'equity risk premium', a rate of return is added to the risk-free rate to reflect the additional risk of equity instruments over risk-free instruments. Additionally, a 'business size premium' is used. In some cases, specific incidents, for instance, a strike by a union at a factory, may require an additional risk premium. Tribunals may be skeptical of measuring such specific or subjective risk components, as these may be used to reduce estimated cash flow when other valuation inputs fail doing tricks. Finally, if a USD-based discount rate is employed to value a business not based in the U.S., the risk-free component of the discount should be adjusted in accordance with so-called sovereign risk, and a country risk premium should be applied in computing the rate due to volatility in that country. Kantor (2008), pp. 146, 148–159, Hooke (2014), pp. 120–121, Stan (2015), p. 102, and also see Marboe (2017), pp. 196–197.

[100] Some scholars define WACC as "*average cost of each dollar of financing, no matter its source, that the firm uses to purchase assets*". For the quoted definition, see Stan (2015), p. 162, WACC is also defined as the market-based method, which calculates the rate for this particular asset from market rates for assets of similar risk and also defined as the rate used to discount the investment's projected cash flow and terminal value to the present, see respectively; Sabahi (2011), p. 121; Pearl and Rosenbaum (2013), p. 137. *Kantor* states that WACC considers that the proper discount rate should approximate the balance between risks and benefits that arm's-length third party investors and lenders would reach if they made new equity investments and new loans to the company at the valuation date. For the formulation of WACC, see Kantor (2008), p. 161 and Pearl and Rosenbaum (2013), p. 151. Also see Newcombe and Paradell (2009), p. 392.

[101] Hooke (2014), p. 119.

CAPM[102] (Capital Asset Pricing Model) to calculate the expected return on a company's equity.[103]

DCF comprises several steps. The first step is to estimate an explicit forecast[104] of the net cash flow[105] of the asset. The second step is to calculate the present value of those cash flows, taking into account the time value of money and the risks faced by

---

[102] This model is a substitute for the 'subjective risks' component of the build-up procedure and seeks to isolate the risks attributable to a particular business activity. Kantor (2008), p. 164 also see Marboe (2017), pp. 198–199.

[103] The equation of CAPM is as follows: E(ri) = rf + B[E(Rm-rf)] in this formulation E(ri) represents expected or required return for firm or asset, Rf equals to the risk-free rate of interest, Bi stands for the beta for the firm or asset i. and E(rm) is the expected return on the market. See Dukes (2006), p. 4, also, see Pearl and Rosenbaum (2013), p. 154.

[104] Investments, projects with a limited lifespan, relying on a concession, license or a special purpose vehicle having a limited duration, or a right deriving from BOOT(Build-operate-own-transfer) and to be reverted free of cost to the host government at the end of operation period, do not seem to justify a terminal value. In investments or projects with potential for renewal or extension, where fulfilling certain future conditions might be speculative and not easily anticipated, such additional duration should not be taken into consideration in the appraisal. In *CMS v. Argentina* (paras. 196–199) the tribunal came to the following conclusion: "*The parties have also disputed another aspect relevant for the determination of rights and obligations under the contract: the duration of the License. In the Claimant's view, TGN is entitled to an extension of the license beyond the initial period of 35 years ending in 2027. This extension would, under the terms of the License, be for an additional ten years, ending in 2037. The Respondent believes, to the contrary, that the License does not entail a right of automatic renewal and is subject to performance requirements that have not been met by the Claimant, as well as to other conditions set forth in Clause 3.2 of the License. The Tribunal notes that the License provides for the right to an additional ten-year extension, but this right is subject to compliance with performance requirements, and has to be requested by the licensee and approved by the Government. A discussion about performance requirements is unnecessary for the Tribunal to reach a conclusion on this aspect of the dispute. Indeed, the License is very clear about the fact that this right is conditional and subject to a number of steps, both substantive and procedural, which might or might not take place. As it would be impossible to establish at present whether these conditions might be met, the Tribunal is persuaded by the Respondent argument to the effect that no damages should be considered beyond the year 2027. This will therefore be the year which the Tribunal will rely on for its determination of damages.*" Note: In addition to renewal or extension, some investor-state agreements aim to mitigate currency risk by including adjustment clauses that allow for contractual terms to be modified in response to recent economic developments. Such adjustments may also be made through renegotiations. In calculating the cash flow of future incomes, these provisions are taken into consideration. The case mentioned above is an example of such adjustments. Kantor (2008), p. 189, Sabahi (2011), pp. 119–120, see Stan (2015), pp. 132, 145–149 and for renegotiation clauses see Chap. 7.

[105] Kantor (2008), p. 132, Sabahi (2011), p. 121 and Stan (2015), p. 131. The past operations or historical performance of the investment may provide useful insight about the possible benefits it might have generated had it continued its existence. Pearl and Rosenbaum (2013), pp. 141–142; Stan (2015), pp. 136–137. In *National Grid v. Argentina* (para. 276), the tribunal held that "*The DCF method, while not without its drawbacks, has the advantage of realistically assessing the economic value of a going concern by relying on the stream of value that it can generate over its operative life. In order to function properly, the DCF approach requires that the concern in question must have a history of profitable operation.*" Available at https://www.italaw.com/sites/default/files/case-documents/ita0555.pdf accessed 05.09.2024.

the investment. The third step is to estimate the ending/terminal value for the asset[106] (if appropriate) which is used to quantify the remaining value of the investment after the projection period.[107] Calculating the future income for an unlimited period is impossible; therefore, DCF valuation must be limited to a specific period. In addition, investments may experience rapid growth and slowdowns, requiring the calculation of projected cashflows for each term differently.[108]

Finally, country risk can be incorporated into the assessment of damages through the adjustment of the cash flows or through the discount rate.[109] Country risk reflects the difference in running similar businesses in different countries. If the potential investor wants to set a price for an investment or expects a high profit in return for the high-risk exposure associated with investing in a particular country, it ought to consider the nature of the investment, the circumstances under which the investment will operate, its specific characteristics, including the period in which it has been in existence, the proportion of tangible assets in the total investment, and other relevant factors pertinent to the specific circumstances of each case,[110] and so must the assumed 'willing buyers'.

Of the circumstances, the probability of political risks is significant; political risks must be included for the purposes of valuation. The probability of expropriation in the host state can be crucial in determining the discount. One may argue that the state might intentionally depress the value of investment through the threat of a political risk and benefit from lower-expected compensation.[111] However, states' intentional adverse impact on the value is borne in mind in the assessment of damages by tribunals.[112] In *Lemire v. Ukraine*, the tribunal stressed the application of difference country risks to companies located in different companies. Tribunal held that "*same company, situated in the US or in Ukraine, is subject to different political and regulatory risks; to reflect this difference, ceteris paribus the discount rate in Ukraine must be higher (and the valuations lower) than in the US.*[113]"

---

[106] Terminal value represents 'the amount the business would be worth if it was sold at market value at end of the specific projection period, discounted back to a present value as of the valuation date'. Apart from Gordon Growth model, EBIT (Earnings before interest and taxes) and EBITDA (Earnings before interest, taxes, and depreciation) are alternative procedures to estimate terminal value. For detailed explanation, see Kantor (2008), pp. 182, 187–188; Pearl and Rosenbaum (2013), p. 143.

[107] Pearl and Rosenbaum (2013), p. 137 and Stan (2015), p. 127.

[108] Stan (2015), pp. 171, 172.

[109] Burgstaller and Ketcheson (2017), p. 197.

[110] In fact, this is the definition of 'market value' brought by the World Bank in World Bank Guidelines on Treatment of Foreign Direct Investment and employed by several tribunals.

[111] Burgstaller and Ketcheson (2017), pp. 194, 205.

[112] See Dorobantu et al. (2016), p. 113.

[113] See paras. 230 and 280. Available at https://www.italaw.com/sites/default/files/case-documents/ita0454.pdf accessed 06.09.2024. For the analysis of the case, see Faccio (2014). Scholars state that the United States or Germany is used in comparisons as a risk-free country. Domínguez (2016), p. 98 also see Dorobantu et al. (2016), pp. 220, 229.

Although the DCF serves as a cornerstone for valuation techniques, the elements involved in DCF calculation can be of speculative nature,[114] particularly when dealing with commodities traded in volatile markets. The price purportedly offered by a non-existing buyer, or the forecasts from an untested market and uncertain future,[115] may not effectively surrogate for an actual market. Moreover, the calculation is premised on many parameters such as future supply and demand, economic conditions, and estimates of minerals, which are almost impossible to predict with reasonable accuracy. Misapplication of the DCF may cause what scholars call a 'Cinderella effect' (overvaluation of the asset) which took part in the US-Iran claims.[116] The conundrum lies in the fact that any projection about the future is inherently 'speculative'. On the other hand, laws provide a room for adjudicators to determine the quantum of the damage. By way of illustration, the article 7.4.3 (3) of the International Institute for the Unification of Private Law (UNIDROIT) Principles of International Commercial Contracts goes beyond mere innuendo, stating "*Where the amount of damages cannot be established with a sufficient degree of certainty, the assessment is at the discretion of the court.*" Therefore, however valuation adjudicators decide will be unsatisfactory for one party.

The formulation of the DCF[117] can be crucial, tribunals are expected to provide a basis upon which they build the appreciation. In the *MINE* case, Guinea (the

---

[114] Some adjudicators oppose to DCF method, in their view, projection of future profit is speculative to award. See Marzal (2021), pp. 274, 275, 278. For arbitral awards where tribunals were cautious in applying DFC, see Simmons (2012), pp. 222, 227, 228 and 229. Also see *Siemens v. Argentina* (para. 355).

[115] In *Tecmed v. Mexico,* (para. 186) such valuation was disregarded on this basis, tribunal held that "*The non-relevance of the brief history of operation of the Landfill by Cytrar —a little more than two years— and the difficulties in obtaining objective data allowing for application of the discounted cash flow method on the basis of estimates for a protracted future, not less than 15 years, together with the fact that such future cash flow also depends upon investments to be made — building of seven additional cells— in the long term, lead the Arbitral Tribunal to disregard such methodology to determine the relief to be awarded to the Claimant*".

[116] See Stauffer (1996), pp. 472–473, 478, 481–482 and Soderlund et al. (2005), pp. 23, 27, 28. In case of concession agreements, the legitimacy of the investor's expectation that the agreement could be subject to renewal or extension may justify claims for loss of future profits. The admissibility of the claim will be based on the legislation, contract or statement through which the host state provides a specific promise. To put it otherwise, in the lack of the state's commitment in such a manner, the realization of future profits will be in its discretionary hands. See Marzal (2021), pp. 303, 306 and Simmons (2012), pp. 222, 227, 228. Scholars also propose the concept of 'Legitimate Expectations Valuation' (LEV) which is based on the normal profit investment would generate. 'Normal profit' denotes the amount an investor must receive in order to stay in business, is grounded on the idea that total revenues of a company are equal to the total costs in a perfectly competitive market. *Kantor* criticizes this approach due to its fundamental shortcoming, in the author's view, in a petroleum concession if the field is a 'dry hole' and cannot generate cash flow, the strict application of LEV will lead the investor to receive a compensation excessing the market value of the investment. See Kantor (2009), pp. 155–162.

[117] The formulation is as follows; $NPV = \sum_{t=0}^{n} \frac{FCF_t}{(1+k)^t} + \frac{FCF_n*(1+g)}{(k-g)} / (1+k)^{n+1}$ NPV stands for net present value (the DCF value), FCF refers to the free cash flow of the period in question, k is the chosen discount rate, g is the estimated long-term growth rate, t is a discrete time period, and n is the

respondent state) challenged the award upon the tribunal's failure to state the mathematics of the calculation. Guinea claimed that the tribunal did not address every question submitted to it as required by Article 48(3) of the Convention.[118] The committee annulled the portion of the award related to damages on the grounds that the tribunal, while finding the theories "Y" and "Z" submitted to itself "unusable because of their speculative character", did not without explanation and contradicting itself, adopt, one of its own (a "damages theory") which was contrary to the reality of the situation. In the committees' view. "*The requirement to state reasons is satisfied as long as the award enables one to follow how the tribunal proceeded from Point A. to Point B. and eventually to its conclusion, even if it made an error of fact or of law.*[119]" However, whether deliberate or not, the tribunal's omission of the calculation was not a sufficient reason to annul the award for another committee. The annulment committee was satisfied with the reasoning, albeit without a calculation, of the tribunal in *Rumeli Telekom* provided in its decision.[120]

It's worth noting that the amount or rate of interest, when added to the principal, should not go unnoticed, especially when considering the values of investments and the risks that PRI providers carry. The UN United Nations Compensation Commission Governing Council decided that "*interest will be awarded from the date the loss occurred until the date of payment, at a rate sufficient to compensate successful claimants for the loss of use of the principal amount of the awards*".[121] Article

projection period. Due to the complexities in forecasting future cash flows, DCF values are usually not calculated through direct application of this formula. Instead, the net cash flow of each period is discounted individually and summed to reach a net present value. See Sabahi (2011), fn 197. See Waters (2015), p. 374 and for cash flow equations see Hu (1979), pp. 68–74. Simplified formulation can be read as $V = \frac{C_1}{(1+k)} + \frac{C_2}{(1+k)^2} + \ldots + \frac{C}{(1+k)}$ V stands for the value of the investment; C represents the net amount of the cash flow; and k is the rate of return. See Soderlund et al. (2005), p. 24.

[118] Article 48(3) of the ICSID Rules is as follows "*The award shall deal with every question submitted to the Tribunal and shall state the reasons upon which it is based.*" Failure to state the reasons is a ground to request annulment of the award under article 52 (1(e).

[119] See paras. 2.04, 5.09, 6.105, and 6.107 available at https://www.italaw.com/sites/default/files/case-documents/italaw8608.pdf accessed 05.09.2024.

[120] The annulment committee held the following decision "*The figure of US$125 million is baldly stated in the Award, without an explanation of a mathematical calculation undertaken by the Tribunal in arriving at it. The Committee well understands the grounds for the Applicant on Annulment's objection in this regard. It is highly desirable that tribunals should minimise to the greatest extent possible the element of estimation in their quantification of damages and maximise the specifics of the ratiocination explaining how the ultimate figure was arrived at. But, nevertheless, the Committee does not consider that the award of damages is one which it ought to annul, since the Tribunal did not fail to give reasons for its award of damages. On the contrary, the Tribunal examined the position as to damages with considerable care and set out the reasons for its award in terms appropriate to the circumstances of the case and the evidence available to it.*" See para. 178 of the decision of the ad hoc committee, available at https://www.italaw.com/sites/default/files/case-documents/ita0729.pdf accessed 06.09.2024. Also see Simmons (2012), pp. 215–217.

[121] Please visit: https://digitallibrary.un.org/record/505297/files/S_AC.26_2003_18-EN.pdf accessed 06.09.2024.

38(1) and (2) of the ILC's article, further detail the interest which read as follows "*The interest rate and mode of calculation shall be set so as to achieve that result. Interest runs from the date when the principal sum should have been paid until the date the obligation to pay is fulfilled.*" The interest rate and the date interest begins to accrue can be significant, if the loss is less than the cap imposed by the PRI provider. While some insurers may set a maximum duration for the charge of the interest, such as 120 or 180 days, others may take a more insured-friendly approach and accrue an interest beginning from the filing of claim until indemnification. Finally, in PRI, interest rate can be contractual and flat, investments tribunal whereas, may opt to award compound interest (interest on interest).[122]

Cases

ADC v. Hungary: ADC Affiliate Limited - and - ADC & ADMC Management Limited v. The Republic of Hungary, (ICSID Case No. ARB/03/16), Award

Azurix v. Argentina: Azurix Corp. v. The Argentine Republic, (ICSID Case No. ARB/01/12), Decision on the Application for Annulment of the Argentine Republic

Cementownia v. Turkey: Cementownia 'Nowa Huta' SA v. The Republic of Turkey, (ICSID Case No. ARB(AF)/06/2), Award

Chorzow Factory: The Government of Germany v. The Government of the Polish Republic, (Permanent Court of International Justice, Series A. No 17), Judgment

CME v. Czech Republic: CME v. The Czech Republic v. CME v. The Czech Republic, (UNCITRAL Arbitration), Final award

Delagoa Bay Railway Arbitration...

....

Desert Line v. Yemen: Desert Line Projects LLC v. The Republic of Yemen, (lCSID Case No. ARB/OS/17), Award

Europe Cement v. Turkey: Europe Cement Investment & Trade S.A. v. The Republic of Turkey, (ICSID Case No. ARB(AF)/07/2), Award

LAFICO v. Burundi: Libyan Arab Foreign Investment Company (LAFICO) v Republic of Burundi Burundi (1991) 96 ILR 279, Award

Lemire v. Ukraine: Joseph Charles Lemire v. Ukraine (ICSID CASE NO. ARB/06/18), Award

MINE: Maritime International Nominees Establishment v. Government of Guinea (ICSID Case No. ARB/84/4), DECISION on the Application by Guinea for Partial Annulment of the Arbitral Award

National Oil Corporation: National Oil Corporation v. Libyan Sun Oil Company, Civ. A. No. 89-415-JLL.United States District Court, D. Delaware

[122] In the scholars' view, investors can receive compound interest through investment vehicles thus, compound interest in arbitral awards aligns with economic reality. See Simmons (2012), p. 221.

National Grid v. Argentina: National Grid plc v. The Argentine Republic, (UNCITRAL Arbitration), Award

Pey Casado v. Chile: Victor Pey Casado and Foundation 'PRESIDENTE ALLENDE' v. The Republic of Chile, (ICSID Case No. ARB/98/2), Award

Rainbow Warrior: Rainbow Warrior arbitration between France v. New Zealand

Rubber Improvement: Rubber Improvement Ltd v Daily Telegraph Ltd.

Rumeli Telekom: Rumeli Telekom A.S. and Telsim Mobil Telekomunikasyon Hizmetleri A.S. v. Republic of Kazakhstan, (ICSID Case No. ARB/05/16), Award and Decision of the Ad Hoc Committee on Annulment Proceedings

Siemens v. Argentina: Siemens A.G. v. The Argentine Republic, (ICSID Case No. ARB/02/8), Award

Starrett Housing v. Iran: Starrett Housing International, Inc v. The Government of the Islamic Republic of Iran, Bank Markazi, Others, (IUSCT Case no. 24), Final Award, Award No. 314-24-1 and See; Interlocutory Award No ITL 32-24-1

Tecmed v. Mexico: Tecnicas Medioambientales Tecmed S.A. v. The United Mexican States, (ICSID Case No. ARB (AF)/00/2), Award

Unglaube v. Costa Rica: Marion Unglaube and Reinhard Unglaube v. Republic of Costa Rica, (ICSID Case No. ARB/08/1 and ICSID Case No. ARB/09/20), Award

Von Pezold v. Zimbabwe: Bernhard Friedrich Arnd Rüdiger Von Pezold and others v. Republic of Zimbabwe, (ICSID Case No. ARB/10/15), Award

Online Database

https://www.investmentpolicy.unctad.org
https://www.italaw.com
https://www.jusmundi.com
https://www.law.justia.com
https://www.legal.un.org
https://www.rics.org
https://www.oecd.org
https://www.rics.org
https://www.trans-lex.org
https://www.un.org
https://www.uncc.ch/sites
https://www.uni-marburg.de

References

Born G (2021) International arbitration: law and practice, 3rd edn. Kluwer Law International

Burgstaller M, Ketcheson J (2017) Should expropriation risk be taken into account in the assessment of damages? ICSID Rev 32(1):193–215

Cohen J, Grgeta E, Temerlin F (2019) CASE COMMENT In all probability: an economic reading of damages under factory at Chorzów. ICSID Rev 34(3):577–584
Domínguez MDG (2016) Calculating damages in investment arbitration: should tribunals take country risk into account. Ariz Law J 34(1):96–122
Dorobantu FA, Dupont N, Maniatis MA (2016) Country risk and damages in investment arbitration. ICSID Rev 31(1):219–231
Dukes WP (2006) Business valuation basics for attorneys. J Bus Valuat Econ Loss Anal 1(1):1–19
Dumberry P (2010) Compensation for moral damages in investor-state arbitration disputes. J Int Arbitr 27(3):247–276
Dumberry P (2012) Satisfaction as a form of reparation for moral damages suffered by investors and respondent States in Investor-State arbitration disputes. J Int Dispute Settlement 3(1)
Eggers PM (2016) The place of subrogation in insurance law: the deceptive depths of a difficult doctrine. In: The Modern Law of Marine Insurance: Vol. 4
Faccio S (2014) The application of the principle of proportionality to assess compensation: some reflections arising from the case of Joseph Charles Lemire v. Ukraine. Law Pract Int Courts Tribunals 13(2):199–222. https://doi.org/10.1163/15718034-12341275
Gultutar D (2021) Moral damages under international investment law: the path towards convergence, international arbitration law library, vol 62. Kluwer Law International
Hooke JC (2014) M&A: a practical guide to doing the deal. John Wiley & Sons, Incorporated, New York. Available from: ProQuest Ebook Central
Hu HTC (1979) Compensation in expropriations: a preliminary economic analysis. Va J Int Law 20(1):61–95
Kantor M (2008) Valuation for arbitration: compensation standards, valuation methods and expert evidence. Kluwer Law International, Alphen aan den Rijn, The Netherlands
Kantor M (2009) New age compensation for expropriation. J World Energy Law Bus 2(2):155–162. https://doi.org/10.1093/jwelb/jwp005
Kryvoi Y (2012) Counterclaims in investor-state arbitration. Minn J Int Law 21(2)
Marboe I (2017) Calculation of compensation and damages in international investment law (2nd edn). Oxford International Arbitration Series. Oxford University Press
Marzal T (2021) Quantum (in)justice: rethinking the calculation of compensation and damages in ISDS. J World Invest Trade 22(2):249–312
Merrill TW (2002) Incomplete compensation for takings. N Y Univ Environ Law J 11(1):110–135
Newcombe A, Paradell L (2009) Law and practice of investment treaties: standards of treatment. Kluwer Law International
Parish MT et al (2011) Awarding moral damages to respondent states in investment arbitration. Berkeley J Int Law 29(1)
Pearl J, Rosenbaum J (2013) Investment banking: valuation, leveraged buyouts, and mergers and acquisitions. John Wiley & Sons, Incorporated, New York
Pirim CZ (2020) Reparation by pecuniary means of direct moral damages suffered by states as a result of internationally wrongful acts. J Int Dispute Settlement 11(2)
Reinisch A (2008) Legality of expropriations. In: Reinisch A (ed) Standards of investment protection. Oxford University Press. https://doi.org/10.1093/acprof:oso/9780199547432.003.0009
Reisman WM, Crawford JR et al (eds) (2014) Foreign investment disputes: cases, materials and commentary, 2nd edn. Kluwer Law International
Rubins N, Kinsella NS (2005) International investment, political risk and dispute resolution "a practitioner's guide". Oxford University Press
Sabahi B (2011) Compensation and restitution in investor-state arbitration: principles and practice. Oxford University Press, Oxford
Salacuse JW (2016) The law of investment treaties, 3rd edn. Oxford University Press, Oxford
Saldarriaga A, Kantor M (2009) Calculating damages: arbitrators, counsel, and experts can do better than they have in the past. In: Lu KW et al (eds) Investing with confidence: understanding political risk management in the 21st century. World Bank, Washington DC, pp 196–238

Simmons JB (2012) Valuation in investor-state arbitration: toward a more exact science. Berkeley J Int Law 30(1):196–250

Soderlund C et al (2005) The valuation of lost profits: finding it right. J World Invest Trade 6(1): 23–38

Sprankling JG (2014) The international law of property, 1st edn. Oxford University Press, Oxford

Stan GO (2015) Valuation approaches in investment arbitration: an analytical and comparative study. Doctoral Thesis, King's College London, Dickson Poon School of Law

Stauffer TR (1996) Valuation of assets in international takings. Energy Law J 17:461–488

The Black's Law Dictionary

van Sliedregt E (2012) Individual criminal responsibility in international law. Oxford University Press, Oxford

Waters JJ (2015) A comparative analysis of public and private political risk insurance policies with strategic applications for risk mitigation. Duke J Comp Int Law 25(3):361

Wittich S (2002) The International Law Commission's Articles on the responsibility of states for internationally wrongful acts adopted on second reading. Leiden J Int Law 15(4)

Wittich S (2004) Non-material damage and monetary reparation in international law. Finnish Yearb Int Law 15:321

Chapter 11
Subrogation

11.1 In General

Subrogation is the substitution of one person in place of another as the possessor of any rightful claim.[1] Aside from insurance contacts, subrogation is also applied in suretyship or guarantee contracts wherein the surety or the guarantor discharges a debt owed to a third party in order to benefit the security and personal rights of the third party against the debtor.[2] While compensation aims to put the insured in the same position it was in prior to the occurrence of the risk, subrogation allows the insurer to step into the shoes of the insured. It is a process whereby the insurer seeks reimbursement from the wrongdoer to collect the portion of the sum that was paid to the insured. PRI contracts provide a ceiling for the compensation amount, and the cap concerned is lesser than the loss investor may sustain.[3] The purpose ascribed to a requirement is that the investor will act as a coinsurer[4] for a portion of its investment and retain some risk is twofold; to assure that the investor steers its business away

[1] Sheldon (1882), p. 1, the author provides another definition for the civil law context, according to the definition subrogation is *"a change by which another person has been put into the place of a creditor, and which makes the rights of the creditor and any securities that he holds pass to the person who, by being subrogated to him, enters into his right"*. Ibid, p. 3. Likewise, the Black's Law Dictionary defines as *"the substitution of one party for another whose debt the party pays, entitling the paying party to rights, remedies, or securities that would otherwise belong to the debtor"*.

[2] Eggers (2016), p. 241.

[3] For instance, MIGA grants guarantees up to 90 per cent of equity investment and 95 per cent of the principal when it comes to loans. See Muchlinski et al. (2008), p. 545. Also see Hyder and Attanasio (2021), pp. 459–460.

[4] Insurance policies define this mechanism as 'self-insurance' where the insured is obliged to bear some portion of the risk throughout the duration of the period.

Ö. Tosun, *The Law of Political Risk Insurance*, AIDA Europe Research Series on Insurance Law and Regulation 12, https://doi.org/10.1007/978-3-031-74675-8_11

from risky countries and, to the extent applicable, it takes all reasonable efforts to protect the investment and avoid exposing the insurer to additional risks.[5]

The insurer can take over the insured's interest in the subject matter in three different ways. Subrogation may stem from a juridical declaration, the law (the legal subrogation) or as a result of an agreement to that effect. In a conventional assignment parties enter into an express agreement.[6] Hence, the insurer must ensure that the contract concluded between the investor and the host state does not involve a waiver clause or a provision prohibiting the assignment. In legal subrogation, the insurer is entitled to the insured's rights by operation of law. The principle of 'statutory assignment', which is applied in some jurisdictions,[7] may serve several purposes within the PRI context; it may protect subrogated rights, preclude the sovereign from avoiding responsibility to the insured, and finally, prevent the insured, from unjustly enriching itself.

Enrichment or '*double dipping*' by insured claimants[8] is prohibited in insurance.[9] This concise statement carries significant weight. In investments insured against political risks, the debtors upon whom rests the obligation to rectify the insureds' situation are either the sovereign or the insurer. Hence, for the insured, the party paying for the sovereign's wrongdoings is of no importance.[10] However, the insurer is entitled to reimburse from the insured any benefits received from the sovereign in diminution of the loss.[11]

Thus, the insured must account to the insurer for the proceeds previously received, and the insurance claim must be reduced by that amount. If the insured has been fully indemnified by the sovereign for the same loss, he/she must reject the insurer's compensation offer. Conversely, if the insured has been fully indemnified by the insurer, the sums to be received from the sovereign must be held in trust and handed over to the insured. Finally, one may need to note that in case of partial payment by the sovereign, the insurer will still be liable to the insured within the limits of its policy for the full amount of the loss after deducting the sum from the recovery.[12]

In *Hochtief v. Argentina* the insured received a payout from the insurer, and Argentina argued that, since Germany was subrogated to the insured's rights, the insured would no longer pursue its claim. However, the tribunal agreed with the

[5]Contract frustration policies provide that insurer will bear %10 to %15 of the risks of an uninsured basis, Budd (1993), p. 307. Also see Martin (1967), p. 307.

[6]Sheldon (1882), p. 5.

[7]For instance, in Turkish Law, irrespective from the existence of a specific assignment contract, upon payment of the indemnification, the insurer is entitled to the insured rights by operation of law. First sentence of the art. 1472(1) of TCC is as follows: "*The insurer shall legally succeed the insured upon payment of the insurance indemnity*".

[8]For the expression see Merkin and Steele (2013), p. 111, fn 72.

[9]Eggers (2016), p. 241.

[10]Also see Schill (2010), pp. 47–49.

[11]Merkin (2013), p. 175.

[12]See Sheldon (1882), p. 269, similarly, Merkin (2013), p. 191.

claimant's request that there should be no deduction to be made in respect of the payment that it received under the political risk insurance. The tribunal held that "*the insurance payment is a benefit which Claimant arranged on its own behalf, and for which it paid. It does not reduce the losses caused by Respondent's actions in breach of the BIT: it is an arrangement that had been made by Claimant with a third party in order to provide a hedge against potential losses. The Tribunal does not consider that any principle of international law requires that such an arrangement, to which Respondent was not a party, should reduce Respondent's liability.*[13] However, in *İçkale v. Turkmenistan*, the tribunal did take into account of the presence of insurance agreement and compensation, and held that "*the Claimant must be assumed to have recovered the value of these assets from insurance.*[14]"

While the findings and conclusion in the latter case are accurate, the conclusion of the tribunal in *Hochtief v. Argentina* was unfortunate and problematic within the sense of subrogation and could lead to unjust enrichment of the insured or a double punishment of the sovereign for the same action. That being said, some BITs explicitly pave the way for the enrichment of the investor, article 13(2) of the Canada–China BIT 2012 provides that "*contracting party shall not assert, as a defence, counterclaim, right of setoff or otherwise, that the disputing investor has received or will receive, pursuant to an insurance or guarantee contract, indemnification or other compensation for all or part of its alleged damages.*[15]"

The *non bis in idem* or *double jeopardy*, the doctrines, although applied in criminal law, refer to prevention of a person from being tried again on the same subject-matter following the pronouncement of a sentence for the same crime. In a scenario where the loss the investor incurred is 100 units, and the insurer, without a cap, pays this amount to its insured, the insurer will be entitled to seek reimbursement of 100 units from the sovereign. If the payout worth 100 units is not appraised in the calculation of loss by the tribunal, the sovereign may face a 100 units award in the investor's favour along with a claim of 100 by the insurer as a result of subrogation.

It is worth noting that the insurer (assignee) is also precluded from obtaining better rights than those of the insured (assignor). As mentioned earlier, since the amount of insurance coverage is often less than the value of the transaction or the investment, the statutory assignment can be detrimental to the insured. To illustrate;

[13] See *Hochtief v. Argentina*, para 308–309. Available at https://www.italaw.com/sites/default/files/case-documents/italaw4101.pdf. Some BITS specifically preclude their parties from asserting a defense, set-off or counterclaim on the grounds that the foreign investor has received or will receive an insurance indemnification for the alleged damages. See for instance art. 6(7) of Kazakhstan - United States of America BIT (1992) available at https://investmentpolicy.unctad.org/international-investment-agreements/treaty-files/1792/download accessed 06.09.2024.

[14] See *İçkale v. Turkmenistan*, para. 373–375

[15] The BIT is available at https://edit.wti.org/document/show/d2554820-6f2a-439a-982f-87ef12f12348. Also see article 18 of the China – Mexico BIT 2008, available at https://investmentpolicy.unctad.org/international-investment-agreements/treaty-files/759/download both accessed 06.09.2024. Also, see SUN (2020).

in a case where the loss is 150, and the coverage rate is %90, the compensation amount will be 135 (150 × 0,9) leaving the insured with a remaining loss of 15. In such a case, since both parties to the insurance contract, in theory, will be entitled to seek reimbursement from the wrongdoer (the host state), the insured will assume a duty towards the insurer that will require him to take insurer's interest into account and not to settle for an amount detrimental to the insurer's benefit. Hence, public PRI providers often take over the entire sum through an assignment contract prior to indemnification. In doing so, the insurer brings proceedings on its own account and in its own name.[16] If the sum collected from the wrongdoer exceeds the amount of insurance coverage, depending on the wording employed in the assignment contract, the insurer may either return to the insured the collected sum up to the value of the investment or it may share it with the insured based on the coverage rate.

Finally, one must note that the insurer, as subrogee, succeeds in the insured's (cedent's) rights and remedies in respect of the subject matter for which he/she paid for. The insurer will face the same defenses that the sovereign could have raised against the cedent. Hence, PRI policies may require the cedent(investor) to assign and transfer all its rights free from any defense, counterclaim, encumbrance or right to set off. The cedent will be relieved from liability to the extent that it delivers to the insurer the investment contract, documents or means necessary to prove the existence of the receivable.

11.2 Exercise of Jurisdiction Over Another State

11.2.1 In General

The '*act of state*' and '*state immunity*' are doctrines that share a similar nature and have the common element of comity. Both doctrines originated from the principle of equality among sovereign states[17]and the concept of territoriality-comity.[18] According to the territoriality-comity, every sovereign possesses exclusive jurisdiction and the right to rule within its own territory.[19] All the nationals of the sovereign, irrespective of whether they reside permanently or temporarily within the territories, are the subjects of that sovereign.

The act of state doctrine mostly covers cases where illegal taking is concerned. It removes the judiciary capacity of the courts of a country to sit in the judgment of acts

[16] *Merkin* states that in assignment, the insurer can proceed without the cooperation of the insured. Merkin (2013), p. 189. In PRI practice, this opinion will find supporters only if the entire receivable/contract is assigned to the insured. In partial subrogation, the insurer will still be in need of the insured's presence throughout the process.

[17] According to the principle of sovereign equality, states have a duty to refrain from interfering in the areas of exclusive jurisdiction of other states. Salacuse (2013), p. 76.

[18] Cooper (1980), p. 195, fn 6 and p. 207.

[19] Also see Mooney (1967), p. 11.

undertaken by a foreign sovereign (host state) on its own territory.[20] Whereas the state immunity, in brief, is a concept where a foreign state will not be subject to suit without its consent.[21] Immunity is limited to instances where the sovereign acts in a public capacity. Be that as it may, both doctrines serve to show the difference of one state to the acts of another and to protect the sovereignty of one state from infringement by other states.

11.2.2 Act of State

A court of a state is not empowered to apply, within its territory, any laws other than those of its own government. Additionally, the court cannot question the legality of the acts of another state insofar as they affect property situated within that state when the legislation takes effect.[22] The courts of a state are not entitled to supervise or scrutinize the acts of another. Therefore, what is of crucial importance is not the legality of the acts, but rather whether they have been committed by the sovereign.[23]

Of particular importance in the doctrine of act of the state is the case *Banco Nacional*,[24] in which a dispute arose out of the nationalization of American sugar interests in Cuba.[25] The illegal expropriation of assets gives rise to a rightful claim for redress. However, as far as the doctrine was concerned, the U.S. Supreme Court rejected to order compensation to a U.S. investor and did avoid passing judgment on the expropriatory actions of the Cuban state. This decision was criticized for dealing a blow to the U.S. position since the U.S. supported the principle of full compensation in expropriation claims, and arbitration decisions had been supporting this rule.[26] A communist sovereign may not accord special treatment to property rights. Neither must the sovereign be expected to provide an alien's property with protection

---

[20] Gordon and Saunders (2021).

[21] The solemn dignity can be impaired when a state is allowed to sue another without its consent. Cooper (1980), pp. 194, 199.

[22] *Shearer* concludes that "*the court of one State may not question the validity or legality of acts of another sovereign country or of its agents and that such questioning must be done, if at all, through diplomatic channels*" quoted from Barker et al. (1998), p. 957. Similarly see Allen and Viscusi (1976), p. 154.

[23] Cooper (1980), p. 206.

[24] The distinction between Act of State and Sovereign Immunity was made in *Banco Nacional* "*immunity relates to the prerogative right not to have sovereign property subject to suit; fairness has been thought to require that when the sovereign seeks recovery, it be subject to legitimate counterclaims against it. The act of state doctrine, however, although it shares with the immunity doctrine a respect for sovereign states, concerns the limits for determining the validity of an otherwise applicable law.*" Also see Cooper (1980), p. 234.

[25] For the detail of the case, please see Mooney (1967), p. 77 et seq and similarly, see Cooper (1980), p. 217 et seq and visit: https://supreme.justia.com/cases/federal/us/376/398/ accessed 06.09.2024.

[26] DeLeonardo (2005), pp. 760–761.

over the property of its national. Although the case concerns nationalization, and the court refrained from assessing the merits due to its jurisdictional capacity, at the time of rendering this decision, states may not have agreed on whether compensation was a requirement.[27] However, as international consensus is reached with regard to the standards protecting aliens(investors), the importance of political risk insurance once again comes to the fore.

11.2.3 Sovereign Immunity

11.2.3.1 In General

The immunity of a sovereign (its instrumentality or agency) from the jurisdictions of the courts of another state is a general principle of international law.[28] The rationale for the immunity rests on the idea of the status of equality attaching to the independent sovereign and non-intervention in the internal affairs of other states.[29] The court in *Germany v. Italy* described in broad the function of the immunity. According to the court's view "*the rules of State immunity determine whether or not the courts of one State may exercise jurisdiction in respect of another State. They do not bear upon the question whether or not the conduct in respect of which the proceedings are brought was lawful or unlawful*".[30]

The expression of immunity covers not only 'jurisdictional immunity' but also the immunity from the home state's exercise of its administrative or executive powers.[31] The foreign state's assets in the host state are protected from attachment

[27] ILC's articles on states' responsibilities were adopted almost four decades after this decision. Also see Mooney (1967), p. 84 et seq.

[28] Under article 5 of the United Nations Convention on Jurisdictional Immunities of States and Their Property (hereinafter 'the Immunities Convention') "*A State enjoys immunity, in respect of itself and its property, from the jurisdiction of the courts of another State subject to the provisions of the present Convention.*" Full text of the Convention is available at https://treaties.un.org/doc/source/recenttexts/english_3_13.pdf as of 06.09.2024. For the background and the history of this article, see Fox and Webb (2013), pp. 304–306. Also see European Convention on State Immunity, available at https://rm.coe.int/16800730b1 8 countries had either ratified or accepted the European Convention. For detail also visit: https://treaties.un.org/pages/showDetails.aspx?objid=08000002800c8eb2 and https://treaties.un.org/Pages/ViewDetails.aspx?src=IND&mtdsg_no=III-13&chapter=3&clang=_en both accessed on 06.09.2024. Also, ICSID awards are subject to local rules of state immunity for the state assets. See Lord Lloyd-Jones (2019), p. 267.

[29] Gaukrodger (2010), p. 13.

[30] See para. 93. available at https://www.icj-cij.org/public/files/case-related/143/143-20120203-JUD-01-00-EN.pdf accessed 06.09.2024.

[31] Please see commentary to art.1 of the "*Draft articles on Jurisdictional Immunities of States and Their Property*". In jurisdictions like France and the United States, assets subject to execution are required to have a link with the claim. See Gaukrodger (2010), p. 21.

or executions.[32] An attempt to enforce a court decision that is directed at the assets of the foreign state will only serve to generate tension between states.

Under Foreign Sovereign Immunities Act of the USA (FSIA), foreign sovereigns enjoy a presumptive immunity from suit in U.S. federal and state courts.[33] However, as governments engage in commercial activities, private parties are no longer able to seek judicial remedies, and the immunity provides an unfair advantage in competing with private commercial enterprises.[34] Although states enjoy almost absolute immunity from actions in *personam,*[35] the United States has developed a restrictive theory[36] in which states can be held accountable before U.S. courts[37] for activities of the kind that were carried on by private persons.[38] The FSIA sets out several exceptions, one of which concerns commercial activities conducted by a foreign state. If these activities are carried on in the territory of the United States or elsewhere but have a direct effect in the United States, the foreign state cannot enjoy immunity.[39]

FSIA sets out the exceptions where the foreign state shall not be immune from the jurisdiction of courts of the United States. Of all the exceptions set out under FSIA, the exception of expropriation deserves special attention.[40] The two limbs of this

[32] As one author states "*to judge a foreign state is one thing, to subject it to coercive measures of execution is another.*" For the distinction between adjudicative immunity and enforcement immunity and also for the quotation, please see Gaukrodger (2010), p. 20.

[33] Frischknecht et al. (2018), p. 310. Also see Dolzer and Schreuer (2012), pp. 311–312.

[34] https://travel.state.gov/content/travel/en/legal/travel-legal-considerations/internl-judicial-asst/Service-of-Process/Foreign-Sovereign-Immunities-Act.html accessed 06.09.2024.

[35] Lloyd-Jones (2019), p. 248.

[36] A federal statute that determines whether the sovereign is entitled to immunity in a given case, and which is the exclusive basis for U.S. courts (state or federal) to exercise jurisdiction over foreign sovereigns or their property. See Frischknecht et al. (2018), p. 309.

[37] In the UK, prior to the enactment of the SIA (Sovereign Immunity Act) although the doctrine of absolute immunity had been applied, the courts gradually shifted towards denying immunity of states' separate trading entities. For detail, please see Fox and Webb (2013), pp. 137–141.

[38] Similarly, according to the article 10 of the Immunities Convention, the state (or one of its forms defined thereunder) cannot invoke immunity from that jurisdiction in a proceeding arising out of that commercial transaction.

[39] The second probability of the nexus is that the act as well as the activity are carried on outside the United States. *Fox and Webb* describe the third nexus as "*an act performed in the United States in connection with a commercial activity carried on elsewhere*". Fox and Webb (2013), p. 264.

[40] To see the list of the exceptions, please visit: https://www.govinfo.gov/content/pkg/STATUTE-90/pdf/STATUTE-90-Pg2891.pdf also visit https://www.law.cornell.edu/uscode/text/28/1605 accessed 06.09.2024. For expropriation exception, see section 1605(a)(3) of the FSIA and also see Fox and Webb (2013), p. 427. Arbitration is another exception to sovereign immunity. On August 16 2024, the U.S. Court of Appeals for the D.C. Circuit issued a decision holding that U.S. courts have jurisdiction under the Foreign Sovereign Immunities Act (FSIA) to enforce arbitral awards. See the *NextEra*, *9REN*, and *AES Solar* cases. Also visit: https://www.iarbnews.com/members/?token=YWnrHJVd4UlycHQvIKyDhO1sTlicS25W&action=signin&r=https%3A%2F%2Fwww.iarbnews.com%2Fu-s-court-of-appeals-confirms-jurisdiction-to-enforce-icsid-awards-

exception are that expropriation be in violation of international law[41] and the presence of a jurisdictional link with the United States. To put the latter in a different way, there must be an adequate commercial nexus to justify the courts of the United States in exercising jurisdiction over the defendant.[42] The jurisdictional condition will be satisfied if the property taken in violation of international law is present in the U.S. territory and is in connection with a commercial activity carried on by an agency or instrumentality of the foreign state. If it is located outside, property itself must be proven to be used by the state agency for commercial purposes within the U.S.[43]

11.2.3.2 Enforcement of Sovereign Assets: Awards and Measures on Sovereign Immunity

Immunity is of relevance in terms of PRI. After being subrogated to the rights of the foreign investor, the PRI provider will bring legal proceedings against the host state, and when it obtains the court ruling or the award, it will seek to enforce it in the jurisdictions where state in question has assets. Bankruptcy regime offers individuals and firms a shield from enforcement and a means to overcome collective action problems; in other words, as *Choi et al* state, creditors rarely can travel a simple path to recovery.[44] Sovereigns on the other hand have already immunity to shield themselves.[45] Sovereigns' assets are inexhaustible; the bankruptcy regime sovereigns are subject to does not end with the liquidation of assets and the dissolution of the sovereign. Hence, even if the amount of the sovereign's liability exceeds its assets and the sovereign becomes insolvent, the 'bad state[46]' is still expected to pay its debts.[47]

In order to manage their funds and diversify their economy, resource-rich countries may establish autonomous or semi-autonomous authorities, often in the form of

---

against-spain-but-overturns-district-courts-anti-suit-injunctions-over-international-comity-concerns%2F accessed 30.08.2024.

[41] As we discussed in the previous chapters, to claim the illegality of the expropriation within the PRI context, the taking must be discriminatory, not for a public purpose and not accompanied by prompt, adequate and effective compensation.

[42] The nexus requirement can be satisfied without the presence of the expropriated asset in the United States. If the asset in question is controlled by the state entity, agency or instrumentality that has engaged in commercial activity within the United States, that organ of the state will not be granted immunity from the courts of the United States. For detail, please see Tattersall (2019), pp. 181–195, similarly see Fox and Webb (2013), pp. 242–243, 265.

[43] For detail, see Fox and Webb (2013), pp. 269, 427.

[44] Choi et al. (2012), p. 134.

[45] Gelpern (2013), p. 1104.

[46] According to *Choi* et al., the country, not able to repay its debts in full or in some portion is the "bad state". See Choi et al. (2012), p. 134.

[47] Hagan (2008), pp. 198–199, see Brown (2015), p. 730.

'sovereign wealth funds', and allocate funds at their disposal. The question then may be posed whether the degree of control exercised by the state, or the function the wealth-fund serves is of relevance within the meaning of immunity. Under the restrictive doctrine, the state agency is entitled to immunity if it performs acts in the exercise of sovereign authority.[48] In other words, the agency enjoys immunity to the same extent as the state it represents.

A distinction must be drawn between central banks'[49] exercise of sovereign authority and conducting commercial operations. The commercial activities of central banks, such as guarantees given to finance hospitals or the issuance of a letter of credit or a promissory note, have nothing to do with the exercise of sovereign authority and were held to be commercial activities; thus, they could not benefit from immunity.[50] Likewise, in *Trendtex,* the court found that although the central bank of Nigeria was established by the state under statute as a separate legal entity, there was no clear expression of intent that it should have governmental status and therefore, it was not entitled to immunity.[51]

In *AIG v. Kazakhstan*, AIG obtained an ICSID award[52] and sought to enforce the award as a judgment by obtaining final Third-Party Debt and Charging Orders against cash and securities of the Kazakhstan's National Fund, which were held by third parties in London (London assets). Since the central bank of Kazakhstan used to carry out the trust management of the National Fund, it intervened in the proceedings and asserted that the cash and securities were part of its property and were subject to immunity from enforcement under the Sovereign Immunity Act of the UK (SIA). According to section 3 of the SIA,[53] sovereigns are not immune for their commercial transactions. The domestic court, however, discharged the orders.

[48] Fox and Webb (2013), p. 355.

[49] Article 2(1)b of the Immunities Convention reads(b) "State" means: (i) the State and its various organs of government; (ii) constituent units of a federal State or political subdivisions of the State, which are entitled to perform acts in the exercise of sovereign authority, and are acting in that capacity; – 2 – (iii) agencies or instrumentalities of the State or other entities, to the extent that they are entitled to perform and are actually performing acts in the exercise of sovereign authority of the State; (iv) representatives of the State acting in that capacity. Although the Convention did not provide a specific attention to central banks in the definitions, it ranks its assets as immune from execution under article 21 (1)c, also see Fox and Webb (2013), p. 372. Courts treat quasi-public entities [such] as national banks as organs under FSIA. Frischknecht et al. (2018), p. 312.

[50] Fox and Webb (2013), p. 408.

[51] Fox and Webb (2013), pp. 141, 178, 370.

[52] AIG and a Kazakhstan company formed a joint venture to develop a project for a residential housing complex and to this end purchased a property and concluded contracts. However, the government of the Republic of Kazakhstan announced that the land concerned was required for a national arboretum. Then city officials of Almaty expelled the joint venture's contractors from the construction site and seized the property. For the case, please visit: https://www.italaw.com/sites/default/files/case-documents/ita0022.pdf accessed 06.09.2024.

[53] For the legislation please visit: https://www.legislation.gov.uk/ukpga/1978/33#:~:text=Immunity%20from%20jurisdiction&text=(1)A%20State%20is%20immune,in%20the%20proceedings%20in%20question accessed 06.09.2024.

Amongst other considerations, the court found that the London assets were not, at any time, either in use or intended for use for 'commercial purposes' within the meaning of section 13(4) of the SIA.[54] By contrast, in the court's view they must enjoy complete immunity from the enforcement process in the UK courts.[55]

According to some scholars, issuing a foreign currency regulation is an action peculiar to a state (and therefore not 'commercial'), whereas contracting to purchase goods (even if for a public interest) is a 'commercial' activity, because private companies can similarly use sales contracts to acquire goods.[56] *Fox and Webb* draw a similar line between commercial and public activity. In the authors' belief, a contract to construct a government building constitutes commercial activity, and the same would be true of a contract to make repairs on an embassy building.[57]

These opinions can find supporters when the sovereign explicitly acts in the manner of a commercial player. The fact is that the acts complained of must have a private nature. A contract may appear on its face as simply 'an amalgamation of impetus to achieve a commercial result'; in fact, even if one were to consider that the purpose of the transaction is of crucial significance, it may not be an oversimplification to presume that all contracts ranging from sales of military equipment to construction of infrastructure, that sovereigns conclude, by their nature, (including the ones expected to generate pecuniary profit) aim to safeguard the populace's well-being. By way of illustration, an SOE may run its operations on a not-for-profit basis and undertake social dwellings for its nationals, who cannot otherwise afford decent housing from the private market or who suffer from homelessness. Its activity will have undisputedly served the public needs. Thus, 'the purpose test' expands immunity in favor of the state and is insufficient to make a concrete distinction between commercial and public activity.[58] If the sovereign has exercised the attributes of statehood by constructing or repairing a facility (such as an embassy) for its external agents, the activity should be treated the same and regarded as having lost its commercial character.

If AIG had obtained PRI coverage, would the reaction of the UK court have been the same when the insurer stepped into the shoes of AIG? AIG is a U.S. corporation, and if it had been assured by a US insurer, the Kazakhstan - United States of America BIT (1992) would have applied. However, the BIT in question is silent on

[54] The court relied on the privileges stated under article 13(2)(b) and 13(4) of the SIA which read respectively as follows; "*the property of a State shall not be subject to any process for the enforcement of a judgment or arbitration award or, in an action in rem, for its arrest, detention or sale.*" and "*Subsection (2)(b) above does not prevent the issue of any process in respect of property which is for the time being in use or intended for use for commercial purposes; but, in a case not falling within section 10 above*".

[55] See para. 95 of the court's decision.

[56] See Frischknecht et al. (2018), p. 322. Also see Lord Lloyd-Jones (2019), p. 248, similarly, Fox and Webb (2013), p. 261.

[57] Fox and Webb (2013), p. 259.

[58] Fox and Webb (2013), p. 406.

recognition of the subrogatory rights of both parties' insurers.[59] Even if the republic of Kazakhstan had recognized AIG's assignment of its claims to a U.S. insurer under the same BIT, in our opinion, the BIT could not have been interpreted as an 'recognition of a debt'.

As this study was being drafted, the U.S. and its allies, in response to Russia's actions in Ukrainian territory, mounted an unprecedented reaction and imposed several sanctions on Russian central bank, financial institutions, and citizens.[60] Many countries had given preponderant weight to reducing Russia's financial capacity. The assets of Russia's central bank were frozen through OFAC. The blocking of Russian's central bank's assets[61] was in a manner akin to expropriation, and Russia responded with a counter regulation that could have led to the nationalization of foreign companies.[62]

The SIA accords special treatment to central banks,[63] and not coincidentally, unlike U.S. policymakers, the court of the UK granted immunity from enforcement to the central bank of Kazakhstan. Some scholars are of the opinion that OFAC's sanction do not fall within FSIA's scope, and neither are they in the nature of attachment or execution.[64] The underlying purpose of OFAC's decision was to hinder Russia from reaching the financial means necessary to support its operations. It is vague whether the duration of the decision is temporary; however, it is clear that OFAC's decision is arbitrary and politically driven. Questions may arise as to extent to which states are entitled to interfere with the ownership rights of another. In its furtherance, can states that are supposedly third parties to the conflict pursue enactments upon a sound legal basis against the actual parties to the same conflict?

11.2.3.3 Waiver of Immunity

In the era of global economy, it is not fortuitous that the host state may happen to maintain assets or some of its national wealth situated within different countries

[59] The only reference made to insurance is in article 8 which provides for an exemption. According to the article, the dispute settlement mechanism set out in the BIT will not be applied to the insurance programs of the US Exim. Readers will recall that the US provides insurance to its exporters/investors through two different entities, the US Exim and DFC. The DFC concludes specific inter-governmental agreements with the host-states. For the BIT, please visit: https://investmentpolicy.unctad.org/international-investment-agreements/treaty-files/1792/download accessed 06.09.2024.

[60] Anderson et al. (2022).

[61] Please visit: https://www.whitehouse.gov/briefing-room/statements-releases/2022/02/26/joint-statement-on-further-restrictive-economic-measures/ also see Directive 4 under Executive Order 14024. Available at https://ofac.treasury.gov/media/918806/download?inline all accessed 06.09.2024.

[62] Please visit: https://www.clydeco.com/en/insights/2022/03/expropriation-and-other-recent-measures-aimed accessed 06.09.2024.

[63] For the decisions of the UK courts, see Fox and Webb (2013), pp. 182, 371.

[64] Wuerth (2022).

(third-party state). Hence, in order for collecting its receivables, the PRI provider will likely need to track the location of these assets. In the ordinary course of enforcement law, taking a measure of constraint is sufficient if the asset is located in the territory over which the court has jurisdiction or where the award can be enforced. When the assets of the sovereign concerned, as the nature of conservatory measures, measures against the host state's assets are confined into the extent that they immobilize those assets located in the forum state.[65] The immunity of the sovereign bars the PRI provider from seeking relief through the arrest or attachment of the asset unless the sovereign has waived from its immunity[66] and conferred competence on the national courts of the third-party state. Waiver of sovereign immunity may offer a safe passage to lenders; thereby, PRI providers may bring lawsuits before the municipal courts.[67]

The question is whether a separate waiver from immunity of execution will be necessary if a waiver has already been given in relation to adjudication. In essence, article 20 of the Immunities Convention lifts doubts and provides a clear indication that an additional consent is imperative.[68] If the host state has agreed to arbitrate according to the institutional rules, can it be construed as willingness and therefore extend to the execution of the award? According to some scholars, if a sovereign is a signatory to an international treaty that calls for the enforcement of the award in other signatory states, the agreement to arbitrate will constitute an implicit waiver of immunity.[69] Adherence to treaties leads us to think that the ratification of the ICSID

[65] Fox and Webb (2013), p. 496.

[66] Article 7 of the Immunities Convention enunciates that explicit consent can be in the following forms: international agreement, a written contract or a declaration before the court or a written communication in a specific proceeding. Silence, inaction on the part of the state or a mere implication cannot be presumed to be instances amounting to consent of the state unless to the contrary is justified. Article 8 of the same text deals with the conducts of the state which are capable of evidencing the presence of its consent. According to the said article, if the state itself instituted the proceedings or took steps in the merits of a case, the state in question is precluded from invoking immunity. If it satisfies the court that it could not have acquired knowledge of facts on which a claim to immunity can be based until after it took such a step or if it invoked immunity in the proceedings, such instances would not operate as bar to invoke immunity.

[67] Nevertheless, the municipal courts will likely refuse hearing the case or the state will disrespect enforcement of the judgments. Waiver must be aligned with lifting other impediments before enforcement of a court order or arbitral award. In other words, the sovereign, in the first place, should grant a waiver including enforcement of the judgement, so that lender can collect on its debts. In so doing, the lender will have avoided incurring the denial of justice risk and will not be prevented from seizing the sovereign's assets. Choi et al. (2012), pp. 138–139. The author examines immunity from the perspective of lenders. PRI providers, acting as subrogors of lenders, will possess the same rights as lenders. Therefore, such an example can be applied identically to PRI providers.

[68] Mentioned article reads "*Where consent to the measures of constraint is required under articles 18 and 19, consent to the exercise of jurisdiction under article 7 shall not imply consent to the taking of measures of constraint.*"

[69] See Frischknecht et al. (2018), p. 316, for the supportive views of other scholars, see Fox and Webb (2013), p. 387.

Convention constitutes a form of 'waiver of immunity' in relation to arbitral proceedings to which state itself is a party. In fact, in an ICC case, the state's conduct in arbitral proceedings was construed as impairing sovereignty, and similarly, the enforcement of an ICC award in the United States was denied on the grounds that the losing state in the arbitral proceedings had not signed the New York Convention; therefore, the state in question did not intend to waive its sovereign immunity in the United States.[70]

The adjudication and enforcement stages of the proceedings must be considered in an entirety, and the latter stage is the corollary of procedural law. Otherwise, the intention of a disputing party will be reduced merely to obtaining an award on the merits in its favor, and a denial of jurisdiction at the stage of enforcement will render the adjudicatory jurisdiction meaningless. However, while it is incumbent upon all state parties to the ICSID Convention to recognize awards as binding,[71] the Convention preserves states' immunity from enforcement[72] and leaves the issue of state immunity to the discretion of municipal courts, limiting the scope of the enforcement to the properties used for commercial purposes. In other words, although some may consider states' claiming their immunity as a mere procedural bar and violation of international law, ratification of the ICSID Convention is not sufficient form of waiver so as to override the laws of the third-party state as regards the state immunity in execution.

11.3 Incorporation of Subrogation by Reference

'Recognition of subrogation' clause set out in BITs is of preemptive nature, functioning as a 'no-objection clause'.[73] The clause assumes that it grants the PRI provider the authority to pursue the rights of the investor, thereby precluding the host state from claiming the incapacity of the PRI provider. States retain the freedom to pursue their public purpose and manage their own affairs.[74] This freedom also

---

[70] Under article 35(6) of the ICC Rules, parties submitting their dispute to arbitration "*shall be deemed to have waived their right to any form of recourse in so far as such waiver can validly be made.*" Also see Meessen (2004), pp. 392, 395.

[71] As discussed in the following pages, the signatory state in the courts of which the enforcement is sought must treat the ICSID award as if its domestic judgment against which no judicial remedy is available. Also see Fox and Webb (2013), p. 257.

[72] Article 54(3) of the ICSID Convention provides that execution of an award against assets of a state is "*governed by the laws concerning the execution of judgments in force in the State in whose territories such execution is sought.*" Likewise, Article 55 of the Convention provides that enforcement is subject to "*the law in force in any Contracting State relating to immunity of that State or of any foreign State from execution.*" Also see Born (2021a), p. 493 and finally, see Fox and Webb (2013), p. 490.

[73] Konrad (2013), p. 38.

[74] Fox and Webb (2013), p. 481.

involves the management of the assets they own. However, a BIT containing such a clause should entitle the insurer to interfere with the state's property and take coercive measures against its property, thus remove the state's discretion over the fate of at least some of its assets.

The right of subrogation is recognized either by an investment guarantee agreement concluded between states or by a specific clause in a BIT.[75] BITs may provide for subrogation rights limited to home state or its agency[76] or some BITS require the agency of the home state to assign its subrogated rights to a 'fiduciary agent[77]'. Therefore, as seen in the examples of MIGA or ICIEC, multinational insurers cannot enjoy the privileges designed in BITs; therefore, they require member countries to recognize subrogation.[78] All property and assets that belong to MIGA or ICIEC are free from restrictions, regulations, controls and moratoria. However, the assets MIGA acquired via subrogation are free from applicable controls of the host country only to the extent that the investor was entitled to such treatment.[79] In addition, the assets MIGA acquires via subrogation are exempt from taxes.[80]

Some model agreements and BITs lift the rules that require the insurer to be owned or controlled by a specific authority.[81] By way of illustration, the Netherlands

---

[75] Radi (2020), p. 238, similarly Tan (2015), p. 184.

[76] For instance, art. 9 (1) of the UK – China BIT reads as: "*If one Contracting Party or its designated Agency makes a payment to its national or company under an indemnity given in respect of an investment made in the territory of the other Contracting Party, the latter Contracting Party shall recognize the assignment to the former Contracting Party or its designated Agency by law or by legal transaction of all the rights and claims of the national or company indemnified and that the former Contracting Party or its designated Agency is entitled to exercise such rights and enforce such claims by virtue of subrogation, to the same extent as the national or company indemnified the former Contracting Party or its designated Agency may assume the obligations related to the investment.*"

[77] Article 3 of the BIT between the U.S. and Ecuador was as follows: "*if the Issuer makes payment to any party under Coverage, the Government of Ecuador ...... shall recognize as well the appointment of the natural or juridical person to whom, as fiduciary agent or holder of the Issuer in Ecuador, the Issuer has assigned any right, title, privilege, claim, or cause of action existing or which may arise in connection with said payment and which constitutes an effective right in favor of the Issuer over all currency, credits, assets, or investment*" For the treaty, see Weisenfeld (1985) and also, see Diaconis (1989), p. 278.

[78] See art. 18 of MIGA Convention and similarly art.24 of ICIEC Article of Agreement.

[79] See art. 45(b) of MIGA Convention, art. 69 of the Commentary on the MIGA Convention and similarly, art. 53 of ICIEC Article of Agreement.

[80] See art. 47 of MIGA Convention, art. 71 of the Commentary on the MIGA Convention and similarly art. 26 of DHAMAN Convention.

[81] Article 7 of the Mexico - Netherlands BIT (1998) is as follows: "*If the investments of a national of the one Contracting Party are insured by a wholly privately owned and controlled insurance corporation (hereinafter referred to as "insurance corporation"), against noncommercial risks or otherwise give rise to payment of indemnification in respect of such investments under a system established by law, regulation or government contract, any subrogation of the insurance corporation to the rights of the said national pursuant to the terms of such insurance or under any other indemnity given shall be recognized by the other Contracting Party. Only the national or the insurance corporation shall be entitled to exercise such rights and to engage in a dispute with*

Model Investment Agreement[82] and the Norway Model BIT[83] recognize the insurer's rights regardless of whether the insurer is a state agency or a private company. Similarly, the UK-Turkey BIT (1991) does not provide specific reference to the ownership of the insurer.[84]

The importation of any protection contained in another BIT through an MFN clause is prevalent. The question is whether the importation of subrogation by operation of an MFN clause is admissible and whether the MFN standard can allow the insurer to take advantage of the host state's 'recognition of subrogation' as found in another treaty. Put simply, one should raise the question of whether PRI providers can benefit from treaty-shopping.

As readers will recall, the presence of an MFN clause in a BIT is intended to grant investors the right to avail themselves of substantive guarantees explicitly outlined in third-party treaties. The subjects of MFN clauses are the nationals or the companies of the contracting parties, and the actions to which the host state must not afford less favorable treatment are those which are in relation to management, maintenance, use or disposal of investments. Put it another way, the incorporation by reference has been applied as far as a protection which is exclusive to investor (and therefore to its investment) was concerned.

However, neither subrogation constitutes an international standard of protection, nor is the insurer the party that is being protected by BITs unless they contain a subrogation clause and even in that case, the protection captures exclusive to the

---

respect to those rights." Available at https://investmentpolicy.unctad.org/international-investment-agreements/treaty-files/3276/download accessed 06.09.2024.

[82] Art. 14 of the Agreement is as follows "*If the investment of an investor of a Contracting Party is insured against noncommercial risks or otherwise give rise to payment of indemnification in respect of such investment under a system established by law, regulation or government contract, any subrogation of the insurer or re-insurer or agency designated by that Contracting Party to the rights of the said investor pursuant to the terms of such insurance or under any other indemnity given shall be recognized by the other Contracting Party.*"

[83] Art. 22 of the BIT provides that "*If the investments of an investor are insured against non-commercial risks, any subrogation of the claims of the investor pursuant to this Agreement, shall be recognized by the other Party.*"

[84] Article 10 of the BIT is as follows: "*(1) Where an investment in the territory of one Contracting Party of a national or company of the other Contracting Party is insured against non-commercial risks under a system established by law and a payment is made by an insurer under an indemnity given in respect of that investment, the former Contracting Party shall recognize the assignment to the insurer by law or by legal transaction of all the rights and claims of the national or company indemnified. (2) The insurer shall be entitled to exercise all such rights and enforce all such claims by virtue of subrogation to the same extent as the national or company indemnified and shall be entitled also in all circumstances to receive the same treatment in respect of those rights and claims and any payments received under them as the national or company indemnified was entitled to receive by virtue of this Agreement in respect of the investment concerned and its related returns. (3) Any payments received by an insurer in pursuance of the rights and claims acquired shall be freely available to that insurer for the purpose of meeting any expenditure incurred in the territory of the Contracting Party on whose territory the investment is.*" Available at https://investmentpolicy.unctad.org/international-investment-agreements/treaty-files/2355/download accessed 06.09.2024.

recognition of the mechanism. If one were to read out the principle of incorporation by reference in narrow, she/he may rule out importing 'the acceptance by the host state the subrogatory rights that of the insurer' into the treaty by its MFN clause. In fact, discussions held on the importation of clauses are irrelevant to international standards of protection, such as dispute settlement clauses.

Every BIT is negotiated under different circumstances, and in case law, the language of the BIT is of significant assistance if it indicates, even in its preamble, explicit or implied terms referring to a protection desired to be imported.[85] *Schill* points out that an investor, the rights of whom are intended to be extended through the use of' borrowing a provision', may be prevented from doing so if the basic bilateral treaty contains a clause explicitly circumventing the operations of the MFN. According to the author, MFN clauses will not bypass the scope of the application of the basic treaty and will not override the clear intent of the parties thereto. By way of illustration, the definition of the investor or the investment under the BIT cannot be bypassed by means of an MFN clause within the same BIT.[86]

In essence, by acknowledging the MFN clause, the host state reveals its intention to allow the importation of a more favorable clause from a third-party treaty. If the dispute resolution mechanism of the basic treaty is different from that of the third-party treaty and stipulates a requirement to pursue domestic remedies, the MFN clause may serve for a fork in the road clause. In other words, due to the fact that arbitration is in the best interest of the investor in comparison with local courts, the investor is likely to opt for arbitration to address a claim that would otherwise need to be pursued in local courts.

The dilemma is that in most investor-state disputes, tribunals were not satisfied with the presumption of the host state's consent to arbitrate,[87] by contrast, they sought the explicit consent, which, according to tribunals cannot be incorporated through an MFN clause.[88] To give an instance, in its decision on jurisdiction, the tribunal in *Plama v. Bulgaria* concluded that "*It is a well-established principle, both*

[85] For detail, see Dumberry (2017), pp. 116–137.

[86] For detail, see Schill (2009), pp. 142, 146.

[87] The tribunal in the *Wintershall v. Argentina* (para 173), after discussing the extension of dispute resolution clause by interpretation, came to the conclusion that "*a dispute resolution clause is a specific provision reflect[ing] the precise will of the contracting parties*". Similarly, the tribunal in *Menzies v. Senegal* explained that investor cannot submit its dispute to arbitration unless the host state explicitly agreed otherwise. See paras. 142–145. Available at https://www.italaw.com/sites/default/files/case-documents/italaw7483.pdf accessed 06.09.2024.

[88] In the view of tribunal in *Plama v. Bulgaria* incorporation by reference to dispute settlement and thus the consent of the state to arbitrate had to be clear and unambiguous. However, the tribunal was against expansive interpretation and dubious as to whether the reference in the basic treaty fit this requirement. The tribunal went further and found it unachievable to harmonize the dispute settlement provisions. In the tribunal's view, the presence of various dispute settlement provisions in BITs that host state has concluded would create a chaotic situation and the host state could be confronted with a large number of permutations deriving from these provisions. See paras. 200 and 219. Also see Schill (2009), pp. 66–168. However, the tribunal in *RosInvest v. Russia* (para. 132), within the context of MFN protection, found no reason to reject transferring arbitration clauses

in domestic and international law, that such an agreement should be clear and unambiguous. In the framework of a BIT, the agreement to arbitrate is arrived at by the consent to arbitration that a state gives in advance in respect of investment disputes falling under the BIT.[89]"

Schill posits that investor's right to recourse to arbitration should not be treated separately in terms of the MFN's operation. The host state's consent to arbitrate, as set out in a third-party treaty, can be construed as a valid offer by means of the MFN clause of the basic treaty and can, therefore, be extended to the investor covered by that treaty.[90] An MFN clause offers an automatic alteration of a BIT without the need for state's further approval, promoting competition on equal terms among foreign investors. The question is which intention of the states should carry more weight. In our opinion, an MFN clause cannot serve as a means to import states' consent to arbitrate.[91] Arbitration requires the parties' firm and unequivocal consent, as a matter of fact, some BITS prevent extension of MFN clause to dispute settlements.[92]

Many BITs are not silent on the subrogatory rights of insurers. In the assumption that states are deemed to have granted consent via the incorporation by reference of provisions from other BITs, a state may also be compelled to recognize the rights of insurers from the states with which it has concluded a BIT. An illustration can be provided by using the following hypothetical example:[93] Three states, A, B and C conclude BITs between each other. All BITs contain an MFN clause, however, only BIT A-C contains recognition of a subrogation clause. The current application of MFN standard and the interpretation of the characteristic of the investment protection impede the importation of subrogation. However, the subrogation clause, along with boosting the investment, also serves to protect the investor. Because as previously stated, PRI has a dissuasive effect on the host state, and offers a less cumbersome and time-consuming indemnification process in comparison to investment arbitration. While the PRI provider of the state C is entitled to claim its insured's rights by virtue of the subrogation clause, the PRI provider of state B will be prevented from doing so in its reimbursement from state A. In our opinion, such an approach would not be in consonance with the ends pursued in accepting

---

offered by other investment treaties. Available at https://www.italaw.com/sites/default/files/case-documents/ita0719.pdf accessed 06.09.2024. Also see Schill (2009), pp. 172, 173.

[89] See. para. 198, available at https://www.italaw.com/sites/default/files/case-documents/ita0669.pdf accessed 06.09.2024.

[90] Schill (2009), pp. 181, 182.

[91] Also see Pérez-Aznar (2019), p. 190.

[92] Art. 4(4)(c) of the the Turkey-Ukraine BIT (2017) is as follows: "*Most Favored Nation treatment referred to in paragraphs 1 and 2 does not include treatment accorded to investors of a non-Contracting Party and their investments by provisions concerning the settlement of investment disputes provided for in this Agreement or in other international agreements concluded between a Contracting Party and a non-Contracting Party.*" BIT is available at https://investmentpolicy.unctad.org/international-investment-agreements/treaty-files/6080/download accessed 06.09.2024, similarly, see Art. 4(4)(c) of the Belarus-Turkey BIT (2018).

[93] For the example see Dumberry (2017), p. 118.

standards to protect investors. The investor from state B must enjoy the benefit of a clause which compels the host state to act in a cautious manner towards him/her. Hence, if state A rejects the incorporation of subrogation, it would treat the investor (insured) from state B less favorably. Finally, the timing of the conclusions of the BITs is irrelevant. Even if the BIT A-C is concluded before BIT A-B and state A's presumed intention was to 'deliberately omit a subrogation clause', by signing the latter BIT, state A must endure the consequences associated with its choice of accepting an MFN clause. Thus, the nationality of the PRI provider can be just as crucial as the nationality of the investor in determining which BIT is applicable, as the relevant BIT may contain an MFN clause.

11.4 Subrogation in PRI

11.4.1 In Expropriation

The insurer may decide whether to bear the risk by presuming the value of the investment or what may remain of it in the event of a risk occurrence. In conventional insurance, title to the asset is vested by the abandonment in the insurer. Expropriation is the only risk in which the insured is forced to abandon the investment to the sovereign. In a dispute between the insurer and the sovereign, the insurer may seek reimbursement for the amounts it paid to the insured in return for the loss of proprietary rights to the expropriated asset.[94] Although, as per the commentary to the MIGA Convention, in exceptional cases, the agency may acquire non-cash assets and convert them into cash expeditiously,[95] insurers will be prone to obtain cash rather than deliverance of the investment forcibly abandoned.

The Berne Union stresses *'forced abandonment'*, a term that is less frequently referred in investment arbitration decisions. It provides a coverage against losses sustained as a consequence of forced abandonment of operations or the investment itself due to events of political violence nature. Another event addressed in some PRI policies is 'forced divestiture'. Likewise, this coverage protects against losses that arise due to host state's measures, at the end of which the investor is prevented from retaining its shares or to operating, whether in part or in full. Forceful and involuntary deprivation of possession or any property rights are outcomes of political risks. These events are not the cause of the harm; on the contrary, they occur as a result. Therefore, it's challenging to draw a distinction between these events and expropriatory events. It appears that underwriters may wrongfully list these events as if they are diversified in scope and constitute a specific risk.[96]

[94] In the latter case the salvage value may need to be deducted from the disputed value.

[95] See art. 71 of the Commentary on the MIGA Convention.

[96] Please visit: https://www.berneunion.org/Stub/Display/17 accessed 06.09.2024.

It is also worth noting that, in order to file a claim, the investor will be required to go through a waiting period.[97] The waiting period differs from grace periods and cooling periods typically found in BITS. In conventional insurance, a grace period may denote the duration during which the insured is enabled to delay the premium payments beyond the maturity dates without being charged for the delay. On the other hand, cooling period in BITs mandates that the investor waits for six months following notice of a dispute.[98] In our opinion, the waiting period signifies the timeframe during which the insured may receive indemnification from the host state before the insurer, and it's the time during which the insured must complete its investigation and decide on the claim. In expropriation, the waiting period ranges from six to twelve months from the date of loss,[99] which is the date when the investor is deprived of its proprietary rights.

11.4.2 *In Political Force Majeure*

11.4.2.1 Strict Liability

The concept of strict or absolute liability is typically associated with environmental law and requires the investor's liability, as a polluter, which does not necessitate intent or negligence on the investor's part. However, this concept can be applied to host states under several circumstances. In theory, states are not responsible for the actions of private persons or groups.[100] The traditional doctrine of state responsibility is based upon fault,[101] with exceptions including political force majeure events and, under ILC articles, states being held responsible for private conduct if it is attributable to the state.

The requirement of fault in state responsibility refers to an objectively identifiable malfunction in the state's conduct and is defined as 'fault in service'. The state may be answerable if the fault in its service was carried out with a delay or in a defective manner, and provided that the resulting consequences are significant. A routine mistake that could be made by any administrative body does not constitute a fault in service.

In earlier times, in order to limit states' burden of compensation, gross negligence in their service was required to establish liability. Under this framework, a state could escape liability by demonstrating that it had taken the utmost care and precautions in preventing the harm. However, the developments in the concept of

[97] Under BITs, instead of "waiting period" an ambiguous wording such as "unreasonable amount of time" might be employed. In that case, that might be up to discretion of arbitrators whether governments acted otherwise. See: Ginsburg (2013), pp. 955–956.

[98] Born (2021a), p. 508.

[99] Williams (1993), p. 109.

[100] Please also see Proulx and Simma (2012), pp. 168, 239.

[101] Kelson (1972), p. 200 and see Gözübüyük and Tan (2021), p. 718.

constitutional states and the transformation of liberal states into social states entailed a shift towards the principle of strict liability.[102] Today, states are required to compensate their citizens for damage that befalls its citizens, resulting from activities associated with their status as a state, when such activities are carried out by their organs or instrumentalities.

According to the principle of '*social danger and risk*', the risk is distributed among society, and the state can be held liable even if there is a break in the chain of causation between the action and the damage. Strict liability is the apogee of this view, it removes the necessity of fact-finding investigations as to fault and identifying the person responsible for the damage.[103] One may need to know that the losses citizens incur do not derive from negligence in their activities,[104] by contrast, they may stem from the social disturbance that takes place in the society to which citizens belong as a consequence of their 'citizenship' status. Accordingly, the prerogative of entitlement to compensation is the outcome of the legal relation between the state and her citizen.

11.4.2.2 Scope of the Host State's Liability to Foreign Investor

It will be trite to say that the state must come to grips with the loss that only her nationals incur. Investors may claim strict liability of the state in reliance upon full protection and security (FPS) treatment found in relevant BITs. If one were to ponder whether FPS standard imposes a strict liability on the host state and whether states are under strict liability to foreign investors given that the state is in charge to prevent the events of extra ordinary and specific nature, the reason may lie within the interpretation of FPS. In the tribunal's opinion in *AAPL v. Sri Lanka, "the language of BIT imposing on the host State obligation to provide protection and security cannot be construed as creating a strict liability."* According to the tribunal "*the State into which an alien has entered… is not an insurer or a guarantor of his security… It does not, and could hardly be asked to, accept an absolute responsibility for all injuries to foreigners*".[105] In a similar vein, the tribunal in *Tecmed v Mexico* concluded that the full FPS standard is not absolute and does not impose strict liability upon the state that grants it.[106] In a case where an Italian claimant asserted compensation on account of forced loans exacted of him by revolutionary troops, the umpire closed the door for the strict liability, in his view, "*revolutionary*

[102] Gözübüyük and Tan (2021), pp. 699, 700 and Proulx and Simma (2012), p. 200.

[103] Kelson (1972), p. 208.

[104] Gözübüyük and Tan (2021), pp. 729–736.

[105] See *AAPL v. Sri Lanka,* para. 49, also see *Wena Hotels v. Egypt,* para. 84. Latter case is available at https://www.italaw.com/sites/default/files/case-documents/ita0902.pdf accessed 06.09.2024.

[106] See *Tecmed v. Mexico*, para. 177.

acts commit to destroy governments, and no one should be held responsible for the acts of an enemy attempting his life.[107]"

Kelson states that the acceptability of strict liability in international law, may to some extent, be determined by the degree to which there is a coherent consensus on a rule of strict liability in municipal law systems.[108] The question that must be raised is, whether host states should grant rights to the foreign investors broader than those granted to their own citizens. This can be discussed in light of BITs. When political force majeure is concerned, for instance German – Turkey BIT provides that the contracting party must not accord foreign investors less favorably than it accords its own national.[109] The UK – Turkey BIT goes further to detail and indicates that the contracting party must afford the same compensation for injury as it affords to its own nationals.[110]

If the foreign investor is accorded the same treatment as the nationals of the host state, the insurer may take the view that claim determination must be made in accordance with municipal laws. This argument appears persuasive on subrogation grounds. To illustrate; the municipal law may have produced a solution of curative character whereby the state ensures compensation only if the act that caused harm to the citizen is that of the state. If the PRI policy has not shifted burden of exculpation onto the insurer, as the principle of 'he/she who alleges must prove[111]', the insured will be expected to first prove that the loss was caused by a listed peril and exhaust the local remedies by proving whether, by intention or negligence, the activities were committed by the host state. Moreover, the municipal law may not provide compensation in cases of a citizen's willful, malicious, negligent, or reckless conduct. Hence, the insured who used the same degree of care may be treated the same way,

---

[107] See U.N. Reports of International Arbitral Awards, Vol X. pp. 511–513. Available at https://legal.un.org/riaa/cases/vol_X/477-692.pdf accessed 06.09.2024. The case is known as "Sambiaggio".

[108] Kelson (1972), p. 202.

[109] Art. 3(3) of the German – Turkey BIT (1962) provides the following: "*Nationals or companies of either Contracting Party whose investments suffer losses in the territory of the other Contracting Party owing to war or armed conflict or to any acts likely to disturb the public order, shall be accorded treatment no less favorably by said other Contracting Party than that party accords to its own nationals and companies as regards all compensation*". Available at https://investmentpolicy.unctad.org/international-investment-agreements/treaty-files/1438/download accessed 06.09.2024.

[110] Art. 4 of the UK – Turkey BIT states that "*Nationals or companies of one Contracting Party whose investments in the territory of the other Contracting Party suffer losses owing to war or other armed conflict, a state of national emergency, revolt, national or local insurrection or riot in the territory of the latter Contracting Party shall be accorded by the latter Contracting Party treatment, as regards measures it adopts in relation to such losses, including restitution, indemnification and compensation, no less favourable than that which the latter Contracting Party accords to its own nationals or companies or to nationals or companies of any third State. whichever is the more favourable to the investor.*" Available at https://investmentpolicy.unctad.org/international-investment-agreements/treaty-files/2355/download accessed 06.09.2024. For a similar provision, see Article 12 of the Georgia - Japan BIT (2021).

[111] Merkin and Kullmann (2006), pp. 6–8, 13–15.

and the portion of the loss which is caused by the aforementioned conduct might go uncompensated.

If the imposition of strict liability is a solution of last resort, the strength of a state's responsibility will lie in its potential to prevent the political force majeure event from occurring.[112] By way of illustration, municipal law may have stated that imputation of responsibility can be made to the state if it knew or could be presumed to have forestalled the probability of the event. In this case, the insured will be required to prove that the host state could have used the means at its disposal and averted the political force majeure event via due diligent conduct.[113] Failure to thwart such an event may be perceived as having engendered by it.[114] Furthermore, according to *Proulx and Simma*, a state having the capacity to prevent terrorism but failed to do so may not have fulfilled the duty stated in art. 2(4) of the UN Charter.[115]

11.4.2.3 States' Contribution to Risk Management

Members of society must be equal before any public burden, and it would be unfair if only some suffer the consequences of the event. When the insured incurs a loss, indemnification is drawn from a fund composed of other insureds' premiums. This so-called *risk pooling* allows insurer to spread, whether correlated or not, the risk, among other insureds or in some cases re-insurers and prevent massive payouts.[116] In the time of war or terrorist attacks, as in Churchill's own words "*it is unfair for British society to place the entire burden of the destruction on those unlucky enough to be hit*"[117] and hence, states may employ a concept that functions on the same basis as risk pools do and compensate individuals through the taxes of those remained unharmed. According to scholars, sharing the burden of war by the citizens and taxpayers may boost the public morale and respond to the failure of the private insurance market.[118]

---

[112] Proulx and Simma (2012), pp. 13, 270.

[113] According to *Alvarez*, "*every State is considered as having known, or as having a duty to have known, of prejudicial acts committed in parts of its territory where local authorities are installed; that is not a presumption, nor is it a hypothesis, it is the consequence of its sovereignty*". See Separate opinion by Judge Alvarez in *Corfu Channel*, p. 44. Available at https://www.icj-cij.org/en/case/1 accessed 06.09.2024.

[114] Proulx and Simma (2012), p. 169.

[115] Proulx and Simma (2012), p. 25. The mentioned article is as follows: "*All Members shall refrain in their international relations from the threat or use of force against the territorial integrity or political independence of any state, or in any other manner inconsistent with the Purposes of the United Nations.*" Available at https://www.un.org/en/about-us/un-charter/full-text accessed 06.09.2024.

[116] According to *Merkin and Steele*, risk pool assists to lessen the burden of misfortune on any individual by sharing its cost. Merkin and Steele (2013), p. 25.

[117] Levmore and Logue (2003), p. 288, fn 63 and also visit: https://publications.parliament.uk/pa/ld200506/ldhansrd/vo051121/text/51121-19.htm accessed 06.09.2024.

[118] Levmore and Logue (2003), p. 287.

State law may require insurers to provide coverage against political force majeure events or may encourage them to do so by providing reinsurance.[119] Terrorism Risk Insurance Act of 2002 of United States established a program providing a compensation mechanism for insureds' losses resulting from acts of terrorism.[120] With respect to claims paid to her nationals, the U.S. was entitled to subrogatory rights. The regulation was designed to be a temporary and terminated at the end of 2005 but was later extended to the end of 2027.[121] Under The War Risks Insurance Act of UK 1939[122] which was extended by The War Damage Act of the UK 1941,[123] the government acted as a reinsurer. The Riot (Damages) Act 1886, repealed by the Riot Compensation Act of 2016, also provided compensation to property owners who sustained damages from war or riots.[124] The latter regulation conferred on the insurer a statutory right of subrogation against the police authority that was imposed with liability to prevent the riot.[125] The liability was strict, however could be deduced to the extent that the claimant failed to take precautions.[126] In addition, in order for covering terrorism risk, Reinsurance (Acts of Terrorism) Act of 1993[127] was introduced, and the government of UK acted as the insurer of last resort. The State-backed terrorism reinsurer '*Pool Re*' which is also funded by the member insurers,[128] was formed in 1993.[129] The slight difference is that Pool Re does not

---

[119] Merkin and Kullmann (2006), p. 18. For the terrorism risk insurance programs OECD countries with government participation, please visit: https://www.oecd-ilibrary.org/finance-and-investment/terrorism-risk-insurance-in-oecd-countries_9789264008748-en accessed 06.09.2024.

[120] https://home.treasury.gov/policy-issues/financial-markets-financial-institutions-and-fiscal-service/federal-insurance-office/terrorism-risk-insurance-program accessed 06.09.2024.

[121] For the regulation and amendment thereto see https://www.govinfo.gov/content/pkg/PLAW-107publ297/html/PLAW-107publ297.htm and https://www.congress.gov/bill/116th-congress/house-bill/1865/text both accessed 06.09.2024.

[122] According to The Marine and Aviation Insurance (War Risks) Act 1952 that repealed The War Risks Insurance Act 1939, the government was empowered to act as reinsurer as well as insurer if the prospective insured cannot find and insurer in the market. For the legislation, please see https://www.legislation.gov.uk/ukpga/Geo6and1Eliz2/15-16/57/contents/enacted accessed 06.09.2024. Also see Merkin and Steele, Insurance and the law of obligations, p. 160.

[123] Legislation is available at https://www.legislation.gov.uk/ukpga/1941/12/pdfs/ukpga_19410012_en.pdf According to article 1 of the War Damage Act of 1965, the Crown was exempted from liability, and persons were disallowed from requesting compensation in respect of damage to, or destruction of, property if the acts of the Crown was lawful. Legislation is available at https://www.legislation.gov.uk/ukpga/1965/18 both accessed 06.09.2024.

[124] Levmore and Logue (2003), p. 288.

[125] Hjalmarsson and Merkin (2007), p. 696; Merkin and Steele (2013), p. 158.

[126] Merkin and Steele (2013), p. 158.

[127] The act has its origins in a bomb explosion in London in 1992 that resulted in the withdrawal of reinsurers from the market and the inability of property owners to obtain coverage. Hjalmarsson and Merkin (2007), p. 714, similarly, see Merkin and Steele (2013), p. 160.

[128] Some scholars opine that the funds for the Pool Re are collected from premiums as well as a 3% levy on all household and motor vehicle policies written in Great Britain. Levmore and Logue (2003), p. 302.

[129] https://www.poolre.co.uk/reinsurance/ accessed 06.09.2024.

operate as a guarantor for uninsured properties that are damaged by terrorist acts; instead, it serves as a reinsurer for the assureds.

The sound reason for governments to offer a subsidy is be to induce commercial players who otherwise would not have availed themselves of coverage against those risks. However, such an insurance/reinsurance of last resort concept must be mandated and the premiums insurers offer must be somewhat available at a price that insureds can afford; otherwise, prospective assured will opt not to buy coverage, and insurance of such risks may remain as unavailable as it was prior to enactment of laws.

Under Turkish Jurisdiction, Law no. 5233 on Compensation for Losses Resulting from Terror and Combating Terrorism deals with the principles and methods of compensating losses incurred by individuals as a result of terror or actions to combat terrorism. In a case, an insurer sought from Turkish Republic, reimbursement for the portion of the indemnification paid to its insured due to a political force majeure event. Amongst factors considered by the court, the position of the requesting party bears a distinctive consideration. In rejecting the insurer's arguments, the High Court expressed that the claims must be directed at those who are responsible for the harm. According to the court, this kind of subrogation does not enable the insurer to invoke the principle of equality, which only applies to individuals and where the burden is shouldered by society. In its finding, the court explained that the recipients of the harm are vested with the entitlement to compensation; hence, the principle cannot be a basis for subrogation claims.[130]

Political risks in general occur as a result of deliberate decisions or actions by states, whereas political force majeure events are those that a state may not be able to avoid or oppose by its own means. Liability insurance[131] may adopt strict liability and provide compensation without seeking fault or determining its degree. From this perspective, a PRI policy covering losses resulting from force majeure events may be viewed as functioning similarly to liability insurance. In political force majeure events, states have an interest in protecting themselves, and they will be concerned with sheltering themselves from responsibility.[132] At first glance, an argument can be advanced that the Turkish case above pertains solely to matters of a state's internal affairs. Although it is a non-PRI case, the court underscored that the recourse to the state must hinge on the insured party. One must not lose sight of the fact that insurers may face this line of thought even if the host states have undertaken to recognize the assignment of investor's rights to the indemnifying party. Thus, when political force majeure is concerned, since the extent and the scope of state liability, as well as state intervention may diversify among jurisdictions, and since insurers

---

[130] See the decision given by the 10 the circuit of the Republic of Turkiye Council of the State, decision number 2008/2685 and decision date 21.04.2008 available at https://kararararama.danistay.gov.tr/ accessed 06.09.2024.

[131] Liability insurance provides cover for loss or damage to another person for which the insured is responsible. See Clarke (2013), p. 61.

[132] Proulx and Simma (2012), p. 98.

will be keen to benefit from the reinsurance of last resort scheme, municipal laws may require a high standard of observation by the insurer.

The final note is that private insurers are profit-oriented, and among other parameters, their risk appetite can be influenced by the salvage value of the investment.[133] The value of the salvage on which the insurer pays a claim and to which it is subrogated is important.[134] While political force majeure events may render investments salvageable, they may still retain a certain degree of worth. In the case of full subrogation, the value of how much can be salvaged from the remains of the investment or the cost of reconstruction will affect the insurer's profit.

11.4.3 In Transfer Restriction and Inconvertibility

The insurer may oblige the insured to deliver the possession of the ineffective money which may be transferrable or convertible at a later date. By doing so, the insured will be deemed to have fulfilled its obligation to mitigate the insurer's loss and protect his/her right to seek reimbursement from the host state, thereby preventing unjust enrichment.[135] *Diaconis* states that if the banking system of the host country does not permit currency conversion, the DFC can purchase the local currency for U.S. dollars and sell it to the U.S. Embassy in the host country for use in operating expenses.[136]

The waiting period, which varies from 60 to 180 days, is the time between the insured's initial attempt to transfer or convert the money and the point at which the currency inconvertibility clause recognizes that a loss has occurred.[137] In article 11 of its convention, MIGA employs the term "reasonable period" and in the commentaries of this article, it is expressed that *In determining what constitutes a 'reasonable period,' the Agency will need to reconcile the investors' interest in a speedy transfer with the fact that certain delays in the processing of applications by governments may be justified.*[138] This approach is of crucial for the insurer for a variety of reasons, such as the host state's regulations in force, political or legal impediments in the transferee state, or the amount of the currency. Transfer or conversion may not take place in the insured's first attempt; hence, the insured will be under the burden of proof to show that the actions of the government causing

---

[133] For salvage value, please see DeLeonardo (2005), pp. 756–757.

[134] See Williams (1993), p. 106.

[135] Also see Newcombe (2005), p. 16.

[136] Diaconis (1989), p. 276.

[137] According to some authors, this period is related to "passive blockage" which comes in the form of excessive delay in converting or transferring the currency. Wagner (2012), p. 106.

[138] See art. 13 of the Commentary on the MIGA Convention.

the damage were nonexistent at the time of the contract[139] and he/she continuously applied for and failed to transfer or convert the currency.[140]

11.4.4 In Denial of Justice and Arbitration Award Default

In DOJ, the insurer will require the investor to have done his/her part properly using the means placed at his disposal. Alternatively, the investor may need to prove the futility of certain procedures, such as the appeal process.[141] One may note that judicial finality is not a substantial barrier to filing claims for loss. In fact, it may be even absurd to expect the investor to pursue access to justice if his attempts are likely to be futile.

Similar to the waiting periods for previously discussed risks, the insured is deemed to have exhausted remedies if such exhaustion is carried out on a continuous basis for a period up to 180 days. For instance, take contracts in which disputes are to be resolved by local courts. If the court impedes a fair and non-discriminatory judicial process or adjourns contrary to the rule of law, it becomes the cause of the insured's failure to exhaust the local remedy and/or undue delay.[142] The same court may not treat with a high degree of courtesy in providing authenticated documents upon request. Thus, at the end of 180 days, submitting a petition and, to the extent applicable, even the written statement of the insured may suffice for the loss claim.[143] Besides, some PRI policies contain a provisional advance payment. The insured, by proving his inability to obtain a court order or arbitral award despite his sustained efforts over time, can receive indemnification (usually up to 50% percent of the claim), on condition that he agrees to return the amount if he loses the case or the difference if the amount awarded is lesser than the advance payment.

In AAD, entitlement to money that is to be collected from the host state in accordance with arbitral award is transferred to insurer. The insurer will seek to

[139] Khachaturian (2006), p. 1056.

[140] More obligations might be required compared to those imposed by BITs, see; Soopramanien (2017), p. 598. For the claims rejected by the US insurer on the grounds that insureds failed to show reasonable efforts, see Ginsburg (2013), p. 957.

[141] See *Chevron* case para. 321–325.

[142] In *Olin Holdings v. Libya* (para. 350) "a three-year delay in court proceedings" was not considered as an undue delay. Available at https://www.italaw.com/sites/default/files/case-documents/italaw9766_0.pdf accessed 06.09.2024. Also see *Toto Costruzioni* case para. 165.

[143] In *Jan de Nul* case, the tribunal held that "*the requirements of exhaustion of local remedies would not have been a bar to a claim of denial of justice on the basis of excessive delays in the judicial proceedings had such delays been deemed a treaty breach. Indeed, it would make no sense to insist on the exhaustion of remedies that are unavailable precisely because the issuance of an appealable decision is delayed. Such insistence might constitute a denial of justice in and of itself.*" See para. 256.

carry out the award by using available legal sanctions[144] which is also known as 'enforcement'. In order to enforce an award, many jurisdictions require that the award be final[145] and binding upon parties. In other words, if the losing party has more room for maneuver and if the award is subject to further examination, the performance of the award may be at risk. Thus, it is of great importance for insurers to obtain an adjudication that neither can be overturned nor set aside. Some may be confused in understanding the difference between appeal and annulment. Appeal may result in replacement of the award,[146] whereas annulment removes the original decision and therefore another tribunal may hear the case.[147]

International conventions secure a considerable degree of uniformity in the recognition and enforcement of awards.[148] *Redfern and Hunter* state that the New York Convention is regarded as being of fundamental importance to the recognition and enforcement of international arbitral awards.[149] According to *Born*, the New York Convention provides for an award's presumptive recognition, subject to only narrow exceptions.[150] The exceptions enumerated in article V are mostly procedural in nature[151] and serve as grounds for denying the recognition of a foreign arbitral award.

---

[144] Redfern and Hunter (2015), p. 611.

[145] Art. 3 of the New York Convention [United Nations Convention on the Recognition and Enforcement of Foreign Arbitral Awards (New York, 10 June 1958)] provides for the finality of the award and "*Each Contracting State shall recognize arbitral awards as binding and enforce them in accordance with the rules of procedure of the territory where the award is relied upon, under the conditions laid down in the following articles.*" And according to the art. V(1)(e) of the same Convention, enforcement of the award may be refused if the award has been set aside or suspended by a competent authority of the country in which, or under the law of which, that award was made" See https://www.newyorkconvention.org/english accessed 06.09.2024.

[146] For instance, under ICSID rules, (53/1) Award shall not be subject to any appeal, but same award, under several circumstances can be annulled.

[147] Dolzer and Schreuer (2012), p. 302.

[148] Redfern and Hunter (2015), p. 616.

[149] Redfern and Hunter (2015), p. 636.

[150] Born (2021a), p. 453 and see Born (2021b) International commercial arbitration, 26.02. (This source has been accessed through an online database and the database provider, due to update of the version, recommends making citation to section headings, rather than page numbers)

[151] Art. V (1) of New York Convention is as follows; 1. Recognition and enforcement of the award may be refused, at the request of the party against whom it is invoked, only if that party furnishes to the competent authority where the recognition and enforcement is sought, proof that: (a) The parties to the agreement referred to in article II were, under the law applicable to them, under some incapacity, or the said agreement is not valid under the law to which the parties have subjected it or, failing any indication thereon, under the law of the country where the award was made; or (b) The party against whom the award is invoked was not given proper notice of the appointment of the arbitrator or of the arbitration proceedings or was otherwise unable to present his case; or (c) The award deals with a difference not contemplated by or not falling within the terms of the submission to arbitration, or it contains decisions on matters beyond the scope of the submission to arbitration, provided that, if the decisions on matters submitted to arbitration can be separated from those not so submitted, that part of the award which contains decisions on matters submitted to arbitration may be recognized and enforced; or (d) The composition of the arbitral authority or the arbitral procedure

Article V (2) of New York Convention provides for the most frequently invoked bases for refusing to recognize awards.[152] According to article V(2)(a), enforcement of an award can be refused if the dispute is not arbitrable. The non-arbitrability ground may be of less importance[153] provided that investment in question falls within the scope of 'investment' as defined in the related BIT. Enforcement of commercial arbitration disputes is mostly refused on public policy grounds, as stipulated in article V(2)(b) of the Convention. The list of purposes which a host state's interference may serve so as to fall within the ambit of the notion of public policy is extensive and it is beyond the scope of this book to review all circumstances however, award; procured trough fraud or other undue means, issued by biased or corrupt tribunal, compelling violation of foreign law may be given as some illustration.[154]

The following case may draw the attention of those who are electric guitar players as I am or interested in music. In *Heavy Metal* case, Chinese Ministry of Culture banned a U.S. heavy metal band's performance due to the band's 'outrageous acts'. As the band sought enforcement of CIETAC award ruling damages for the band's lost income, the Supreme People's Court denied enforcement, on the grounds that "*tribunal's findings were in manifest disregard of the underlying facts that the performance of heavy metal music was against 'national sentiments', and accordingly contrary to the social and public interests*".[155] Heavy metal or hard rock music is mostly a manifestation of objection or disobedience against circumstances such as injustice and discrimination which disrupts social equilibrium and to which society responds in a disturbed manner. Besides, live shows of any music genre may feature

was not in accordance with the agreement of the parties, or, failing such agreement, was not in accordance with the law of the country where the arbitration took place; or (e) The award has not yet become binding on the parties, or has been set aside or suspended by a competent authority of the country in which, or under the law of which, that award was made. 2. Recognition and enforcement of an arbitral award may also be refused if the competent authority in the country where recognition and enforcement is sought finds that: (a) The subject matter of the difference is not capable of settlement by arbitration under the law of that country; or (b) The recognition or enforcement of the award would be contrary to the public policy of that country. As is seen, the grounds set out in the New York Convention are exhaustive and permissible. In fact, the Convention employs quite restrictive language, the term "may be refused" implies an affirmative obligation to recognize foreign and non-domestic awards, subject to specified exceptions. See Redfern and Hunter (2015), p. 623, similarly, see Born (2021b) International commercial arbitration, 26.02, and also, see Dolzer and Schreuer (2012), pp. 301, 303.

[152]The article is as follows: "*Recognition and enforcement of an arbitral award may also be refused if the competent authority in the country where recognition and enforcement is sought finds that: (a) The subject matter of the difference is not capable of settlement by arbitration under the law of that country; or (b) The recognition or enforcement of the award would be contrary to the public policy of that country.*"

[153]For instance, according to art. 1 of Turkey's International Arbitration Act numbered 4686, disputes pertaining to rights in rem on immovable property. See https://www.lawsturkey.com/law/international-arbitration-law-4686 accessed 06.09.2024.

[154]Frischknecht et al. (2018), pp. 166–170.

[155]Redfern and Hunter (2015), p. 645.

irrational or irregular scenes. Not for simplification, however, acts in question were drinking, smoking, splashing water and jumping down from the stage. International courts or tribunals apply laws different from that of the recognition forum's laws and may reach a conclusion which can be contrary to what the domestic court reached;[156] hence, the character of public policy must be treated exceptional. Some jurisdictions may have rigid rules and for instance the concept of 'loss income' may be of a public policy concern. However, as in the above-mentioned case, extending the 'public policy' ground to the performance of art can cast a shadow over the public's access to music, leading to deprivation even if it affects a minority.

Disputes between sovereigns and investors mostly fall within the scope of the ICSID Convention. The annullable errors stated under the ICSID Convention are similar to those stated in New York Convention.[157] The ICSID contains a self-contained review process which replaces judicial challenge of the award.[158] Hence, the principle is that ICSID awards are subject to immediate recognition and enforcement in the courts of Contracting States without set aside proceedings or any other review in national courts.[159]

According to article 52(3) of ICSID Convention, upon the request of a party, it is at the discretion of an ad-hoc committee to annul the award. Parties to ICSID Convention accept to recognize the award as if it were a final judgment of a court in that state[160] and at the time of enforcement, domestic courts cannot examine whether the award is in conformity with the forum state's public policy. An ad hoc committee is rarely explicit about annulling the awards, and the exceptional nature of annulment serves to build a trust in the ICSID judicial system.

Prior to making a claim, the investor should take all reasonable efforts to enforce the award for a period stated in the policy. In other words, during the waiting period, insured on a regular basis, should try collecting the debt or to the extent possible, obtain title to the host state's assets or their proceeds of sale. The subrogation rights accrue upon the insurer's payment, *Ginsburg* states the waiting period will begin to toll as the investor initiates its first attempt.[161]

---

[156] Born (2021a), p. 483.

[157] Art. 52 of ICSID Convention is as follows; *(1) Either party may request annulment of the award by an application in writing addressed to the Secretary-General on one or more of the following grounds: (a) that the Tribunal was not properly constituted; (b) that the Tribunal has manifestly exceeded its powers; (c) that there was corruption on the part of a member of the Tribunal; (d) that there has been a serious departure from a fundamental rule of procedure; or (e) that the award has failed to state the reasons on which it is based.*

[158] Redfern and Hunter (2015), p. 573.

[159] Born (2021a), p. 493.

[160] Art. 54 of ICSID Convention reads as follows; "*Each Contracting State shall recognize an award rendered pursuant to this Convention as binding and enforce the pecuniary obligations imposed by that award within its territories as if it were a final judgment of a court in that State*". See https://icsid.worldbank.org/sites/default/files/ICSID%20Convention%20English.pdf accessed 06.09.2024.

[161] Ginsburg (2013), p. 963.

The prerequisite of the waiting period provides room for further deliberations. Besides, the more attempts insured made, the lesser ways or grounds the host state will have in defending itself at the time of subrogation. A single attempt to enforce an award may be fruitless for some reason and cannot be taken as a token of the host state's reluctance. In the end, frequent attempts will demonstrate that the insured acted bona fide and to the benefit of the insurer. Similar to waiting periods for the occurrence of other risks, PRI providers typically require a waiting period ranging from 90 to 180 days. However, it's essential to note that in the case of this particular risk, waiting for such a duration may be necessary. The success of these attempts is closely linked to the host state's justice system, which is inclined to political risk and can be expected to operate slowly. In other political risk scenarios however, apart from assessing the value of the damage and perhaps negotiating with the host state, waiting for 180 days may be considered lengthy.

Cases

AAPL v. Sri Lanka: Asian Agricultural Products Ltd (AAPL) v. Republic of Sri Lanka, (ICSID Case No ARB/87/3), Final Award

AES Solar: AES Solar and others (PV Investors) v. The Kingdom of Spain, (PCA Case No. 2012-14)

AIG v. Kazakhstan: AIG Capital Partners v. The Republic of Kazakhstan (the High Court of Justice Queen's Bench Division Commercial Court, Case No: 2004/536), Judgment

Banco Nacional: Banco Nacional de Cuba v. Sabbatino, 376 U.S. 398 (1964)

Chevron: Corporation and Texaco Petroleum Company v. The Republic of Ecuador, (UNCITRAL Arbitration, PCA Case No. 34877), Partial Award on the Merits

Corfu Channel: United Kingdom of Great Britain and Northern Ireland v. Albania, (International Court of Justice, Judgment of April 9th, 1949)

Germany v. Italy: Federal Republic of Germany v. Italy, Greece intervening Jurisdictional Immunities of the State, Judgment, ICJ Reports

Heavy Metal case

Hochtief v. Argentina: Hochtief AG v. Argentine Republic, (ICSID Case No. ARB/07/31), Decision on Liability

Jan de Nul: Jan de Nul N.V. Dredging International N.V. v. Arab Republic of Egypt, (ICSID Case No. ARB/04/13), Award

İçkale v. Turkmenistan: İçkale İnşaat Limited Şirketi v. Turkmenistan, (ICSID Case No. Arb/10/24), Award

Menzies v. Senegal: Menzies Middle East and Africa S.A. and Aviation Handling Services International Ltd. v. Republic of Senegal (ICSID Case No. ARB/15/21), Award

NextEra: NextEra Energy Global Holdings B.V. and NextEra Energy Spain Holdings B.V. v. Kingdom of Spain, (ICSID Case No. ARB/14/11)

Olin Holdings v. Libya: Olin Holdings Limited v. State of Libya, (ICC Case No. 20355/MCP) Final Award

Plama v. Bulgaria: Plama Consortium Limited v. Republic of Bulgaria, (ICSID Case No. ARB/03/24), Award

RosInvest v. Russia: RosInvestCo UK Ltd. v. The Russian Federation, (SCC Case No. V079/2005), Award on Jurisdiction

Sambiaggio --

Tecmed v. Mexico: Tecnicas Medioambientales Tecmed S.A. v. The United Mexican States, (ICSID Case No. ARB (AF)/00/2), Award

Toto Costruzioni: Toto Costruzioni Generali S.p.A. v. The Republic of Lebanon, (ICSID Case No. ARB/07/12), Decision on Jurisdiction

Trendtex: Trendtex Trading Corporation v. Central Bank of Nigeria, Date of the decision, of the judgment, 13/01/1977, QB 529

Wena Hotels v. Egypt: Wena Hotels Limited v. Arab Republic of Egypt (ICSID Case No. ARB/98/4), Award

Wintershall v. Argentina: Wintershall Aktiengesellschaft v. Argentine Republic, (ICSID Case No. ARB/04/14), Award

9REN: 9REN Holding S.a.r.l v. Kingdom of Spain,(ICSID Case No. ARB/15/15)

Online Database

http://www.aida.org.uk
https://www.berneunion.org
https://www.clydeco.com
https://www.congress.gov
https://www.danistay.gov.tr
https://www.edit.wti.org
https://www.govinfo.gov
https://www.iarbnews.com
https://www.icj-cij.org
https://www.investmentpolicy.unctad.org
https://www.italaw.com
https://www.law.cornell.edu
https://www.lawfaremedia.org
https://www.lawsturkey.com/law
https://www.legislation.gov.uk
https://www.lexology.com
https://www.newyorkconvention.org
https://ofac.treasury.gov
https://www.oecd.org
https://www.poolre.co.uk
https://www.publications.parliament.uk
https://www.supreme.justia.com

https://www.travel.state.gov
https://www.treasury.gov
https://www.treaties.un.org
https://www.un.org
https://www.whitehouse.gov

References

Allen RM, Viscusi WK (1976) Insuring the expropriation risks of multinational firms. Stanford J Int Stud

Anderson SR et al (2022) What sanctions has the world put on Russia? Lawfareblog online

Barker JC et al (1998) State immunity, diplomatic immunity and act of state: a triple protection against legal action? Int Comp Law Q 47(4):950–958

Born G (2021a) International arbitration: law and practice, 3rd edn. Kluwer Law International

Born G (2021b) International commercial arbitration, 3rd edn. Wolters Kluwer Law & Business, Alphen aan den Rijn

Brown VM (2015) Felonious, erroneous, it's all odious: a story of debt gone wrong. Fordham Law Rev 84(2):725–767

Budd N (1993) Making sense of political risk insurance policies. Int Financ Law Rev 12(6):29–32

Choi SJ et al (2012) The evolution of contractual terms in sovereign bonds. J Leg Anal 4(1): 131–179

Clarke MA (2013) The law of liability insurance. Informa Law from Routledge, New York

Cooper CG (1980) Act of state and sovereign immunity: a further inquiry. Loyola Univ Chic Law J 11(2)

DeLeonardo JM (2005) Are public and private political risk insurance two of a kind? Suggestions for a new direction for government coverage. Va J Int Law 45(3):737

Diaconis JS (1989) Political risk insurance: OPIC's use of a 'fiduciary agent' to facilitate resolution of subrogation claims. Int Lawyer 23(1):271–279

Dolzer R, Schreuer C (2012) Principles of international investment law, 2nd edn. Oxford University Press, Oxford

Dumberry P (2017) The importation of the FET standard through MFN clauses: an empirical study of BITs. ICSID Rev 32(1):116–137

Eggers PM (2016) The place of subrogation in insurance law: the deceptive depths of a difficult doctrine. In: The Modern Law of Marine Insurance: Vol. 4

Fox H, Webb P (2013) The law of state immunity, 3rd edn. Oxford University Press, Oxford

Frischknecht A, Poplinger A et al (2018) Chapter 18: Special considerations with respect to recognition and enforcement of foreign arbitral awards and judgments against sovereigns. In: Frischknecht et al (eds) Enforcement of Foreign Arbitral Awards and Judgments in New York Kluwer Law International

Gaukrodger D (2010) Foreign State Immunity and Foreign Government Controlled Investors. OECD Working Papers on International Investment

Gelpern A (2013) A skeptic's case for sovereign bankruptcy. Houston Law Rev 50(4):1095

Ginsburg R (2013) Political risk insurance and bilateral investment treaties: making the connection. J World Invest Trade 14(6)

Gordon J, Saunders C (2021) Recent Supreme Court Rulings on the Foreign Sovereign Immunities Act. lawfareblog

Gözübüyük AŞ, Tan T (2021) Public Law – General Principles

Hagan S (2008) Designing a legal framework to restructure sovereign debt in current developments. Monet Financ Law 4:195–307

Hjalmarsson J, Merkin RM (2007) Compendium of insurance law. Informa, London

Hyder AA, Attanasio DL (2021) International investment protection of global banking and finance: legal principles and arbitral practice. Kluwer Law International
Kelson JM (1972) State responsibility and the abnormally dangerous activity. Harv Int Law J 13: 197–244
Khachaturian A (2006) Are we in good hands? The adequacy of American and multilateral political risk insurance programs in fostering international development. Conn Law Rev 38(5):1041
Konrad S (2013) Investment treaties and international centre for settlement investment disputes: what investment insurers need to know. In: Verheyen G, Quintrell E (eds) Old risks, new solutions, or is it the other way around?
Levmore S, Logue KD (2003) Insuring against terrorism and crime. Mich Law Rev 102(2)
Lloyd-Jones L (2019) Forty years on: state immunity and the state immunity act 1978. Int Comp Law Q 68(2):247–269
Martin EM (1967) Multilateral investment insurance: the OECD proposal. Harv Int Law J 8(2): 280–338
Meessen KM (2004) State immunity in the arbitral process. In: Horn N (ed) Arbitrating foreign investment disputes. Kluwer Law International
Merkin RM (2013) Insurance law: an introduction. Routledge, London
Merkin R, Kullmann J (2006) The insurance, reinsurance and the impact of terrorism. http://www.aida.org.uk/pdf/questionnaire2.pdf
Merkin RM, Steele J (2013) Insurance and the law of obligations, 1st edn. Oxford University Press, Oxford
Mooney EF (1967) Foreign seizures: Sabbatino and the act of state doctrine. University of Kentucky Press, Lexington, Kentucky
Muchlinski P et al (2008) The Oxford handbook of international investment law. Oxford University Press
Newcombe A (2005) The boundaries of regulatory expropriation in international law. ICSID Rev 20(1):1–57
Pérez-Aznar F (2019) CASE COMMENT Menzies Middle East and Africa SA and Aviation Handling Services International Ltd v Senegal Consent to International Jurisdiction and the Limits of Most-Favoured-Nation Clauses. ICSID Rev 34(1):190–195
Proulx V-J, Simma B (2012) Transnational terrorism and state accountability: a new theory of prevention. Bloomsbury Publishing, Oxford
Radi Y (2020) Insurance against political risks. Rules and Practices of International Investment Law and Arbitration: 231–242
Redfern A, Hunter M (2015) Redfern and Hunter on international arbitration, 6th edn. Oxford University Press, London
Salacuse JW (2013) The three laws of international investment: national, contractual, and international frameworks for foreign capital. Oxford University Press
Schill SW (2009) The multilateralization of international investment law. Cambridge University Press Cambridge International Trade and Economic Law, Cambridge. https://doi.org/10.1017/CBO9780511605451
Schill SW (2010) Part I Chapter 2: private enforcement of international investment law: why we need investor standing in BIT Dispute Settlement. In: Waibel M, Kaushal A et al (eds) The Backlash against investment arbitration. Kluwer Law International
Sheldon H (1882) Law of subrogation. Soule and Bugbee, Boston
Soopramanien RD (2017) Mind the GAP: tailoring the form and substance of political risk insurance in order to bridge the 'enforcement gap' in investment arbitration. Int lawyer 50(3)
Sun H (2020) Political risk insurance. https://www.lexology.com/library/detail.aspx?g=a986a316-31b0-4783-8f13-fc6248c438ba
Tan C (2015) Risky business: political risk insurance and the law and governance of natural resources. Int J Law Context 11(2):174–194
Tattersall L (2019) Derailing state immunity: a broad-brush approach to jurisdiction under claims for the expropriation of cultural property. Int J Cult Prop 26(2):181–195

Wagner D (2012) Managing country risk a practitioner's guide to effective cross-border risk analysis. CRC Press, Boca Raton
Weisenfeld LS (1985) Ecuador-United States: Investment Guaranty Agreement. Int Leg Mater 24(3):566–570
Williams S (1993) Political and other risk insurance: OPIC, MIGA, EXIMBANK and other providers. Pace Int Law Rev 5:59–113
Wuerth I (2022) Does foreign sovereign immunity apply to sanctions on central banks? Lawfareblog online

Chapter 12
Choice of Law and Dispute Resolution

12.1 The Governing Law and the Dispute Resolution in General

Party autonomy is the most prominent and widely accepted international conflict of law rule.[1] The question might be that; how far the principle of party autonomy can be extended? Municipal laws emanate from the sovereign state, covering all transactions within state's jurisdiction.[2] Parties are free to choose the law by which the contract is to be governed, within the limits prescribed by municipal laws. A brief enumeration of these limitations is of interest.[3] By their nature, in contracts relating to immovable, the law of country where immovable is located[4] and similarly, in employment contracts,[5] the law of the habitual workplace of the employee may

[1] Cox et al. (2020), p. 281.

[2] Yntema (1952), p. 344.

[3] Yntema (1952), pp. 353–356.

[4] For instance, according to art. 21 of Act on Private International and Procedural Law(IPL) of Turkey (Act no 5718) "*The law of the place where the property is located which is in force at the moment of transaction shall govern the ownership and other rights in rem to movable and immovable property.*" The Law is available at http://www.lawsturkey.com/law/act-on-private-international-and-procedural-law-5718. According to the REGULATION (EC) No 593/2008 OF THE EUROPEAN PARLIAMENT AND OF THE COUNCIL of 17 June 2008 on the law applicable to contractual obligations (Rome I) parties are entitled to choose the law. According to art. 4 (1) (c) the Rome I regulation, in the absence of choice of law, "*a contract relating to a right in rem in immovable property or to a tenancy of immovable property shall be governed by the law of the country where the property is situated*" See https://eur-lex.europa.eu/legal-content/EN/TXT/PDF/?uri=CELEX:32008R0593&from=EN both accessed 07.09.2024.

[5] For instance, according to the article 27 of IPL of Turkey "*The employment contracts are subject to law which is designated by parties as long as the provisions which foresee the minimal protection due to statutory provisions of his habitual workplace law are reserved*". Under article 8(2) of The Rome I regulation, if the parties have not chosen the governing law, the employment contract shall be governed by the law of the country in which or, failing that, from which the employee habitually

Ö. Tosun, *The Law of Political Risk Insurance*, AIDA Europe Research Series on Insurance Law and Regulation 12, https://doi.org/10.1007/978-3-031-74675-8_12

govern the contract.[6] Choice of law questions in contracts can also be governed by treaties and directives. For instance, in the European Union, according to the article 1 of the Rome Convention, the rules of the Convention apply to contractual obligations in any situation involving a choice between the laws of different countries.[7] On the other hand, some conventions may list the transactions or matters that fall outside its scope.[8] If parties failed to designate the governing law, the law most connected to the transaction may govern the contract. In the context of insurance contracts, since the characteristic performance is the debt of the insurer, the law of the insurer's habitual residence may govern the contract. Should the parties have not explicitly designated a dispute resolution forum, the local courts in the place of respondent's business will be entitled to hear the case.

Party autonomy is also accorded in the context of alternative dispute resolutions. Nevertheless, municipal laws may set out the limits within which party autonomy can be exercised. For instance, due to public policy concerns, disputes arising from criminal matters, bankruptcy law, family law or consumer law may not be appropriate for arbitration. In the same way, despite the ILO's Convention states

---

carries out his work in performance of the contract. The country where the work is habitually carried out shall not be deemed to have changed if the employee is temporarily employed in another country.

[6]The contractual will of the parties is not always accorded primacy, especially when the subject matter is at stake. Autonomy in choosing the scope of the contract is subject to a variety of matters. Contracts subject matter of which are impossible, violating a statutory prohibition, contravening public policy, morality or personal rights can be deemed null and void. For provisions of similar nature, please see art.27 of Turkish Code of Obligations or see Section 134 of German Civil Code which is available at http://www.gesetze-im-internet.de/englisch_bgb/englisch_bgb.html#p4994 accessed 07.09.2024.

[7]Convention on the Law Applicable to Contractual Obligations (the Rome Convention) is available at https://eur-lex.europa.eu/resource.html?uri=cellar:22cc5c49-2b36-4962-aa60-e928a52efa66.0008.02/DOC_1&format=PDF accessed 07.09.2024.

[8]For instance, article 2 of the Convention of 30 June 2005 on Choice of Court Agreements reads as "*(1) This Convention shall not apply to exclusive choice of court agreements – a) to which a natural person acting primarily for personal, family or household purposes (a consumer) is a party; b) relating to contracts of employment, including collective agreements. (2) This Convention shall not apply to the following matters – a) the status and legal capacity of natural persons; b) maintenance obligations; c) other family law matters, including matrimonial property regimes and other rights or obligations arising out of marriage or similar relationships; d) wills and succession; e) insolvency, composition and analogous matters; f) the carriage of passengers and goods; g) marine pollution, limitation of liability for maritime claims, general average, and emergency towage and salvage; h) anti-trust (competition) matters; i) liability for nuclear damage; j) claims for personal injury brought by or on behalf of natural persons; k) tort or delict claims for damage to tangible property that do not arise from a contractual relationship; l) rights in rem in immovable property, and tenancies of immovable property; m) the validity, nullity, or dissolution of legal persons, and the validity of decisions of their organs; n) the validity of intellectual property rights other than copyright and related rights; o) infringement of intellectual property rights other than copyright and related rights, except where infringement proceedings are brought for breach of a contract between the parties relating to such rights, or could have been brought for breach of that contract; p) the validity of entries in public registers.*" Convention is available at https://www.hcch.net/en/instruments/conventions/full-text/?cid=98 accessed 07.09.2024.

otherwise,[9] employment law-related disputes may not be arbitrable in some jurisdictions. In addition, parties may choose arbitration without entirely excluding litigation, allowing specific disputes to be resolved by arbitrators. Finally, dispute resolution mechanism may be multi-tiered with parties seeking amicable solutions prior to commencing litigation or arbitration.[10]

PRI, in essence, consists of two legal relations. The PRI contract is concluded between the insured and the insurer while the contract or the transaction covered by the PRI contract is concluded between the insured and the host state. In the following pages, we will first explore the rationale behind the parties' choice of law and forum in these contracts, then we will discuss how certain PRI providers address this issue and touch upon the contracts of multinational insurers.

12.2 In PRI Contracts

For a variety of reasons, parties to insurance contracts may disagree in choosing the governing law and the place where the dispute will be heard. Apart from the enforceability of the judgment, the speed of proceedings—which will be discussed later—is of particular importance, as is the accuracy and consistency of the judgment. The decision of a judge who is familiar with PRI will be predictable than that of someone who lacks the relevant experience.[11]

In contracts that contain a foreign element, the autonomy attributed to parties must be broad. Hence, a little more need to be said about the Rome Convention and Rome I Regulation. First, the benefit of this unified regime is that, regardless of the jurisdiction, parties domiciled in the European Union will obtain the same outcome.[12] Second, these regulations recognize parties' freedom. The Rome Convention applies to insurance contracts which cover risks situated outside the territories of the Member States.[13] On the other hand, the Rome I regulation applies, in situations involving a conflict of laws[14]in contractual obligations in civil and commercial

[9]Art. 8 of The Termination of Employment Convention, 1982 (No. 158) reads: "*A worker who considers that his employment has been unjustifiably terminated shall be entitled to appeal against that termination to an impartial body, such as a court, labour tribunal, arbitration committee or arbitrator*." See: https://www.ilo.org/dyn/normlex/en/f?p=NORMLEXPUB:12100:0::NO::P12100_ILO_CODE:C158 accessed 07.09.2024.

[10]Born (2021a), pp. 1–8.

[11]For detail, also see Merkin (2013), p. 318.

[12]Cox et al. (2020), p. 208.

[13]See article 1(3) of the Rome Convention.

[14]Needless to say, the residence of the insured or the insurer, or the fact that risk occurs in a country different than that of parties, provide a basis for the conflict of law in PRI.

matters.[15] The same regulation vests in parties of the insurance contract covering a large risk[16] 'the right to choose the governing law[17]'.

Despite PRI's international character, the parties thereto may not necessarily lean toward choosing the law of a third party or an alternative dispute resolution. State-owned or state-backed PRI providers will single out the law and the forum they believe to be the most favorable to them. Hence, for instance, the law governing the PRI contract between the investor and the public ECA will most likely be the municipal laws of the country of its origin, and the forum will be the local courts unless the municipal law permits otherwise.[18]

12.3 In Multinational Insurance

It is to be remarked that multinational insurers offer different types of mechanism. For instance, DHAMAN Convention provides an escalating dispute resolution system. According to article 35 of the Convention, in case of a dispute between contracting country and the Corporation concerning the insured investment, parties

[15] See art. 1(1) of the Rome I regulation.

[16] Large risks are provided for in article 5(d) of the First Council Directive 73/239/EEC of 24 July 1973 on the coordination of laws, regulations and administrative provisions relating to the taking-up and pursuit of the business of direct insurance other than life assurance are ("Council Directive"). According to the article "'*Large risks' means: (i) risks classified under classes 4, 5, 6, 7, 11 and 12 of point A of the Annex; (ii) risks classified under classes 14 and 15 of point A of the Annex, where the policy-holder is engaged professionally in an industrial or commercial activity or in one of the liberal professions, and the risks relate to such activity; (iii) risks classified under classes 3, 8, 9, 10, 13 and 16 of point A of the Annex in so far as the policy-holder exceeds the limits of at least two of the following three criteria: first stage: until 31 December 1992: — balance-sheet total: 12,4 million ECU, — net turnover: 24 million ECU, — average number of employees during the financial year: 500. second stage: from 1 January 1993: — balance-sheet total: 6,2 million ECU, — net turnover: 12,8 million ECU, — average number of employees during the financial year: 250.*" Although the regulation does not explicitly indicate political risks, the risks defined as "credit" or "miscellaneous financial loss" (for instance loss of benefits, loss of market value, loss of rent or revenue and other forms of financial loss in Annex of this regulation) can be deemed variations of political risks. This specific regulation is available at https://eur-lex.europa.eu/legal-content/EN/TXT/?uri=CELEX%3A01973L0239-20070101 accessed 07.09.2024.

[17] Art. 3(1) of the Rome I regulation is as follows: "*A contract shall be governed by the law chosen by the parties. The choice shall be made expressly or clearly demonstrated by the terms of the contract or the circumstances of the case. By their choice the parties can select the law applicable to the whole or to part only of the contract.*" And according to article 7(2) "*An insurance contract covering a large risk as defined in Article 5(d) of the Council Directive shall be governed by the law chosen by the parties in accordance with Article 3 of this Regulation.*"

[18] According to the Sinosure's policy, all disputes between the insured and the Sinosure must be resolved before the China International Economic and Trade Arbitration Commission in accordance with Chinese law. Sun (2020).

must first exhaust settlement by negotiations.[19] If parties fail to reach a settlement, they may then settle the dispute through conciliation. Parties are free to commence arbitral proceedings; if they opt out of conciliation, if the conciliator fails to provide a report within a period of less than six months from the date of commencement of their mission, or if the parties reject the proposal brought by the conciliator.[20]

The multi-tiered dispute resolution process MIGA adopts is slightly more complex. According to article 57(b)(i) and Annex II of the MIGA Convention, in disputes between the member country and MIGA where MIGA acts as subrogee of an investor, MIGA and the member country must attempt to settle the dispute by negotiations prior to conciliation or arbitration.[21] According to art. 3(a) of Annex II parties may bypass conciliation; however, once they agree to use conciliation, submitting their dispute to arbitration is possible only if one of the following occurs: a) the conciliator fails to submit their report within a period not exceeding one hundred and eighty days from the date of their appointment; b) the parties fail to accept all of the proposals contained in the report or fail to agree on a settlement of all controversial issues within sixty days after its receipt; or c) a party fails to express its views on the report.[22]

According to article 57(b)(ii) of the MIGA Convention, MIGA may enter into an agreement with a member country concerning alternative method(s) for the settlement of the disputes. On condition that the agreement in question contains provisions to that effect, MIGA may be required to seek remedies available under the domestic laws of the host country and recourse to arbitration only if it has not obtained relief under such remedies within a specified period of time, or the parties may seek an advisory opinion from the International Court of Justice.[23] Finally, according to article 58, disputes involving holders of a guarantee or reinsurance must be submitted to arbitration to be settled in accordance with the Rules of Arbitration.[24]

[19] Negotiations will be deemed to have been exhausted if the parties cannot reach a settlement within 6 months from the date of the request by any party to enter into such negotiations.

[20] For the entire mechanism, see the Annex of the Convention.

[21] Negotiations will be deemed to have been exhausted if the parties cannot reach a settlement within 120 days starting from the date of the request to enter into negotiation.

[22] In the absence of an agreement on the conciliator, the parties may jointly request either the Secretary-General of ICSID or the President of the International Court of Justice to appoint a conciliator. They may seek the same assistance at the time of the arbitrators' appointment. See article 4(b) of Annex II.

[23] The agreement must be approved by the Board by special majority before MIGA undertakes operations in the territories of the member concerned. See the last paragraph of article 57(b) and also see article 76(c) of the Commentary on the MIGA Convention.

[24] According to art. 3 of the Rules of Arbitration for Disputes under Contracts of Guarantee of the MIGA, the party wishing to institute arbitration must send a notice to that effect in writing to the Secretary-General of the Permanent Court of Arbitration at The Hague. Rules are available at https://www.miga.org/sites/default/files/archive/Documents/Master-Rules-of-Arbitration.pdf accessed 07.09.2024.

The mechanism ICIEC introduced is of a similar nature. According to article 59 of ICIEC's Article of Agreement (AoA), parties can submit the dispute to arbitration if they cannot reach an amicable solution. It is of benefit to the member country to exhaust amicable solutions first. Finally, ICIEC insurance contracts are governed by general principles of Islamic law and include provision of dispute resolution to be settled in accordance with the Rules of Arbitration.

12.4 In Investment Disputes

In discussing the choice of law and dispute resolution mechanism, the distinction has to be made according to the concerns of both parties. As any contracting party, the host state will choose the terms it believes fit for the contract and particularly when national resources are concerned, it can be reluctant to agree on the contract that is governed by the law of a third country. Besides, it may wish to battle on familiar grounds by opting for its municipal laws. The settlement of a dispute before arbitrator(s) may mean a sacrifice of sovereignty over a foreign cash flow. Moreover, in most jurisdictions, the bodies responsible for appointing the state's judges are quasi-independent.

By contrast, the investor may wish to single out the law of a neutral jurisdiction to avoid the disproportionate advantage that the host state might otherwise have from the application of its own laws.[25] If the contract is governed by municipal laws, investors are vulnerable to adverse changes in those laws by the sovereign. Conversely, an investor with greater bargaining power will seek assurance that the host state grants independent and impartial adjudication and permits arbitration for potential claims. Some may believe that local court judges might be biased in favor of the host state.

In addition, if a dispute is settled by local courts, due process might not be exercised in a transparent manner. Hence, securing a fair, prompt, and enforceable award becomes crucial for the investor. The investor may also experience unreasonable delays in obtaining the award and enforcement thereof might be hindered by the local authorities. An arbitration clause can be a game-changer in such circumstances, allowing the prevailing party to enforce the award in multiple jurisdictions. Additionally, due to the absence of appellate review, arbitration tends to be faster and less costly than litigation.[26]

Arbitration agreement can take two forms. The most common is an arbitration clause contained in the principal agreement between the parties. The second form is a separate agreement to submit existing disputes to arbitration.[27] The substance of the

[25] Born (2021a), p. 10, and see Florey (2020), p. 1135.

[26] Born (2021a), pp. 9–10.

[27] Redfern and Hunter (2015), pp. 72–73, similarly, see Born (2021b) International commercial arbitration, p. 251.

contract often takes precedence over procedural matters. Besides, in contract designing, governing law and dispute resolution clauses are generally placed at the end of contracts. As a result, counsel may be fatigued by the time they review these clauses, which can lead to them being given less attention. *Redfern and Hunter* employ the term 'midnight clause' since it is the last clause to be considered in contract negotiations, sometimes late at night or in the early hours of the morning.[28]

Investment treaties often provide for ad hoc arbitration or administrative arbitration such as that administered by ICSID. The benefit of the latter lies in the enforcement of the award since ICSID award will be treated as a final judgment. If the administrative body is other than ICSID, enforcement of the award will be determined within the scope of the New York Convention. The general rule of the ICSID Convention is that in terms of the jurisdiction, it applies to disputes between a state and a national of another state. In the preliminary draft of the Convention, one proposed exception was to extend ICSID's jurisdiction to disputes between states if one of them was subrogated in the rights of its national.[29] According to the first draft, the international organization (MIGA) or a public insurer, after being subrogated to the investor's rights could substitute for the investor in ICSID proceedings.[30] However, the substitution of a state for an investor in ICSID proceedings faced 'vigorous' opposition[31] and the drafting Committee decided to drop this exception on the grounds that the insurer would require the investor having recourse to ICSID prior to insurance indemnification.[32]

Although the term 'national of a state' embraces government owned companies, in cases where a corporation insurer is subrogated to the rights of an investor, determination of whether the dispute falls within ICSID's jurisdiction does not depend upon whether the state controls or owns the corporation in any form. Tribunal rulings can be made on the basis of whether the corporation's activities are of a governmental nature. That is what the tribunal discussed in *CSOB v. Slovak Republic*. CSOB (Ceskoslovenska Obchodni Banka, A.S. 'a commercial bank organized under Czech laws') assigned certain non-performing loan portfolio receivables to Collection Companies one to be established by the Czech Republic, the other by the Slovak Republic. The claimant charged respondent with violation of the Consolidation Agreement which stipulated that each Collection Companies was to pay CSOB for the assigned receivables.

The grounds on which the respondent relied in challenging the tribunal's jurisdiction were that the requirements of article 25(1) have not been satisfied and thus, the claimant should be discharged from stepping into the shoes of CSOB. According to the respondent, the dispute at hand was between two states because "*a) Claimant was a state agency of the Czech Republic rather than an independent commercial*

[28] Redfern and Hunter (2015), p. 72.
[29] Parra (2012), p. 46.
[30] Parra (2012), pp. 71, 82.
[31] Feldman (2016), p. 33.
[32] Parra (2012), p. 91.

entity; and b) the assignment transformed the Czech Republic into the real party in interest to the case.[33]" Tribunal came with a liberal approach and made the following statement "… *for purposes of the Convention a mixed economy company or government-owned corporation should not be disqualified as a 'national of another Contracting State' unless it is acting as an agent for the government or is discharging an essentially governmental function*[34]"

Model agreements or BITs may select diversified ways of dispute resolution. The Norway Model BIT indicates an extraordinary dispute resolution provision. While BITs deal with disputes between national v. contracting party, the model agreement introduces the settlement of the dispute between the insurer and the contracting party.[35] The China – Mexico BIT 2008 however, prevents insurer from arbitrating. Article 9(2) of the BIT states the following "*In case a dispute arises, the Contracting Party which has been subrogated in the rights of the investor may not initiate or participate in proceedings before a national tribunal, nor submit the case to international arbitration in accordance with the provisions of Chapter III (which imposes amicable solution prior to arbitration).*[36] Finally, and interestingly, the Belarus-Turkey BIT (2018)[37] and the Turkey-Ukraine BIT (2017)[38] both specify that disputes between the insurer and the host state will be settled in accordance with the article that deals with dispute resolution between the investor and the contracting state. However, the recognition of subrogation could be sufficient to enable such a mechanism. In other words, if states recognize the subrogation of the insurer through a BIT, the same BIT does not necessarily contain an additional clause stating that the subrogee is entitled to the rights of the investor in settling the dispute.

---

[33] See paras. 10, 15 and 28 of the case, available at https://www.italaw.com/sites/default/files/case-documents/ita0144.pdf accessed 07.09.2024.

[34] See paras. 17–22 of the case.

[35] According to the Annex C; "*1. This Annex applies to legal disputes between an insurer and a Contracting Party, based on Article [Subrogation] of this Agreement, provided that the insurer does not have legal standing under Article 25(1) of the ICSID Convention. 2. Each Party hereby consents to the submission by an insurer of a dispute, in accordance with Article [Subrogation] of this Agreement and Paragraph 1 of this Annex, to international arbitration under the UNCITRAL Arbitration Rules ("UNCITRAL"). 3. The consent under Paragraph 2 and the submission of the dispute by an insurer shall be considered to satisfy the requirements of Article 1 of UNCITRAL. 4. Any arbitral award rendered pursuant to this Annex, shall be final and binding on the parties to the dispute and will be recognized and enforced in accordance with the Convention on the Recognition and Enforcement of Foreign Arbitral Awards, done in New York on 10 June 1958. 5. Articles of this Agreement and the procedural rules of ICSID shall apply to disputes under this Annex mutatis mutandis.*"

[36] Available at https://investmentpolicy.unctad.org/international-investment-agreements/treaty-files/759/download accessed 07.09.2024.

[37] See art. 9(3).

[38] Also see art. 9(3).

Cases

CSOB v. Slovak Republic: Ceskoslovenska Obchodni Banka, A.S. v. The Slovak Republic, (ICSID Case No. ARB/97/4), Decision of the Tribunal on Objections to Jurisdiction

Online Database

https://www.eur-lex.europa.eu
http://www.gesetze-im-internet.de
https://www.hcch.net
https://www.ilo.org
https://www.investmentpolicy.unctad.org
https://www.italaw.com
http://www.lawsturkey.com/law
https://www.lexology.com
https://www.miga.org

References

Born G (2021a) International arbitration: law and practice, 3rd edn. Kluwer Law International
Born G (2021b) International commercial arbitration, 3rd edn. Wolters Kluwer Law & Business, Alphen aan den Rijn
Cox R et al (2020) Private international law of reinsurance and insurance, 1st edn. Informa Law from Routledge, Abingdon
Feldman M (2016) State-owned enterprises as claimants in international investment arbitration. ICSID Rev 31(1):24–35
Florey K (2020) Substance-targeted choice-of-law clauses. Va Law Rev 106(5):1107–1181
Merkin RM (2013) Insurance law: an introduction. Routledge, London
Parra AR (2012) The history of ICSID, 1st edn. Oxford University Press, Oxford
Redfern A, Hunter M (2015) Redfern and Hunter on international arbitration, 6th edn. Oxford University Press, London
Sun H (2020) Political risk insurance. https://www.lexology.com/library/detail.aspx?g=a986a316-31b0-4783-8f13-fc6248c438ba
Yntema HE (1952) "Autonomy" in choice of law. Am J Comp Law 1(4):341–358. https://doi.org/10.2307/837348

Chapter 13
Conclusion

Although it is less likely for a developed country to engage in conduct that is detrimental to the foreign investors, as the catastrophic event of 9/11 presented, in the realm of political risks, unless PRI is in place, regardless of whether the host country has a low-political risk profile or not, the foreign investors may not act with great confidence and may lose out on profitable ventures. PRI contracts serve not only as remedy mechanisms in themselves, but also as vehicles for mutually beneficial exchanges between countries, poverty reduction and bringing the means supposedly necessary for the construction, improvement and welfare of the developing countries. As individuals, somehow, we are all insureds and do not often consider the furtherance of the insurance practice after indemnification. Although PRI takes much of the financial burden off foreign investors' shoulders, one may need to remember that insurance does not prevent the risk-occurring, and the insurer cannot immunize itself from the sovereign. In other words, sooner or later someone needs to confront the sovereign.

It is of great relevance to investigate, with a degree of precision, the political and economic background of the host country as well as the legal framework and the regulations concerning foreign investments. In essence, PRI entails an observation of the phenomenal parameter, which is the propensity of host state for political risks. Admittedly, PRI is a colossal protection, however it should be considered as a last resort, meaning that; buying an insurance coverage implies an acceptance of the probability of risk, and indemnification cannot fully provide the benefits that could have been gained if the risk did not take place. Therefore, foreign investors should also be wary of the abovementioned parameters and conduct their own research.

It is conceivable that nations have not learned the necessary lessons from their past. One way to reduce political risks could have been by narrowing the economic disparities between nations. Currently, migration is often seen as a problem for destination countries. While the current situation may be thought-provoking, it is just one aspect of population change, and its ripple effects may manifest in countries other than the ones in which individuals were born or previously resided. The country of origin may face severe governance issues. Additionally, as financial

Ö. Tosun, *The Law of Political Risk Insurance*, AIDA Europe Research Series on Insurance Law and Regulation 12, https://doi.org/10.1007/978-3-031-74675-8_13

power shifts to Asia and the world transitions to a multipolar international system, and with the increasing number of state-like or micronations, more disputes may be on the horizon for some time to come. The expansion of PRI further supports this concern. Therefore, there is no reason to believe that there will be a radical change in the coming years.

In the beginning, we decided to name the study 'Political risk insurance in a nutshell'. However, a topic bringing together politics, international relations and many fields of law demands a thorough examination and therefore, a title that goes beyond a mere dilemma. Besides, artificial intelligence compels a radical change, thus, insurance and investments may need to change their 'shells' as well. The beginning of the next decade portends a digital transformation. Private insurers compete with one another for more clients and public insurers should conform their mandate, in this regard, PRI underwriters need to spare most of their time to deal with risks that befall digital assets and PRI providers might want to embrace the political and financial shifts and digitalization. The volume of and profits in PRI are relatively small, therefore, PRI providers may suffer from outdated managements and a shortage of necessary human resources. Besides, for the sake of subrogation, PRI requires an internationally constructive policy. Therefore, if the PRI community wishes to be prepared for the next era, it is of great importance to remove the challenges stand in the way.

www.ingramcontent.com/pod-product-compliance
Lightning Source LLC
Chambersburg PA
CBHW072218220525
27162CB00003B/40
9783031746741